EYEWITNESS TRAVEL

CUBA

LONDON, NEW YORK,
MELBOURNE, MUNICH AND DELHI
www.dk.com

PRODUCED BY Fabio Ratti Editoria Srl, Milan, Italy

PROJECT EDITOR Giorgia Conversi
ART EDITOR Paolo Gonzato

EDITORS Carla Beltrami, Barbara Cacciani,
Fernanda Incoronato, Alessandra Lombardi

MAIN CONTRIBUTOR
Irina Bajini

OTHER CONTRIBUTORS
Alejandro Alonso, Christopher Baker, Miguel A Castro Machado,
Andrea G Molinari, Matt Norman, Marco Oliva, Francesca Piana

PHOTOGRAPHERS
Heidi Grassley, Lucio Rossi

CARTOGRAPHERS
Laura Belletti, Oriana Bianchetti, Roberto Capra

ILLUSTRATORS
Marta Fincato, Modi Artistici

ENGLISH TRANSLATION
Richard Pierce

Dorling Kindersley Limited
EDITOR Fiona Wild
CONSULTANT Emily Hatchwell
DTP DESIGNERS Jason Little, Conrad van Dyk
PRODUCTION Joanna Bull

Reproduced in Singapore by Colourscan
Printed and bound in South China

First published in Great Britain in 2002
by Dorling Kindersley Limited,
80 Strand, London WC2R 0RL

Reprinted with revisions 2004, 2007, 2009

Copyright © 2002, 2009 Dorling Kindersley Limited, London
A Penguin Company

A CIP CATALOGUE RECORD IS AVAILABLE FROM THE BRITISH LIBRARY.

ISBN 978 1 40534 440 1

*Front cover main image: Classic American car driving
along the Prado in Havana*

We're trying to be cleaner and greener:

- we recycle waste and switch things off
- we use paper from responsibly managed forests whenever possible
- we ask our printers to actively reduce water and energy consumption

CONTENTS

Ídolo de Tabaco, Museo
Montané, Havana *(see p101)*

INTRODUCING
CUBA

Primary school children in
Santiago de Cuba

◁ A house in Trinidad with characteristic iron grilles; in the insert, the bust of Hatuey at Baracoa

The beach at Guardalavaca, one of the best-known resorts in Cuba

Restored buildings around Plaza
Vieja, Havana

Guava paste and cheese

Dancing at the Casa de la
Tradición in Santiago de Cuba

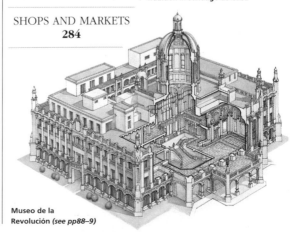

Museo de la
Revolución *(see pp88–9)*

HOW TO USE THIS GUIDE

This guide will help you to get the most out of your visit to Cuba by providing detailed information and expert recommendations. *Introducing Cuba* maps the island and sets it in its historic, artistic, cultural and geographical context. *Havana* and the four regional sections describe the most important sights, with maps, floor plans, photographs and detailed illustrations. Hotels and restaurants, together with night spots and shops, are described in *Travellers' Needs*, while the *Survival Guide* offers tips on everything from transport to phones and local currency.

HAVANA AREA BY AREA

The centre of the city is divided into three areas, each with its own chapter. The last chapter, *Further Afield*, covers peripheral sights. All the sights are numbered and plotted on the *Area Map*. The detailed information for each sight is easy to locate because it follows the numerical order on the map.

Sights at a Glance lists the sights in each chapter by category: Churches, Museums and Galleries, Streets and Squares, Historic Buildings, Parks and Gardens.

All pages relating to Havana have red thumb tabs.

A locator map shows where you are in relation to the other areas of the city.

1 Area map
All the major sights are numbered and located on this map. Those in the historic centre are also listed in the Havana Street Finder *(see pp118–23).*

2 Street-by-Street Map
This gives a bird's-eye view of the most important areas in each chapter.

Stars indicate the sights no visitor should miss.

Suggested routes are shown in red.

3 Detailed Information
The most important monuments and sights in Havana are described individually. Addresses, phone numbers, opening hours and information concerning guided tours and taking photos are also provided.

1 Introduction to the Region

The landscape, history and character of each region are described here, showing how the region has developed over the centuries and what it has to offer to visitors today.

CUBA REGION BY REGION

Apart from Havana, the island has been divided into four regions, each with a separate chapter: Western Cuba, Central Cuba – West, Central Cuba – East and Eastern Cuba.

2 Regional Map

This shows the road network and provides an illustrated overview of the whole region. All the interesting places to visit are numbered in the same order in which they are described, and there are also useful tips on getting around the region by car and by public transport.

Each region can easily be identified by its own colour coding.

3 Detailed Information on Each Sight

All the major cities and other top sights are described in detail. They are listed in order, following the numbering on the Regional Map. Within each town or city there is detailed information on important buildings and other sights.

The Visitors' Checklist provides all the practical information you will need to plan your visit.

Boxes provide further information on the region: leading figures, legends, historical events, local flora and fauna, curiosities, and so on.

4 Cuba's Top Sights

These are given two or more full pages. Historic buildings are dissected to reveal their interiors, while museums have colour-coded floor plans to help you locate their most interesting features, which are shown in photographs with captions.

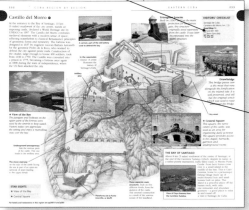

INTRODUCING
CUBA

DISCOVERING CUBA

Cuba is a fascinating island nation. Its lively capital city, Havana, is rich in attractions and steeped in atmosphere. Western Cuba has a dramatic mountain chain, with lush forests and fertile valleys planted with fields of tobacco. Charming Colonial cities are plentiful in Central Cuba, with important wetland habitats on the Caribbean shores in the West, and a string of beach-rimmed isles along the Atlantic seaboard in the East. The rugged mountain terrain of Eastern Cuba is combined with several ancient cities endowed with a strong African heritage. These pages give a brief overiew of the distinctive highlights of each region.

Classic car in Havana

Exuberant carnival scene in the streets of Havana

HAVANA

- **Fascinating museums**
- **Habana Vieja**
- **Captivating nightlife**
- **Evocative fortress**

A vibrant, once cosmopolitan capital city teeming with historic buildings and irresistible allure, Havana boasts dozens of sights of interest, a vibrant nightlife and carnivals. Many sights are concentrated in **Habana Vieja** *(see pp60–77)*, the compact old city centred around cobbled plazas and characterized by Hispanic-Andalusian architecture. The Plaza de la Catedral is surrounded by 18th-century aristocratic buildings and the elegant cathedral, while the Plaza de Armas has a strong Colonial feel.

Centro Habana *(see pp78–95)* includes the area around the Parque Central with the intriguing **Museo de la Revolución** *(see pp88–9)* and the well-stocked **Museo de Bellas Artes** *(see pp92–5)*.

Taxis are useful for exploring **Vedado** *(see pp96–105)* and **Miramar** *(see pp108–9)*, sprawling regions full of Beaux Arts, Art Nouveau and Modernist buildings. The **Hotel Nacional** *(see p98)* is a must-see, as is the **Plaza de la Revolución** *(see p102)*.

On the outskirts of the city, the beaches of **Playas del Este** *(see p113)* and the **Finca La Vigía** *(see p115)* – Ernest Hemingway's Cuban home – are well worth a visit, as is the Parque Histórico-Militar Morro Cabaña in the **Castillo del Morro** *(see p110)*.

WESTERN CUBA

- **Superlative scenery**
- **Valle de Viñales**
- **Lush tobacco fields**
- **Islands and beaches**

With spectacular landscapes, tobacco fields and charming towns that evoke a sense of nostalgia for past times, mountainous Western Cuba invites leisurely exploration. A short distance west of Havana, the **Sierra del Rosario** *(see p136–7)* forms a magnificent setting for Cuba's prime ecotourism resort – Las Terrazas – while westward the Sierra de Órganos are studded with *mogotes* – fantastic limestone formations centered on the **Valle de Viñales** *(see pp142–5)*. Also a centre of tobacco production, this valley offers the most quintessential of Cuban landscapes.

María la Gorda *(see p146)*, at the western tip of Cuba, is a prime dive site. Off the coast are the isles of the Archipiélago de los Canarreos, shimmering with gorgeous beaches. Here, the best diving in all Cuba awaits off the southwest tip of the **Isla de la Juventud** *(see pp148–51)*, while **Cayo Largo** *(see pp152–3)* draws visitors with its stunning sands and turquoise waters – the only place in Cuba to allow nude sunbathing.

The fertile Valle de Viñales with limestone *mogotes* in the background

◁ Mural on the corner of Calle Heredia and Calle Clarín, Santiago de Cuba

The enchanting *casco viejo* (historic core) of Trinidad

CENTRAL CUBA – WEST

- **Parque Nacional Zapata**
- **Revolutionary museums**
- **Famous resort of Varadero**
- **Fireworks battles in Remedios**

With the country's top beach resort and largest national park, plus important museums honoring revolutionary heroes, this region is Cuba at its most varied. With a glorious beach, **Varadero** *(see pp162–3)* makes a fine base

Pink flamingos at the Parque Nacional Zapata

for watersports enthusiasts and for exploring the towns of **Matanzas** *(see pp158–9)* and **Cárdenas** *(see p161)*.

Nature lovers are enticed to the **Península de Zapata** *(see pp164–7)*, part of which has been designated a national park, good for spotting crocodiles and colourful birds, and for sportfishing for bonefish in shallows. Playa Girón (setting for the 1961 Bay of Pigs battle) is off-limits to

visitors but has an evocative museum on the CIA-sponsored invasion. **Santa Clara** *(see pp174–6)* claims another fascinating revolutionary museum,while close by, the colonial town of **Remedios** *(see p177)* is best visited at Christmas for its *parranda* (fireworks battle). With a strong French heritage, **Cienfuegos** *(see pp168–71)* features unique architecture.

CENTRAL CUBA – EAST

- **Gorgeous beaches**
- **Trinidad's historic centre**
- **Flamingoes at Cayo Coco**
- **Lush Sierra Escambray**

Fringed to the north and south by offshore isles, this region claims the most attractive beaches in Cuba. Coral reefs and walls edge the isles, providing tantalizing opportunities for diving and top-notch sportfishing. **Cayo Coco** *(see pp198–9)* is the most developed isle, with a wide choice of luxury all-inclusive hotels.

The beautifully preserved town of **Trinidad** *(see pp182–90)* is the loveliest of Cuba's Colonial cities, its *casco viejo* (historic core) full of cobbled streets. The immediate area is replete with attractions, from steam-train rides to hiking and birding in the **Sierra del Escambray** *(see p173, 191)*.

The main highway, the Carretera Central, links three provincial capitals of modest appeal – **Sancti Spíritus** *(see pp194–5)*, **Ciego de Ávila**

(p196), and **Las Tunas** *(p207)* – and a fourth – **Camagüey** *(pp200–203)*, with restored colonial plazas that are redolent of yesteryear.

EASTERN CUBA

- **Carnival in Santiago de Cuba**
- **Basílica del Cobre**
- **White sands of Guardalavaca**
- **Pre-Columbian sites**

Birthplace of both the independence and revolutionary movements, Oriente (as this region is known) abounds in monuments and museums. Many are in **Santiago de Cuba** *(see pp222–31)*, the most African of Cuban cities, with inspiring architecture and a vivacious spirit, best experienced during July's exciting Carnival.

Visitors are also drawn to Cuba's main pilgrimage site – **Basílica del Cobre** *(see p221)* with its statue of the black Madonna – and to **Parque Baconao** *(see pp234–7)*, a UNESCO biosphere reserve that also contains an unusual range of attractions, from dolphin shows to an antique car museum. Cuba's best pre-Columbian sites are located here too, near the resort of **Guardalavaca** *(see p215)* with its crescent-shaped beach and in **Baracoa** *(see pp242–3)*, the country's oldest city which enjoys a spectacularly lush setting.

The **Sierra Maestra** *(see p220)*, the setting for Castro's guerrilla headquarters, is a beautiful national park.

The glorious white sand beach of Guardalavaca – a major resort

Putting Cuba on the Map

Washed by the Atlantic Ocean, the Caribbean Sea and the
waters of the Gulf of Mexico, Cuba is the largest island in the
Greater Antilles, situated just south of the Tropic of Cancer. It
lies only 180 km (112 miles) from Florida and 210 km (130
miles) from Mexico, while Haiti and Jamaica are slightly less
than 80 km (50 miles) and 140 km (87 miles) away,
respectively. Cuba is not a single island, but a varied
archipelago with a total surface area of 110,922 sq km
(42,815 sq miles). Lying on an east-west axis, the main island, the
elongated Isla Grande, is about 1,250 km (776 miles) long, and 100
km (62 miles) wide on average. Around it are five archipelagoes:
Colorados, Sabana, Camagüey, Canarreos and Jardines de la Reina,
consisting of thousands of *cayos* (keys and small islands). The
largest minor island is Isla de la Juventud. Cuba has about 11
million inhabitants, 2,500,000 of whom live in Havana, the capital.

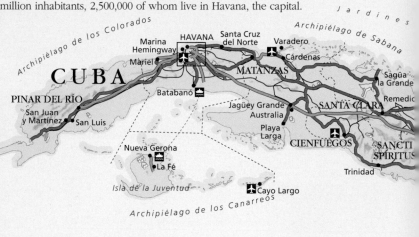

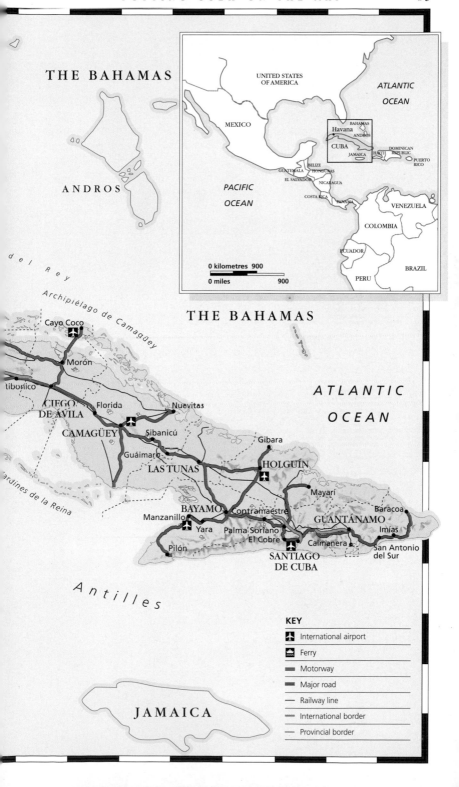

THE BAHAMAS

ANDROS

UNITED STATES
OF AMERICA

MEXICO

ATLANTIC
OCEAN

BAHAMAS
Havana ANDROS
CUBA
JAMAICA HAITI DOMINICAN
REPUBLIC
PUERTO
RICO

PACIFIC
OCEAN

GUATEMALA BELIZE HONDURAS
EL SALVADOR
NICARAGUA
COSTA RICA
PANAMA

VENEZUELA

COLOMBIA

ECUADOR

PERU

BRAZIL

0 kilometres 900

0 miles 900

del Rey

Archipiélago de Camagüey

THE BAHAMAS

Cayo Coco

Morón

Tiburónio

CIEGO
DE ÁVILA

Florida

Nuevitas

ATLANTIC

OCEAN

CAMAGÜEY

Sibanicú

Gibara

Guáimaro

LAS TUNAS

HOLGUÍN

Jardines de la Reina

BAYAMO

Contramaestre

Mayarí

Baracoa

Manzanillo

GUANTÁNAMO

Imías

Yara

Palma Soriano

El Cobre

Caimanera

San Antonio
del Sur

Pilón

SANTIAGO
DE CUBA

Antilles

JAMAICA

KEY

✈	International airport
⛴	Ferry
▬	Motorway
▬	Major road
—	Railway line
—	International border
—	Provincial border

A PORTRAIT OF CUBA

*I*mages of Cuba show hot sun and fields of sugar cane, tall palm
trees and deep, clear blue sea. Cuba is indeed all these things, but
it is also a country with a deep-rooted, complex culture in which
old traditions and new intellectual developments co-exist. It is a young
and vital island, a place of music and colour, which despite severe
economic difficulties in recent years has held on to its unique identity.

Cuba's identity owes a great
deal to the fact that it is
surrounded by sea as well
as to its geographical
position. It is sometimes
called the "key to the gulf"
because of its strategic
location between North and
South America at the entrance
to the Gulf of Mexico, and the island
has been a crossroads since the
beginning of the Colonial period. As
a result, the island's early population
consisted of European settlers, a few
native Indians who had survived
struggles against the invaders,
imported diseases and hard labour,
and thousands of black slaves,
brought over from Africa. Up to the
abolition of slavery in 1886, the
dominant culture was that of the

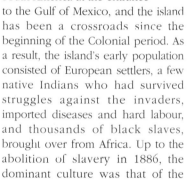

The crest of Cuba,
"key of the gulf"

conquering Spanish, with some
influence from the sailors
and travellers who had
stopped in Cuba. However,
by surreptitious means, the
African slaves managed to
preserve their songs, musical
instruments and dances,
introduced new spices and
tastes to the local cuisine, and
continued to worship their Yoruba
gods *(see pp22–3)*.

The result of this cross-fertilization
is a surprising ethnic mosaic of
whites, blacks, people of mixed race
and Asians (a Chinese community
grew in Havana in the 19th century).
The same mosaic characterizes
Cuban culture too: the bringing
together of vastly different traditions
has produced a unique blend.

Chatting outside the front door, a typically Cuban habit

◁ Students outside their school, illustrating the diverse ethnic mix of the Cuban population

Playing dominoes, a national past time

THE LIFESTYLE

In general, Cubans are outgoing, talkative and sociable. The doors of their houses are always open, a glass of rum or a cup of coffee is there for anyone who passes by to say hello and chat. There is no clear-cut boundary between home and the street: people talk to one another from their balconies, or from the steps or pavement in front of their house.

A trio of musicians playing in the street

The whole day can be spent outside, thanks to the perennial tropical summer. People spend a lot of time outdoors, chatting, playing dominoes, flirting, cycling around the streets buzzing with colour, voices and sounds, or simply sitting. Music is everywhere and is the soul of the island. Melodic thanks to the Spanish heritage, and dynamic due to the hypnotizing rhythm of Afro-Cuban percussion, religious and passionate at the same time, music is a vital part of daily life, like dance. Even the smallest Cuban town

has a Casa de la Trova, now a Cuban institution, where local bands play and young and old alike go to dance. Indeed, there is no single designated venue for dancing in Cuba, and any excuse is good enough to improvise a party. One of the official celebrations is the debut in society of 15-year-old girls, who are dressed up like brides for the occasion. Besides this lively, fun-loving side, Cubans have an equally strong domestic one, and love to spend time at home with the family, in front of the television or chatting from the ever-present rocking chairs.

THE POLITICAL SYSTEM

The present Constitution of the Republic of Cuba, approved by 97.7 per cent of voters (in Cuba people can vote at the age of 16), was promulgated in 1976. In 1992 various amendments were introduced, including guarantees for foreign investments, some flexibility in foreign trade, more religious freedom, and the introduction of direct election by universal suffrage of deputies to the National Assembly. The Constitution states that Cuba is a socialist republic whose supreme

A 15-year-old girl preparing for her debut in society

Fidel Castro, the Líder Máximo, during a rally in Plaza de la Revolución

governmental body is the National Assembly of People's Power (the equivalent of Parliament), elected by universal suffrage every five years. The Assembly in turn elects the State Council, the Council of Ministers, and the president of the State Council, who is the head of state and of the government, as well as the judges of the Supreme Court. There are also the Provincial and Municipal Assemblies of the People's Power (Poder Popular), through which the population expresses its wishes. Since the only political party is the Cuban Communist Party, which by law cannot propose candidates, the citizens directly elect their candidates. Lastly, there are many social organizations, to which most of the citizens belong. These groups are for young people (UJC), children (UPCJM), women (FMC), students (FEEM and FEU), trade unions (CTC), and small private farmers (ANAP). The largest of these groups consists of the Committees for the Defence of the Revolution (CDR), founded in 1960 to watch over the country and tackle social issues.

In spite of the severity of the Castro government, national pride is quite strong, partly thanks to the continued embargo imposed by the US. Fidel Castro (although very ill at present) is still regarded as a charismatic figure by many, and there is general awareness and appreciation of the social reforms achieved since the revolution. It remains to be seen how the introduction of Western affluence will affect the country in the long term.

EL PARTIDO ES HOY EL ALMA DE LA REVOLUCION CUBANA
PCC

Billboard with political propaganda along the Carretera Central

THE ECONOMY

The most important factor in the Cuban economy is tourism. Since 1980 the island has been open to foreign tourists, which has meant that the traditional flow of citizens from Eastern European countries has been

Waving Cuban flags at a rally

Varadero, one of the most popular resorts for international tourism

replaced by the arrival of tourists from western capitalist countries – the only people who can bring strong currencies into the country. The decision to make more of the nation's rich natural and architectural heritage to produce some degree of wealth was crucial for the economy. However, it has also created major changes in the social relationships, habits and customs of millions of people, who after 30 years of semi-isolation have begun to measure themselves alongside Western Europeans, Canadians and even the occasional embargo-defying American. The uneasy dual economy of the

A popular toy made of wood and three wheels

Cuban *peso* and the convertible peso, the result of the boom in tourism, is still a problem to be resolved. Another important item in the local economy is sugar cane: Cuba is still one of the world's leading exporters of sugar, with 156 extraction centres.

EDUCATION AND CHILDREN

José Martí, who was a poet and man of letters, and became a hero of national independence *(see p45)*, stated that the only way to be free was to be educated. The Cuban Revolution has not forgotten this motto and has staked much on fostering free public education. Thanks to the massive literacy campaign of 1961 *(see p52)*, illiteracy was almost completely eradicated within a short time. Today most of the island's people, half of whom are under 30 – that is, born since the Revolution – can read and write the official language, Spanish, and are also taught foreign languages. Throughout the country Casas de la Cultura, or cultural centres, act as venues for exhibitions, performing arts and even dance evenings. Child care is an important component of the

Machines used to harvest sugar cane

nation's educational policy: the government has invested a great deal of effort and funds in the younger generations and is particularly keen on protecting children, who are safeguarded from the exploitation and sweatshop labour so common in many Latin American and Third World countries. Children are well looked after in Cuba: they have the right to attend nursery schools and day-care centres and to education, physical education and recreational activities. All these services are free for everyone and generally of good quality.

HEALTH

The achievements of the government in the field of health have raised the country to the level of the world's most industrialized nations. A great deal has been invested in providing hospitals and medical consultants throughout the island, in free medicine, and in concentrating on prevention (the nationwide vaccination of infants and children has virtually eliminated diseases common on the American continent) and medical research. Cuba has the lowest infant mortality rate and the highest life expectancy rate in Latin America. The health service, which is free for everyone, is excellent despite restrictions imposed by the economic crisis. The presence of highly trained Cuban doctors and the reduced costs of therapy and hospitalization have made the island a centre for "health tourism"; patients from many countries come here for specific treatments, especially for skin and stress problems.

Javier Sotomayor, the gold medallist in the high jump in the 1992 Olympics at Barcelona

SPORTS

Physical activity has always been encouraged by the government via a mass physical education programme and numerous specialist schools that offer talented youngsters the chance to make a name for themselves. As a result, sports standards are high, and Cuba has many Olympic champions. Baseball is the national sport (the Cuban team is one of the best in the world), and athletics, volleyball, basketball and boxing are also popular. Leading figures in sport include boxer Kid Chocolate (1910–88), successful in the US before the Revolution, high-jump champion Javier Sotomayor, Ana Fidelia Quirot, the 800m world champion in 1995 and 1997, and Ivan Pedroso, gold medallist in long-jump in Sydney 2000 and Edmonton 2001.

Boxing training in a Havana gym

Landscape, Flora and Fauna

A land crab, a marsh inhabitant

The Cuban poet Nicolás Guillén once likened his native island to a green crocodile with eyes of stone and water. An aerial view would show the island stretching out in the Caribbean Sea and indeed covered with vegetation and patterned with rivers. Small islands and coral reefs lie just offshore in the sparkling blue sea. In the interior, the landscape is very varied, from plains of red earth to the *mogotes* outcrops of Viñales, from desert cactus to tropical forest. Protected reserves make up 22 per cent of the national territory. There are numerous species found only on Cuba, but no poisonous creatures.

Coral reefs, with their own distinct ecosystem *(see p147)*

MOUNTAINS

The most important ranges are the Sierra de los Órganos to the West, the Sierra del Escambray in the centre and the Sierra Maestra to the southeast. The latter is Cuba's principal range and includes Pico Turquino (1,974 m/ 6,475 ft), the highest peak in the country. The slopes are covered with forests of deciduous trees, pines and tropical plants, and by coffee and cocoa plantations.

PLAINS

Areas of plain occur throughout the island, but are particularly prevalent in the central regions – the provinces of Matanzas, Sancti Spíritus and Camagüey – and in the Pinar del Río area. The land is fertile and planted with sugar cane, palm trees, mangoes and citrus fruit, or left as grazing land for cattle.

Carpintero
(carpenter) is the Cuban name for the woodpecker, which nests in tree trunks.

The *tocororo (Cuban trogon) is the national bird. The colours of the flag of Cuba were inspired by its feathers.*

The *cartacuba (Todus multicolor) is an endemic species only a few centimetres long. It has highly coloured plumage.*

The *tiñosa, or turkey vulture, with its unmistakable red head, flies the plains in search of carrion.*

The cattle egret
follows grazing cows and feeds on insects, both those disturbed by ploughing and others on the cows' hides.

The so-called gulf fritillary
is one of 190 species of butterfly in Cuba, about 30 of which are endemic to the island.

FLORA

The Cuban landscape is characterized by the many varieties of palm tree *(see p173)*, together with the pine in the mountainous areas, and the ceibas in the plains. The *yagruma*, with large dark green and silvery leaves, is also widespread. Three important hardwoods are mahogany, cedar and *majagua*. Splashes of colour are added to the luxuriant green vegetation by flowering hibiscus, bougainvillea and *flamboyán* (royal poinciana). Numerous species of orchid grow here, as well as mariposa, Cuba's national flower.

A *flamboyán* (royal poinciana)

The ceiba tree, sacred to Pre-Columbian peoples

The mariposa, the national flower

MARSHLANDS

The southern part of the island in particular has many lagoons and marshlands, often distinguished by mangrove swamps, and is rich in birdlife. The most important area is the Ciénaga (swamp) de Zapata, in the province of Matanzas *(see p166)*.

Pink flamingoes *live in areas of brackish water from Cayo Coco to Zapata.*

***Buteogallus anthracinus gundlachi** is an endemic hawk that feeds on crabs.*

Mangroves *develop an intricate root system under water. This habitat suits a diverse range of birds and fish.*

TROPICAL FOREST

The Sagüa-Baracoa mountain range in Eastern Cuba, under the influence of northeast trade winds, is one of the most biologically diverse areas in the Caribbean. Here, the heavy rainfall produces thick vegetation.

The tiny *zunzuncito*, *the smallest hummingbird in the world, lives in protected or wooded areas like the Península de Zapata.*

The black anolis *lizard, a forest reptile, reacts to disturbance by inflating the white part under its throat.*

The *Polymita picta*, *an endemic species of snail that lives only in the Baracoa area, has a brightly coloured shell and feeds on plant parasites.*

Santería

Different religions co-exist in Cuba as the result of its history. Both the Catholicism of the Spanish conquerors and the cults imported by the African slaves have survived. The most widespread of the African faiths is santería, also called Regla de Ocha. In order to be able to worship their gods despite the persecution of the Spaniards, Yoruba slaves, originally from Nigeria, merged their gods' identities with certain Catholic saints. Over the years the two religions have almost become blended. Pure Catholicism today is not a widespread religion in Cuba, while santería is so strongly felt that it is an important part of the national identity.

The batá, *three conical drums of different sizes with two skins, accompany the most important santería ceremonies.*

The crown of Changó, the king of the orishas

Rituals *are almost always performed in a domestic context (santería has no temples as such). Rites are inspired by animistic spirituality, although there are elements that share similarities or even merge with Catholicism.*

Fresh fruit, including bananas, Changó's favourite

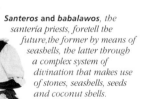

Santeros and babalawos, *the santería priests, foretell the future, the former by means of seashells, the latter through a complex system of divination that makes use of stones, seashells, seeds and coconut shells.*

Agogó (traditional rattles), maracas and bells are played while greeting the gods.

AN ALTAR FOR CHANGÓ

Altars are set up by santería initiates on feast days, such as their "saint's birthday" (the initiation anniversary), and decorated with the attributes of the god to whom they are dedicated. They also contain elements belonging to other *orishas*, such as cloth, devotional objects, flowers, fruit and other special foods.

THE *ORISHAS*

The main santería god is Olofi, the creator divinity, similar to the God of Christianity but without contact with Earth. The gods who mediate between him and the faithful are the *orishas*, who listen to the latter's prayers. Each *orisha* has his own colour and symbols, as well as a ritual characterized by its type of dance, music and costumes: Ochún, for example, wears yellow clothes and loves honey, pale soft drinks and violins.

Obbatalá, *a hermaphrodite god, is the protector of the head as well as the chief intermediary between Olofi and humankind.*

Ochún, *the goddess of love, lives in rivers, and corresponds to the Virgen del Cobre (see p221).*

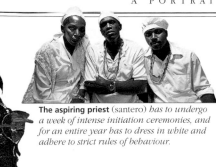

The aspiring priest (santero) *has to undergo a week of intense initiation ceremonies, and for an entire year has to dress in white and adhere to strict rules of behaviour.*

The axe and sword are Changó's two warlike attributes.

The *batea* is a wooden receptacle containing natural elements in which the spirit of the god resides. Only the *santero* may open it.

The *pilón* is the large wooden mortar on which the *santero* sits during the week of initiation, and it is preserved as an object of worship.

Various objects – *Christian, secular or even personal items – are set together on santería altars. Here, three Madonnas are placed alongside plastic horses.*

Elegguá *is the first god to be greeted during ceremonies. He is represented by a stone made to look like a face, with two shells as eyes, and is usually placed behind a believer's front door.*

Fresh flowers are always placed on the altars of the *orishas:* red ones for Changó, yellow ones for Ochún, and white ones for Obbatalá.

Candles

A basket of offerings is on display during ceremonies. The money is used to buy objects of worship.

Yemayá, *sea goddess and mother of* orishas, *wears blue. Capable of great sweetness and great anger, she is linked with the Virgen de Regla (see p112).*

Changó *is the virile and sensual god of fire and war who adores dancing and corresponds to St Barbara.*

OTHER AFRO-CUBAN RELIGIONS

Among the African cults practised in Cuba, two others are also significant: Palo Monte (or Regla Mayombé), in which herbs and other natural elements are used for magical purposes, and Abakuá, more of a mutual aid secret society, for men only. The former, introduced to Cuba by Bantu-speaking African slaves from the Congo, Zaire and Angola, is based on the cult of the dead. The faithful, called *paleros*, perform rites that are sometimes macabre and even verge on black magic. A region between Nigeria and Cameroon was the birthplace of the Abakuá cult. In celebrations the participants, disguised as little devils *(diablitos)*, dance and play music. The *diablito* has become part of Cuban folklore.

An Abakuá *diablito* with his typical headdress

Architecture in Cuba

Formal architecture in Cuba began in the Colonial period. For the entire 16th century all efforts were concentrated on building an impressive network of fortresses; then came the first stone-built *mudéjar*-style houses, which replaced simple wooden dwellings with tiled roofs. The 18th century was a golden age of civic architecture, characterized by the Baroque style imported at a late stage from Europe, which in turn made way for Neo-Classical buildings in the 19th century. The mixture of styles typical of the *fin de siècle* was followed, in 1900–30, by Art Deco architecture, a forerunner of the 1950s skyscrapers. Ugly pre-fabricated buildings characterize the post-1959 era.

The courtyard *was a typical feature of Colonial architecture and the centre of domestic life. Above, the Conde de Jaruco's Havana residence (see p76).*

THE 17TH CENTURY

The tropical climate, with high temperatures and heavy rain, influenced the local architecture. Many private homes had thick walls, tiled roofs and windows protected by shutters.

A typical wooden ceiling at Calle Tacón 4, in Havana

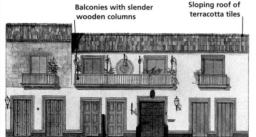

Balconies with slender wooden columns

Sloping roof of terracotta tiles

The house at Calle Obispo 117–19 (p72), *with its characteristic central courtyard and wooden balconies, shows a clear Spanish influence in the structure itself and in the building techniques used.*

THE 18TH CENTURY

More rooms were added to houses with a central courtyard, more houses were built, and some wonderful examples of civic architecture were created. Three highlights of light Cuban Baroque in Havana are the Palacio de los Capitanes Generales *(pp70–71)*, Palacio del Segundo Cabo *(p66)* and Havana Cathedral *(p64)*. Trinidad also has many 18th-century Colonial buildings.

The mezzanine, a structural element introduced in the 1700s

The arcade on the ground floor, which was the external equivalent of the inner courtyard, was an 18th-century innovation. As trade increased, mansions like this housed growing numbers of servants, who lived in the lower part of the building.

Stained-glass windows

Arches supported by columns and pilasters distinguish 18th-century buildings.

Limestone façade

Palacio de los Capitanes Generales *is a typical Cuban Baroque mansion, with thick stone walls, an abundance of arches, columns, porticoes and balconies, and a large central courtyard with dense vegetation.*

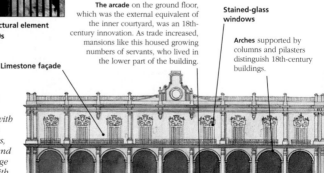

An elegant arched *mediopunto* window

MEDIOPUNTO

These stained-glass windows were created in the mid-18th century to protect houses from the glare of the tropical sun. They became popular in the 1800s, when mansion windows were decorated with glass set into a wooden frame. The original geometric motifs were later replaced by others drawing inspiration from tropical flora and fauna.

THE 19TH CENTURY

The widespread use of porticoes with columns and lintels, wrought iron and decoration inspired by Classical antiquity or the Renaissance, is the distinguishing feature of 19th-century Cuban Neo-Classical architecture. Grilles across windows and shutters helped air to circulate inside (previously the central courtyard performed this function). Buildings that best represent Cuban Neo-Classicism are the Palacio de Aldama in Havana *(p84)* and the Teatro Sauto in Matanzas *(p158)*.

Wrought- or cast-iron grilles

Shutters and *mediopuntos* protected rooms from bright light.

Ionic pilasters

Palacio de Aldama, *designed by Manuel José Carrera in 1840 for the wealthy Don Domingo de Aldama, is the most important Neo-Classical building in Havana. Rejecting Baroque exuberance, it echoes the austerity and purity of line of Classical architecture*

Doric columns

In the portico the arch is replaced by the lintel.

BRIDGING THE 19TH–20TH CENTURIES

The architectural value of many Cuban cities derives from the mixture of different styles.This is seen in buildings such as the Neo-Moorish Palacio de Valle in Cienfuegos *(p170)*, the Capitolio in Havana *(pp82–3)*, and at Paseo and Calle 17, Havana's so-called "millionaires' row", with splendid mansions such as the Casa de la Amistad, built in 1926 *(see p99)*.

Detail of the façade of the Palacio Guasch, Pinar del Río (p136)

Palacio de Valle *in Cienfuegos, designed by the Venetian architect Alfredo Colli in 1912 for Acisclo del Valle, combines Moorish and Venetian Gothic elements with references to Beaux Arts forms – a typical example of the eclectic style's use of a range of prevailing architectural motifs and elements.*

THE 20TH CENTURY

The early 20th century saw the construction of a few examples of Art Nouveau and Art Deco buildings, paving the way for the major urban development that took place in Havana in the 1950s. This period witnessed the building of some very tall, modern skyscrapers and hotels such as the Riviera and the Habana Libre (then called the Habana Hilton, *p98*). In parallel with this came the rise of a style that was reminiscent of Rationalist architecture.

Edificio Bacardí *(1930) in Havana, designed by E Rodríguez, R Fernández and J Menéndez, is a splendid example of Art Deco. It is clad in granite and limestone, with motifs in terracotta.*

Painting in Cuba

The history of Cuban painting can be divided into three basic stages. The first began in 1818 with the foundation of the San Alejandro Fine Arts Academy, run by Jean-Baptiste Vermay, a French Neo-Classical painter. The second began over a century later, in the 1930s, when, thanks to great artists such as Wifredo Lam, René Portocarrero and Amelia Peláez, a movement influenced by the European avant-garde created a universally comprehensible idiom that expressed the unique essence of Cuban identity. Thirdly, after 1959, as part of a programme of art education that promoted avant-garde artists, the National School of Art and the Institute for Advanced Art Studies were founded. Cuban painting has always brimmed with vitality and painters of recent generations have achieved international recognition, helped by shows like the Havana Biennial.

Víctor Manuel García, *one of the fathers of modern Cuban art, created the archetypal* Gitana Tropical *(1929).*

Wifredo Lam *(1902–82), lived for a while in Europe and worked with Pablo Picasso in Paris. He developed a new pictorial language that went beyond national boundaries. He painted extraordinary pictures such as* La Jungla (The Jungle), *now in the Museum of Modern Art, New York,* La Silla *(see p93), and* The Third World *(1966), seen here, which cast a dramatic light on the elements in Cuban religions.*

Amelia Peláez *(1897–1968) blended still life motifs with the decorative elements in Cuban Colonial architecture such as stained glass and columns, as seen here in* Interior with Columns *(1951).*

René Portocarrero *(1912–86) expressed the essence of Cuba through a Baroque-like vision of the city, painting domestic interiors and figures of women, as in* Interno del Cerro *(1943). He made use of bold colour and was influenced by the European avant-garde and Mexican mural painting.*

Raúl Martínez *and Guido Llinás were leading exponents of the abstract art movement that came to the fore in the 1950s–60s and later adopted the Pop Art style in representions of current-day heroes, as exemplified by* Island 70 *(1970) by Raúl Martínez, seen here.*

Alfredo Sosabravo *(b. 1930) – a painter, illustrator, engraver and potter – tackles the themes of nature, man and machines with an ironic twist. A leading figure, he has been active since the 1960s, together with Servando Cabrera Moreno, a Neo-Expressionist, Antonia Eiriz, a figurative artist, and Manuel Mendive, whose subject is Cuba's African heritage.*

Flora Fong *– along with Ever Fonseca, Nelson Domínguez, Pedro Pablo Oliva, Tomás Sánchez and Roberto Fabelo – represents a strand of 1970s painting, which tended towards abstraction without quite losing sight of objective reality. Her* Dimensiones del Espejo *is seen here.*

GRAPHIC ART

Graphic design, which first flourished during the Colonial period, when it was used in the sugar and tobacco industries, with time became an independent art form, with the creation of prestigious periodicals such as *Social*. During the 20th century the growing importance of marketing produced different types of graphic art. In the 1960s, in the wake of the enthusiasm for the victorious revolution, well-designed graphic posters became a natural part of the main political and cultural campaigns, and designs became ever more sophisticated. Use of graphic art is still very visible in Cuba's towns and cities and at the roadside all over the island.

Poster by Alfonso Prieto for July 26 celebrations

CERAMICS

In 1950, the physician Juan Miguel Rodríguez de la Cruz brought together leading painters such as Wifredo Lam, René Portocarrero and Amelia Peláez in Santiago de las Vegas, near Havana, so that they could all work on ceramic designs. It marked the beginning of a new artistic genre in Cuba that today ranges from crockery to sculpture, and also includes installations and works for home interiors. Wonderful examples of Cuban ceramics can be found in the Museo Nacional de la Cerámica in the Castillo de la Real Fuerza (p68) and in the Hotel Habana Libre (p98).

Decorated plate, Havana Ceramics Museum

Cuban Literature

A frequent theme in the literature of Cuba has always been the question of national identity, and the genre has evolved with a marked interest in social problems and questions about reality. The works of the great 20th-century Cuban authors are regarded as classics, and younger authors are beginning to attract attention on the international scene. The Revolution was a golden era for publishing, because production costs for books were very low. However, the trade was plunged into sudden crisis in the early 1990s and many publishers are only now slowly regaining their former status. Every year Havana plays host to an International Book Fair, a major literary event involving authors and publishers from all over the world.

An expressive portrait of the great Cuban poet Nicolás Guillén

THE 19TH CENTURY

The birth of Cuban literature is usually dated from *Espejo de Paciencia*, an epic poem written in the early 1600s by Silvestre de Balboa, originally from the Canary Islands. However, truly national literature only began to emerge in the 19th century, with the call for an end to slavery and for Cuban independence from Spain.

Félix Varela, writer-philosopher

Among the literary figures of that time, various names stand out. Father Félix Varela (1787–1853) was an eclectic philosopher and patriot who wrote a pamphlet extolling the "need to stamp out the slavery of the blacks on the island of Cuba, which would also be in the interests of their owners". José María de Heredia (1803–39) was a romantic poet who introduced the American landscape into New World literature and was forced to live in the US and Mexico because of his nationalist stance. Gertrudis Gómez de Avellaneda (1814–73), another romantic, lived for a long time in Spain and defended the black population in her novel *Sab*. Cirilo Villaverde (1812–94) was a patriot and author of *Cecilia Valdés*, a famous abolitionist work which was made into a *zarzuela* (operetta) in the 20th century by the Cuban composer Ernesto Lecuona.

However, the towering figure in the 19th century was the great José Martí (1853–95), an intellectual, journalist and author who expressed his nationalist ideas in elegant literary form (*Ismaelillo* and *Versos Sencillos* are his best-known works), and became a leading exponent of Latin American modernism.

Another figure in this movement was Julián del Casal, a decadent, symbolist writer. The premature deaths of these two brought the development of innovative literature to a halt.

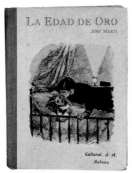

La Edad de Oro, José Martí's children's periodical

THE 20TH CENTURY

The leading interpreters of 20th-century Cuban literature were the poet Nicolás Guillén (1902–89) and the novelist Alejo Carpentier (1904–80), both of whom were sent into exile because of their opposition to Gerardo Machado's regime and their fierce criticism of Batista's dictatorship.

Guillén, who was of mixed race, spoke for the black population, exposing among other things the brutal working conditions of the *macheteros*, the labourers who cut sugar cane on the plantations. After Castro's victory, Guillén was proclaimed as "national poet" and asked to head UNEAC, the Cuban writers' and artists' union. Taking as his starting point the rhythms of dance and traditional musical genres such as *son* (*see p30*), grafted onto the classical Spanish octosyllable, Guillén's stylistic studies gave rise to bold experiments as early as 1931 in works like *Songoro Cosongo, poemas mulatos*.

Alejo Carpentier, an architect, musicologist and writer acutely

José Lezama Lima

aware of the realities of Cuba's situation, was one of the most original and innovative authors in 20th-century world literature. Using a blend of irony and respect, he gave voice to the myths of his country, anticipating the destructuring of the post-modern novel. Among his major works are *The Kingdom of This World*, *The Lost Steps*, *Concierto Barroco* and *The Age of Enlightenment*.

Two other leading figures of the same period are the dramatist Virgilio Piñera (1912–79), a reformer, who had a marked taste for experimental theatre, and José Lezama Lima (1910–76), a poet of elegance, also a novelist and chief editor of the magazine *Orígenes*. From 1944 to 1956 this leading periodical printed works by the best Cuban writers and artists of the time. It became one of the key publications in Latin America. Lima is internationally known as the author of *Paradiso* (1966).

A famous novel by Alejo Carpentier (1974)

In general, the literary scene in revolutionary Cuba has been characterized by creative fervour, in poetry and in novel-writing. Among the "veterans", people who lived through the experience from the outset, mention should be made of the poets Eliseo Diego, Cintio Vitier, Pablo Armando Fernández and Fina García Marruz; and the novelists Félix Pita Rodríguez, Mirta Aguirre, and Dulce María Loynaz. The works of Loynaz were not published in Cuba until the late 20th century, just before her death. These authors were followed by the younger writers Miguel Barnet, Antón Arrufat, López Sacha and César López, committed writers in favour of the revolution.

Among the anti-Castro authors writing in exile, the leading name was the late Guillermo Cabrera Infante (1929-2005), whose works include *Infante's Inferno* and *Three Trapped Tigers*.

Author Dulce María Loynaz, pictured in her twenties

CONTEMPORARY WRITERS

Present-day authors worthy of mention include Abel Prieto, the Minister of Culture, a brilliant and perceptive author of several novels, including *The Cat's Flight*. Another name is Abilio Estévez, a dramatist and novelist of extraordinarily expressive intensity, with a lyrical and visionary tone. Marylin Bobes and Mirta Yáñez both write from the feminist angle. Senel Paz wrote the story that inspired the film *Strawberry and Chocolate*; and detective-story writer Leonardo Padura is known abroad for a quartet of mystery novels set in Havana.

CUBAN CINEMA

The founding of the Instituto Cubano del Arte y la Industria Cinematográficos (ICAIC) in 1959 virtually marked the birth of cinema in Cuba. The aim of this institution was to disseminate motion picture culture throughout the country, and thus encourage the formation of Cuban directors, to work on documentary films in particular. Fostered by the revolutionary government, Cuban cinema experienced a golden age in the 1960s and has been evolving ever since. Today Havana is the capital of new Latin American cinema thanks to the annual film festival organized by ICAIC. Gabriel García Márquez, winner of the Nobel Prize for Literature, is president of the Fundación del Nuevo Cine Latinoamericano, which also runs the Escuela Internacional de Cine film school, based in San Antonio de los Baños. Among Cuba's many directors, who include Julio García Espinosa, Manuel Octavio Gómez and Pastor Vega, there are three particularly outstanding names: Santiago Alvarez, who has made fine documentaries; Humberto Solás, director of the classic *Lucía* and of *Cecilia*; and the late Tomás Gutiérrez Alea, who found fame abroad in 1993 thanks to *Fresa y Chocolate (Strawberry and Chocolate)*, which he made with Juan Carlos Tabío, which courageously dealt with the themes of homosexuality and dissent.

Symbol of the ICAIC

Poster for the film *Strawberry and Chocolate*

Music and Dance

Anything can be used to make music in Cuba: two pieces of wood, an empty box and a tyre rim are enough to trigger an irresistible rhythm, anywhere and at any time of day, on the bus, on the beach or in the street. There are top classical music composers and interpreters, but it is popular music, a fusion of Spanish melodies and African rhythm, that is the very essence of Cuba. The success enjoyed by mambo and cha-cha-cha in the 1950s was followed by the worldwide popularity of *son*, rumba and salsa. Dance, too, is an essential part of life here. No-one stays seated when the music starts: feet and hands start to move with the rhythm, and bodies sway and rock.

Compay Segundo, the famous *son* singer and songwriter

Salsa *is dance music which maintains the rhythmic structure of* son *while adding new sounds borrowed from jazz and other Latin American genres.*

The guitarist is often also the accompanying voice, while the solo singer plays a "minor" percussion instrument such as the maracas or *claves*.

Traditional maracas are made from the fruit (gourd) of the *güira* tropical tree.

Bongo

Double bass

Tres

SON

This genre is a type of country music that originated in Cuba in the 19th century, a blend of African rhythm and Spanish melody, which then greatly influenced Latin American music as a whole. In around 1920 *son* began to be played in towns in Eastern Cuba, where, along with other genres, it produced the *trova tradicional*, a ballad-style song with guitar.

THE MUSICIANS

Ernesto Lecuona

Three great 20th-century composers and musicians are pianist Ernesto Lecuona (1896–1963), Ignacio Villa (or "Bola de Nieve"), and Pérez Prado, in whose orchestra Benny Moré sang *(see p171)*. In the 1920s there was the star Rita Montaner and the Trío Matamoros, the top *trova* band in Santiago. Others were Sindo Garay, a bolero writer, and César Portillo de la Luz, a founder of *feeling* music in the 1960s. Contemporaries include the *salsero* Issac Delgado and Afro-Cuban jazzman Chucho Valdés.

Bola de Nieve *(1911–71), or "snowball", is the stage name that Rita Montaner gave to her pianist Ignacio Villa. This husky-voiced musician also wrote and sang very moving love songs.*

Dámaso Pérez Prado *(b.1922), the king of mambo, became an international success with his orchestra in the 1950s.*

Guaguancó, *a fast variation of rumba, enacts a breezy battle between a man and woman who tries to parry his insistent advances. In effect, this dance is a thinly disguised simulation of the sexual act.*

The voice was the original element of the rumba, which began as song. The percussion instruments, the basis of this musical genre, were added at a later stage.

A *batá* covered with canvas and seashells

Tumbadora or conga

CUBAN MUSICAL INSTRUMENTS

Claves

Tres

Güiro

There are several exclusively Cuban musical instruments. Among the stringed instruments are the *tres*, a small guitar, always used in *son* bands, with three pairs of metal strings, and the *requinto,* another small, high-pitched guitar that is used in trios to play melodic variations.

Typical Cuban percussion instruments are the *tumbadora*, a tall wooden and leather drum played with the hands, which is used in all musical forms, including jazz; the *bongó,* two small round drums; the *claves*, two wooden cylinders played by striking them against one another; the *güiro*, the gourd of the güira fruit which is stroked with a small stick; and the *marímbula*, a rarely used small piano.

RUMBA

The African soul of Cuban music, the rumba originated in poor neighbourhoods as a voice of rebellion against slavery and segregation. It then became a form of political satire and social criticism, as well as the poignant expression of an unhappy love affair. *Columbia* is country-style rumba, while *yambú* and *guaguancó* are the urban varieties, with a dance rhythm that can be sensual and dynamic, or sad and slow.

Los Van Van *have dominated the Cuban musical scene for over 30 years and are world-famous for their new rhythms and sounds (they invented a new genre, the* songo*).*

Silvio Rodríguez, *a singer and songwriter who defends the ideals of the Cuban revolution, founded the Nueva Trova with Pablo Milanés (right) in the late 1960s, revitalizing the style and repertory of the* trova, *a rural musical genre.*

Buena Vista Social Club, *Wim Wenders' film (1998), brought into the limelight traditional* son *interpreters over 80 years old, such as the late guitarist and singer Compay Segundo, the late pianist Rubén González, and the late singer Ibrahim Ferrer.*

Cuban Cigars

The cigar is an inextricable part of Cuba's culture, history, and even, for some, its essence. It is known that cigars were used by the native Indians. After Columbus's voyage, tobacco, regarded in Europe as having therapeutic qualities, was imported to Spain. However the first smokers were imprisoned, because people believed that cigar smoke produced diabolical effects. Even so, tobacco grew in popularity and was later exported to other European nations, where government agencies were set up to maintain a monopoly over the product. After the revolution, the US embargo had a serious effect on the international sale of cigars *(puros)*, but since the 1990s the fashion for cigar smoking has given a boost to sales.

Tobacco (cohiba) *was used by Cuban Indians during religious rites to invoke the gods. They either inhaled the smoke through a tubed instrument called a* tabaco, *or smoked the rolled leaves.*

The *tripa* is the inside, the "core" of the cigar with the filler leaves. In hand-made cigars, the *tripa* consists of tobacco leaves which have been selected in order to obtain a particular flavour.

The *capa* is the wrapper leaf on the outside of the cigar. It gives it its smooth, velvety look as well as its colour.

The head (or top part of the cigar) is cut off before smoking.

Foot

The *capote* is the binder leaf that holds the inner part together and keeps it compact.

THE PARTS OF A CIGAR
Cigars can be either hand-made or machine-made. With hand-made cigars the inside consists of whole tobacco leaves, while machine-made cigars are made up of leaves that are blended and then shredded.

BRAND NAMES
There are 32 brands of Cuban cigar on the market today. Below are four, each represented by a *marquilla*, or label, which is placed on the cigar box to identify the brand. Some designs have not changed since first marketed.

Montecristo (1935)

Cohiba (1966)

Cuaba (1996)

Vegas Robaina (1997)

The *anilla*, *the band that goes around the central part of the cigar and bears its brand name, has a curious history. It is said that in the 18th century, Catherine the Great of Russia, a heavy smoker, had her cigars wrapped with small bands of cloth so they would not leave stains on her fingers. Her eccentricity soon became fashionable. The first commercial cigar band was produced in 1830 by the manufacturers Aguila de Oro. Above is a band produced by the Cuban cigar-maker Romeo y Julieta in 1875.*

HOW CIGARS ARE MADE

Cigar manufacturing is a real skill that Cubans hand down from generation to generation. This sequence of photographs shows how Carlos Gassiot, a highly skilled *torcedor* (cigar roller), makes a cigar, from selecting the loose tobacco leaves to the final touches.

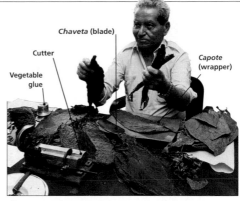

Chaveta (blade)

Cutter

Capote (wrapper)

Vegetable glue

1 *Having placed the* capote *(wrapper leaf) on the tablet, the* torcedor *chooses the filler leaves he wants to use for the core of the cigar: three leaves from different parts of the plant – seco, volado and* ligero *(see p139).*

2 *He begins to roll (*torcer *in Spanish, hence the term* torcedor*) the leaves. The* capote *is wrapped around the filler leaves selected for the* tripa, *which in turn is covered by the* capa, *which is smooth and regular. This determines the appearance of the cigar.*

3 *Once the wrapping is complete, the final touches are added. First the wrapper leaf is worked until it is completely smooth. Then comes the trimming. The cigar tip is finished off by wrapping the end with a last tobacco leaf.*

Chaveta

Tableta (tablet)

4 *Once the cigar is finished, the* torcedor *checks its diameter with a special gauge stamped with the various standard sizes established for every kind of cigar. The same instrument is also used to measure the pre-established length, after which the cigar is cut to this size using the cutting machine.*

THE SHAPE AND SIZE

Cigars are made in different sizes (heavy, standard or slim ring gauge) and shapes (they may be regular or tapered, *figurado*). Fatter cigars tend to have a fuller flavour, which connoisseurs prefer. The best hand-rolled Cuban cigars benefit from ageing, like fine wine.

Cuaba Exclusivo, *figurado* cigar

Trinidad Fundador, regular-shaped cigar

CUBA THROUGH THE YEAR

Because of its tropical climate, Cuba does not really have a high or low season, although officially, peak season is from December to the end of March and in July and August, when hotel rates are higher and flights are packed. Except for the peak of summer, when temperatures can be searingly hot, and September and October, when hurricanes are likeliest, any month is suitable for a visit. It is warm at the beach even in winter, because the *frentes fríos* (cold fronts)

A Carnival outfit

generally last only a couple of days and even then the temperature hardly ever drops below 10°C (50°F). The cooler, drier months from November to March are the best for sightseeing.

Thanks to the climate, and the Cubans' love of music and cultural events, there are open-air concerts, festivals, and religious and folk festivities all year round. However, the most interesting and eventful months are July, during Carnival, and December, when the festivities in Remedios and Havana's two famous cinema and ballet festivals take place.

SPRING

During this season there is an escalation of dance and theatre performances. The beaches are crowded, but mainly with visitors – the Cubans usually go to the seaside only in summer.

MARCH

Festival de Monólogos y Unipersonales, Havana *(Mar)*. A competition for actors, authors, directors, dancers and choreographers from all over Cuba. It also features monologues by foreign performers.
Taller Internacional de Teatro de Títeres, Teatro Papalote, Matanzas, *(Mar–Apr)*. Performances by leading puppet theatres, with seminars, conferences and workshops.

APRIL

La Huella de España, Gran Teatro de la Habana and Castillo de La Real Fuerza, Havana *(Apr)*. A festival of Cuban culture of Spanish derivation: concerts, classical dance, flamenco and theatre.
Festival Internacional de Percusión, Havana *(Apr)*. Concerts, courses, conferences, lectures and documentary film screenings, all revolving around Cuban percussion instruments.
Bienal del Humor de San Antonio de Los Baños, Museo del Humor, San Antonio de los Baños *(1–15 Apr)*. Festival of Humour, with exhibits, lectures and performances.

Festival de Arte Danzario, Havana and Camagüey *(Apr–May)*. Festival featuring all types of dance, from traditional to contemporary experimental. Also includes lectures, seminars, educational activities and workshops held by Cuban and visiting international dancers and scholars.

A batá player at the Percussion Festival

Los Días de la Danza *(Apr–May)*. Festival featuring Cuban dance groups. On 29 April, International Dance Day, the Premio Nacional de la Danza, a national prize, is awarded in Teatro Mella, Havana.

MAY

Primero de Mayo, Havana *(May 1)*. Rallies, marches and parades are held in every city in the country. The most important one takes place, of course, in Havana: the citizens gather in Plaza de la Revolución for speeches and patriotic songs.
Feria Internacional del Disco Cubadisco (International Record Fair), Pabellón Cuba, Havana *(mid-May)*. Records on display and for sale; conferences and concerts.
Fiesta Nacional de la Danza, Santa Clara *(Apr–May)*. The best local dancers perform in the towns of this province. The fiesta ends with a great celebration in Santa Clara.

The First of May Parade in Plaza de la Revolución, Havana

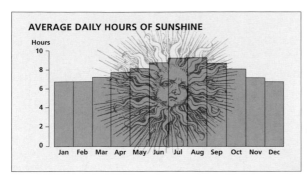

AVERAGE DAILY HOURS OF SUNSHINE

Hours: 10, 8, 6, 4, 2, 0

Jan Feb Mar Apr May Jun Jul Aug Sep Oct Nov Dec

Sunshine
This chart shows the average daily hours of sunshine in Cuba. In the winter the days are short: at 6pm the sun has already set. In the summer the sun is strong and you should protect your skin and wear a hat and sunglasses, even if only taking a short stroll in town.

SUMMER

There are various festivals and festivities during the summer months, especially in Havana and Santiago. Almost every evening there are open-air concerts along the Malecón in Havana, particularly in the square known as the Piragua, which is transformed into an open-air dance floor (free of charge). If you plan to include the Carnival in your visit, book accommodation well in advance in both cities.

JUNE

Festival Boleros de Oro, Santiago, Morón, Havana *(mid-Jun)*. String of concerts by the best Cuban and international performers of bolero songs, lectures.
Encuentro de Bandas de Concierto, Plaza de la Revolución, Bayamo *(Jun 1–15)*. Outdoor concerts by national and international bands. Lectures, workshops.

Walking on stilts in Morón during the Fiesta del Gallo

Fiesta del Gallo, Morón *(end of Jun)*. Parade through town based on theme of the cockerel, symbolic here.
Jornada Cucalambeana, Encuentro Festival Iberoamericano de la Décima, Las Tunas *(end of Jun, biennial)*. The most important festival of Cuban rural culture. Concerts and performances by poets, musicians and *repentistas* (improvisers). Lectures and literary meetings, exhibits of local handicrafts, theatre.
Havana Carnival *(Jun–Jul)*. A parade of floats in the city streets, going from the Hotel Nacional to Calle Belascoaín, and live music performances by *comparsas* (processional groups who prepare all year long) in various parts of the city. At weekends, free concerts are held at the Piragua. The parades can be viewed from a grandstand.

JULY

Fiesta del Títere, Havana *(first week of Jul)*. Puppet shows in different parts of the old town.
Fiesta del Fuego, Santiago de Cuba *(first half of Jul)*. Annual festival celebrating the music, poetry, figurative art, religions and history of the Caribbean nations. Meetings, shows, exhibits, round tables, concerts, poetry readings and festivities throughout the city.
Festival Internacional de Música Contemporánea de Camagüey, Camagüey *(Jul)*. A major contemporary music festival with concerts,

A group of dancers from a Havana *comparsa*

seminars and round table discussions on Cuban and foreign composers.
Santiago Carnival, Santiago de Cuba *(second half of Jul)*. Parade of floats along the city streets, live music performed by *comparsas*, and a show from the Tropicana in Santiago *(see p229)*. For the most important parades there is a grandstand for spectators.
"26 de julio" *(held every year in a different city)*. The official commemoration of the attack on the Moncada barracks *(see p230)*, with a speech by president Raúl Castro and other political leaders in the main square of a Cuban city, accompanied by children who recite poetry and by concerts.

AUGUST

Festival Internacional de Música Popular "Benny Moré", Cienfuegos, Lajas and Havana *(end of Aug, biennial)*. Survey of Cuban popular music and its most important figures, with lectures and meetings centred around the figure of Benny Moré *(see p171)*.

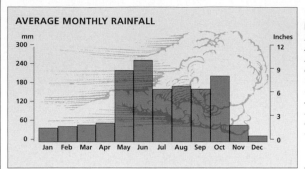

AVERAGE MONTHLY RAINFALL

mm		Inches
300		12
240		9
180		6
120		3
60		0
0	Jan Feb Mar Apr May Jun Jul Aug Sep Oct Nov Dec	

Rainfall
*In Cuba, the dry
season (from
November to April)
alternates with the
rainy season, when
brief but heavy
showers fall. In the
Baracoa and Moa
area at the eastern tip
of the island, rainfall
is heavier because the
mountains block the
Atlantic winds.*

AUTUMN

After the August heat, when
everything to do with work
seems to slow down, life
starts to pick up again. In
autumn the schools reopen
and work returns to a normal rhythm. The number of
tourists – Europeans in
particular – decreases.

SEPTEMBER

**Fiesta de la Virgen
del Cobre**, El Cobre, Santiago
de Cuba *(8 Sep)*. On the
feast-day of the Virgin there
is a surge in the regular
pilgrimage to this site from
all parts of the island.
The statue of the Virgin
is borne in procession
through the streets.

**Festival de Teatro
de La Habana**, Havana
(second half of Sep). This
biennial theatre festival
features a wide range of
performances, including
opera, dance, puppet
theatre, street
shows and
pantomime.
The theoretical
aspects of theatre
are also discussed,
and experts from all
over the world
participate.
Matamoros Son,
Santiago *(Sep)*. A
biennial festival
given over to *son*
(see p30).
**Festival de Teatro
de Camagüey**, Camagüey
(Sep–Oct). A national theatre
competition dedicated to

Gertrudis Gómez de
Avellaneda *(see p28)*, with
the added participation of
various foreign companies.
As well as productions there
are seminars, discussions,
lectures and conferences.

OCTOBER

**Festival de La Habana
de Música
Contemporánea**, Havana
(first half of Oct). Concerts
with top conductors and
soloists, world
premières, lectures
and meetings with
contemporary
Cuban and foreign
composers.
**Fiesta de la
Cultura Iberoamericana**,
Holguín *(second half of Oct)*.
A festival given over to
Spanish culture, with
concerts, exhibitions,
festivities and lectures.
**Festival Internacional
de Ballet de La Habana**,
Teatro García Lorca, Havana
(second half of Oct). A
wide-ranging survey of
classical ballet, organized by
the Ballet Nacional de Cuba
headed by Alicia Alonso.
Famous international artists
take part as well.

**Alicia Alonso
performing at the
Teatro García Lorca**

NOVEMBER

**Salón de Arte Cubano
Contemporáneo**, Centro
Desarrollo de las Artes
Visuales, Havana *(biennial)*.
An expo-competition of
contemporary art works, with
prizes awarded at the end.
Also conferences, lectures,
round table discussions.

HURRICANES

Hurricanes form when masses of hot air with low central
pressure move upwards in a spiral, pulling cold air in towards
the centre from the surrounding atmosphere. They cause
high tides, extremely strong winds, and very heavy and per-
sistent rainfall resulting in floods. The areas most vulnerable
to these storms are the coasts, areas with little surface
drainage, the valleys, the mountain areas and the cities.
Most of the natural disasters in Cuba in the last 100 years
have been caused by these
storms. In 2008, Hurricanes
Gustav and Ike hit the
island eight days apart. Over
three million people were
evacuated and thousands of
homes and crops were
destroyed, making them the
costliest hurricanes to ever
hit Cuba. September and
October are the most likely
months for Caribbean
hurricanes to occur.

**Satellite photograph of
Hurricane Gustav over Cuba**

AVERAGE MONTHLY TEMPERATURE

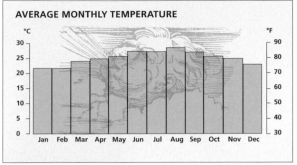

°C		°F
30		90
25		80
20		70
15		60
10		50
5		40
0	Jan Feb Mar Apr May Jun Jul Aug Sep Oct Nov Dec	30

Temperature

The chart covers the entire island. In practice, Eastern Cuba, especially the Santiago area (except for the mountainous zones) is hotter. On the cayos *the annual temperature range varies little. The humidity level goes from 81 per cent in summer to 79 per cent in winter.*

Dancing at the Festival de Raíces Africanas, Guanabacoa

Festejos de San Cristóbal de La Habana *(Nov).* Festivities and concerts to commemorate the foundation of Havana.
Festival Internacional de Coros, Sala Dolores, Teatro Heredia, Santiago de Cuba *(biennial).* Concerts by choral groups from all over the world.
Festival de Raíces Africanas "Wemilere", Guanabacoa *(second half of Nov).* A festival of folk events, with closing prize-awarding ceremony.
Festival Cubadanzón, Teatro Sauto, Matanzas *(second half of Nov).* Performances by *danzón* orchestras and dancers, courses and conferences.

WINTER

The most active season of the year from a cultural point of view, with many top conferences and festivals, the majority held in the capital. The events calendar is not generally disrupted by the holiday season, because although Christmas has been an official holiday since 1997,

it is in fact little celebrated. New Year's Day is usually celebrated at home with the family or with close friends, rather than being the focus for public events.

DECEMBER

Festival Internacional del Nuevo Cine Latinoamericano, ICAIC, Havana *(first half of Dec).* This is the most important cinema festival and competition of the year, attracting famous international guests. The main cinemas in the capital present screenings of the Latin American films in the competition, as well as retrospectives of Cuban and international filmmakers.
Fiesta a la Guantanamera, Guantánamo *(first half of Dec).* Performances of, and lectures on, Afro-Cuban religion. Visits to the French *cafetales* (old coffee plantations) and the stone zoo.
Día de San Lázaro, Santiago

Festival Internacional del Nuevo Cine Latinoamericano poster

de Las Vegas, El Rincón *(17 Dec).* The faithful and the sick come on pilgrimage to the church of Rincón; many come from Havana on foot. **Parrandas de Remedios**, Remedios *(8–24 Dec).* Cuba's most popular folk festival begins with a children's parade and ends with floats, fireworks and exuberance on Christmas Eve *(see p177).*

JANUARY

The Feria Internacional del Libro logo

Feria Internacional de Artesanías, Pabexpo, Havana *(Jan–Feb).* Handicrafts fair. Stands from different countries; meetings and lectures.

FEBRUARY

Feria Internacional del Libro, Fortaleza de San Carlos de La Cabaña *(first half of Feb).* Book fair featuring a different nation each year. New Cuban and foreign publishing initiatives presented and sold. Round tables, conferences, poetry readings, events and concerts.

NATIONAL HOLIDAYS

New Year's Day/ Liberation Day (1 Jan)
Labour Day (1 May)
National Rebellion Day (26 July)
Start of First War of Independence (10 Oct)
Christmas Day (25 Dec)

THE HISTORY OF CUBA

First inhabited in Pre-Columbian times, Cuba was later conquered by the Spanish, who ruled here for four centuries. The island gained independence in 1899, only to come under the virtual control of the US, with the help of dictators Machado and Batista. The revolution headed by Fidel Castro and Che Guevara, who defeated Batista on 1 January 1959, was a turning point for the country. The new political system achieved major social results and Cuba is now finally emerging from decades of isolation.

Before the arrival of the Spanish, Cuba was inhabited by three Amerindian ethnic groups: the Guanajatabey, Siboney and Taíno. The first were gatherers who lived in caves. The Siboney, hunters and fishermen, left behind the most interesting Pre-Columbian rock paintings in the country, more than 200 pictures in the caves of Punta del Este on Isla de la Juventud *(see p151)*. The Taíno were farmers and hunters thought to be from present-day Venezuela, and their culture, the most advanced of the three, achieved a primitive form of social organization.

Indo-Cuban find, Museo Bani *(see p215)*

On 28 October 1492, Christopher Columbus landed in Cuba during his first voyage of discovery in the New World *(see p214)*. He named it "Juana" in honour of the king of Spain's son, but the natives continued to call it "Cuba". From 1510 to 1514 Diego Velázquez de Cuellar, upon commission from Columbus's son, set about annexing the island to Spain. This proved to be a straightforward enterprise, because the Indians put up little resistance, with the exception of a few episodes. The chief Hatuey led a rebellion in 1511–12, but was taken prisoner and burnt at the stake *(see p219)*.

Diego Velázquez then turned to colonization. He founded the city of Baracoa, the first capital of the island, in 1512; San Salvador (present-day Bayamo) in 1513; San Cristóbal (Havana), Santísima Trinidad (Trinidad) and Sancti Spíritus in 1514; and Santiago de Cuba and Santa María del Puerto del Príncipe (present-day Camagüey) in 1515. The native population was decimated despite vigorous defence by Friar Bartolomé de las Casas, so-called "Protector of the Indians", and the Spanish soon had to import slaves from the western coasts of Africa to fulfil the need for labourers. Later, dissatisfied with the lack of gold in Cuba, the Spanish began to use the island both as a base from which they set out to conquer other American territory, as well as a port of call for ships taking the riches of the New World back to Spain.

TIMELINE

Pre-Columbian age	1490	1500	1510

Before 1492 Cuba inhabited by Guanajatabey, Siboney and Taíno Indians

Diego Velázquez de Cuellar

1511 Indian resistance led by Hatuey, who is killed by the Spanish

1514 San Cristóbal (present-day Havana), Santísima Trinidad (Trinidad) and Sancti Spíritus founded

Bust of Columbus, Museo de la Revolución, Havana

28 October 1492 Christopher Columbus lands on the island

1510 Diego Velázquez de Cuellar begins conquest of Cuba

1512 Foundation of Baracoa, first city in Cuba

1515 Foundation of Santiago de Cuba and Santa María del Puerto del Príncipe (Camagüey)

◁ **Detail from the painting *Siempre Che* (Che Forever) by Raúl Martínez**

PIRATES AND BUCCANEERS

By the mid-1500s the population of Cuba had dwindled considerably because the native Indians had been virtually annihilated by forced labour and diseases, and the Spanish had left for other parts of the New World in search of gold. However, the island was still important strategically as one of the defensive bastions of the Spanish colonies in America against the expansionist policies of France, Britain and the Netherlands.

Havana, the chief dock for vessels transporting treasure from America to Spain, soon drew the attention of pirates, who were plying the Caribbean Sea by the second half of the 16th century. In 1555, the French buccaneer Jacques de Sores sacked and burned Havana, triggering the construction of an impressive fortification system. Pirate raids became more and more frequent in the 17th century. The first buccaneers were French, then came the turn of the British (including Francis Drake and Henry Morgan) and

Henry Morgan, the British buccaneer

the Dutch, who attacked Spanish galleons loaded with treasure as well as the Cuban ports.

In order to deprive Spain of her colonies, France, Britain and the Netherlands joined in the "corsair war" – essentially state-sanctioned piracy – by financing attacks on Spanish merchant ships. The Spanish crown took several measures to defend its possessions, but to no avail. In 1697 the Ryswyk Treaty signed by Spain, France and Britain finally put an end to this unusual war in the West Indies.

In the meantime Havana had become the new capital of Cuba, thanks to its well-protected bay, and the constant ebb and flow of men and precious cargo imparted a vitality unknown to most of the other cities in the New World. However, the rest of the island was isolated from this ferment, even though agriculture was developing rapidly as the Spanish encouraged the large-scale cultivation of sugar cane and tobacco, which soon became desirable commodities in Europe *(see p32)*. Cuba, a major hub of maritime traffic, was compelled to trade only with the parent country, Spain. Within a short time the island became a haven for smuggling, which was a boost for the island's economy, stimulating the exchange of Cuban sugar and tobacco for the products of the Old World.

THE BRIEF BRITISH DOMINION

Although in the 17th century the Cuban population, concentrated around Havana, had increased with the arrival of Spanish settlers and African slaves, in the early 18th century the island was

The French buccaneers led by Jacques de Sores sacking the city of Havana

---

TIMELINE

16th-century Spanish galleon

1586 Havana again risks being attacked by Francis Drake's British buccaneers

The coat of arms of Havana: the key of the Gulf, with its fortresses

1550	1600	1650

1555
Havana sacked and burned by French buccaneers under Jacques de Sores

1607 Havana becomes the island's capital

The British fleet attacking Havana in the summer of 1762

still a minor colony. In the summer of 1762 Havana was conquered by the British under the leadership of George Pocock and Lord Albemarle, who ruled for about a year. However, even in this short period the British occupation changed the economic and social organization of the island. The trade restrictions imposed by Spain were abolished, and Cuba began to trade openly with British colonies in North America. The slave trade intensified with Africans being used as labourers on the sugar cane plantations. As a result of the Treaty of Paris, drawn up in 1763, Havana was returned to the Spanish in exchange for Florida.

THE RISE OF NATIONAL IDENTITY

The 18th century marked the birth of a Creole aristocracy. These people, Cuban-born of Spanish descent, commissioned the fine buildings which can still be seen today, and led a Colonial lifestyle based on a combination of local, Indian and African traditions. At the end of the century, a cultural movement promoted by the intellectuals De Heredia, Varela and Villaverde *(see p28)* aimed at establishing a Cuban national identity. In the early 19th century, Spain, forced to recognize the independence of other American colonies, granted some freedom to Cuba, but then gave the island's governors dictatorial powers. Years of revolts, which the Spanish subdued mercilessly, then ensued. However, the new Creole middle class no longer had vested interests in the Spanish crown, and was determined to gain independence for the island.

The new Havana middle class taking a carriage ride

1697 The Treaty of Ryswyk ends the "corsair war" in the West Indies	1762 The British attack and occupy Havana		1830 Cuba replaces Haiti as the world's leading producer of sugar
1700	**1750**		**1800**
	1763 The Treaty of Paris marks the end of British occupation and Havana is given back to the Spanish	*Captain General Luís de las Casas, governor of Cuba 1790–96*	1837 First Cuban railway line opens, beginning at the port of Havana

Sugar, Slaves and Plantations

At the beginning of the 19th century the Cuban sugar industry was booming, thanks to the growing demand for sugar in Europe and America. The growth of the industry was made possible by the labour of slaves brought from Africa in their greatest numbers from the late 18th to the early 19th centuries. About one million men and women were brought to Cuba, and by around 1830 black Africans, including slaves and legally freed slaves, made up more than half the population of Cuba. The island became the world's leading sugar manufacturer, overtaking Haiti, and the industry continued to thrive after the abolition of slavery. Life on the sugar plantations therefore became a key feature of the island's history and life.

Bells *marked the daily routine of life in the* ingenio*: at 4:30am the Ave Maria was played to wake the workers; at 6am the assembly marked the beginning of work proper. At 8:30pm the last bell sounded to announce bedtime.*

Cimarrones *were runaway slaves who hid in the mountains or forests to avoid the* rancheadores, *whose job it was to find and capture them, dead or alive. These fugitives organized frequent revolts, which were almost inevitably suppressed with bloodshed.*

Storehouses, stables and cattle sheds were built around the *ingenio* area.

The sugar refining area stood in the original core of the sugar factory, the *trapiche* or mill.

The first stret ch of railway on the island, which actually preceded the introduction of trains in Spain, was inaugurated in 1837 to transport sugar cane to the port of Havana.

Slaves were used *in all phases of sugar manufacture, and not only as field labourers. This old illustration shows the* sala de las calderas, *where the cane juice was boiled before being refined.*

Carlos Manuel de Céspedes, *the owner of an estate near Manzanillo, freed his slaves on 10 October 1868, thus triggering the Cuban wars of independence. In his manifesto he asked for the abolition of slavery.*

The dances and music *that are thought to have given rise to the rumba (see p31) were performed in the ingenio, accompanied by the drumming of cajones, wooden boxes used to transport goods. Every year on 6 February the plantation owners allowed their slaves to celebrate their origins by dancing in the streets dressed in traditional costumes.*

The *barracones* (the slaves' dormitories) were rectangular buildings divided into small rooms and with only one grilled door.

THE *INGENIO*

The sugar factory *(ingenio)* was in reality an agro-industrial complex, in the middle of which stood the owner's house. This was usually an elegant building, often embellished with arches and wrought-iron grilles. The sugar factory owner would stay here during the long inspection periods. The *batey*, an Amerindian term used to describe collectively all the buildings on an *ingenio*, included a sugar cane mill, refinery rooms, a distillery, an infirmary, stables and cow sheds, vegetable gardens, storehouses, and the slaves' *barracones*, or sleeping quarters.

The ethnologist Fernando Ortiz *(1881–1969) was the first person to seriously analyze the social condition of the blacks in Cuba, emphasizing the cultural bonds with African traditions.*

A CULTURAL MELTING POT

Symbol of the Abakuá religion

The *ingenio* was a place where landowners, farmers and slaves, white and black, men and women, had to live and work together. The African slaves came from different ethnic groups and spoke different languages, but they managed to keep their religious practices alive by meeting in the *cabildos* (mutual aid associations), where they continued to pray to their gods, "concealing" them in the guise of Catholic saints *(see pp22–3)*. The Spanish themselves ended up assimilating elements of the very traditions they had been trying to suppress. Present-day Cuban music and dances were widespread in the *batey*, and the original songs and literature constantly refer to the *ingenio*, since it was here that the cultural crossover typical of Cuba evolved.

THE TEN YEARS' WAR AND THE ABOLITION OF SLAVERY

On 10 October 1868, at his La Demajagua estate *(see p219)*, the landowner Carlos Manuel de Céspedes launched the *grito de Yara* (war-cry from Yara), calling upon his fellow Cubans to rebel against Spanish rule. After conquering Bayamo, the rebels set up a revolutionary government and chose Céspedes as President of the Republic. On that occasion, the Cuban national anthem was sung for the first time. The new republic, however, was short-lived. The Spanish came back with a vengeance and the rebels – known as *mambises* (villains) – responded with the famous "machete assaults". In the meantime, the struggle had spread to other provinces, but differences among the rebels certainly did not help the cause.

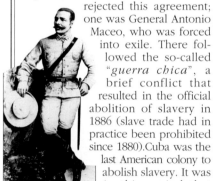

Máximo Gómez

The Ten Years' War – during which the first Cuban constitution was written (1869) – ended in 1878 with the Treaty of Zanjón, at which the rebels capitulated. Some revolutionaries rejected this agreement; one was General Antonio Maceo, who was forced into exile. There followed the so-called *"guerra chica"*, a brief conflict that resulted in the official abolition of slavery in 1886 (slave trade had in practice been prohibited since 1880).Cuba was the last American colony to abolish slavery. It was in this period that trade relations with the US developed.

General Maceo, who was exiled in 1878

RESUMPTION OF HOSTILITIES AND THE END OF THE WAR

Towards the end of the 1800s, despite the rebellions, living conditions on the island had remained basically the same and none of the promised reforms had been enacted. In 1892, the Cuban intellectual José Martí (1853–95), in exile in the US, made a major contribution to the struggles that would follow: he founded the Partido Revolucionario Cubano, which united the Cuban forces in favour of independence.

The war against Spanish repression resumed on 24 February 1895. The leading figures were Martí – the real author and coordinator of Cuba's struggle for independence, who died in battle on 19 May, Máximo Gómez (recruited by Martí himself, who went to Santo Domingo to meet him) and Antonio Maceo. These last two had already distinguished themselves in the Ten Years' War. There was an escalation in the war and Spain sent reinforcements, but the situation was already out of control. Gómez and Maceo extended the war from the east to the west, gradually liberating the island. Not even the arrival of the Spanish general Valeriano Weyler, who was granted extraordinary powers, did any good: the war had taken a decided turn for the worse for the Spanish.

On 15 February 1898, when the Cubans had practically won, the American cruiser *Maine*, officially sent to the bay of Havana to protect US citizens and property in Cuban territory, exploded mysteriously, causing the death of about 250 marines. The US accused Spain of being responsible for the tragedy and, with public opinion

TIMELINE

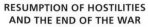

Road sign for *La Demajagua*, Céspedes' estate

10 February 1878
The Treaty of Zanjón marks the capitulation of the rebels and the end of the Ten Years' War (1868–78), the first stage in the struggle for independence

1870	1875	1880	1885

10 October 1868
From Yara, Carlos Manuel de Céspedes launches the "cry" that triggers the revolt

The machete, the symbolic weapon of the rebellion

1886
Formal abolition of slavery

The US battlecruiser *Maine* in Havana Bay in 1898, with the Castillo del Morro on the right

on their side at home, intervened in the war. On 3 July the US Navy defeated the Spanish fleet, with the obvious intent of taking part in the peace treaty. On 10 December the Treaty of Paris – which involved Spain and the US, but not Cuba – marked the end of Spanish Colonial dominion in America. On 1 January 1899 the last Spanish governor, Jiménez y Castellanos, officially handed the keys of Havana to US general John Brooke. From this point onwards, Cuba became inextricably linked with the United States.

US SUPERVISION

In February 1901 the Constituent Assembly approved the first Cuban constitution and Tomás Estrada Palma was elected president. However, the delegates were forced to accept the Platt Amendment, formulated by US senator Orville Platt and added to a bill in Congress. Officially this provision aimed at safeguarding peace on the island, but its underlying purpose was to sanction the right of the US to intervene in Cuban affairs and to supervise trade relations between Cuba and other nations. In addition, the US was granted the right to establish naval bases on the island, including the one at Guantánamo in Eastern Cuba, which it still maintains *(see p239)*.

Although formal independence was granted to Cuba on 20 May 1902, in the years that followed American involvement in the local economy increased and, on the pretext of safeguarding their citizens and investments, the US sent marines to the island on many occasions.

JOSE MARTI

In 1895, when he died in battle at Boca de dos Ríos, José Martí was only 42. Despite this, he had had years of experience of living in exile and revolutionary struggle, besides writing a number of poems, articles and essays that would be the envy of a veteran author. Martí was born in Havana in 1853 to Spanish parents. By the time he went to secondary school he was already participating in anti-Spanish conspiracies. This activity led to his being deported in 1868, and exiled in 1878, after which he lived in the US, Spain, Mexico, Guatemala and Venezuela. As an essayist and journalist, Martí was known for his vigorous style. He was also a modernist poet *(see p28)*. He was an activist, a great politician and a sensitive interpreter of the impulses of the human soul.

José Martí, a national hero

1890		1895		1900	
	1895–8 José Martí heads resumption of hostilities against the Spanish	**15 February 1898** Explosion of the battlecruiser *Maine*		**25 February 1901** First constitution	*Tomás Estrada Palma, first president of Cuba*
1892 José Martí, in exile in the US, founds the Partido Revolucionario Cubano	**19 May 1895** José Martí dies in combat	**7 December 1896** Antonio Maceo dies in combat	**10 December 1898** Paris Treaty marks end of Spanish dominion and beginning of American control		**20 May 1902** Cuba obtains formal independence

THE EARLY PERIOD OF THE REPUBLIC

In its first 25 years, the Cuban Republic was headed by various presidents who did relatively little for the country. The second incumbent, José Miguel Gómez, who was nicknamed *tiburón* (shark), is at least to be credited for having introduced free public education and freedom of association and speech, as well as the separation of Church and State, and laws regarding divorce. In the early 1900s, sugar cane production increased to the point where sugar became virtually the only crop grown, and several new sugar factories were built. Havana, especially in the 1920s, saw the development of entire urban areas.

A popular uprising against the corrupt, inefficient government of Gerardo Machado

However, in general, independence had not really benefited the population at large, and protest demonstrations, repressed with force, began to increase. The first trade and student unions were set up, and in 1925 the Cuban Communist Party was founded. The leading figure in the party was the Marxist intellectual Julio Antonio Mella, leader of the Havana student movement and key to Latin American left-wing politics. Mella was arrested in Cuba but then freed because of the massive demonstrations that took place after he went on hunger strike; he was then sent into exile in Mexico. However, on 10 January 1929, Mella was assassinated in Mexico City by hired killers in the pay of the dictator Gerardo Machado. He became a national hero.

The Marxist intellectual Julio Antonio Mella

GERARDO MACHADO'S REGIME

In 1925 Gerardo Machado became president of Cuba, later changing the Constitution so he could rule for a further term, which he did with iron force until 1933. This period was marked by violence and tyranny; the people demonstrated their discontent by means of continual strikes, and the situation worsened with the Great Depression. A long general strike and the loss of the support of the army forced Machado to flee to the Bahamas on 12 August 1933.

After a brief period of progressive government, from early 1934 onwards there were various presidents who were little more than puppets, placed there by Sergeant Fulgencio Batista – who himself became president from 1940 to 1944. From 1934 to 1940 various social reforms came into being: the Platt amendment was revoked, women were allowed to vote, an eight-hour working day was instituted, and a new constitution was enacted.

1907 Birth of Independent Colour Party, which demands equality between whites and blacks

1910–20 Architectural boom in Havana

1925 Gerardo Machado becomes president

1929 Economic crisis

1905	1910	1915	1920	1925	1930

29 September 1906 Intervention of US Marines, who police Cuba until 1909

Havana railway station (1912)

1925 Founding of Cuban Communist Party

BATISTA'S DICTATORSHIP

After World War II the Orthodox Party led by Eduardo Chibás became popular, supported by the more progressive members of the middle class. This party might have won the election that was to take place on 1 June 1952, but on 10 March Fulgencio Batista staged a coup. Protest demonstrations followed, consisting mostly of students, which were ruthlessly repressed. The university was then closed. Batista's government, having the official support of the US, abandoned its initial populist stance and became an out-and-out, violent dictatorship indifferent to the needs of the Cuban people. In fact, vast areas of land were sold to American and British firms, and the money was pocketed. As the dictator's cronies became rich, the population became poorer, and the country more and more backward. Cuba was becoming a "pleasure island" which held an overpowering fascination, especially for Americans.

By the 1950s Cuba was famous for glamour – its music and cocktails, its splendid prostitutes, cigars, drinking and gambling, and the sensual tropical life attracted mafiosi and film stars, tourists and businessmen, in equal

Fulgencio Batista (left) with American vice-president Richard Nixon

measure. However, there was a high price to pay: Cuba had not only become a land of casinos and drugs, it had also fallen into the hands of the American underworld, which ran the local gambling houses and luxury hotels, used for money laundering.

THE CUBAN REVOLUTION

After Batista's coup, a young lawyer, Fidel Alejandro Castro Ruz, an active student leader who associated with the Orthodox Party, denounced the illegitimacy of the new government to the magistracy, without effect. Since peaceful means did not work, on 26 July 1953 Castro made an unsuccessful attempt to capture the Moncada army barracks at Santiago (see p230). He was one of the few fortunate surviving rebels and was tried and sentenced to imprisonment in the Presidio Modelo, on Isla de Pinos (currently Isla de la Juventud). Thanks to an amnesty, he was freed two years later and went into exile in Mexico, where he set about organizing the revolutionary forces, and was joined by a young Argentine doctor, Ernesto "Che" Guevara. This famous collaboration proved to be decisive for the success of the Revolution. In 1959, after years of armed struggle, the island was freed from dictatorships (see pp48–51).

Dancers at the Tropicana in the 1940s

12 August 1933 At night, Machado flees with a load of gold to the Bahamas	1940–4 Fulgencio Batista obtains presidential mandate thanks to a coalition of forces		1953–9 The Revolution liberates Cuba from dictatorship
1935	**1940**	**1945**	**1950**	**1955**

January 1934
Start of a period with a series of puppet presidents manoeuvred by the Cuban Army sergeant Fulgencio Batista

Sergeant Fulgencio Batista

10 March 1952
Coup d'état by Fulgencio Batista

The Cuban Revolution

In exile in Mexico after the attack on the Moncada army barracks, on 25 November 1956 Fidel Castro left for Cuba on the yacht *Granma* with 81 other revolutionaries, including Che Guevara. Three days later they were attacked by Batista's troops, and only a few managed to escape to the Sierra Maestra, where they began to organize their guerrilla war. The miserable living conditions of the people, and the ever increasing corruption and repression, lent impetus to their struggle. The rebel army, which included farmers, students, women and regular army deserters, defeated Batista's troops after two years of fighting.

The attack against the Moncada barracks
took place on 26 July 1953 (the 100th anniversary of José Martí's birth). The rebels took advantage of the Carnival festivities to move unseen in the crowds, but the attack was a failure.

KEY

– – Raúl Castro's march

– – Che Guevara's march

– – Camilo Cienfuegos' march

Havana was occupied by Che Guevara's guerrillas, while Castro entered Santiago de Cuba (1 January 1959).

Santa Clara was the scene of the battle that marked the triumph of the revolution. After the rebels' victory, Batista fled to Santo Domingo (31 December 1958).

Havana

Matanzas

Pinar del Rio

Santa Clara

Cienfuegos

Isla de la Juventud

Sierra del Escambray was reached by Che Guevara after an exhausting march; his men were without food or shoes and extremely weary but they were victorious (October 1958).

Radio Rebelde
was the guerrillas' radio station, set up in the Sierra Maestra by Che Guevara in February 1958. Its programmes were listened to avidly all over the island.

THE PHASES OF THE WAR

The advance of two columns of guerrillas from the Sierra Maestra – one led by Che Guevara and Camilo Cienfuegos to the west (October 1958), the other by Raúl Castro bound for Guantánamo – marked the climax of the revolutionaries' struggle. After the battle of Santa Clara, conquered by Guevara's troops at the end of December, Batista escaped to Santo Domingo. On 1 January 1959 victory was declared by the revolution.

The Landing of the *Granma*
in Cuba took place on 2 December 1956. Due to some problems at sea, the yacht landed on 2 December and not 30 November as planned. Three days later they were attacked by Batista's troops. Those captured were killed, while the survivors (including Castro) took refuge in the Sierra Maestra.

Castro entered Havana *on 8 January 1959 and on 16 February was elected prime minister. At the time the president was Manuel Urrutia, elected after Batista's escape. The revolutionary government immediately abolished racial discrimination and reduced rents and the cost of electricity.*

Young women, *including Haidée Santamaría, Celia Sánchez and Vilma Espín, participated actively in the revolutionary war. After Havana was captured, they were entrusted with guarding strategic points.*

On the Sierra Maestra, *Cuba's largest mountain range, the rebels organized guerrilla warfare, recruiting soldiers from among the population (above, Castro recruiting farmers). The strategy was to ambush Batista's troops and take their supplies and weapons.*

Camagüey

Holguín

Playa Las Coloradas was where the *Granma* landed on 2 December 1956.

Bayamo   Santiago de Cuba

Guantánamo

The attack at La Plata, a military barracks, was the rebels' first success (17 January 1957).

In the Sierra Maestra Fidel Castro, Che Guevara and the other survivors of the *Granma* worked out a strategy of guerrilla warfare with a growing number of *barbudos*, students, army deserters and reinforcements sent by the urban branch of the Movimiento 26 de Julio.

At Santiago de Cuba the rebels won an important victory on 17 January 1957.

TIMELINE

October 1953 Castro condemned to 15 years' imprisonment in Presidio Modelo	**30 November 1956** Bloody repression of revolt at Santiago	*Che Guevara*	**31 August** Che and Cienfuegos leave east to conquer central regions	**1 January** Che and Cienfuegos enter Havana; Castro, Santiago
1953	**1956**		**1958**	**1959**
26 July 1953 Attack on Moncada barracks	**15 May 1955** Castro freed, goes to Mexico in exile *Castro leaving prison*	**2 December 1956** Landing of *Granma* **1956–58** Guerrilla war in Sierra Maestra	**24 February** Radio Rebelde set up **31 December** Santa Clara falls, Batista flees	**8 January** Castro enters Havana in triumph

The Heroes of the Revolution

The success of the revolution can be partly explained by the moral stature of the heroes who headed it, and partly by the unity of the movement – an entire population was determined to obtain freedom. After their triumphal entrance into Havana, the revolutionary leaders were entrusted with the task of realizing their objectives: the reorganization of the country's agriculture, afflicted with large landed estates and monoculture; the battle against illiteracy and unemployment; industrialization; the construction of homes, schools and hospitals. Fidel Castro became Prime Minister and Che Guevara was appointed Minister of Industry and president of the National Bank. The revolution continued, with its heroes and ideals.

Ernesto "Che" Guevara *was an Argentinian who met Castro in Mexico. Unpretentious, straightforward and ascetic, and an uncompromising idealist, he believed the Third World could be freed only through armed rebellion (see p176).*

The straw hats worn by the *barbudos* were those commonly used by farmers.

Camilo Cienfuegos, *a commander whose courage was legendary, was a direct, spontaneous person with a great sense of humour. He played a crucial role in the armed struggle, but took part in the government only for a brief period. He disappeared on 28 October 1959 while returning in his small plane after arresting guerilla commander Hubert Matos, who had betrayed the Revolution, in Camagüey, and was never seen again.*

Horses were the most common means of transport used by the revolutionaries.

Frank País *(seen here with his mother and fiancée), head of the Movimiento 26 de Julio, was entrusted with organizing a revolt in Santiago de Cuba that would coincide with the landing of the Granma on 30 November 1956. But because of the delay in the landing the revolt was repressed. País died in Santiago during the armed revolt, in an ambush set up by the chief of police.*

Raúl Castro, *Fidel's brother, currently President of Cuba, was one of the few survivors of the landing of the* Granma. *He took part in the guerrilla war and became a member of the government, adopting a radical stance. As Minister of Defence he signed, with Khrushchev, the agreement for the installation of the nuclear missiles in Cuba that caused the 1962 crisis.*

The Cuban flag, used after the wars of independence, has the colours of the French Revolution. The three blue stripes represent the old provinces of the island.

Fidel Castro with Juan Almeida *(left), one of the strategists of revolutionary guerrilla warfare. Castro, a great orator and political strategist, the* Líder Máximo *and an uncompromising patriot, personified the Cuban state. As poet Nicolás Guillén wrote, "he accomplished what José Martí had promised". Born on 13 August 1926 in Mayarí in Eastern Cuba, the son of Spanish immigrants, he studied with the Jesuits and took a degree in law. He began to fight for the cause while at university.*

THE BARBUDOS

The rebels were referred to as *barbudos* (bearded men) because during their time in the mountains, they all grew long beards. A large number of farmers joined their famous marches. This photograph, taken by the Cuban photographer Raúl Corrales, expresses the epic and team spirit of the revolution.

Guillermo García Morales *was one of the first Cuban farmers to join the revolutionary war of the Movimiento 26 de Julio. A guerrilla in the Sierra Maestra together with Castro, he was named Commander of the Revolution for his distinguished service.*

Celia Sánchez Manduley *espoused the revolutionary cause at an early age and fought in the Sierra Maestra. Considered Fidel Castro's right-hand "man" and companion, after 1959 she filled important political positions. Celia died of cancer in 1980, while still young.*

ERADICATING ILLITERACY, AGRICULTURAL REFORM

One of the first acts of the revolutionary government was a campaign against illiteracy, initiated in 1961: thousands of students travelled throughout the countryside, teaching the rural population to read and write. Che Guevara, who during the guerrilla warfare in the mountains had encouraged his men to devote some time to study, participated in the campaign. In a short time illiteracy was eradicated.

Marines arriving at the US naval base of Guantánamo during the missile crisis

The next step was agrarian reform, which began with the abolition of ownership of large landed estates, especially those in foreign (in particular American) hands. US landholdings were drastically reduced. This marked the beginning of hostilities between the two countries. In October 1960 the US declared an economic boycott that blocked the export of petroleum to Cuba and the import of Cuban sugar. After nearly two years of growing tension, Cuba secured closer economic and political ties with the Soviet Union, Eastern Europe and China. In the meantime, the struggle against counter-revolutionary guerrillas in the Sierra del Escambray continued.

Participants in the campaign against illiteracy in 1961

against Cuba, which heralded a boycott by most other countries in the Americas (except Mexico and Canada). These countries also severed diplomatic relations with the island, as the US had done. The result was the establishment of even closer ties between Cuba and the communist world. A year later, when the US discovered the presence of nuclear missile sites in Cuba, President Kennedy ordered a naval blockade around the island and demanded that the missile installations be dismantled immediately. At the height of the crisis, with the world poised on the brink of nuclear war, the Soviet president Nikita Khrushchev ordered the missiles to be taken back to the Soviet Union.

THE EMBARGO AND MISSILE CRISIS

On 17 April 1961 a group of Cuban exiles and mercenaries trained by the CIA landed at Playa Girón, in the Bay of Pigs, to invade the island. But the attack failed because, contrary to the expectations of the US, Cuban civilians did not rise up against Castro (see p167). Eight days later President Kennedy declared a trade embargo

FROM THE *ZAFRA* CAMPAIGN TO THE EMIGRATION OF THE *"MARIELITOS"*

During the early stages, the government had aimed to create as much diversity in the economy as possible. However, in 1970, in order to inject life into the flagging economy, all efforts were concentrated on promoting the

TIMELINE

1961 April 17: landing at Bay of Pigs; US embargo begins on April 25

1962 Missile crisis

1965 Only legal political party is the Cuban Communist Party

1975 First congress of the Cuban Communist Party

1960

1970

1980

1961 January 3, diplomatic relations with US are broken

1967 Death of Che Guevara

1970 The *zafra* campaign

1980 125,000 Cubans emigrate from the small harbour at Mariel

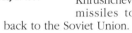

zafra (sugar cane harvest) campaign. A target was set of ten million tons, but in the end only 8,500,000 were harvested. In the same period some Latin American countries resumed diplomatic relations with Cuba. While the revolution had achieved a great deal in social terms, the country's economic problems had by no means been resolved. 1980 saw the emigration of 125,000 Cubans, the so-called *marielitos* – named after the small harbour of Mariel, near Havana, where they set off for Miami.

Pope John Paul II and Castro during his visit to Cuba

THE *PERÍODO ESPECIAL*

The dismantling of the Berlin Wall in 1989 and the subsequent collapse of Communism in Eastern Europe deprived Cuba of economic partners; and Castro did not conceal his dislike of Gorbachev's *perestroika* policy. The suspension of Soviet aid was a crippling blow for the Cuban economy, and triggered a crisis that the government faced by imposing a programme of austerity. In 1990 the island went through one of the most difficult phases in its history, the Período Especial. Many sectors of industry came to a standstill due to a lack of fuel, imports were reduced, interruptions in the supply of electricity and water became part of everyday life, transport virtually came to a halt, food rations were reduced, and wages were lowered. In 1991 the Soviet Union also withdrew its troops and technicians. The economic crisis continued to worsen until 1994.

THE ECONOMIC RECOVERY

At a time when more and more *balseros* (refugees who travelled on makeshift rafts, *balsas*) were fleeing to Miami, the first signs of change appeared. The government began to encourage foreign investment, private enterprise was granted a certain degree of freedom, relations were resumed with Eastern European nations, and the use of the US dollar in transactions was legalized. In the meantime Castro emerged from isolation and undertook official visits to a number of European countries. A sign of the change was Castro's visit to the Vatican to meet Pope John Paul II in 1996, and the Pope's visit to Cuba two years later. By the late 1990s, tourism had become the strongest sector of the economy. Today it is both a resource, and a cause for concern, in that the dual economy of the Cuban *peso* and the convertible peso has created its own particular social problems. Cuba today faces all kinds of challenges, not least, how to change without losing its identity.

Empty shelves in a shop during the crisis period

90 Beginning of the Período Especial	*Rations coupon booklet*	1996 In November, Castro visits Pope John Paul II in the Vatican	2006 July: Castro is taken seriously ill and his brother, Raúl, becomes Acting President	2008 Hurricanes Gustav and Ike hit Cuba and are the costliest storms in recent history
1990			**2000**	**2010**
1991 The Soviet Union withdraws ops and technicians	1996 The Helms-Burton law tightens economic embargo	1998 Pope John Paul II's visit to Cuba (21–25 January), a significant turning point	2000 1,774,000 tourists visit Cuba in one year *Seaside tourism*	2008 Raúl Castro becomes President of the Cuban Council of State

HAVANA
AREA BY AREA

Havana at a Glance

The crest of Havana

Havana is a lively, colourful capital city, full of bustle and entertainment, with some splendid architectural gems from the Colonial period and beyond, and numerous other sights. The city alone is worth the trip to Cuba. Many attractions are concentrated in three quarters: Habana Vieja (Old Havana), Centro Habana and Vedado. In the following pages Habana Vieja, the Colonial centre within the old city walls, is described first, followed by Centro Habana and the area known as Prado. The western part of the city is covered in the chapter called Vedado and Plaza. For map references for major sights in Havana, refer to the Street Finder (*see pp118–23*).

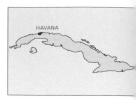

HAVANA

0 kilometres   1

0 miles   1

VEDADO AND PLAZA
(see pp96–105)

Necrópolis de Colón (see pp104–5) *is Havana's city cemetery as well as a national monument. Many famous people are buried here, often in striking tombs, and the site has become a place of pilgrimage for many.*

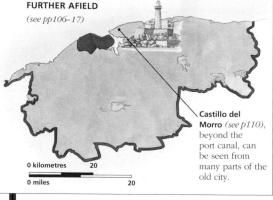

FURTHER AFIELD
(see pp106–17)

0 kilometres   20

0 miles   20

Castillo del Morro *(see p110)*, beyond the port canal, can be seen from many parts of the old city.

Martí Memorial (see p103) *in Plaza de la Revolución is one of the symbols of Cuba. The white marble statue of the great patriot forms a focal point for national celebrations.*

◁ Havana at sunset, with the dome of Capitolio rising up over the rooftops

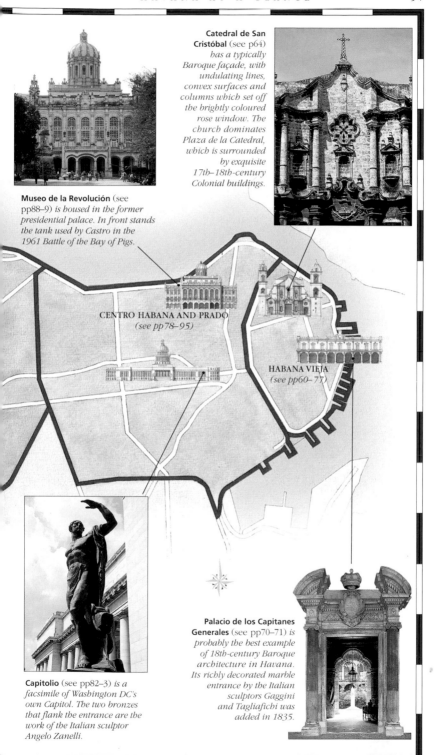

Catedral de San Cristóbal (see p64) *has a typically Baroque façade, with undulating lines, convex surfaces and columns which set off the brightly coloured rose window. The church dominates Plaza de la Catedral, which is surrounded by exquisite 17th–18th-century Colonial buildings.*

Museo de la Revolución (see pp88–9) *is housed in the former presidential palace. In front stands the tank used by Castro in the 1961 Battle of the Bay of Pigs.*

CENTRO HABANA AND PRADO
(see pp78–95)

HABANA VIEJA
(see pp60–77)

Capitolio (see pp82–3) *is a facsimile of Washington DC's own Capitol. The two bronzes that flank the entrance are the work of the Italian sculptor Angelo Zanelli.*

Palacio de los Capitanes Generales (see pp70–71) *is probably the best example of 18th-century Baroque architecture in Havana. Its richly decorated marble entrance by the Italian sculptors Gaggini and Tagliafichi was added in 1835.*

The Malecón

No other place represents Havana better than the Malecón, and no other place thrills tourists and locals so much. This seafront promenade winds for 7 km (4 miles) alongside the city's historic quarters, from the Colonial centre to the skyscrapers of Vedado, charting the history of Havana from past to present. The busy seafront boulevard is lined with many attractive buildings, but it is the overall effect that is striking – and the Bay of Havana looks truly spectacular at sunset. In addition, the Malecón means tradition and religion to the people of the city: offerings to the gods *(see p23)* are thrown from the parapet into the sea.

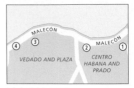

LOCATOR MAP
See Street Finder pp120–23.

① **The Caryatid Building** *is one of the most important structures in the first stretch of the Malecón. Built in the early 20th century and recently restored, it was named after the Art Deco-style female figures that support the entablature of the loggia.*

② **The area between Prado and Calle Belascoaín,** *which has been scrupulously restored, is known for its pastel buildings. In the same part of the street, at No 51, is the "Ataúd" (the coffin), a 1950s skyscraper whose name derives from the shape of its balconies.*

Varied decoration

Balconies with Neo-Moorish decorative patterns

ARCHITECTURE

The Malecón is lined with buildings whose pastel hues have faded in the sun and salty air, as well as early 20th-century structures, often with two or three storeys and a loggia on the upper floor, in a mix of different architectural styles.

Edificio Focsa

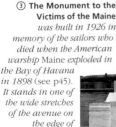

③ **The Monument to the Victims of the Maine** *was built in 1926 in memory of the sailors who died when the American warship* Maine *exploded in the Bay of Havana in 1898 (see p45). It stands in one of the wide stretches of the avenue on the edge of Vedado.*

Hotel Nacional

④ **Between Calle 23 and Calle G** *is the stretch of the Malecón that borders the Vedado quarter to the north. Dominated by Havana's tallest buildings, this is the seafront of a modern metropolis.*

On stormy days *the waves break against the rocks and crash over the sea wall onto the street. Children love it when this happens. Storms are also a source of inspiration for followers of* santería, *who view it as the wrath of Yemayá, the sea goddess (see p23).*

Fishing *on the Malecón is a popular pastime among the locals. Others are playing music, strolling, or simply sitting on the low wall and watching the horizon.*

ATMOSPHERE
The Havana seafront is especially magical at sunset, when the colours of the buildings are accentuated. The Malecón is at its busiest on Sundays, when the Havanans who cannot get to the Playas del Este flock here.

Young people love to gather along the Malecón, to meet friends, socialize, swim, sunbathe and drink rum.

The striking setting *of the Malecón, facing the sea and with the city behind it, makes it a popular place for romantic young couples. There is also the occasional single person on the lookout for female or male companionship.*

A WALK BY THE OCEAN: THE HISTORY OF THE MALECÓN

On 4 November 1901, the US authorities then occupying Cuba planned the Malecón as a tree-lined, pedestrian promenade to begin at the Castillo de la Punta. However the strong wind and rough sea obliged the engineers to change their original project and it was an American engineer named Mead, and Frenchman Jean Forestier, who came up with a more practical plan. In 1902 the open space in front of the Prado was completed with a municipal bandstand. Hotels and cafés were built near the old city, while bathing facilities were concentrated in Miramar. In 1919 the Malecón stretched as far as Calle Belascoaín, and in 1921 as far as Calle 23. It soon became a fast link between the old and modern cities – so much so that in the 1950s it was virtually abandoned by pedestrians. Today, despite the traffic, its original function has been partly revived.

The Malecón in the early 1900s

HABANA VIEJA

The historic heart of Havana, which was declared part of the "cultural heritage of humanity" by UNESCO in 1982, is the largest Colonial centre in Latin America. After two centuries of neglect, restoration work under the direction of Eusebio Leal Spengler, the *historiador de la ciudad* (Superintendent of Cultural Heritage), is reviving the former splendour of this district. Habana Vieja is characterized by

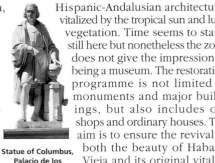

Statue of Columbus, Palacio de los Capitanes Generales

Hispanic-Andalusian architecture, vitalized by the tropical sun and lush vegetation. Time seems to stand still here but nonetheless the zone does not give the impression of being a museum. The restoration programme is not limited to monuments and major buildings, but also includes old shops and ordinary houses. The aim is to ensure the revival of both the beauty of Habana Vieja and its original vitality and everyday activities.

SIGHTS AT A GLANCE

Museums and Galleries
Museo de Arte Colonial ❷
Museo del Ron ⓭
Museo José Martí ⓲

Historic Buildings
Bodeguita del Medio ❹
Castillo de la Real Fuerza ❺
Palacio de los Capitanes Generales pp70–71 ❽
Seminario de San Carlos y San Ambrosio ❸
El Templete ❻

Historic Streets and Squares
Calle Obispo ❾
Calle Oficios ❼
Casa de Africa ⓫
Casa de la Obra Pía ❿
Plaza de San Francisco ⓬
Plaza Vieja ⓮

Churches and Monasteries
Catedral de San Cristóbal ❶
Convento de Santa Clara ⓯
Iglesia de Nuestra Señora de la Merced ⓱
Iglesia del Espíritu Santo ⓰

KEY
- Street-by-Street map *pp62–3*
- Street-by-Street map *pp66–7*
- 🛈 Tourist information
- 🚢 Ferry

0 metres 300
0 yards 300

GETTING THERE
The easiest way to reach this quarter is by taxi, or by *cocotaxi (see p315)*, which is cheaper. A tourist bus also explores the area *(see p314)*. Habana Vieja can be easily explored either on foot or by hiring a rickshaw or carriage. These can be found behind the Castillo de la Real Fuerza, at the corner of Calle Mercaderes and Calle Empedrado.

◁ Colonial buildings in Plaza Vieja *(see p76)*

Street-by-Street: Plaza de la Catedral

Dominated by the elegant profile of its church, Plaza de la Catedral is one of the symbols of Habana Vieja. In 1592, the Zanja Real, the city's first aqueduct (and the first Spanish aqueduct in the New World), reached the square. Water was channelled from the Almendares river, 11 km (7 miles) away. The Zanja Real was built to provide water to ships docking in the harbour, as well as to local residents. A 16th-century plaque in the square marks the spot where the Zanja Real was located. In the 18th century the aristocratic buildings and present-day Cathedral were built here. Plaza de la Catedral is an unmissable attraction for anyone visiting the historic centre, with women in Colonial costume who stroll under the arcades and read fortunes, and a bar-restaurant where you can relax in the shade and listen to music.

A woman in Colonial costume on the Cathedral steps

Former entrance to the seminary

Centro Wifredo Lam, housed in an 18th-century palazzo, promotes contemporary art with exhibitions and lectures.

CALLE SAN IGNACIO

Seminario de San Carlos y San Ambrosio
The modern entrance of this 18th-century building echoes the Baroque decorative motifs of the Cathedral ❸

Palacio de los Marqueses de Aguas Claras was built in the second half of the 18th century. In the 1900s it housed the París Restaurant and then the offices of the Banco Industrial. It is now a bar-restaurant, El Patio, with tables in the inner courtyard as well as in the picturesque square.

CALLE EMPEDRADO

KEY

– – – Suggested route

STAR SIGHTS

★ Catedral de San Cristóbal

★ Museo de Arte Colonial

★ Bodeguita del Medio

Casa de la Condesa de la Reunión, a 19th-century building surrounding a splendid courtyard, is the head-quarters of the Alejo Carpentier Foundation. This well-known 20th-century Cuban writer (*see p29*) set his novel *Siglo de las Luces* here.

LA BODEGUITA DEL MEDIO

★ **Bodeguita del Medio**
This restaurant is legendary thanks to the writer Ernest Hemingway, who came here to drink mojitos ❹

For hotels and restaurants in this region see pp252–6 and pp276–9

LOCATOR MAP
See Street Finder, pp120–23,
map 4

★ Catedral de San Cristóbal
*The Baroque façade of this church, declared
a national monument, is considered one of
the most beautiful in the Americas* ❶

Palacio del Conde Lombillo (1746)
is now home to the offices of the
Historiador De La Habana and hosts
temporary exhibitions of photographs
and lithographs.

CALLE TACÓN

CALLE EMPEDRADO

CALLE MERCADERES

PLAZA DE LA CATEDRAL

Plaza
de Armas
*(see
pp66–7)*

**Palacio de los Marqueses
de Arcos**, built in the 1700s,
houses an art gallery where
handicrafts and prints are
on sale. The building was
once the main post office
and the original letter box is still
visible on the outside wall.

| 0 metres | 40 |
| 0 yards | 40 |

CALLEJÓN DEL CHORRO

CALLE SAN IGNACIO

**The Taller Experimental de
Gráfica** (1962) holds theoretical
and practical courses in graphic
art for Cubans and foreigners, and
houses a Gallery of Engravings.

★ Museo de Arte Colonial
*Dating from 1720, this is one of the
city's finest examples of early Colonial
domestic architecture. It houses an exhibition of Colonial furniture and objects* ❷

Catedral de San Cristóbal ❶

Calle Empedrado 156. **Map** 4 E2.
Tel (7) 8617 771. ☐ 10am–4:30pm
Mon–Fri, 10am–2pm Sat, 9–11:30am
Sun. ✝ 6pm Mon–Fri, 3pm Sat,
10:30am Sun. ⊙

The austere nave of Catedral de San Cristóbal

Construction of the Catedral de San Cristóbal (Cathedral of St Christopher) began in 1748 under the supervision of Jesuit priests, but after they were expelled from Cuba following conflict with the Spanish crown, the church was finished by Franciscans in 1777. It became a cathedral after the collapse of the old Parroquial Mayor *(see p70)*, which was caused by the explosion of a ship in the nearby port.

In 1789, present-day San Cristóbal was consecrated as Catedral de la Virgen María de la Inmaculada Concepción, and the small square where it stands gained its current status. In 1796 it was renamed Catedral de San Cristóbal de La Habana, because, according to popular belief, from that year until 1898 it housed the relics of Christopher Columbus himself. A plaque to the left of the pulpit tells the same story, though there is no official historical record.

The architecture is in keeping with other Jesuit churches throughout the world: a Latin cross layout, chapels on the sides and to the rear, the nave higher than the side aisles. The Cuban Baroque façade is grandiose, with two large, asymmetrical bell towers and an abundance of niches and columns, which Cuban author Alejo Carpentier described as "music turned into stone".

In comparison, the Neo-Classical interior is rather disappointing. Large piers separate the nave from the aisles, which have eight chapels. The largest one is the Sagrario chapel; the oldest (1755), designed by Lorenzo Camacho, is dedicated to the Madonna of Loreto and contains quaint, tiny houses used as ex votos.

The three frescoes behind the high altar are by Giuseppe Perovani, while the original wooden and plaster ceiling, demolished and then rebuilt in 1946–52, was the work of Frenchman Jean Baptiste Vermay, who founded the San Alejandro Fine Arts Academy *(see p26)*. The high altar was created by Italian artist Giuseppe Bianchini in the 1800s. To the right is a huge wooden statue of St Christopher, carved by the Seville sculptor Martín de Andújar in 1636. The legs are out of proportion with the trunk, as they were cut in order to allow the statue to pass through the portal.

On 16 November, the saint's feast day, a solemn mass is held here, during which the faithful, who have to stay quiet during the service, file past the statue to silently ask for his blessing. This blessing is given as long as worshippers do not utter a word until they have left the church.

Statue of St Christopher

Pope John Paul II in front of the Cathedral

POPE JOHN PAUL II'S VISIT

Pope John Paul II visited Cuba from 21–25 January 1998 *(see p53)*. This carefully planned event was of great historical significance to Cuba and was greeted with enthusiasm not only by Catholics, but by virtually the entire population. The Cuban government had shown signs of favouring dialogue with the Church and greater religious tolerance in the 1990s. The Pope's visit and the outdoor masses were broadcast on television and the government also officially recognized Christmas Day as a holiday. On 25 January the "Celebration of the Word" was held in the Cathedral, during which the Pope met Cuban priests. Journalists from all over the world attended, and the Pope also held an audience with the faithful in Plaza de la Revolución.

Museo de Arte Colonial ❷

Calle San Ignacio 61. **Map** 4 E2. **Tel**
(7) 8626 440. 🕙 9am–5:30pm Tue–
Sat, 9am–noon Sun. 🔴 10 Oct. 📷
🎫 📷 (with charge).

This 18th-century mansion,
built by Don Luis Chacón,
governor of Cuba, has been
the home of a fascinating
museum dedicated to Colonial
art since 1969. The building is
a fine example of a Colonial
residence and is constructed
around an elegant courtyard.

The 12 rooms on the ground
floor and first floor contain
furniture, chandeliers,
porcelain and other decorative
pieces from various 18th–19th-
century middle-class and
aristocratic houses in Havana,
in which European, Creole
and Colonial traditions are
combined. Besides a remarkable collection of furniture
made of tropical wood,
the museum has an
exceptional collec-
tion of stained
glass windows
(mediopunto),
typical of
Cuba's Creole
craftsmen *(see
p25)*.

**Museo de Arte Colonial: an arched
mediopunto window**

There is also a 13th room
where exhibitions of contemporary artand crafts inspired
by Colonial art are held. During the week the museum
organizes tours for school-
children and leisure activities
for the elderly in the area.

A small adjacent theatre,
which has its own entrance on
Calle San Ignacio, puts on a
busy and wide-ranging
programme of concerts and
plays at weekends.

Seminario de San Carlos y San Ambrosio ❸

Calle San Ignacio 5. **Map** 4 E2. **Tel** (7)
8626 989. 🕙 8am–5pm Mon–Fri.
🔴 1 Jan, 26 Jul, 10 Oct, 25 Dec. 📷

This building was erected
by the Jesuits in the mid-
18th century to house a
seminary first founded in
1689. Famous Cuban patriots

**Colonial furniture in the Museo de
Arte Colonial**

and intellectuals studied here.
One of them was Padre Félix
Varela (1788–1853), who laid
down the theoretical bases
for the Cuban war of independence *(see p28)*.

Besides the old portal on
Calle San Ignacio, built in
the Churrigueresque
style which was
common in Spain
and her colo-
nies in this
period, there
is also anoth-
er entrance in
20th-century
Neo-Baroque style on the
Avenida del Puerto.

The large central courtyard
is the only one of its kind in
Cuba: it has galleries on three
levels, the first with simple
columns, the second with
double columns, and the third
with plain wooden piers. The
lavishly decorated inner
stairway leading to the first
floor has trapezoidal motifs
instead of the more common
arch, and fine black mahogany
banisters. The seminary is still
functioning, but is open to
the public for visits.

Bodeguita del Medio ❹

Calle Empedrado 207. **Map** 4 E2.
Tel (7) 8671 374. 🕙 noon–12:30am
daily. 📷

Standing exactly at the
halfway point in a typical
small street in old Havana,
a few steps away from the
Cathedral, the Bodeguita del
Medio (literally, "little shop in
the middle") has become a
big attraction.

The place was founded in
1942 as a food shop. A bar
serving alcoholic drinks was
added, and the place became
a haunt for intellectuals, artists
and politicians. Today it is
no longer a shop but a good
restaurant offering typical
Creole dishes, with a bustling
bar serving shots of rum and
Cuban cocktails. The walls are
plastered with photographs,
drawings, graffiti and visitors'
autographs, including those
of famous patrons such as the
singer Nat King Cole, poets
Pablo Neruda and Nicolás
Guillén, and the writers
Gabriel García Marquez, Alejo
Carpentier *(see p29)*, and
Ernest Hemingway, who
was a regular here.

The Bodeguita del Medio with its memento-covered walls

Street-by-Street: Around Plaza de Armas

The elegant, spacious Plaza de Armas is lined with Baroque buildings, giving it a delightful Colonial atmosphere. The space overflows with tropical vegetation and is enlivened by the stalls of the second-hand book market *(see p69)*. The plaza was built in the 1600s to replace the old Plaza Mayor, the core of Havana's religious, administrative and military life, and up to the mid-1700s it was used for military exercises. After its transformation in 1771–1838, it became a favourite with rich Havana citizens and popular as an area for carriage rides. Careful restoration work has been carried out over recent years, and the square now attracts throngs of visitors and locals, many of whom simply gather here to sit and relax.

Palacio del Segundo Cabo (1776), the former residence of the Spanish lieutenant governor, is now the home of the Cuban Book Institute.

★ Palacio de los Capitanes Generales
This fine Baroque palace, now the Museo de la Ciudad, was built for Cuba's old Colonial rulers. A statue of Columbus stands in the courtyard, beneath towering royal palms **8**

Plaza de la Catedral *(see pp62–3)*

STAR SIGHTS

- ★ Castillo de la Real Fuerza
- ★ El Templete
- ★ Palacio de los Capitanes Generales
- ★ Calle Obispo

Hotel Ambos Mundos

Former Ministerio de Educación

Farmacia Taquechel

★ Calle Obispo
Like an open-air museum of Colonial architecture, this street is lined with buildings of interest dating from the 16th–19th centuries, including old groceries and historic shops **9**

Casa de la Obra Pía
This large 17th-century mansion is well-known for its elaborate Baroque doorway, which was reputedly sculpted in Spain **10**

★ Castillo de la Real Fuerza
This 16th-century castle, with its broad moat and characteristic angular ramparts, is the oldest military construction in Havana. A copy of the Giraldilla, the symbol of the city, stands on one of its towers ❺

LOCATOR MAP
See Street Finder, pp120–23, map 4

Calle Enna is Havana's narrowest and shortest street. It was named after a general active in the Colonial period.

★ El Templete
This Neo-Classical building, shaded by a majestic ceiba tree, evokes memories of the city's foundation ❻

AVENIDA CARLOS M. DE CÉSPEDES (AVENIDA DEL PUERTO)

CALLE O'REILLY

PLAZA DE ARMAS

CALLE BARATILLO

CALLE OFICIOS

CALLE JÚSTIZ

Hotel Santa Isabel is in the former home of the Conde de Santovenia, built between the 18th and 19th centuries and recently opened after lengthy restoration *(see p253).*

La Casa de los Arabes housed the city's first school in the 17th century.

Calle Oficios
This perfectly restored Colonial street houses a number of shops and museums, including a vintage car museum ❼

0 metres		60
0 yards		60

KEY

– – – Suggested route

Stairway leading to the battlements, Castillo de la Real Fuerza

Castillo de la Real Fuerza 🄹

Calle Tacón e/ Calle Obispo y O'Reilly.
Map 4 F2. **Tel** (7) 8616 130.
⬤ *Closed for restoration until late 2008.* 🄳 🄼 🄾 *(with charge).*

This fortress *(castillo)* was built in 1558–77 to protect the city from pirate attacks, following a raid by the French buccaneer Jacques de Sores in 1555, in which the original fort was destroyed and Havana devastated *(see p40)*. But despite the moat surrounding it and its thick walls, the castle soon proved to be quite inadequate as a defensive bulwark because of its poor strategic position, too far inside the bay. The castle then became the residence of governors, military commanders and leading figures, as well as a safe place to store

The tower with its copy of the 17th-century weathervane

LA GIRALDILLA

There are various theories as to the meaning of the bronze weathervane sculpted by Gerónimo Martín Pinzón in 1630–34 and modelled on the one crowning La Giralda in Seville. Some people say it is the symbol of victory, others think it is the personification of Seville, the final destination of ships going to Europe. But others say the statue represents Inés de Bobadilla, wife of the Spanish governor Hernando de Soto. According to legend, she spent hours gazing at the horizon, waiting for her husband to return from his exploration of Florida and other parts of the US (in vain, since he died on the banks of the Mississippi). This is said to be the reason why the statue was placed on the highest point of the fortress dominating the port entrance.

Painted pottery, Ceramics Museum

treasures brought from America and en route to Spain. In 1634, a weathervane known as La Giraldilla was placed on the lookout tower, which soon became the symbol of Havana. The original is now on display in the Museo de la Ciudad *(see pp70–71)* and a copy has been placed on the tower. Today, the Castillo houses the **Museo Nacional de la Cerámica Cubana**, which houses a collection of ceramics, sculpture, mosaics and painted panels by modern and contemporary Cuban artists.

El Templete 🄺

Plaza de Armas, Calle Baratillo y O'Reilly. **Map** 4 F2. ◯ *9am–7pm daily.* ⬤ *1 Jan, 1 May.* 🄳 🄼 🄾 *(with charge).*

Small and austere, this Neo-Classical building, resembling a temple, stands on the spot where, according to legend, the city of San Cristóbal de La Habana was founded in 1599. Here, under a leafy ceiba – a tropical tree considered sacred by all the natives of Central America – the first meeting of the local government *(the cabildo)* and the first mass reputedly took place. A majestic ceiba tree still stands in front of El

View of the Castillo de la Real Fuerza: the drawbridge and entrance, the moat, and the Giraldilla tower (left)

For hotels and restaurants in this region see pp252–6 and pp276–9

Templete, although it is not the original. Next to it is the Columna de Cacigal, a column named after the governor who ordered its construction in 1754.

El Templete, completed in 1828, was modelled after a monument in the Basque town of Guernica in northern Spain. Inside are three enormous canvases by Jean-Baptiste Vermay (see p26), depicting scenes from the history of Havana: the local authorities inaugurating the building, the first cabildo, and the first mass, which was celebrated by Bishop Juan José Díaz Espada y Land, who blessed the city as part of the ceremony.

The First Mass, one of Vermay's paintings in the Templete

Calle Oficios ❼

Map 4 F2.

This street was originally a link between the military centre of Plaza de Armas and the commercial and harbour activities centred around Plaza San Francisco. Together with Calle Obispo, this is one of the most atmospheric streets in Old Havana and should be toured slowly (don't miss the many interesting façades).

Approaching from Plaza de Armas, there are three buildings well worth visiting. The first, at No. 8, is the home of the **Museo Numismático**, built in the late 1700s and for a long time the premises of the Monte de Piedad bank. According to legend it was inhabited by the ghost of a Colonial lady dressed in white. It has a rich collection of coins, banknotes, old lottery tickets, medals, and Cuban and foreign bank documents.

At No. 16 is the 18th-century **Casa de los Arabes**, with displays of 18th- and 19th-century Hispanic-Arab bronzes, fabrics, rugs and furniture: the largest ethnographic display of Arab objects in Cuba, evidence of the presence of an old Lebanese, Syrian and Palestinian colony on the island. The building also houses the only mosque in Cuba and an Andalusian restaurant.

The third interesting and curious museum on the street is the **Museo del Auto Antiguo**, featuring vintage Cadillacs, Rolls-Royces, Packards and Fords dating from the 1930s, as well as the Bel-Air Chevrolet that once belonged to Che Guevara.

🏛 **Museo Numismático**
Tel (7) 8615 811. ◻ 9:15am–5:15pm Tue–Sat; 9am–1pm Sun. ●
1 Jan, 26 Jul, 10 Oct, 25 Dec. 🖼🎥

The Casa de los Arabes patio, with narrow balconies and a Moorish-style fountain

🏛 **Casa de los Arabes**
Tel (7) 8615 868.
◻ 9am–5pm Mon–Sat, 9am–noon Sun. 🖼📷

🏛 **Museo del Auto Antiguo**
Tel (7) 863 9942.
◻ 9am–4:30pm Tue–Sat, 9am–12:30pm Sun. ● Mon.
🎥✓📷 (with charge).

THE MARKET IN PLAZA DE ARMAS

Since the early 1990s, when small businesses were officially authorized, this plaza (see p67) has been filled with colourful stalls. In the streets that surround it is a market with second-hand books and periodicals of every kind, magazines published in the 1940s and 1950s, newspapers from the time of the revolution and Cuban classics now out of print. Next to the San Carlos y San Ambrosio Seminary and behind the Castillo is the tourist handicrafts market, where skilfully made objects created from papier mâché and glass take their place alongside the more traditional and familiar ceramics and carved wood.

Second-hand books at the daily market in the Plaza de Armas

Palacio de los Capitanes Generales ❽

Early 19th-century marble bathtub in the bathroom

Construction of this palace, a splendid example of Cuban Baroque *(see p24)*, took from 1776 to 1791. It was commissioned by the governor Felipe Fondesviela and designed by engineer Antonio Fernández de Trebejos y Zaldívar. The Palacio originally housed the Chapter House and the governor's residence as well as a house of detention, which until 1834 occupied the west wing. The seat of the Cuban Republic in 1902, the building became the Museo de la Ciudad (City Museum) in 1967, but the original structure of the sumptuous residence and political centre has not been altered. The complex as a whole offers an overview of the history of Havana, from the remains of the old Espada cemetery and Parroquial Mayor church to mementoes from the wars of independence.

Hall of Heroic Cuba
This hall contains objects from the independence wars, including the flag of Céspedes (see p42).

The Cabildo Maces
Considered the first major example of Cuban goldsmithery, these maces, by Juan Díaz (1631), are on display in the Sala del Cabildo, the room where local town council meetings were held in the governor's palace.

★ Cenotaph from the Parroquial Mayor Church
In 1557 the oldest Colonial monument in Cuba was placed in the old Parroquial Mayor (parish church), which then stood on this site. It commemorates the death of a young woman who was killed by accident while she was praying.

★ La Giraldilla
At the foot of the steps leading to the mezzanine is the oldest bronze statue in Cuba. It was commissioned by the governor, Juan Bitrián de Viamonte, for the lookout tower of the Castillo de la Real Fuerza (see p68).

STAR SIGHTS

★ Cenotaph from the Parroquial Mayor Church

★ La Giraldilla

★ Salón de los Espejos

Gallery
The monumental gallery, which overlooks a large, leafy courtyard, features a collection of busts of illustrious figures, the work of the Italian sculptor Luigi Pietrasanta in the early 1900s.

VISITORS' CHECKLIST

Plaza de Armas, Calle Tacón
e/ O'Reilly y Obispo.
Map 4 E2. **Tel** (7) 8615 779,
8615 062. ◯ 9am–7pm daily.
⬤ 1 Jan, 1 May.
▨ ▥ ▣ (with charge) ▯

The White Room
has on display the escutcheons of Bourbon Spain and the city of Havana, and is decorated with 18th- and 19th-century Meissen porcelain.

Throne Room
Modelled on the large salon in the Palacio de Oriente in Madrid, this room was originally built for a Spanish monarch, but never used. It was restored in 1893 for the visit of Princess Eulalia of Bourbon.

The stained-glass windows brighten the grey of the *piedra marina*, a limestone encrusted with coral fossils.

The Espada Cemetery Room
has relics from the first city cemetery, founded by Bishop Juan José Díaz de Espada in 1806. They include the tomb of the French artist Vermay *(see p26)*.

★ Salón de los Espejos
The end of Spanish rule was proclaimed in 1899 in this light-filled salon with its 19th-century Venetian mirrors, and in 1902 the first president of the Republic of Cuba took office here.

The portico pavement, made of *china pelona*, a hard, shiny stone, dates from the 18th century.

Casa del Agua la Tinaja, vendor of purified well water

Calle Obispo ⑨

Map 4 E2.

The liveliest and most characteristic street in Old Havana is like a long, narrow bridge linking the two architectural souls of the historic centre, the Colonial and the Art Nouveau-eclectic. At one end is the Plaza de Armas, the Baroque heart of the old city, while at the other is Avenida de Bélgica and the famous El Floridita restaurant, which mark the start of the more modern district. The street is called Calle Obispo because in the past the city bishop (obispo) resided in the building situated on the corner of Calle Oficios.

Old filter, Taquechel pharmacy

Thanks to the recent restoration work promoted by the Oficina del Historiador de la Ciudad, headed by the charismatic Eusebio Leal Spengler, aimed at salvaging the best buildings in the old area, Calle Obispo has retained the elegance, vivacity and colours of the Colonial period. Newly installed street lighting makes for enjoyable evening strolling.

A plaque on the left-hand side of the Palacio de los Capitanes Generales bears quotations made by the great Cuban patriot José Martí concerning Garibaldi's stop at Havana. Opposite is the small

shop window of the **Casa del Agua la Tinaja**, which for centuries has been selling well water purified by very old but still quite efficient ceramic filters. Next door, **La Mina** restaurant serves food and cocktails outdoors and brightens up the whole block with live traditional music *(see p276)*.

Among the most fascinating shops in this part of the street is the old pharmacy called **Taquechel**, which sells cosmetics and natural and homeopathic products, all created and produced in Cuba. Quaint shelves boast a pretty collection of 17th- and 18th-century glass and Italian majolica jars, as well as alembics and antique pharmaceutical and medical objects. No. 117–19 is the oldest house in Havana *(see p24)*.

One of the major sights in the street is the restored **Hotel Ambos Mundos** *(see p253)*. This charming, eclectically decorated hotel is rich in literary memories. The writer Ernest Hemingway stayed here for long periods from 1932 to 1939 *(see p114)*, and began writing his famous novel *For Whom the Bell Tolls* in room 511.

Towards the end of the street, near the small Obispo y

Wooden *"azul avana"* blue doors of the Colonial house at No. 117

Bernaza square, there are more modern shops offering everything from embroidered shirts to books.

Next is **El Floridita** restaurant *(see p277)*, known as "the cradle of the daiquiri". It was here, in the 1930s, that barman Constante (his real name was Constantino Ribalaigua) perfected the original cocktail mixed by Pagluchi *(see p275)*. The new-style daiquiri, a blend of white rum, lemon, sugar and a few drops of maraschino and ice, was devised with the help of Ernest Hemingway, who was a regular. Today, in El Floridita's luxurious interior, besides Constante's classic cocktails you can feast on lobster and shellfish in the company of a bust of the great novelist. It was sculpted by Fernando Boada while Hemingway was still alive.

An old letter box at No.115

Typical majolica jars on the shelves of the former Sala Museo

The upper gallery of the Casa de la Obra Pía, with its frescoed walls and polished wood balustrade

Casa de la Obra Pía ⑩

Calle Obrapía 158 esq. Mercaderes. **Map** 4 E2. **Tel** (7) 8613 097. ⭕ 9am–5pm Tue–Sat, 9:30am–12:30pm Sun. ⬤ 1 Jan, 1 May, 26 Jul, 10 Oct. 🎟 📷

Calle Obrapía (literally Charity Street) was named after this mansion, whose own name commemorates the pious actions of Martín Calvo de la Puerta y Arrieta, a wealthy Spanish nobleman who took up resi-dence here in the mid-17th century. Every year he gave a generous dowry to five orphan girls for them to use to get married or enter a convent. A century later the residence became the home of Don Agustín de Cárdenas, who was given the title of marquis for taking Spain's side in 1762 during the British occupation of Havana *(see p40)*. In 1793 new decoration, and the elaborate arch leading to the loggia on the first floor, were added to the building.

La Casa de la Obra Pía is regarded as one of the jewels of Cuban Baroque archi-tecture, and its luxurious salons were used for young noblewomen to make their debut in society.

CALLE DE LA OBRA-PIA

Majolica tile street sign for Calle de la Obrapía

Many colourful legends survive concerning the building's past. It was said that incredible treasures were hidden in its walls and that wailing and weeping could be heard from one of the rooms on the upper floor.

At the corner of Calle Obrapía and Calle Mercaderes is the **Casa de México**, a cultural centre that shows the close links between Mexico and Cuba. It has a library with more than 5,000 books and a museum displaying handmade glass, silver, fabric, terracotta and wooden objects. Lastly, on the other side of the street is the **Casa de Guayasamín**, named after the Ecuadorean painter whose works are on display.

Palo Monte objects *(see p23)*, Casa de Africa

Casa de Africa ⑪

Calle Obrapía 157 e/ San Ignacio y Mercaderes. **Map** 4 E2. **Tel** (/) 8615 798. ⭕ 9am–5pm Tue–Sat, 9am–1pm Sun. ⬤ 1 Jan, 26 Jul, 10 Oct, 25 Dec. 🎟 🎟 📷 (with charge).

Opposite the Casa de la Obra Pía is a 17th-century building that was rebuilt in 1887 to accommodate a family of plantation owners on the upper floor and a tobacco factory, worked by slaves, on the ground floor. It is appropriate that the building is now a museum containing more than 2,000 objects linked to the history of sub-Saharan Africa and the various ethnic groups that were taken to Cuba on slave ships. Many of these items belonged to the ethnographer Fernando Ortíz, a specialist in the African roots of Cuban culture. Together with the section on religion, which includes objects from the various Afro-Cuban cults *(see pp22–3)*, there are instruments of torture used on the slaves, batá drums, and paintings of plantation life. The museum also has a well-stocked library.

Plaza de San Francisco ⑫

Map 4 F2. **Basílica Menor de San Francisco de Asís** *Tel (7) 862 9683.* ◯ *9:30am–5:30pm Mon–Fri, 11:30am–7pm Sat.* ● *1 Jan, 1 May, 26 Jul, 10 Oct, 25 Dec.* 🖼 🎫 📷

Bordering the port, this picturesque square has an Andalusian character and evokes images of a distant age when galleons loaded with gold and other cargo set sail for Spain. In the middle of the square is the **Fuente de los Leones**, modelled on the famous fountain in the Alhambra in Granada. This work by the Italian sculptor Giuseppe Gaggini was donated in 1836 by the fiscal superintendent, Don Claudio Martínez de Pinillos, the Count of Villanueva, and for many years it supplied the ships docked here with drinking water.

The original commercial nature of the area can be seen in two buildings: the Aduana General de la República (the old customs house), built in 1914, and the **Lonja del Comercio** (the former stock exchange, 1908), with a dome crowned by a statue of Mercury, god of commerce. Restored in 1995, this building houses the offices of some of the top foreign firms now operating in Cuba.

The most important building in the square, however, is the **Basílica Menor de San Francisco de Asís**, built in

The Fuente de los Leones, Plaza de San Francisco

1580–91 as the home of the Franciscan community and partly rebuilt in the 1700s. The three-aisle interior has a Latin cross layout and contains some paintings by unknown 18th-century Cuban artists and a wooden statue of St Francis dating from the same period, again by an unknown artist. The basilica also has the remains of major Havana citizens, from the Marquis González, who died during the British siege of 1762, to José Martín Félix de Arrate, an illustrious historian of the Colonial period. Because of its exceptional acoustics, this church was recently converted into a concert hall for choral and chamber music *(see p125).*

Attached to the church is a large, 42-m (138-ft) high bell

Logo of the Havana Club Foundation

tower that affords a lovely view of the city. Originally a statue of St Francis of Assisi stood on the top, but it was badly damaged by a cyclone in 1846.

In the cloister and rooms of the adjacent monastery, which dates back to 1739, is a museum of holy art with 18th–19th-century missals, a collection of votive objects made of precious metals, and 16th–18th-century majolica and ceramics.

Museo del Ron ⑬

Calle San Pedro 262. **Map** 4 F3. *Tel (7) 862 3832, 861 8051.* ◯ *9am–5pm Mon–Thu, 9am–4pm Fri–Sun.* 🖼 🎫 📷 🏠 💻 **www.**havanaclubfoundation.com

The distilleries of Havana Club, the most famous brand of Cuban rum, are open to the public, allowing visitors to see the production process of the spirit described as the "cheerful child of sugar cane" by Cuban writer and journalist Fernando Campoamor, a friend of Ernest Hemingway.

The organized tours begin in the Colonial courtyard of the Havana Club Foundation. After watching a brief videotape on the history of sugar cane and its cultivation, visitors are taken to see the fermentation, distillation (in a room with old alembics), filtration, ageing, blending and bottling processes. In the central hall, heavy with the intense smell of fermented molasses, is a model of an *ingenio (see pp42–3),* or sugar plantation, which also includes a miniature steam train. Tours end in a bar where visitors can relax and sample the three year-old rum. The bar, which also serves excellent cocktails and often has live music, is open from 9am to midnight. The shop sells rum, glassware and souvenirs.

Interior of the basilica of San Francisco, now used for chamber music concerts

For hotels and restaurants in this region see pp252–6 and pp276–9

Cuban Rum

The history of rum dates back to the early 1500s, when an impure distillate was first obtained from sugar cane. With the arrival of Facundo Bacardí *(see p228)*, a new technique of distillation was introduced, and Cuban rum *(ron)* went on to enjoy international success. Rum is part of everyday life in Cuba: a constant companion at parties and festivities, the main ingredient in cocktails, and an

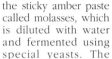

Seal of guarantee of Cuban rum

offering that is frequently given to the gods of *santería*. Rum-making begins with the main by-product of sugar, the sticky amber paste called molasses, which is diluted with water and fermented using special yeasts. The "must" thus obtained is then distilled and filtered to produce an eau de vie. Purified water and pure. alcohol are then added 18 months later to produce Silver Dry, a young, clear rum.

Distillation, *which used to be effected by means of alembics (left), is now carried out by using a series of connected tubes in which the molasses vapour is channelled until it condenses and is transformed into a colourless liquid that is then aged in special barrels.*

The *mezcla* process *is carried out under the expert guidance of a master taster and consists of mixing the new rum with other rums. Once blended, the rum rests for a few weeks in special vats until the right balance of taste and aroma is obtained.*

Special oak barrels *are used for the ageing process which takes at least three years. With time the rum becomes richer in colour and more full-bodied, like the seven-year añejo. The temperature, humidity level and ventilation in the ageing cellars are carefully regulated.*

THE TYPES OF RUM

Besides Silver Dry, which is normally used in cocktails, the market offers rum aged for three years *(carta blanca)*, five years *(carta oro)*, and seven years *(añejo)*, or even longer. Old rum, which is the most highly prized, should be drunk neat and at room temperature, while *carta blanca*, which is the most commonly seen, can be used in many ways and is often drunk with ice. There are assorted brands of Cuban rum, not all of which are internationally known like Havana Club.

Silver Dry   **Carta Blanca**   **Carta Oro**   **Añejo**

The cloister of the convent of Santa Clara, filled with tropical plants

Plaza Vieja ⑭

Map 4 E3.

This square was laid out in 1559 and was originally called Plaza Nueva (New Square). In the 19th century, after the widening of Plaza de Armas and the creation of other urban areas, it lost its role as the city's main public square and was renamed Plaza Vieja. From the 1950s to the 90s it was a car park, but it has now been restored to its original appearance.

The plaza is surrounded by arcades and a number of historic buildings from four different centuries. The most important of these is the **Casa del Conde Jaruco**, built in 1733–37. This was the home of the Countess de Merlin, a Cuban romantic novelist who became a French citizen and also wrote a travel book about Cuba. The house is now used for art exhibitions. The spacious salon on the first floor, with its fine large stained-glass windows or *mediopuntos* (see p25), is well worth a visit.

Next door are two 17th-century buildings, and at the corner of Calle Muralla and Calle Inquisidor is the eye-catching Art Nouveau Hotel-Palacio Cueto. It was first built as a hotel in 1908, then later turned into apartments and is now being restored as a five-star hotel.

A fountain designed in 1796 stands in the middle of the square. It bears the crest of the city and of the Count of Santa Clara, then the city's governor. Nearby are two cultural institutions: a centre for visual arts and a photo gallery.

Convento de Santa Clara ⑮

Calle Cuba 610 e/ Sol y Luz. **Map** 4 E3. **Tel** (7) 8613 335. ☐ 8:30am–5pm Mon–Fri. ● 1 Jan, 26 Jul, 10 Oct, 25 Dec. 🖼 ✗ 🖻 🖸 (with charge).

The Convent of Santa Clara is one of the oldest and most typical Colonial religious buildings in the New World. The convent occupies a considerable area of Habana Vieja and was founded in 1644 by Sister Catalina de Mendoza from Cartagena de Indias, to offer refuge for the wealthy girls of the city.

The plain exterior, with its simple windows, makes a striking contrast to the interior, which has a colonnaded courtyard with elaborate inlaid wooden ceilings. Two of the three original cloisters have stood the test of time. In one of them, overflowing with luxuriant tropical vegetation and with an 18th-century fountain known as "The Samaritan", is the Centro Nacional de Conservación, Restauración y Museología, a body which coordinates the preservation and restoration of Cuba's historic architecture.

The second cloister is now part of a charming hotel decorated in Colonial style. Parts of the building are open to the public but it cannot be seen in its entirety.

Façade of Casa del Conde Jaruco, with typical *mediopunto* stained-glass windows on the first floor

The nave of the Iglesia de la Merced, illuminated by small light bulbs

Iglesia del Espíritu Santo ⑯

Calle Cuba esq. Acosta. **Map** 4 E3. **Tel** (7) 862 3410. ◯ 3–6pm Mon–Sat, 9am–noon Sun. ◢ ✚ 6pm Thu, 5pm Sat, 10:30am Sun.

The Church of the Holy Ghost (Espíritu Santo) is of historical importance as one of the oldest Catholic churches in Havana. It was built in 1637 by some freed African slaves. Thanks to a papal bull and a royal decree from Carlos III, in 1772 it acquired the exclusive right to grant asylum to all those persecuted by the authorities.

From an architectural standpoint, the building's most striking feature is the tower, which is almost as tall as the one on the Basilica of San Francisco (see p74). The church was radically rebuilt in the 19th century, retaining its Hispanic-Arab look only in the characteristic double pitch roof. The main chapel, with its stone vaulting and a crypt, was built by Bishop Jerónimo Valdés in 1706–29.

The area around the church plays host to one of the most picturesque religious markets in the city, in which the yerberos, or herbalist-healers, sell votive objects and various herbs that are used mostly in the local Afro-Cuban religious rites (see pp22–3).

Iglesia de Nuestra Señora de la Merced ⑰

Calle Cuba 806. **Map** 4 E3. **Tel** (7) 8638 873. ◯ 8am–noon, 3–5pm daily. ◙ ✚ 9am daily.

Construction of this church began in 1637 but ended only in the following century, while the lavish decoration in the interior dates from the 19th century. The church is popular among those who follow santería, or local Afro-Cuban religion (see pp22–3). According to the beliefs of this cult, Our Lady of the Merced corresponds to a Yoruba divinity known as Obbatalá, principal figure among the gods and the protector of mankind, who imparts wisdom and harmony. On the Catholic saint's feast day, 24 September, santería followers come dressed all in white – the colour associated with Obbatalá.

Museo José Martí ⑱

Calle Leonor Perez 314, esq. Egido. **Map** 4 E4. **Tel** (7) 8613 778, 8615 095. ◯ 9:30am–5pm Tue–Sat, 9am–1pm Sun. ◙ 1 Jan, 1 May, 26 Jul, 10 Oct, 25 Dec. ◢ ✚ ◙ (with charge). **www**.cult.cu/patrim/cnpc/museos/marti

This modest 19th-century building in the Paula quarter became a national monument thanks to the special historic importance attached to José Martí (see p15), who is the object of great patriotic veneration. The author and national hero, who died in combat on 19 May 1895 during the wars of independence against the Spanish, was born here in 1853. After his death, his mother Leonor Pérez lived in the building, and when she died it was rented to raise money to bring up her grandchildren. In 1901 it was purchased by the municipality after city-wide fund raising, and was turned into a museum in 1925, but government funding only became sufficient with the advent of Castro.

The house has been restored beautifully, and visitors can view furniture, paintings, and first editions of the writer's works. There are also objects of great historic value such as the inkpot and ivory pen used by Generalissimo Máximo Gómez and José Martí to sign the Manifesto de Montecristi, which officially marked the beginning of the war against Spain. Everyday objects are also on display, such as the penknife Martí had in his pocket when he died, and the album with dedications and signatures from friends during his wedding to Carmen Zayas-Bazán.

Portrait of José Martí by Herman Norman in the museum

CENTRO HABANA AND PRADO

Centro Habana has the air of an impoverished aristocrat – a noble creature whose threadbare clothes belie a splendid past full of treasures. This varied quarter developed beyond the city walls (which ran parallel to present-day Avenida Bélgica and Avenida de las Misiones) during the 1800s and was initially built to provide houses

Remains of the old walls

and greenery for the citizens. Most construction took place after 1863, when the walls began to be demolished to make more land available. The work was finally completed in the 1920s and 30s, when French architect Forestier landscaped the area of the Paseo del Prado, the Parque Central, the Capitolio gardens and Parque de la Fraternidad.

SIGHTS AT A GLANCE

Historic Buildings
Capitolio pp82–3 ❸
Castillo de San Salvador
  de la Punta ❽
Hotel Inglaterra ❶
Palacio de Aldama ❻
Real Fábrica de Tabacos
  Partagás ❺

Historic Streets and Plazas
Avenida Carlos III ⓯
Callejón de Hammel ⓰
Parque de la Fraternidad ❹
Paseo del Prado pp86–7 ❼
City Walls ⓱

Quarters
Barrio Chino ⓭

Theatres
Gran Teatro de La Habana ❷

Churches
Iglesia del Ángel Custodio ❿
Iglesia del Sagrado
  Corazón ⓮

Museums
Museo Nacional de la Música ❾
*Museo de la Revolución
  pp88–9* ⓫
Museo Nacional de Bellas
  Artes pp92–5 ⓬

KEY

▨ Street-by-Street map *pp80–81*

🚉 Railway station

GETTING THERE
The easiest way to get to this quarter is by taxi; and the best way to explore it is on foot. When map reading, bear in mind that the commonly used names of the streets differ from the official ones *(see p118)*.

Estación Central

| 0 metres | 800 |
| 0 yards | 800 |

◁ **The bustling arcade alongside the Museo de la Música** *(see p85)*

Street-by-Street: Around the Parque Central

Lying on the border of the old city and Centro Habana, between the Capitolio and the Prado promenade, the Parque Central was designed in 1877 after the old city walls were demolished. A statue of Isabella II was put in the middle of the square but was later replaced by one of José Martí. The park is surrounded by 19th- and 20th-century monumental buildings and adorned with palm trees, and is the heart of the city centre, a popular meeting place. Towards evening, when the air is cooler, people gather here to talk until the small hours of the night about baseball, music and politics.

★ **Gran Teatro de La Habana**
With one of its rooms named after the great Spanish poet, García Lorca, who stayed in Havana for a few months in 1930, the theatre is a mixture of influences with slender, angular towers ❷

Real Fábrica de Tabacos Partagás
This elegant red and cream-coloured building is home to a prestigious cigar factory ❺

Parque de la Fraternidad
The park was laid out in 1892 to celebrate the 400th anniversary of the discovery of America ❹

CALLE SAN MARTÍN (SAN JOSÉ)

CALLE INDUSTRIA

PASEO DE MARTÍ (PRADO)

CALLE DRAGONES

CALLE BRASIL

The Cinema Payret, Cuba's first motion picture theatre, opened in 1897, a year after the Lumière brothers presented their invention in Paris.

STAR SIGHTS

- ★ Capitolio
- ★ Gran Teatro de La Habana
- ★ Hotel Inglaterra
- ★ Paseo del Prado

★ **Capitolio**
The dome of one of the most imposing buildings in Latin America towers over the urban landscape of Havana ❸

★ Hotel Inglaterra
This historic hotel has retained its 19th-century atmosphere. Despite the British name, the architectural elements and decoration are clearly Spanish-inspired ❶

LOCATOR MAP
See Street Finder, pp120–23, map 4

Calle San Rafael, known as *Boulevard,* is a narrow street for pedestrians only. Up to the 1950s it was famous for its luxury shops and boutiques.

The Hotel Parque Central was built recently. Its style and decor blend in well with the surroundings *(see p254).*

★ Paseo del Prado
This avenue, the locals' favourite for strolling, is lined with lovely buildings with recently restored arcades ❼

The statue of José Martí, Cuba's national hero, was sculpted in Carrara marble in Rome by José Vilalta y Saavedra and inaugurated on 24 February 1905 by Generalissimo Máximo Gómez.

CALLE NEPTUNO

PARQUE CENTRAL

CALLE SAN RAFAEL

| 0 metres | 100 |
| 0 yards | 100 |

KEY

– – – Suggested route

The Manzana de Gómez, a 19th-century building, was once a major commercial centre, and gradually shops are returning here.

Palacio del Centro Asturiano, with the characteristic towers on its corners, was designed by Spanish architect Manuel del Busto and opened in 1928. It is home to the Museo de Bellas Artes' international art collection *(see pp92–5).*

The Hotel Plaza, built in the 19th century as a private residence, became a hotel in 1909. It was frequented by great artists of the time, from Isadora Duncan to Enrico Caruso and Anna Pavlova *(see p254).*

Hotel Inglaterra ❶

Paseo de Martí (Prado) 416, esq. a San Rafael. **Map** 4 D2. *Tel* (7) 860 8594. *See p254.*

Although this hotel is built in the style of late 19th-century Havana Neo-Classical architecture, its soul is *mudéjar* (Moorish): the fine ochre, green and gold majolica tiles in the interior were imported from Seville, the foyer is decorated with Andalusian mosaics, and the wooden ceilings are reminiscent of Moorish inlay. Plus, one of the columns in the *salón-café* bears a classical Arabic inscription: "Only Allah is the victor". The Hotel Inglaterra dates

from 1875, when a small hotel merged with the lively Le Louvre night spot and its adjacent ballroom. The pavement outside the hotel, known as the "Louvre sidewalk", was an animated meeting point for Havana liberals. It was here that the young José Martí *(see p45)* advocated total separation from Spain, as opposed to more moderate liberal demands for autonomy. General Antonio Maceo, a hero of the wars of Cuban independence, prepared plans for insurrection in this hotel.

Among many illustrious guests were the great French actress Sarah Bernhardt and the Russian ballet dancer Anna Pavlova.

Gran Teatro de La Habana ❷

Paseo de Martí (Prado) y San Rafael, Central Havana. **Map** 4 D2. *Tel* (7) 8613 078. ☐ 9am–5pm daily. ● 1 Jan, 1 May, 26 Jul, 10 Oct, 25 Dec. ✍ ☑ ◉ (with charge).

One of the world's largest opera houses is part of the monumental Palacio del Centro Gallego (1915), designed by Belgian architect Paul Belau to host the social activities of Havana's large and affluent Spanish community.

The magnificent façade is decorated with four sculpture

The staircase of honour, originally reserved for MPs

Capitolio ❸

A symbol of the city, the Capitol (Capitolio) combines the elegance of Neo-Classicism with Art Deco elements. Inaugurated in 1929 by the dictator Gerardo Machado, it is a loose imitation of the Washington DC Capitol, but is even taller. It stands in an area once occupied by a botanical garden and later by the capital's first railway station. The home of government until 1959, the Capitol has seen major historic events: in 1933 the police fired on a crowd gathered here during an anti-Machado demonstration. Today the building houses the Ministry of Science, Technology and the Environment, but is open for tours, which include the former government chambers and the magnificent library.

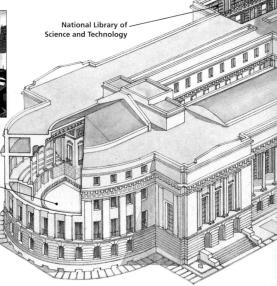

National Library of Science and Technology

Chamber of Deputies
The Chamber still has its original furnishings and is decorated with bas-reliefs by the Italian artist Gianni Remuzzi.

STAR SIGHTS

★ Salón de los Pasos Perdidos

★ Dome

Façade of the former Centro Gallego building, now home to the Gran Teatro

this was the venue for performances by world-famous artists, including the Austrian ballet dancer Fanny Essler, who made her debut here on 23 January 1841. In the mid-19th century Antonio Meucci, the inventor of the "talking telephone", worked here as a stagehand, and his invention was patented in the US, thanks to the support of the Gran Teatro's impresario.

The theatre was inaugurated on 22 April 1915 with a performance of Verdi's *Aida*, and became a stage for great dramatic occasions. Sarah Bernhardt performed here in 1918, and the pianist Arthur Rubinstein the following year. Cuban composer Ernesto Lecuona and the great Spanish guitarist Andrés Segovia have also appeared.

In 1959 the Gran Teatro, though continuing in its role as a concert hall and theatre, became the "home" of Alicia Alonso, the great Cuban ballet dancer. She founded the Ballet Nacional, which is the dance company and school known for organizing a famous annual ballet festival *(see p125)*.

groups by the Italian sculptor Giuseppe Moretti, depicting Charity, Education, Music and Theatre. The building lies over the foundations of the Teatro Nuevo or Tacón. From 1837 to the early 20th century

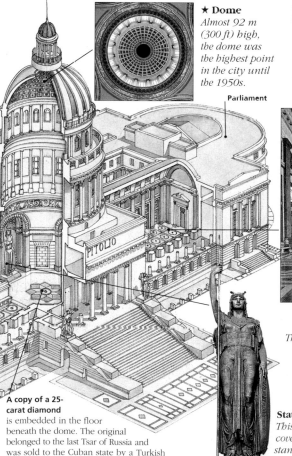

★ **Dome**
Almost 92 m (300 ft) high, the dome was the highest point in the city until the 1950s.

Parliament

A copy of a 25-carat diamond
is embedded in the floor beneath the dome. The original belonged to the last Tsar of Russia and was sold to the Cuban state by a Turkish jeweller. It was stolen and, mysteriously, later turned up on the President's desk.

VISITORS' CHECKLIST

Paseo de Martí (Prado) esq. a San José. **Map** 4 D3.
Tel (7) 863 7861, 861 5519.
9am–6pm daily
(with charge).

★ **Salón de los Pasos Perdidos**
This sumptuous hall, with fine marble floors and gilded lamps, takes its name ("Hall of Lost Steps") from its unusual acoustics.

Statue of the Republic
This work, cast in Rome and covered with 22-carat gold leaf, stands 17 m (56 ft) high and weighs 49 tons. It is the third tallest statue in the world.

Parque de la Fraternidad ❹

Map 4 D3.

The spacious area of greenery behind the Capitol was called Campo di Marte (Parade Ground) in the 19th century, because it was near the Paseo Militar, used frequently for army drill. As the Parque de la Fraternidad (since 1928), it commemorates Cuba's common roots with the other people of the Americas, with monuments to major figures such as the Argentine José de San Martín, the Venezuelan Simón Bolívar, and US president Abraham Lincoln.

In the middle of the park is a gate with a plaque bearing an exhortation by José Martí: "It is time to gather and march together united, we must go forward as compact as the silver in the depths of the Andes. Peoples unite only through bonds of friendship, fraternity and love." Beyond the gate is a monument to American friendship and solidarity: a large ceiba – a tree sacred to both the Amerindians and the African slaves taken to the New World – planted here around 1920.

In front of the square is a white marble fountain, sculpted in 1831 by Giuseppe Gaggini. The fountain is known as the "Fuente de la India" or "La Noble Habana" – an allegorical representation of the city.

Nowadays the Parque de la Fraternidad is usually full of old American cars, most of which operate as private taxis.

The Fuente de la India symbolizing Havana

Façade of the Partagás cigar factory with its prominent pediments

Real Fábrica de Tabacos Partagás ❺

Calle Industria 524. **Map** 4 D3.
Tel (7) 863 5766. ◻ 9–11am, 12–2pm Mon–Fri. ● 1 Jan, 1 May, 26 Jul, 10 Oct, 25 Dec. ☑ 🖼 🚪 🖥

Cuba's largest cigar factory, with its Neo-Classical façade, is a good example of 19th-century industrial architecture. It was founded in 1845 by the ambitious Catalan businessman Jaime Partagás Ravelo. However, he never revealed the sources of his tobacco leaves or how they were processed. The only information that survives is that he was the first person to use wooden barrels to ferment the leaves in order to heighten the aroma.

Neon sign at the Partagás cigar factory

With the profits made from his high-quality cigars, Partagás bought a plantation in the province of Pinar del Río. He wanted to oversee all aspects of the cigar-making process personally, from growing the plants to the placing of a wrapper leaf around the filler and binder leaves rolled by the *torcedor (see p33)*. However, Partagás was assassinated in mysterious circumstances

and the project failed. His factory was then purchased by another shrewd businessman, Ramón Cifuentes Llano.

Dozens of people work in the aroma-filled interior. Nowadays, there is no longer someone reading aloud to alleviate the monotony of the work by entertaining and educating the workers, as was the case in the 19th century (Partagás himself introduced this custom to Cuba).

However there is a loudspeaker that alternates reading passages with music and news on the radio. Connected to the factory is La Casa del Habano, an excellent shop with a back room that is used for sampling cigars.

Palacio de Aldama ❻

Avenída Simón Bolívar (Reina) y Máximo Gómez (Monte). **Map** 4 D3. ● to the public.

This mansion *(see p25)* was designed by Manuel José Carrera and built in the middle of the 19th century, having been commissioned by the rich Basque industrialist Domingo de Aldama y Arrechaga. He had to depend on his influential friends in order to obtain permission to build his residence in front of the Campo di Marte, or Parade Ground, which was

For hotels and restaurants in this region see pp252–6 and pp276–9

reserved for military and administrative buildings. The monumental grandeur of this Neo-Classical building, considered the finest example of 19th-century architecture in Cuba, is still striking. The mansion is now the seat of the Instituto de Historia de Cuba. Sadly, it is not yet officially open to the public, but upon request the porter allows visitors to go into the courtyard to admire the impressive marble staircases, Baroque arches, splendid wrought iron with Imperial motifs and the two inner gardens with fountains made of Carrara marble.

The monument to General Máximo Gómez

Paseo del Prado **7**

See pp86–7

Castillo de San Salvador de la Punta **8**

Malecón y Paseo de Martí (Prado). **Map** 4 D1. **Tel** (7) 8603 196. ⬜ 10am–4:30pm Tue–Sat, 10am–1:30pm Sun. 📷 📷

A modest fortified block on the west bank of the port entrance, this fortress *(castillo)* makes an ideal setting for political speeches and concerts because of its elevated position near the road. In the past it played a crucial role in the defence system of the capital but today it is a naval museum.

Designed by Giovanni Battista Antonelli, Juan de Tejeda and Cristóbal de Roda and built in 1589–1610, it was part of the city's first line of defence together with the much larger Castillo de los Tres Reyes del Morro on the other side of the bay.

A large floating chain of wooden and bronze rings, an ingenious device added by the Italian engineer Antonelli in the late 16th century, connected the two fortresses. It was stretched tightly as soon as an enemy ship was sighted, to block access to the port. In the open space in front of the Castillo are the three cannons to which the chain was tied.

The large forecourt has several monuments that are more important historically than artistically. In the middle is the equestrian statue of Generalissimo Máximo Gómez, the hero of the wars of independence, by Italian sculptor Aldo Gamba (1935). Behind this, a dilapidated chapel is used daily for stamp exhibitions and history lectures. It originally belonged to the Real Cárcel prison, where José Martí was kept for 16 years for subversive activities against the Spanish crown. Some cells still stand, as does a section of the wall against which some medical students were executed on 27 November 1871 as punishment for rebelling against Spanish rule. A cenotaph in their honour stands in the Columbus cemetery *(see p104).*

The Museo de la Música, an example of eclectic architecture

Museo Nacional de la Música **9**

Calle Capdevila 1, e/ Habana y Aguiar. **Map** 4 E1. **Tel** (7) 8619 846, 8630 052. ⬤ Closed for restoration until approximately late 2009. 📷 📷 📷

The building (1905) that houses the National Music Museum is a mixture of different styles, a perfect example of 20th-century eclectic architecture. It was the residence of a family of opera lovers, whose guests included such illustrious figures as the great Italian tenor Enrico Caruso and the Spanish poet Federico García Lorca.

The museum was founded in 1971, and contains the largest collection of traditional musical instruments in Cuba, gathered by the ethnologist Fernando Ortiz, a pioneer in the study of Cuba's African roots. Besides the most complete collection of African drums in the world, there is the piano of singer and composer Bola de Nieve *(see p30)* and 40 guitars used by legendary figures of 20th-century Cuban music, such as the Trío Matamoros and Sindo Garay. Also on show are gramophones and phonographs, photos and famous composers' original manuscripts. In the foyer is a music stand with the score of the Bayamo, the Cuban national anthem. Visitors can consult specialist Cuban and foreign periodicals, as well as the archive of rare musical documents.

The Castillo de la Punta ramparts and the Morro fortress behind

Paseo del Prado 7

The most picturesque boulevard in Havana is popular in
the daytime for a gentle stroll and gossip in the shade
of the trees, and at sunset is one of the locals' main
haunts. The Marquis de la Torre had the Paseo laid out
in 1772 outside the city walls, and it rapidly became the
favourite spot for city aristocrats to take their carriage
rides. Bands were positioned in five spots along the
boulevard to play for their enjoyment. The Paseo was
used for military and carnival parades in the 19th
century, when the paving was redone. In 1927 the
French architect Forestier designed the Prado as
we see it today: it was widened and lined with
bronze lions and marble benches.

Lions
*Eight lions, symbolizing
Havana, were added in
1927, together with the
marble benches near the
Teatro Fausto.*

Neo-Moorish Building
*The building at the
corner of Calle Virtudes,
richly decorated and with
mudéjar arches, shows
many architectural
influences and is typical
of Havana.*

Casa del Científico,
residence of JoséMiguel
Gómez, second President
of the Republic of Cuba,
is nowa small hotel.

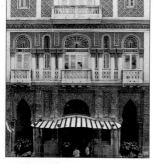

Hotel Sevilla
*This historic hotel opened in
1908 and a ten-storey tower was
added in 1918. It is a homage to
Moorish architecture: the façade
and hall decoration are* mudéjar
(see p24) in style.

Palacio de los Matrimonios
*Named after the civil weddings celebrated on
the first floor, this Neo-Baroque building was
inaugurated in 1914 as the Casino Español.*

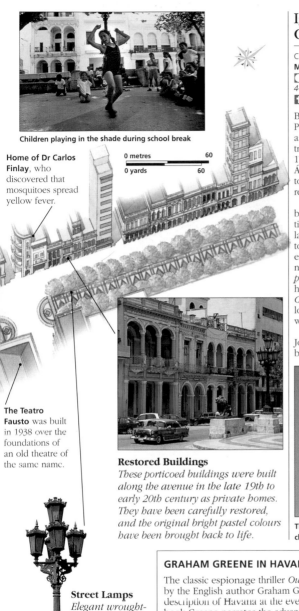

Children playing in the shade during school break

Home of Dr Carlos Finlay, who discovered that mosquitoes spread yellow fever.

0 metres 60
0 yards 60

The Teatro Fausto was built in 1938 over the foundations of an old theatre of the same name.

Restored Buildings
These porticoed buildings were built along the avenue in the late 19th to early 20th century as private homes. They have been carefully restored, and the original bright pastel colours have been brought back to life.

Street Lamps
Elegant wrought-iron street lamps were added in 1834, together with the multi-coloured marble pavement.

Iglesia del Ángel Custodio ⑩

Calle Compostela 2, esq. Cuarteles.
Map 4 D2. **Tel** (7) 8610 469.
◯ 9am–noon & 3–7pm Tue–Fri,
4–7pm Sat, 9–10:30am Sun.
✝ 4–7pm Sat, 9–10am Sun.

Built in 1693 on the Peña Pobre or "Loma del Ángel" hill as a hermitage and then transformed into a church in 1788, today the Neo-Gothic Ángel Custodio looks rather too white and unreal as a result of vigorous "restoration".

Standing in a key position between the former presidential palace (now the Museo de la Revolución) and the old town, it exudes literary references. The 19th-century Cuban novelist Cirilo Villaverde *(see p28)* used the Loma del Ángel hill as the setting for his story *Cecilia Valdés* about the tragic love affair between a Creole woman and a rich white man.

Félix Varela *(see p28)* and José Martí *(see p45)* were both baptised in this church.

The bell tower and spires of the church of Ángel Custodio

GRAHAM GREENE IN HAVANA

The classic espionage thriller *Our Man in Havana* (1958), by the English author Graham Greene, is an excellent description of Havana at the eve of the Revolution. In the book Greene narrates the adventures of a vacuum cleaner salesman who becomes a secret agent against his will. The novel is imbued with a dry sense of humour, and is set against an intriguing environment filled with casinos and roulette wheels, New York skyscrapers and decadent Art Nouveau villas, cabarets and prostitution. The Hotel Sevilla is a constant presence in the background.

Graham Greene (1904–91)

Museo de la Revolución ⓫

The idea of putting the Museum of the Revolution in the former presidential palace of the dictator Fulgencio Batista was clearly symbolic. Designed by the Cuban architect Rodolfo Maruri and the Belgian architect Paul Belau, the building was inaugurated in 1920 by Mario García Menocal, and it remained the residence for 25 other presidents until 1965. The building has Neo-Classical elements, and was decorated by Tiffany of New York. It contains works by the leading Cuban decorators of the early 1900s and by sculptors such as Juan José Sicre, Esteban Betancourt and Fernando Boada. The museum features documents, photographs and memorabilia presenting an overview of the Cubans' struggle for independence, from the Colonial period on, but focusing in particular on the Revolution, from the guerrilla war to the Special Period in the 1990s.

Statues of Che Guevara and Camilo Cienfuegos
These life-size wax statues depict the two heroes in combat.

The third floor contains photos and memorabilia from colonial times to 1959.

The side wing of the palace was home to Batista's office.

GRANMA MEMORIAL

The large glass and cement pavilion in the tree-lined plaza behind the museum contains the yacht *Granma* (named after its first owner's grandmother). In 1956 this boat brought Fidel Castro and some of his comrades from Mexico to Cuba to begin the armed struggle against Batista *(see p48)*. There are also objects and vehicles relating to the invasion of the Bay of Pigs (1961), remains of an American spy plane shot down in 1962 during the missile crisis, and the delivery truck that was used by revolutionaries to attack the palace in 1957.

The remains of a plane's engine

STAR FEATURES

★ Salón de los Espejos

★ Main Staircase

The Dome

The inside of the dome, visible from the staircase, consists of multicoloured ceramics. It includes four panels, decorated by Esteban Valderrama and Mariano Miguel González, against a gold leaf background.

VISITORS' CHECKLIST

Calle Refugio 1, e/ Avenida de las Misiones y Zulueta.
Map 4 D2. *Tel* (7) 862 4091.
◯ 10am–5pm daily.

The second floor displays the President's desk, the Council of Ministers and memorabilia from 1959 to the present day.

★ Salón de los Espejos

Lined with vast mirrors (espejos), the reception hall of the former presidential palace has ceiling frescoes by Cuban painters Armado Menocal and Antonio Rodríguez Morey.

The tall windows are similar to those in the Gran Teatro de La Habana, and were designed by the same architect, Paul Belau.

The terrace opposite the Salón de los Espejos has a fine view of the Bay of Havana.

Entrance

★ Main Staircase

The monumental staircase, which leads to the first floor, still bears marks of the bullets shot here on 13 March 1957, during an attack by some revolutionary university students on a mission to kill Batista. The dictator managed to save his life by escaping to the upper floors.

Museo Nacional de Bellas Artes ⑫

See pp92–5.

Barrio Chino ⑬

Map 3 C3.

The Chinese quarter of Havana, the Barrio Chino, which now occupies a small area defined by San Nicolás, Dragones, Zanja and Rayo streets, developed in the 19th century. In its heyday, in the early 1900s, there was a cultural association performing plays and operas, and a casino. The colourful streets were full of vendors of fritters and other Asian specialities, and people came to buy the best fruit and freshest fish in the city.

Today, all the Chinese shops are concentrated in the so-called Cuchillo de Zanja area (the intersection of Zanja and Rayo), a mixture of the oriental and the tropical; the architecture, however, is not particularly characteristic, except for the quarter gate, which has a

The austere interior of Iglesia de la Caridad

pagoda roof. Another, much more impressive Ming and Ching-style portico was erected in 1998 at the corner of Calle Dragones and Calle Amistad. It is almost 19 m (62 ft) wide and was donated to Cuba by the Chinese government.

The Barrio Chino is also home to the **Iglesia de la Caridad**, dedicated to Cuba's patron saint *(see p221)*. The church also has a popular statue, a Virgin with Asian features, brought here in the mid-1950s.

Iglesia del Sagrado Corazón ⑭

Avenida Simón Bolívar (Reina) 463.
Map 3 B3. **Tel** *(7)* 8624 979.
🕒 *7:30am–noon, 3–6pm daily.*
✝ *8am, 4:30pm Mon–Sat, 8am, 9:30am, 4:30pm Sun.* 🖼 🎥 📷

With its impressive bell tower, 77 m (253 ft) high, the Church of the Sacred Heart can be seen from various parts of the city. It was designed in the early 1900s by the Jesuit priest Luis Gorgoza and consecrated in 1923, and is a rare example of the Neo-Gothic style in Cuba.

Dominating the façade is a figure of Christ resting on three columns decorated with a capital depicting the parable of the prodigal son. The interior has elaborate stained-glass windows narrating the life of Christ and a wealth of stucco-work and pointed arches. A Byzantine-style Sacred Heart with sculptures of saints and prophets is on the high altar.

Entrance to the Iglesia del Sagrado Corazón, with its statue of Christ

THE CHINESE COMMUNITY IN HAVANA

The first Chinese arrived in Cuba in the mid-1800s to work in the sugar industry, and they were treated like slaves. The first to gain their freedom began to cultivate small plots of land in Havana. In one of these, near the present-day Calle Salud, they grew Cuba's first mangoes, which were an immediate, spectacular success. Chinese restaurants began to appear in the area after the second wave of Chinese immigrants arrived from California (1869–75), armed with their American savings. Without losing any of their cultural traditions, the Chinese community has become assimilated into Cuban society, accepting and sharing the island's lot. A black granite column at the corner of Calle Linea and Calle L remembers the Chinese who fought for Cuban independence.

Avenida Carlos III ⑮

(Avenida Salvador Allende) **Map** 3 B3.

Laid out in 1850 during redevelopment under the supervision of Captain Miguel de Tacón, this boulevard (official name Avenida Salvador Allende) was designed to allow troops and military vehicles to go from the Castillo del Príncipe – built on the Aróstegui hill in the late 1700s – to their parade ground in the present-day Parque

Entrance gate to Barrio Chino, the Chinese quarter in Havana

Callejón de Hammel, famous for its exotic and colourful murals

de la Fraternidad. The middle section of the boulevard was reserved for carriages, while the two side avenues with their benches, trees and fountains were for pedestrians. First named Alameda de Tacón or Paseo Militar, it was renamed Avenida Carlos III in honour of the Spanish king who encouraged Cuban commerce and culture in the 18th century.

One of the most curious buildings on the street is the Grand National Masonic Temple, with a world map on the roof, built in the mid-1900s.

Callejón de Hammel ⑯

Map 3 A2.

This street in the working-class Cayo Hueso quarter is a curious open-air Afro-Cuban sanctuary. Its name derives from a legendary French-German resident called Fernando Hammel, a wealthy arms dealer-turned-merchant, who took the entire quarter under his wing. The colourful, 200-m (656-ft) mural here, for which the street is now famous, is the work of naive painter Salvador González. He wanted to

Representation of Ochún, the goddess of love

pay homage to his varied cultural roots by representing all the religious cults and movements of African origin that are still active in Cuba, hence the many symbols, writings, and images of African gods and Abakuá devils (see p23). He began this enormous project in 1990.

This alley has everything: from small shops selling hand-crafted religious objects to a *Nganga*, the large cauldron-like pot which forms the basis of Palo Monte, the religion of former Bantu slaves from the African Congo. On Sundays Callejón Hammel becomes the venue for rumba shows, popular with the locals and tourists alike.

City Walls ⑰

Avenida del Puerto Map 4 D5.

The old colonial city of San Cristóbal de La Habana was encircled and fortified by a 9-m (30-ft) high wall with nine bastions and a moat. Construction began in 1671 and took over a century to complete, finishing in 1797.

Once finished, the gates were closed every evening and access to the bay was blocked by a chain. Cannon shots were fired every night from a ship anchored in the bay, informing the inhabitants that the gates were closing (see p111). By the early 19th century, the city was expanding so fast that finally in 1863 the walls had to be torn down. Today, the best remaining sections are opposite the Museo de la Revolución (see pp88–9) and by the train station.

Remaining section of the old City Wall near Estación Central

Museo Nacional de Bellas Artes ⑬

The National Fine Arts Museum was founded on 23 February 1913 thanks to the efforts of the architect Emilio Heredia, its first director. After frequent moves, the collections eventually found a definitive home in the block once occupied by the old Colón market. The original design was changed when the arcades of the building were demolished and in 1954 the new Palacio de Bellas Artes was inaugurated, a Rationalist building with purely geometric lines designed by the architect Rodríguez Pichardo. The museum is now divided between two buildings: the original palacio dedicated to Cuban art, and the Palacio del Centro Asturiano, by the Parque Central, dedicated to international art.

LOCATOR MAP
See Street Finder, map 4, p123

Virgin and Child
This triptych by Hans Memling (1433–94) exemplifies the vivid style and masterful spatial construction that made this artist one of the great masters of Flemish painting.

Sagrada Familia
The Holy Family *by the Spanish artist Bartolomé Esteban Murillo (1618–82), who enjoyed great fame during his lifetime, is a calm, meditative scene.*

PALACIO DEL CENTRO ASTURIANO
European painting and sculpture, together with the collection of ancient art, are on display in the Centro Asturiano, designed in 1927 by the architect Manuel Bustos.

STAR SIGHTS

★ La Silla by Wifredo Lam

★ La Habana en Rojo by René Portocarrero

★ Panathenaean Amphora

★ **Panathenaean Amphora**
This terracotta amphora in the black figure style is one of the most important pieces in the museum's collection of ancient Greek vases, which once belonged to the Count de Lagunillas.

★ **La Habana en Rojo (1962)**
Havana in Red *is part of a long series that René Portocarrero dedicated to the capital. This painting in particular expresses the passionate Baroque spirit that characterizes all of Portocarrero's work.*

VISITORS' CHECKLIST

Palacio del Centro Asturiano, San Rafael, e/ Zulueta y Monserrate. **Palacio de Bellas Artes**, Calle Trocadero, e/ Zulueta y Monserrate. **Map** 4 D2. *Tel* (7) 861 3858, 863 9484. *Fax* (7) 862 9626. ☐ 10am–6pm Tue–Sat, 10am–2pm Sun. ● 1 Jan, 1 May, 26 Jul, 10 Oct, 25 Dec.

The permanent collection is displayed in chronological order on the first and second floors.

Entrance

PALACIO DE BELLAS ARTES
The Palace of Fine Arts is entirely given over to Cuban art. Sculptures line the perimeter of the central courtyard, which houses service rooms for cultural education, the auditorium and the library. The two upper floors feature galleries divided into three sections: Colonial, academic and 20th-century art (divided into decades from the 1930s to the 1990s).

Form, Space and Light (1953)
This marble sculpture by Rita Longa, in the museum entrance, is characterized by a fluid concept of volume. Two male figures create a harmonious counterpoint.

★ **La Silla (1943)**
One of several fine works in which Wifredo Lam combines Cubism and Surrealism and adds a distinctively Cuban stamp: a Cubist chair with a vase on it is set in the magical context of the jungle.

Exploring the Museo Nacional de Bellas Artes

During the reassessment of many of Cuba's cultural institutions after 1959, a large number of works were added to the original museum collection – the result of the confiscation of property that had been misappropriated. The collection was divided into two sections: Cuban and international art. The first consists of paintings, prints, drawings, and sculptures; the second has paintings, sculptures and drawings primarily from Europe, the US and Latin America, with some works dating from the Egyptian to the Roman age.

Clotilde en los Jardines de la Granja by Joaquin Sorolla

PALACIO DEL CENTRO ASTURIANO (INTERNATIONAL ART)

The building designed as the home of the collection of international art has maintained its original architectural elements, with furnishings, iron grilles, stained-glass windows and chandeliers. Besides the gallery, the place also has communal areas for the public, study rooms, a book shop, café, a video room and an auditorium.

The collection of international art comprises paintings and sculptures displayed in sections: the Middle Ages, Italy, Germany, Flanders, the Netherlands, Great Britain, France and Spain. There are also works from various European schools, the United States and Latin America.

Head of the god Amon, ancient Egyptian sculpture

Among the finest works in the collection are the Flemish paintings and the 19th-century Spanish pictures, including one by Joaquín Sorolla: *Entre Naranjos* (1903). In this the artist depicts a banquet in the countryside, using the play of the figures, light and shadow to create an Impressionist-like atmosphere. The same can be said of the movement of the water and the garden in the background in *Clotilde en los Jardines de la Granja*, which is a portrait of the artist's wife. Other Spanish artists represented are Murillo and Zurbarán. Then there are works by Constable, Bouguereau and Van Mieris.

The Italian collection includes a group of landscape paintings, including one by Canaletto: *Chelsea College, Rotunda, Ranelagh House*

and the Thames (1751), in which the painter brilliantly renders the atmosphere of London. There is also a scene of Venice by Francesco Guardi, *The Lagoon in front of the Fondamenta Nuove*, a youthful work with the delicate rendering that characterized his later production. Other Italian works are *St Christopher* by Jacopo Bassano (ca. 1515–92), *Alpine Landscape with Figures* by Alessandro Magnasco (1667–1748), and *The Spinstress* by Giovanni Battista Piazzetta. *The Reception of a Legation* by Vittore Carpaccio (1490) has a rigorously symmetrical composition.

The ancient art section is also fascinating: Greek, Roman and Egyptian works, as well as Mesopotamian, Phoenician and Etruscan finds. The 5th-century BC Greek amphora and the Fayoum portraits are especially interesting.

PALACIO DE BELLAS ARTES (CUBAN ART)

The permanent exhibition of 18th–21st-century Cuban art offers a complete overview of works by individuals and schools, and highlights the leading trends in each period. The temporary exhibition of prints and drawings, as well as of paintings, adds variety and

One of the many views that Canaletto painted of London

richness to the permanent collection, which has works by the great masters of contemporary Cuban art.

Two of the major figures are painter Wifredo Lam (*La Silla*, 1943) and sculptor Agustín Cárdenas, who were both influenced by the European avant-garde and African art. The free play of volumes in the wooden sculpture *Figure*, less than 1 m (3 ft) high, expresses to the full the African-derived sensuality that informs Cárdenas's style.

Cuban art in the 19th century, characterized by its technical skill, is represented by the portraits of Guillermo Collazo, an academic and painter, and landscapes by the Chartrand brothers. Other artists with an academic background are Armando García Menocal and Leopoldo Romañach, a painter and lecturer at the Academy.

The pioneers of modern Cuban art are particularly interesting. One of these is Víctor Manuel García, an exceptional landscape painter who conveys peaceful atmospheres with silently flowing rivers and figures with sinuous movements. García is the creator of the "mestizo" archetype: *Gitana Tropical* (Tropical Gypsy, 1929) includes a figure of a woman

El Malecón by Manuel Mendive, an extraordinary Naive painting

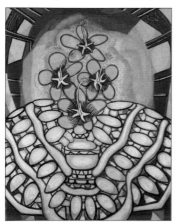

Figure (1953) by Augustín Cárdenas

against the background of a barren landscape, which has become a symbol of Cuban painting *(see p26)*. There are several works by Amelia Peláez, who revived the still-life genre by merging Cubism and specifically Cuban motifs; among these are *Naturaleza Muerta sobre Ocre*, executed in 1930 in Paris, and *Flores Amarillas*, a mature work that marks a return to more simple compositions after a "Baroque" period.

El Rapto de las Mulatas (1938), by Carlos Enríquez, is a dream-like "tangle" of human figures, horses and landscape that echoes the classical theme of the rape of the Sabine women.

It is considered emblematic of Cuban painting and of this artist's oeuvre. The sensuality of the human bodies and the tropical atmosphere in this work provide a key to the interpretation of the motifs of traditional art.

The chronological display of works illustrates the development of Cuban art. In the 1950s there was a move away from figurative art, as seen in the work of Guido Llinás and Hugo Consuegra.

After the victory of the revolution in 1959, Cuban art embraced extremely varied styles. Servando Cabrera first took guerrillas as his subject and then made an erotic series. Antonia Eiriz was a particularly powerful Neo-Expressionist, and Raúl Martinez began with abstract art and then absorbed elements of Pop Art.

Another renowned contemporary artist is Manuel Mendive who, in embracing Cuba's African heritage, searches for the hidden depths of existence. *El Malecón* (1975), one of his most significant works, depicts the city's famous promenade as if it were an almost sacred site where people mingle with African gods. The style here is at once naive and sophisticated.

Of the leading artists of the 1970s there are works by Ever Fonseca, Nelson Domínguez, and the unique illustrator Roberto Fabelo. Among the younger artists (all graduates of the historic San Alejandro Academy and Escuela Nacional de Arte), Tomás Sánchez, with his archetypal landscapes, and José Bedia, with his bold installations, stand out. The artists who continue to emerge on the Cuban art scene – thanks to the Biennial Show – exhibit their works in the many temporary shows.

Of the considerable number of works in its possession, the museum now exhibits many paintings, drawings, prints and sculptures.

Flores Amarillas (1964), a still life dating from Amelia Peláez's mature phase

VEDADO AND PLAZA

The unusual grid plan of Vedado was the design of the engineer Luis Yboleón Bosque in 1859. It called for pavements 2 m (6 ft) wide, houses with a garden, and broad straight avenues. The name Vedado ("prohibited") arose because in the 1500s, in order to have full view of any pirates approaching, it was forbidden to build houses and streets here. In the late 19th and early 20th century the quarter was enlarged, becoming a prestigious residential area for many of the city's leading families. Vedado has two different roles. It is Havana's modern political and cultural centre, with the city's main hotels, restaurants, shops, theatres, cinemas, offices and ministries; and it is also a historic quarter with a wealth of gardens and old houses with grand Colonial entrances. Plaza de la Revolución, the venue for major celebrations, is the political centre of Havana and the whole of Cuba, as well as a highly symbolic place.

Sculpture at the corner of 23 and 12 Street

SIGHTS AT A GLANCE

Museums and Galleries
Museo de Artes Decorativas ❸
Museo Napoleónico ❺

Historic Buildings
Casa de las Américas ❷
Quinta de los Molinos ❻
Universidad de La Habana ❹

Monuments
Memorial José Martí p103 ❽

Streets and Squares
Plaza de la Revolución ❼

Cemeteries
Necrópolis de Colón
pp104–5 ❾

Walks
A Walk through
Vedado
pp98–9 ❶

KEY

Walk pp98–9

Coach station

GETTING THERE

This area is huge, but getting around on foot can be a rewarding experience if you have time. Otherwise, the best alternative is to go by taxi. In order to orientate yourself you will need to know how the street names work *(see p118)*.

0 metres 1000
0 yards 1000

◁ The end of the Malecon in Vedado with the mouth of the Rio Almendares

A Walk through Vedado ❶

This walk takes in the broad avenues which are typical of Vedado, providing a taste of the district's odd architectural mix of ugly 1950s high-rises and crumbling Neo-Classical mansions. There is only one museum on this route (Vedado has few conventional attractions), leaving you free to simply stroll and look around. Calle 23, modern Havana's most well-known street, is the main reference point for the walk. The most famous section is the first few blocks, known as La Rampa.

The Hotel Habana Libre, with the mosaic *La Fruta Cubana* (1957)

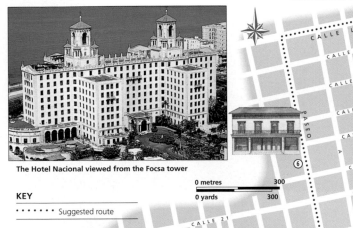

The Hotel Nacional viewed from the Focsa tower

KEY

• • • • • • • Suggested route

0 metres   300
0 yards   300

Malecón

The stretch of the Malecón where this walk begins is dominated by the headland occupied by the Hotel Nacional ①. This gem of Art Deco architecture opened in 1930 (see p255). Many famous guests have stayed here including Winston Churchill, Fred Astaire, Buster Keaton and Walt Disney. The hotel park offers lovely views across the bay.

La Rampa

Head briefly south to reach La Rampa (the first rising stretch of Calle 23 between the seafront and Calle N). Modern and lively, lined with offices, restaurants and bars with old-fashioned neon signs, La Rampa would pass for a typical 1950s street were it not for the façade of the Ministry of Sugar (or Minaz) with its revolutionary mural

and the "futuristic" Pabellón Cuba, which hosts exhibitions. This part of the walk is accompanied by the unmistakable profile of the Edificio Focsa ②, a skyscraper built in the 1950s.

This route also takes you by a small open-air crafts market and the Centro de Prensa Internacional, which caters to foreign journalists.

Calle 23

In the middle of the park at the corner of Calle 23 and L is the Coppelia ice-cream parlour ③, a large glass and metal building (1966). This classic location in Havana was made famous by Tomás Gutiérrez Alea's film *Strawberry and Chocolate (see*

The statue of Don Quixote by Sergio Martínez (1980)

p29). Coppelia is the most popular ice-cream parlour in the city (hence the queues).

On the other side of Calle 23 is the impressive Hotel Habana Libre (see p255), with a tiled mural by renowned Cuban artist Amelia Peláez. The hotel first opened in 1958, and a year later was requisitioned from the Americans and became Fidel Castro's headquarters. Inside are two mosaics by Portocarrero and Sosabravo (see pp26–7). At the intersection with Calle J is the Parque El Quijote ④, a tree-filled area with a modern statue of a nude Don Quixote on horseback by Sergio Martínez. Further along Calle 23 the buildings lessen in height and are more varied in style.

ITINERARY

Hotel Nacional ①
Edificio Focsa ②
Coppelia ③
Parque El Quijote ④
Museo de la Danza ⑤
Casa de la Amistad ⑥
ICAIC ⑦

The constant queue for the
Coppelia ice-cream parlour

VISITORS' CHECKLIST

Departure: Hotel Nacional.
Arrival: corner of 23 y 12.
Length: 3.5 km (2 miles).
Where to eat: Coppelia ice-
cream parlour, Casa de la
Amistad, one of the bars at the
corner of 23 y 12. Plan stops
and museum visits for the (hot)
middle of the day. **Museo de la
Danza** *Tel* (7) 8312 198. ☐
10:30am–6pm Tue–Sat,
10:30am–1pm Sun. ● 1 Jan, 1
May, 26 Jul, 25 Dec. 📷 📷 📷

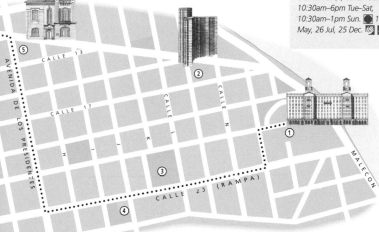

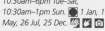

Avenida de los Presidentes
The tour continues by turning
right at Calle G (Avenida de los
Presidentes), a wide, tree-lined
avenue with luxurious 19th-
and 20th-century French-style
buildings. In the middle of
the street are benches and
flower beds. Behind the
statue of Simón Bolívar
is the junction with
Calle Línea.

Calle Línea
The first street to
be laid out in the
Vedado quarter
owes its name to
the tramline *(línea)* that once
ran from here to the historic
centre. Calle Línea also has
many French-style buildings
as well as Colonial houses
with stained-glass windows.
    The recently restored build-
ing at the corner of Calle G
is the Museo de la Danza ⑤,
run by the legendary ballerina
Alicia Alonso, founder of the
Ballet Nacional *(see p83)*. The
only dance museum in Latin
America, it has mementoes of

Alicia Alonso's shoes,
Museo de la Danza

famous dancers who have
visited Cuba, drawings of stage
sets, historic photos, and
works by contemporary artists.

Paseo
Continue along Calle Línea to
the junction with one of the
loveliest streets in Havana:
Calle Paseo, which is like a
long, thin park running
up to the Plaza de la
Revolución *(see
p 102)*. It is lined
with elegant build-
ings with splendid
gardens: mostly
ministries and
public administra-
tion offices. The
Casa de la Amistad ⑥, at No.
406 between Calle 17 and 19,
is a cultural centre with a bar
and restaurant, and part of a
lavish Art Deco building
given by the wealthy Pedro
Baró to his mistress Caterina
Lasa, grande dame of Havana
high society. They were
forced to flee to Europe by
the scandal caused by their
affair, but returned in 1917,
when Lasa managed to get a
divorce from her first husband.

23 y 12
Continue on Calle Paseo back
to Calle 23, six blocks away
from the busy central intersection where this walk ends. A
plaque declares that on 16
April 1961, on the eve of the
American invasion at the Bay
of Pigs *(see p167)*, Fidel Castro
announced that the Cuban
Revolution was Socialist.
    At Calle 23 y 12 there are
restaurants and bars, shops,
and cinemas like the Chaplin
Cinematheque and the Cuban
Institute of Cinematographic
Arts and Industry (ICAIC) ⑦
(see p29), with an art gallery
featuring contemporary artists.

The permanent poster exhibition
in the ICAIC building

The Art Deco building that is the home of the Casa de las Américas

Casa de las Américas ❷

Calle 3ra, esq. G. **Map** 1 C1.
Tel (7) 838 2706, 838 2707.
◯ *10am–5pm Mon–Fri.* ● *1 Jan, 1 May, 26 Jul, 10 Oct, 25 Dec.* ✍

On the Malecón, beyond the Monument to the Victims of the *Maine (see p58)*, there is a kind of secular temple, with a bell tower but no cross. This is the Casa de las Américas, a cultural institution, which was built in just four months after the triumph of the Cuban Revolution. Haydée Santamaría, one of the heroines of the stuggle, founded the Casa with the aim of promoting exchanges among artists and writers on the American continent.

The centre features Arte Nuestra América, the most comprehensive collection known of Latin American painting and graphic art from the 1960s to the present.

Museo de Artes Decorativas ❸

Calle 17, 502. **Map** 2 D2. *Tel (7) 8309 848.* ◯ *10:30am–4:30pm Tue–Sat, 9am–1pm Sun.* ● *1 Jan, 1 May, 25 Dec.* ✍ ▢ ◎ *(with charge)* ▢
www.cult.cu/patrim/cnpc/museos

The wonderful Museum of Decorative Arts is housed in the former residence of one of the wealthiest Cuban women of the 20th century: the Countess de Revilla de Camargo, sister of José Gómez Mena, the owner of

the Manzana de Gómez *(see p81)*. The mansion was built in 1927, and is well worth a visit for its French Rococo-Louis XV furnishings, as well as for the inner gardens.

The collection reveals the sophisticated and exotic tastes of the ruling classes and wealthy collectors of the Colonial period. Major works of art here include two paintings by Hubert Robert, *The Swing* and *The Large Waterfall at Tivoli*, and two 17th-century bronze sculptures in the foyer.

The main hall on the Louis XV-style ground floor has 18th-century Chinese vases, Meissen porcelain, a large Aubusson carpet dating from 1722 and paintings by French artists.

A bedroom on the ground floor holds a collection of Chinese screens, while the Countess's room features a secretaire that once belonged to Marie Antoinette.

Last but not least is the pink marble Art Deco bathroom, which should not be missed.

Chinese porcelain, Museo de Artes Decorativas

Universidad de La Habana ❹

Calle 27 de Noviembre (Jovellar) y Ronda. **Map** 2F2. **Museo Antropológico Montané**, Felipe Poey Bldg, Plaza Ignacio Agramonte. *Tel (7) 8793 488.* ◯ *9am–noon, 1–4pm Mon–Fri.* ● *1 Jan, 1 May, 26 Jul, 10 Oct, 25 Dec.* ✍ ▢ ◎

The University of Havana was founded under the auspices of a papal bull in 1728 and was initially housed in the Dominican monastery of St John Lateran, in the heart of Habana Vieja. In 1902, a few days after the proclamation of the Cuban Republic, it was transferred to the Vedado area to a site which had been utilized as an explosives store in the Colonial period.

The new university, housed in various buildings, was built between 1906 and 1940. In front of the main entrance, now the venue for political demonstrations and concerts, is the Alma Mater, the symbol of Havana

The Neo-Classical foyer of the Museo de Artes Decorativas

The austere façade of the University of Havana, with the statue of the Alma Mater at the top of the staircase

University. This statue, of a woman with her arms outstretched in a gesture of welcome, was cast in 1919 in New York by the Czech sculptor Mario Korbel. It was installed at the top of the broad granite stairway that forms the entrance to the complex in 1927. The student entrance to the university is in Calle San Lázaro, which broadens out into an open space where the ashes of Julio Antonio Mella (see p46) are kept, before sloping upwards.

In the Science Faculty, the Felipe Poey Museum of Natural History is open to visitors. Of much greater interest, however, is the **Museo Antropológico Montané**, in the Mathematics Department. Founded in 1903, this museum has exceptional pre-Columbian archaeological finds from Cuba, such as the Idolo del Tabaco found on the eastern tip of the island, the Idolo de Bayamo, one of the largest stone sculptures in the entire Caribbean area, and the Dujo de Santa Fe, a wooden ceremonial seat.

Idolo de Tabaco, Museo Montané

The oldest building on the hill is the Great Hall, with an austere façade behind which are allegorical paintings by Armando Menocal. The hall itself contains the old University of San Gerónimo bell, used to convene the professors, and the remains of Félix Varela (see p28), brought to Cuba in 1911 from Florida, where the Cuban intellectual had died.

Museo Napoleónico ⑤

Calle San Miguel 1159, esq. a Ronda. **Map** 2 F3. **Tel** (7) 8791 412, 8791 460. ⬤ closed for restoration until approximately mid-2009.
📷 🎞 📷 (with charge). 🚻
www.cult.cu/patrim/cnpc/museos

The surprising presence of a Napoleonic museum in Cuba is due to the passion of a sugar magnate, Julio Lobo. For years he sent his agents all over the world in search of Napoleonic mementoes. In 1959, when Lobo left Cuba, the Cuban government bought his collection.

Every room in this curious museum contains fine examples of imperial-style furniture as well as all sorts of surprising Napoleonic memorabilia, including one of the emperor's teeth and a tuft of his hair. There are two portraits, one by Andrea Appioni, painted in Milan during Napoleon's second Italian campaign, and another by Antoine Gros. There is also his death mask, cast two days before Napoleon's death by Francesco Antommarchi, the Italian physician who had accompanied him to the island of St Helena and who later settled in Cuba.

The mansion itself was built in the 1920s by Oreste Ferrara, counsellor to the dictator Gerardo Machado, who furnished it in a Neo-Florentine Gothic style.

Quinta de los Molinos ⑥

Avenida Carlos III (Salvador Allende) y Luaces. **Map** 2 F3.
Tel (7) 8798 850.
⬤ Closed for restoration until early 2010.

A typical 19th-century villa in the Vedado quarter, the Quinta de los Molinos was built as the summer residence of the captains-general in 1837. The villa stands in a leafy area with two tobacco mills (molinos).

The rambling grounds around the villa were filled with tropical vegetation from the Botanical Garden, which was then in the Capitol area but was dismantled after the Parque Central was enlarged. The park is popular among local musicians, who come here to practise.

In 1899, General Máximo Gómez, Commander in Chief of the liberation army, stayed here, which is why it is now a museum dedicated to this hero of the wars of independence (see p44).

A stained-glass window in the Quinta de los Molinos

A parade in front of the Ministerio del Interior, Plaza de la Revolución

Plaza de la Revolución ❼

Map 2 E5.

Plaza de la Revolución has been Cuba's political, administrative and cultural centre since 1959. The square was designed in 1952 under the Batista regime, and most of the buildings visible today also date from the 1950s. What had been known as the Plaza Cívica was renamed Plaza de la Revolución following Fidel Castro's victory in 1959.

Though it does not distinguish itself by its architecture or design, the square is nonetheless an important place to visit because of its historic and symbolic importance. It was the venue for the first mass rallies following the triumph of the revolution and of the festivities for the campaign against illiteracy in 1961.

Since 1959, military parades and official celebrations have often attracted crowds of over a million people. During these events the area fills with people, and the speakers, including president Fidel Castro, take their place on the podium next to the statue of José Martí, at the foot of the obelisk.

On 25 January 1998 Pope John Paul II celebrated mass from this podium together with thousands of worshippers *(see p53)*.

🏛 Ministerio del Interior
Calle Aranguren.
The façade of the Ministry of the Interior, which stands directly opposite the statue of Martí, is almost completely covered by a huge bronze wire sculpture of Che Guevara, which was completed in 1995. (The guerrilla fighter had his office in this building in the early 1960s.) This striking and symbolic image was inspired by the world-famous photo-graph taken by the press photographer Alberto Korda *(see p176)*. Under the bust are the words: "Hasta la victoria siempre" (keep striving for victory). The façade is illuminated at night.

🏛 Museo Postal Cubano
Ave Rancho Boyeros, 19 de Mayo y 20 de Mayo. *Tel* (7) 882 8223. ◯ *8am–5:30pm Mon–Fri.* ● *1 Jan, 1 May, 26 Jul, 10 Oct, 25 Dec.* 🖼 🖋 📷 *(with charge).*
This fascinating postal museum has occupied a small corner of the Ministry of Communications since 1965. Through the medium of stamps, it illustrates the last two centuries of Cuban history, from the end of the Colonial period to the years following the fall of the Berlin Wall, including the wars of independence, and figures like Machado, Batista and Che Guevara.

The most curious item on display is a fragment of a "postal missile". In 1939, a group of Cubans decided to use a missile for "express airmail deliveries" from Havana to Matanzas, but the crude device exploded a few minutes after "take-off".

The Teatro Nacional seen from Martí's memorial

🏛 Palacio de la Revolución
Calle Martí.
The former Ministry of Justice (1958) behind the Martí Memorial now houses the offices of the Council of State, the Council of Ministers and the Central Committee of the Communist Party. It was here that Fidel Castro received Pope John Paul II on 22 January 1998.

The elegant wooden card-index files in the Biblioteca Nacional

🏛 Biblioteca Nacional José Martí
Plaza de la Revolución.
Tel (7) 855 5442. ◯ *8:15am–6pm Mon–Sat.* ▣
The José Martí National Library has over two million books and is particularly strong in the humanities. The United States embargo, plus the Special Period crisis, have slowed the development of a library computerization programme, but all services are being modernized.

🎭 Teatro Nacional
Paseo y 39.
Tel (7) 8796 011, 8793 558.
Built with a striking convex façade, the National Theatre is Cuba's most important cultural complex. It was inaugurated in June 1959. There are two auditoriums: the Avellaneda, with a seating capacity of 2,500, and the Covarrubia, which seats 800 and has a mural by Cuban artist René Porto-carrero *(see p26)*. Theatre pro-grammes include lectures, courses, theatre festivals, guitar and jazz concerts, and ballet. There is also a *café chan-tant* and a piano bar with live shows *(see p124)*.

Memorial José Martí ⓢ

Work on this monument in the middle of the Plaza de la Revolución began in 1953, on the 100th anniversary of the birth of Cuba's national hero. The memorial was finished in 1958. It consists of a 109-m (358-ft) tower representing a five-pointed star and is built of grey marble from the Isla de la Juventud. At the foot stands a huge statue of José Martí in a meditative pose. The actual Martí Memorial is in the interior of the base, which also houses the Sala de Actos, an auditorium used for concerts, lectures and poetry readings.

★ **Panorama**
On clear days, the mirador on top of the tower, the highest point in Havana, affords a view of the entire city. The panorama shown here stretches from the Ministerio del Interior to the sea.

A lift goes to the top of the tower, which reaches a height of 139 m (458 ft) – the monument stands on a hill 30 m (100 ft) above sea level.

VISITORS' CHECKLIST

Plaza de la Revolución.
Map 2 E5.
Tel (7) 859 2347.
🕘 9am–5pm Mon–Sat.
♿ 🔲 📷 🛍

★ **The Memorial**
Two rooms contain manuscripts, portraits and mementoes of Martí; the third room describes the history of the monument and the square, while a fourth puts on contemporary art exhibitions. The mural in the lobby features the patriot's thoughts.

STAR FEATURES

★ Panorama

★ The Memorial

Statue of José Martí
The 18-m (59-ft) high, white marble statue, carved on site by Juan José Sicre, is surrounded by six half columns.

Necrópolis de Colón ❾

Havana's monumental Columbus Cemetery is one of the largest in the world, occupying an area of 56 ha (135 acres) with 53,360 plots, where some two million people have been buried. It was designed in the 1860s by the Spanish architect Calixto de Loira, who based the layout on the rigorously symmetrical plan of Roman military camps. It was built between 1871 and 1886. Because of its many sculptures and monuments in different styles – from eclectic to the boldest expressions of contemporary art – the Necrópolis has been proclaimed a national monument. However, although it is full of fascinating funerary art, it is still the cemetery for and of Havana's citizens. People come here to visit their loved ones or simply to stroll around.

The Osario General, the ossuary built in 1886, is one of the cemetery's oldest constructions.

Martires del Asalto al Palacio Presidencial
This avant-garde memorial (1982) honours the students killed during their attack on Batista's Presidential Palace in 1957.

La Milagrosa

The Pantheon of Catalina Lasa *(see p99)* was commissioned by her second husband, Juan Pedro Baró, who had her embalmed and brought from Paris to Havana.

★ **La Piedad de Rita Longa**
This delicate marble bas-relief pietà adorns the black marble tomb of the Aguilera family, which was built in the 1950s.

Chapel of the Six Medical Students

★ **Main Entrance**
The statue in Carrara marble of the three theological virtues, Faith, Hope and Charity, was sculpted in 1904 by the Cuban artist José Villalta de Saavedra in "Neo-Romantic" style.

JANUA SUM PACIS

Tomb of the author Alejo Carpentier (1904–80)

Entrance

Fuerzas Armadas Revolucionarias Monument (1955)
This pantheon houses the heroes of the Revolutionary Armed Forces.

VISITORS' CHECKLIST
Calle Zapata esq a Calle 12.
Map 1 C5.
Tel (7) 830 4517.
⬤ 8am–5pm daily.

Panteón de los Prelados

Capilla Central
Built in the late 1800s in the middle of Avenida Colón, the cemetery's main avenue, this chapel contains frescoes by the Cuban artist Miguel Melero.

The Falla Bonet Pantheon
is a truncated grey granite pyramid with a statue of Christ by the Spanish sculptor Mariano Benlliure.

★ Las Víctimas de la Caridad
A monumental pantheon with the tombs of the victims of an accident that occurred in 1890 in the Isasí hardware store. The monument was designed by the Spanish architects Agustín Querol and Julio Zapata.

Tomb of Generalissimo Máximo Gómez
(see p44)

A mother placing flowers on the statue of La Milagrosa

LA MILAGROSA
"The Miraculous One" is the tomb of Amelia Goyri de la Hoz, who died in childbirth in 1901, along with her baby. She was only 24. In keeping with the custom of the time, she and the child were buried together. According to popular legend, a few years later the tomb was opened and she was found intact, holding her baby in her arms. This "miracle", and the fact that the bereaved husband went to her tomb every day and never turned his back to it, made Amelia a symbol of motherly love. She became the protector of pregnant women and newborn children, and her tomb is a pilgrimage site for future mothers, who ask for her blessing and leave without turning their back to the tomb. The statue placed at the tomb in 1909 is by José Villalta de Saavedra.

STAR SIGHTS
- ★ Main Entrance
- ★ La Piedad de Rita Longa
- ★ Las Víctimas de la Caridad

FURTHER AFIELD

Beyond the city of Havana, sights of interest are rather more scattered. The Miramar quarter lies to the west of the city, and the Castillo del Morro and Fortaleza de La Cabaña defence fortresses, evidence of Havana's strategic importance, are physically separated from the city but linked to it historically. Cubans are enthusiastic beachgoers and the long golden beaches at Playas del Este, east of Havana, are especially popular destinations at the weekend. Among the sightseeing highlights are the favourite haunts of Ernest Hemingway, including Finca La Vigía, the villa where he wrote some of his best novels, and the fishing village of Cojímar.

SIGHTS AT A GLANCE

Museums
Finca La Vigía ❿

Monuments and Churches
Castillo del Morro ❸
San Carlos de La Cabaña ❹
Santuario de San Lázaro ⓭

Parks and Gardens
Jardín Botánico Nacional ⓬
Parque Lenin ⓫

Beaches
Playas del Este ❾

Towns and Suburbs
Casablanca ❺
Cojímar ❽
Guanabacoa ❼
Regla ❻

Historic Places
Tropicana ❷

Walks
A Walk through Miramar (pp108–9) ❶

KEY
▨	Historic centre
▢	Built-up area
✈	Airport
⛴	Ferry
━	Motorway
━	Major road
══	Minor road

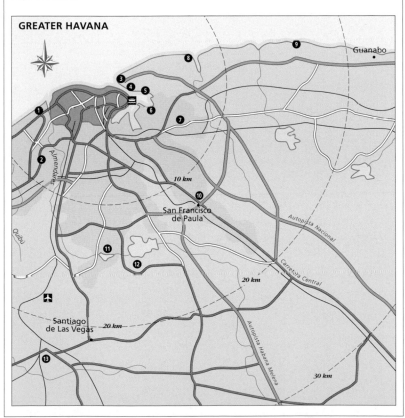

◁ The lighthouse at Castillo del Morro, which can be seen from many parts of the old city

A Walk through Miramar ❶

Miramar is the most elegant part of Havana – as it was before the Revolution, when the city's richest inhabitants lived here. Life in this quarter revolves around the busy Avenida 5, a broad, tree-lined avenue flanked by splendid early 20th-century villas and now boasting a number of luxury hotels. Administratively, Miramar belongs to the municipality of Playa, as does the adjacent Cubanacán quarter, where many foreign embassies are located.

Looking down Avenida 5, the main avenue in Miramar

The compact Fuerte de la Chorrera

Arriving from Vedado

This walk begins at the Fuerte de Santa Dorotea de la Luna en la Chorrera fort ❶, a national monument. The fort, designed by Giovanni Battista Antonelli and built in 1645, was crucial to the city's defence system *(see p110)* for over two centuries. Opposite the fort is the 1830 ❷, a restaurant *(see p278)* in a house that once belonged to Carlos Miguel de Céspedes, Minister of Public Works under President Machado.

Along Avenida 5 (Quinta Avenida)

From here, follow the northernmost tunnel under the Almendares river to reach Avenida 5, a broad, tranquil avenue with shrubs and benches in the middle. On both sides of it are large, imposing mansions built in the early decades of the 20th century and many Art Deco and eclectic-style houses, most of which were abandoned by their owners after Fidel Castro took power. The Cuban government has turned many of these buildings into ministries, embassies and even orphanages (an example is the residence of the former President of the Republic Grau San Martín at the corner of Calle 14). Further down the Avenida, at the corner of Calle 26, is the modern Iglesia de Santa Rita ❸, with three

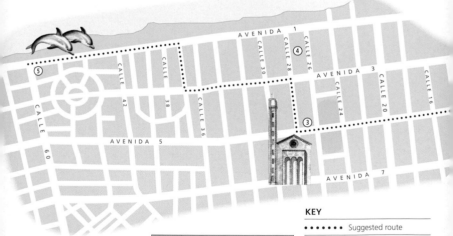

KEY

•••••• Suggested route

0 metres   400
0 yards   400

ITINERARY

Fuerte de Santa Dorotea de la Luna en la Chorrera ❶
Restaurante 1830 ❷
Iglesia de Santa Rita ❸
Maqueta de La Habana ❹
Acuario Nacional ❺

Dolphins performing at the Miramar aquarium

VISITORS' CHECKLIST

Point of departure: Fuerte de la Chorrera, Malecón.
Length: 5 km (3 miles).
Stops: Mesón La Chorrera, Calle Calzada 1252, before the tunnel; Cafetería Rumbos, Playita 16; Bar Media Noche, Calle 4 e/ Ave 3 y 5; Bar Dos Gardenias, Ave 7 y Calle 28.

For hotels and restaurants in this region see pp252–6 and pp276–9

distinctive tall arches on its façade. Pop in to see the statue of St Rita by Cuban sculptress Rita Longa, to the left of the entrance. Walk up Calle 28 to Avenida 3 (*"tercera"*). In the block above is the fascinating Maqueta de La Habana museum ④, a detailed model of Havana measuring about 10 sq m (108 sq ft), with different areas colour-coded according to construction date, showing how the city developed from Colonial times onwards. Continue the walk along Avenida 3, taking in the stylish architecture, and then turn right to walk one block up to Avenida 1.

Statue by Rita Longa, Church of Santa Rita

The Seafront

Avenida 1 (*"primera"*) lacks the liveliness and fascination of the Malecón, but the water is clear and there are peaceful spots for sunbathing, such as Playita 16 (at the end of Calle 16). At the corner of Calle 60 is the unmistakable pale blue building housing the Acuario Nacional ⑤, the city aquarium. Here, large saltwater tanks reproduce an assortment of Caribbean and ocean habitats. About 3,500 specimens represent 350 different species of sea fauna. The most spectacular section is the tank of *Tursiops truncatus* dolphins, more commonly known as bottle-nosed dolphins. Dolphin shows are also performed here at regular intervals. The aquarium complex is open from 10am to 6pm every day except Monday.

The model of Havana: in the foreground, Castillo del Morro, behind, the Malecón

The early 20th-century Fountain of the Muses at the Tropicana

Tropicana ❷

Calle 72 e/ 41 y 45. Marianao.
Tel (7) 2671 717, 2670 110.

The most famous nightclub in Cuba, America and perhaps the world is located in the outskirts of Havana, in the Marianao district. Many legendary figures of the 20th century have performed here, including Josephine Baker, Bola de Nieve, Rita Montaner and Nat King Cole.

The Tropicana was originally a farm estate belonging to Mina Pérez Chaumont, the widow of a wealthy man named Regino Truffin. In the 1930s she transformed her property into a vast nightspot with a restaurant and casino featuring extravagant floor shows with lavish costumes. The nightclub opened on 31 December 1939.

Perhaps surprisingly, given the change of regime, the Tropicana is still alive and kicking. Fortunately, the trees in the original estate were left intact, so that today the Tropicana stands in the middle of an extraordinary tropical forest. At night, floodlights illuminate the palm trees, partly hidden by clouds of artificial smoke. A reminder of the Tropicana's golden age is the enormous "Bajo las Estrellas" ballroom. With its capacity of 1,000 it is one of the largest of its kind.

At the main entrance is the Fountain of the Muses (1952). The garden's statue of a ballet dancer, by Rita Longa (1952), is now the symbol of the club.

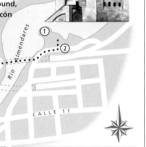

RÍO ALMENDARES

The Almendares river is no longer crystal-clear, but it must have been cleaner in the past, because in the 17th century a Spanish bishop called Almendáriz came to Havana in bad health and fully recovered after a stay along its banks. The river's name was changed from Casiguaguas to Almendares in the bishop's honour. Along its west bank, by the Calle 23 bridge from Vedado, is the Parque Almendares, an area filled with tropical plants and vegetation.

Thick vegetation in the Parque Almendares, Havana's "forest"

Aerial view of the Castillo del Morro, situated on a rocky headland at the entrance to the bay of Havana

Castillo del Morro ❸

Carretera de la Cabaña, Habana del Este. **Parque Histórico Militar Morro Cabaña** *Tel* (7) 8620 617-19, 8627 623. ☐ 10am–10pm daily.

Construction of this fortress, which was designed by the Italian military architect Giovanni Battista Antonelli, began in 1589 at the request of the governor, Juan de Texeda. The function of the Castillo de los Tres Reyes del Morro (its full title) was to detect the approach of any enemy (pirates especially). Various treasures of the New World were periodically concentrated in the port when ships docked

The old lamp in the Morro lighthouse

in Cuba on their voyage to Spain, and it was necessary to protect them.

The original lighthouse on the "Morrillo", the highest point of the hill, was rebuilt several times, until General Leopoldo O'Donnel ordered a new one to be built in 1845. This still stands today. It is made entirely of stone, and has its original lamp, the rays of which shine for a radius of 30 km (20 miles). Today the Castillo del Morro is open to visitors as the Parque Histórico-Militar. Many tourists and locals come simply to admire the outlook, as the fortress affords a magnificent view of the city and port of Havana.

Access to the castles is through an impressive gallery,

where plaques indicate the spot where the British opened a breach in 1762, allowing them to take the Morro and all of Havana after a 40-day siege.

On the northern side of the complex is the Plataforma de la Reina, with defence walls and a flight of steps leading to the upper terrace. From here visitors can gain an overall view of the fortress.

San Carlos de La Cabaña ❹

Carretera de la Cabaña, Habana del Este.
☐ See Castillo del Morro.

After the British conquest of Cuba in 1762, it was 11 months before the Spaniards regained Havana. The bitter experience of foreign occupation convinced them of the need to fortify the hill

HAVANA'S DEFENCES

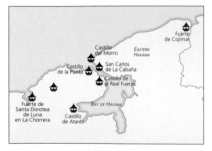

Havana was the most important port in the New World in the 1700s. It was a highly prized target for enemies and pirates because of its extremely favourable strategic position in the Caribbean, and it was also the most fortified city in any Spanish colony. Beyond the maritime canal affording access to the Bay of Havana were the two large fortresses of Morro and Cabaña. These two, together with the castles of Real Fuerza, Punta, Atarés and Príncipe and the city walls, constituted for centuries the city's impressive defence and attack system. From the outlying forts of Cojímar and La Chorrera, to the east and west respectively, any enemy approach could be sighted.

dominating the port in a more effective manner, so, on 4 November 1763, construction work began on the new Cabaña fortress. No fewer than 4,000 men laboured on the project, including Mexican and Indian prisoners transported from the Yucatán peninsula in conditions of semi-slavery.

The new fortification cost 14 million pesos, a sum so large that, according to an old legend, when King Carlos III of Spain was informed of the expense, he asked for a spyglass and reputedly commented: "Such an expensive construction should be visible from Madrid."

La Cabaña, which extends for more than 700 m (2,300 ft) along the entrance canal of the bay, is a huge 10-ha (25-acre) polygon designed in keeping with the principles of French military schools, but with detailing by the Spanish engineer Silvestre Abarca. With its crown-shaped plan, it is considered a fine example of a bastion-type defence fortification.

A visit to the fortress offers a variety of experiences. The fortress's central thoroughfare leads up to the Baluardo di San Ambrosio bastion and the

Entrance to the de La Cabaña parish church, which stands in the fortress parade ground

Terraza de San Agustín, where the poet Juan Clemente Zenea was executed in 1871 for his separatist ideas in 1871. In the same area some Soviet nuclear missiles, left over from the 1962 Cuban Missile Crisis *(see p52)*, are on display.

The **Museo Monográfico** illustrates the history of the fortress through documents and photographs. The **Museo de Armas y Fortificaciones** is a military museum.

However, the one museum not to miss is the **Comandancia del Che**: on 3 January 1959 the *barbudos* (as Castro and his bearded revolutionaries were known) occupied La Cabaña and set up their headquarters in the 19th-century building that was once the residence of the Spanish military governor. Today it is a museum containing various items that belonged to Che Guevara, including his weapons, glasses and camera. The revolutionary's original office, which has been left intact, is also open to visitors.

Casablanca ❺

Regla (Havana). 🚢 *from Muelle de Luz, La Habana Vieja, every 30 mins.* **Tel** *(7) 797 7473.* 🚩

This fishing village was built in the 1700s on the other side of the Bay of Havana from the city. Casablanca is best known for the huge Cristo de la Habana, an 18-m (60-ft) tall white marble statue of Christ, which looms over the village. The work of the Cuban sculptress Jilma Madera (1958), it was commissioned by President Batista's wife, Marta. She had made a vow that she would finance a large statue of Christ if her husband survived the attack by students on the presidential palace in 1957, during which he risked his life. The statue was completed a week prior to the Revolution. It can be seen from many parts of the city and is familiar to all Cubans.

The colossal Cristo de La Habana

THE CAÑONAZO

Every evening, at 9pm exactly, the picturesque "Cañonazo" ceremony is held in the La Cabaña fortress. On the hour, a volley of cannon shots is fired by a group of young soldiers of the Revolutionary Armed Forces, dressed in 18th-century uniforms. This theatrical ceremony is interesting from the historical point of view: in the Colonial period, a volley of cannon shots was fired at the end of each day to tell citizens that the city gates were closed and access to the bay had been blocked by a chain *(see p85)*.

The Cañonazo ceremony, a commemoration in historic costume

Regla ❻

Havana. 🏠 47,000. 🚢 from
Muelle de la Luz, Habana Vieja, every
30 mins; (7) 977 473.

Regla lies on the east coast of
the Bay of Havana, a few
minutes by ferry from Muelle
de la Luz. The town was
founded in 1687 and over the
years grew in economic
importance as a fishing port
and centre for huge sugar
warehouses. In the 19th
century freed slaves settled in
Regla, and there is still a
strong Afro-Cuban culture
here today.

The church of **Nuestra
Señora de la Virgen de
Regla** was built here in 1687.
A modest structure, it stands
on a small hill from which
there are views of the bay.
The humble interior includes

**Interior of the Regla church with its
ornate high altar**

an ornate golden altar into
which is incorporated the
figure of the dark-skinned
Virgen.

The Liceo Artístico y
Literario was opened by
José Martí in 1879 with a
famous speech on Cuban
independence.

Guanabacoa ❼

Havana. 🏠 100,000. 🚌

After its foundation in
1607, this town became
an obligatory port of call
for the slave traffic,
which explains its fame
as a city associated with
Afro-Cuban culture.
Its name, of Indian
origin, means
"land of many
waters": there
are several
springs in this area
which at one time
encouraged wealthy
Habaneros to build
homes here. Today,
Guanabacoa is proud of its
Colonial houses and of having
been the birthplace of three
leading 20th-century Cuban
musicians: pianist and
composer Ernesto Lecuona,
singer Rita Montaner, and
chansonnier Ignacio Villa,
better known as Bola de Nieve.

**The Mano Poderosa in
the Guanabacoa
Municipal Museum**

Guanabacoa has several
interesting churches. Of these,
the **Ermita de Potosí** in
particular is well worth a visit.
Built in 1644, it is one of the
oldest and most original
Colonial period churches.

The interesting **Museo
Municipal de Guanabacoa**,
located in a well-restored
Colonial house, illustrates
the history of the town. The
dominant figure is that of
Pepe Antonio, the local
hero in the struggle
against the British in
the 18th century.
The museum places
particular emphasis on the
santería and Palo
Monte religions and
on the rituals of
the Abakuá cult
(see p23). An
impressive piece
in this section is
the *Mano poderosa*,
a multicoloured
wooden sculpture
that stands approxi-
mately 1 m (3 ft)
high. According to legend,
the sculpture belonged to
a woman who was able to
make contact with the dead.
Traditional Afro-Cuban
events are sometimes held
in the courtyard.

🏛 **Museo Municipal
de Guanabacoa**
Calle Martí 108, esq. Versalles.
Tel (7) 797 9117. ⊙ 10am–6pm
Tue–Sat, 9am–1pm Sun. 🎞 📷 📷

Cojímar ❽

Havana. 🏠 20,100.
🛈 Hotel Panamericano Resort,
(7) 766 1010.

A charming village with one-
storey wooden houses –
often with a garden, small
porch and courtyard at the
back – Cojímar was once
inhabited only by fishermen.
Now there are also many
elderly people, including
writers and artists, who have
chosen to leave the capital for
a more peaceful life.

In the 1950s however, there
was only one author to be
seen on the streets of Cojímar:
Ernest Hemingway. Many of

LA VIRGEN DE REGLA

The Virgin of Regla has been the
patron saint of fishermen and
Havana since 1714. The Neo-
Classical sanctuary dedicated
to her contains an icon of a
dark-skinned Virgin holding a
white child that the faithful
call "La Negra". The icon's
origins are not known but one
legend suggests it acquired its
colour while being taken
across the Black Sea. The
statue was brought from Spain
by a hermit in 1696, and in the
1900s was watched over by a
certain Panchita Cárdenas,
whose modest home next to
the church is now open to
worshippers. For followers of

**La Virgen de Regla, the
protector of fishermen**

santería the Virgen de Regla is also Yemayá, the patroness of
the sea and mother of all men, to whom food, flowers,
candles and sweets are offered. On her feast day (Sep 8) the
icon is borne through the town.

The 17th-century fort at Cojímar

the local fishermen were his friends and he liked to play dominoes and drink rum while listening to their stories. He made this village the setting for his famous novel *The Old Man and the Sea*.

In the small square named after Hemingway there is a monument featuring a bust of the author – a faithful copy of the one in El Floridita *(see p72)*. It is here thanks to the author's fishermen friends, who donated anchors, hooks and tools to pay for the casting.

Nearby, on the seafront, is a small fort, which was built as the easternmost defence point of Havana in 1646. It was designed by Giovanni Battista Antonelli, architect of the Castillo del Morro *(see p110)*.

Cojímar is also the home of Hemingway's favourite restaurant, La Terraza *(see p278)*. It is still as elegant and well-run as it was during Hemingway's time. The cocktail lounge has a splendid wooden bar and is an ideal spot to enjoy a drink.

Playas del Este ❾

Havana.

Havana is one of the few cities in the world to have sizeable beaches only a 20-minute drive from the city centre. The Playas del Este consist of a stretch of about 50 km (31 miles) of fine sand and crystal-clear water, easy to reach via a good, fast road, with hotels, villages and tourist facilities of every kind. The beaches can offer a good compromise for people who want to spend some of their holiday at the seaside during

their visit to Havana. Bear in mind, however, that this area is also a popular haunt of *jineteros (see p300)*, though in places security guards have been drafted in to deter them.

Arriving from central Havana, the first beach is **Bacuranao**, a peaceful spot and a favourite with families. However, the loveliest places on the riviera are **Santa María del Mar** and **Guanabo**. Santa María del Mar is the most popular with tourists. It has the best beach, lined with pine and coconut trees, as well as a good choice of hotels and sports. Guanabo is more traditional, with small houses, restaurants and shops; at weekends this is the liveliest place along the coast when Habaneros arrive by the hundred. The Bajo de las Lavanderas, close to the shore, is a delight for scuba and skin divers, and deep-sea fishing trips can be arranged at the **Marina Veneciana**.

A small island, **Mi Cayito**, lies at the mouth of the Itabo river. There are fine views from Mirador Bellomonte.

One of the Playas del Este beaches popular with Havana residents

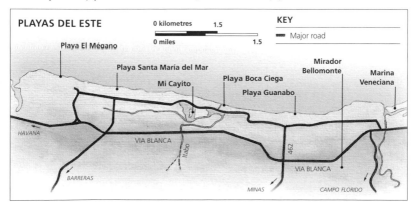

PLAYAS DEL ESTE

0 kilometres 1.5
0 miles 1.5

KEY

━━ Major road

Playa El Mégano
Playa Santa María del Mar
Mi Cayito
Playa Boca Ciega
Playa Guanabo
Mirador Bellomonte
Marina Veneciana
HAVANA
VIA BLANCA
Itabo
462
VIA BLANCA
BARRERAS
MINAS
CAMPO FLORIDO

Ernest Hemingway in Cuba

The great American author fell in love with Cuba on his first visit in 1932, attracted initially by the marlin fishing. It was not until 1939, however, that Hemingway decided to move to the island, initially settling down in the Ambos Mundos hotel in Old Havana *(see p253)*. Having decided to stay on, he found a quiet villa outside the town in which to write, Finca La Vigía, where he lived at first with journalist Martha

Period print of the Ambos Mundos hotel

Gellhorn (whom he married in 1940). His bond with Cuba lasted 20 years, through the Batista period and the beginning of the Revolution, and longer, in fact, than his relationship with Martha Gellhorn. Hemingway's last wife, Mary Welsh (married in 1946), joined the writer in Cuba and lived with him at Finca La Vigía. The villa is now a museum *(p115)*. He eventually returned to the US in 1960, a year before his suicide.

A lover of cocktails, *Hemingway was a regular at Bodeguita del Medio (see p65) and El Floridita (see p72). Both bars were a stone's throw from his room on the fifth floor of the Ambos Mundos Hotel. The writer helped to invent the daiquiri.*

Hemingway wrote *his most famous novels in Cuba. He was at Finca La Vigía in 1954 when he found out that he had received the Nobel Prize. "This prize belongs to Cuba, since my works were created and conceived in Cuba, with the inhabitants of Cojímar, of which I am a citizen." With these words, Hemingway placed the prize at the foot of the Madonna del Cobre (see p221).*

THE SEA AND FISHING

Hemingway loved the sea and was passionate about swordfish and marlin fishing. He practised the sport with great commitment and courage – not on a luxury yacht, but on a small fishing boat, the famous *Pilar* – together with a fisherman, Gregorio Fuentes, who also became a good friend. The boat was moored at the picturesque village of Cojímar.

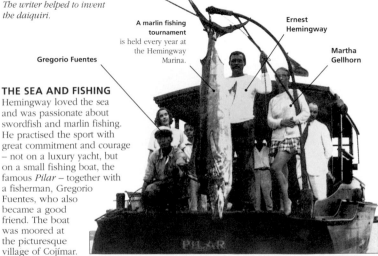

Gregorio Fuentes

A marlin fishing tournament is held every year at the Hemingway Marina.

Ernest Hemingway

Martha Gellhorn

Finca La Vigía ⓾

Calle Vigía y Stheinhard, San Francisco de Paula, Havana. 🚉 *San Francisco de Paula.* **Tel** *(7) 691 0809.* 🕐 *10am–5pm Mon–Sat, 10am–1pm Sun.* 📷 📷 *(with charge).* 🅿 🖥

At San Francisco de Paula, on the outskirts of Havana, is the only residence Ernest Hemingway ever had outside the US. He lived here, in the periods between his various foreign trips, for almost 20 years.

The villa, built in 1887 to a design by Catalan architect Miguel Pascual y Baguer, was bought by Hemingway on 28 December 1940. It was made a public museum in 1962, as soon as news of the writer's suicide in the US reached Cuba.

Everything in the villa is in the same meticulous order it was in when Hemingway lived here. There is his library with its more than 9,000 books; various hunting trophies from African safaris hanging in the living room; the author's personal possessions, such as his weapons and typewriter, and valuable artworks, including a ceramic plate by Picasso. The fact that all these objects have been left just as they were creates the atmosphere of a lived in house rather than a museum.

Two curious features in the garden are the pet cemetery (Hemingway had about 50 cats during his lifetime), and the *Pilar*, the author's fishing boat, which was transferred

The façade of Finca La Vigía, surrounded by tropical vegetation

from Cojímar to the museum and placed in a specially built pavilion in the former tennis court. The *Pilar* was a comfortable and fast boat made of black American oak, and the author loved ploughing through the waves on fishing expeditions with his friend Gregorio Fuentes. During World War II he used it to patrol the sea north of Cuba, on the lookout for Nazi submarines that were in the area to sink ships laden with sugar intended for the Allied troops.

Environs

Near Hemingway's villa is the village of **Santa María del Rosario**, founded in 1732 by Count Don José Bayona y Chacón on the estate of his large sugar factory. A real gem here is the church of the same name (it is also known as Catedral de los Campos de Cuba), notable for its splendid *mudéjar* ceilings.

The church was designed in 1760–66 by architect José Perera. The austere façade is reminiscent of the Spanish missions in the western US, while the interior contains some unusually lavish elements, such as the extravagantly gilded high altar, and paintings attributed to Nicolás de la Escalera, one of Cuba's early artists.

The living room of Hemingway's villa, with hunting trophies on the walls

For hotels and restaurants in this region see pp252–6 and pp276–9

Parque Lenin ⑪

Calle 100 y Cortina de la Presa, Arroyo Naranjo, Havana. *Tel* (7) 644 8880, 643 1868. 🕐 9am–5pm Tue–Sun. 🄯 ⑪ 🖥 🏛 **ExpoCuba** *Tel* (7) 697 9318. 🕐 Wed–Sun. 📷 **Parque Zoológico Nacional** *Tel* (7) 664 7637, 644 7613. 🕐 9am–3pm Wed–Sun. 📷

Lenin Park, 20 km (12 miles) south of Central Havana, occupies an area of 745 ha (1,840 acres). It was created in the 1970s as an amusement park for children and an area of greenery for a city in continuous expansion.

In the same period, thanks to an initiative by Celia Sánchez, Castro's personal assistant during the Revolution, the Russian architect Lev Korbel designed the vast monument honouring the Soviet leader. The statue of Lenin, which weighs 1,200 tons and is 9 m (30 ft) high, was completed in 1982 under the supervision of Antonio Quintana Simonetti, who also designed the park.

The most enjoyable way of getting around Parque Lenin is to take the narrow-gauge train which follows a route of 9.5 km (6 miles) in 45 minutes, making several stops. The train's old steam engines were used until a few years ago by Cuba's sugar factories to transport sugar cane. New open carriages allow passengers to

The impressive monument to Lenin designed by Lev Korbel

admire the scenery. The park is popular with Habaneros, who love to walk among the palm, cedar, pine and araucaria trees. There is also a freshwater aquarium, stables, outdoor cinema, art gallery, swimming pools, café and the Las Ruínas restaurant. The latter occupies a 1960s building that incorporates the crumbling walls of an old plantation house.

Environs
Near the park, among gardens and tree-lined paths, is the largest exhibition centre in Cuba, **ExpoCuba**, which stages various exhibitions and shows all year round. In autumn the pavilions are occupied by the famous Feria Internacional de La Habana, which offers an overview of Cuba's economic and socio-political life. From

Parque Lenin it is also easy to reach the 340-ha (840-acre) **Parque Zoológico Nacional,** where animals live freely in various natural habitats, often without cages. The savannah area is populated with zebras, hippopotamuses, giraffes and antelope. Another area is the habitat of lions.

Jardín Botánico Nacional ⑫

Carretera del Rocío km 3, Calabazar, Arroyo Naranjo (Havana). *Tel* (7) 643 7278, 697 9364. 🕐 9am–4:30pm daily. 🄯 1 Jan, 26 Jul, 25 Dec. 📷 🎫 📷

This enormous 600-ha (1,500-acre) botanical garden, set in an area of woods and cultivated fields, contains

The tranquil Japanese Garden, part of the Jardín Botánico Nacional

For hotels and restaurants in this region see pp252–6 and pp276–9

plants from all over the world. These are on display to the public and are also studied by specialists. The huge gardens are divided into geographical zones – Cuba, America, Africa, Asia and Oceania. The Caribbean section, which takes up one-fifth of the garden, has 7,000 flowering plants, half of which are unique to Cuba. There are also curiosities such as the Archaic Woods and the Palmetum. The former has plants descended from species that thrived in ancient geological eras, such as the *Palma corcho*, a fossil species that can still be found in the Pinar del Río region. The Palmetum has a large collection of palm trees from all tropical latitudes.

A must is the cactus area near the entrance. However, the most interesting part of this rather sparse park is the Jardín Japonés, a Japanese garden with artificial waterfalls and a pond with a gazebo. It was donated to Cuba by the local Asian community in 1989.

Another fascinating sight here is the orchid garden, with numerous varieties.

The Sanctuary of San Lázaro at El Rincón

Santuario de San Lázaro ⓭

Calzada de San Antonio km. 23, El Rincón, Santiago de las Vegas (Havana). **Tel** 683 2396. ⬤
7am–6pm daily. ✝ 9am Wed, Fri & Sun. 📷 Feast Day of St Lazarus, Dec 16 and 17.

This sanctuary, dedicated to St Lazarus, the patron saint of the sick, lies in the small village of El Rincón, outside Santiago de las Vegas, next to an old lepers' hospital (now a dermatological hospital).

In Afro-Cuban religions Lazarus corresponds to Babalú Ayé. Both saints are represented in folk iconography as old men in tatters and covered with sores. In the case of the African saint, the skin disease was supposedly punishment from Olofi, the father of all the gods *(see p22)*, for the saint's adulterous and libertine past.

On 17 December, the simple white sanctuary welcomes thousands of worshippers, who flock here to make vows or ask the saint to intercede for them. Before the high altar, or in front of the image of St Lazarus (who is called *milagroso*, or "the miraculous one"), at a side altar, pilgrims light candles, leave flowers and make offerings.

The water from the fountain to the right of the sanctuary, considered miraculous by believers, is used to cure diseases and ease pain.

ITALO CALVINO AND CUBA

Santiago de las Vegas, most famous for its San Lázaro sanctuary, was also the birthplace of the great Italian novelist Italo Calvino (1923–1985). His father Mario was an esteemed agronomist who went to Cuba in 1918, following his appointment as director of the Estación Experimental de Santiago de las Vegas. This experimental field station covered 50 ha (123 acres) of land and employed 100 university graduates and 63 office workers. While in Cuba, Mario Calvino found ways of making genetic improvements to sugar cane and introduced new plants, including pumpkin and lettuce. He also worked on tobacco, corn and sorghum, while his wife Eva wrote articles exhorting Cuban women to emancipate themselves and acquire new dignity through education and training.

When the Calvino family returned to San Remo in Italy, they took not only a son who would become a great writer, but also mango, avocado, flamboyant, cherimoya and even sugar cane seeds, which they cultivated at the San Remo Experimental Agriculture Station. In 1964 Italo Calvino was named a member of the jury for the Casa de las Américas prize *(see p100)* and visited Cuba, where he returned to his birthplace and also met Che Guevara.

Author Italo Calvino, born at Santiago de las Vegas

The altar of St Lazarus with flowers left by worshippers

HAVANA STREET FINDER

Street sign, corner of Calle 13 and Ave de los Presidentes

The page grid shown on the *Area by Area* map below shows the parts of Havana covered by maps in this section. All map references in this guide refer to the maps in the *Street Finder* section. Addresses are indicated in keeping with the system used in Cuba so that people will understand your requests for information. The street name (and sometimes house number) is followed by either "e/" (*entre*, or "between") and the names of the two streets between which the address you want is located, or "*esq.*" (*esquina*, or "corner") followed by the name of the street on the crossroad where the address is located.

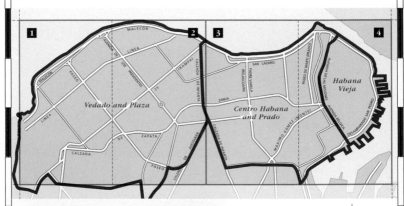

0 metres 700
0 yards 700

SCALE OF MAPS

0 metres 300
0 yards 300

KEY

	Major sight
	Place of interest
	Other buildings
P	Parking
i	Tourist information
	Hospital
	Police station
	Church
	Post office
	Coach station
	Train station
	Ferry

CUBAN STREET NAMES

Tile street sign in Habana Vieja

Since many streets changed name after the revolution, some have both an official name and an unofficial, more commonly used one. Where this occurs in this guide, the latter is followed by the former in brackets. In Vedado the streets are divided into neat 100-m (109-yd) long blocks or *cuadras*. The grid layout of the streets in this district is easy to follow. The streets parallel to the seafront are named with odd numbers, while the cross streets are indicated either with letters (from A to P) or even numbers. Street signs in the form of small stone blocks (see above) give coordinates at every corner.

Street Finder Index

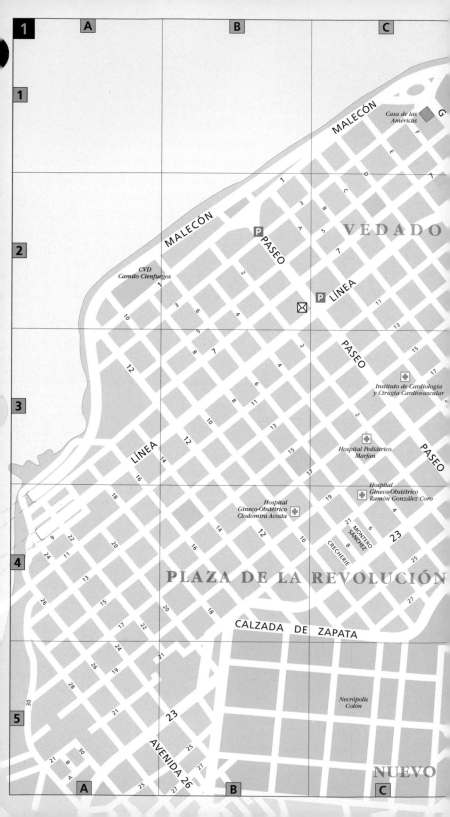

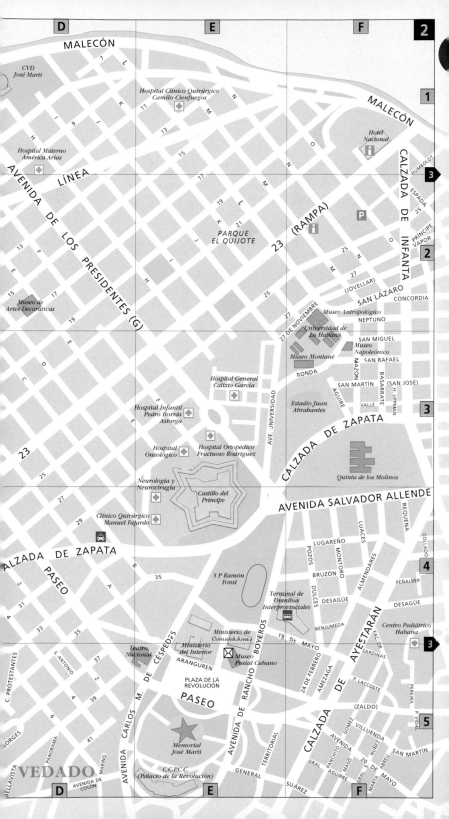

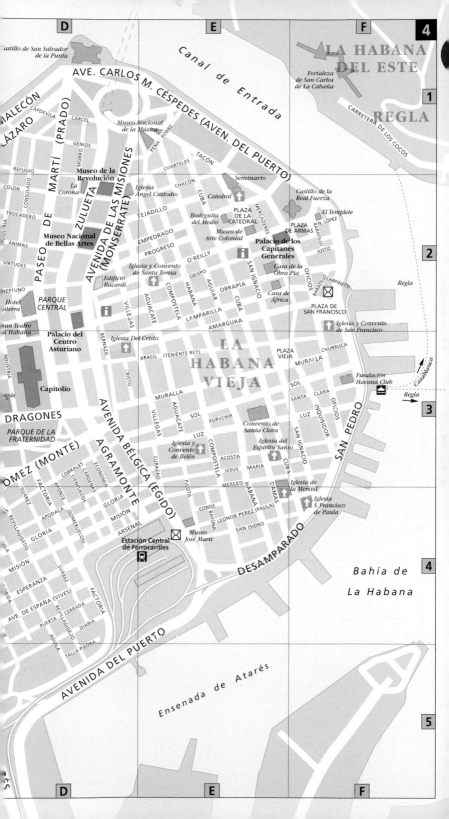

ENTERTAINMENT IN HAVANA

The lively, pleasure-loving capital of Cuba offers entertainment to suit visitors of all ages and tastes. Theatres, cinemas and concert halls are active year-round, while the city's annual ballet, cinema and jazz festivals draw admirers from afar. Havana has the biggest and best nightclubs in the country, offering all kinds of music from salsa and jazz to bolero to rap. The cabaret scene

Ballet Nacional de Cuba dancer

is world-class. You can dance 'til dawn in the discos, while those who prefer more traditional entertainment can investigate the neighbourhood Casa de la Trova or Casa de la Cultura. The bar scene is somewhat desultory, and many venues that pre-date the revolution are rough around the edges, but this adds atmosphere to Havana's sense of a *temps perdu*.

The National Symphony performing in Havana

INFORMATION

The airport, hotels and travel agents all distribute information brochures. *Bienvenidos a Cuba* is a small guide giving details of the most important shows and events. *Cartelera,* a bi-weekly newspaper and the monthly *Guia Cultural de la Habana* provide addresses of nightclubs and other venues, with details of shows. The *Granma* daily lists major events, which are also broadcast on Cubavisión (channel 6) Thursdays at 10:25pm. Visitors can tune into Radio Taíno (93.3FM), which broadcasts in Spanish and English.

Havana's thriving underground scene requires seeking out. The corner of Calles 23 and L (outside Cine Yara) is a good place to find out about impromptu parties and shows – especially for the gay scene.

BUYING TICKETS

To avoid long queues for festivals and other major events, visitors can purchase tickets

in advance from the venue's ticket office, from tourist agencies in the hotels or through **Paradiso: Promotora de Turismo Cultural**.

Tickets for cabaret shows at the world-famous Tropicana nightclub and Cabaret Parisienne can be obtained at the tour bureaus of any tourist hotel. For smaller shows and events, you will need to stand in line on the day or night of the performance.

THEATRE

Theatre has a long and illustrious tradition in Havana, though the range of offerings has been severely curtailed for political reasons since the Revolution. The *Festival Internacional del Teatro,* held every two years, offers both mainstream and experimental theatre, and some companies, such as El Público, have their own venues. Havana's most important and active theatres are located mostly in the Vedado quarter and are presented exclusively in Spanish.

The Teatro Nacional de Cuba, a complex with several auditoriums *(see p102)*, often hosts major international companies. The **Teatro Hubert de Blanck** specializes in contemporary drama, while the **Teatro Mella** has a more varied programme. The **Teatro Trianón** and **Teatro El Sótano** are committed to presenting experimental theatre. The **Café Teatro Brecht** opens only at weekends to a limited audience.

Cuban comedy tends towards bawdy slapstick. The best venues are **Casa de la Comedia**, offering shows at weekends, **Teatro Fausto** and **Café Teatro Brecht**.

CLASSICAL MUSIC & OPERA

There are two main classical music venues in Havana. The recently restored **Teatro Amadeo Roldán** is home to the National Symphony Orchestra.

The impressive exterior of the Gran Teatro de la Habana

The Gran Teatro de la Habana *(see p82)*, which has excellent acoustics, hosts opera and other productions.

The lovely Basilica de San Francisco de Asís *(see p74)* is an atmospheric venue for choral and chamber music concerts. The Agrupación Anfitriona de Música Antigua 'Ave Longa' puts on Renaissance and Baroque concerts in the **Iglesia de San Francisco de Paula**. The tiny **Museo Nacional de la Música** hosts classical concerts at weekends.

A traditional *son* band performing on the street

BALLET

Classical dance is popular in Cuba thanks to the promotion of the **Ballet Nacional de Cuba**, founded by the international ballet star Alicia Alonso. This institution organizes an annual international ballet festival and promotes specialist courses for foreign dancers. Performances take place in the Gran Teatro de la Habana *(see p82)*. Visitors are often shocked to discover that many performances feature taped music. The **Teatro Mella** hosts occasional ballet shows.

La Zorra y El Cuervo – a popular and crowded jazz venue

FOLK & TRADITIONAL MUSIC

Traditional Cuban music covers a broad range of styles including rumba, *guanguancó, son, danzón,* bolero and *punto guajiro (see pp30–31).*

Some of the best performances are based on Afro-Cuban forms, as perfected by the **Conjunto Folklórico Nacional**, which performs an open-air rumba every Saturday and hosts lessons for Cubans and foreigners. Similar performances are hosted on Sundays at the **Asociación Cultural Yoruba de Cuba**, and at **Rumba del Callejón de Hamel** in Centro Habana, one of the city's most popular weekend venues.

Visitors are also welcomed at **Salón de Ensayo Benny Moré**, where folkloric groups practise *danzón, guanguancó* and other dances.

RAP, ROCK & JAZZ

Rap is very popular in Cuba, and an international festival is held every August in Alamar, where the **Casa de la Cultura Alamar** hosts live performances, as do the **Teatro América** in Centro Habana and **La Madriguera** in the once-lovely botanical gardens.

The **Teatro Karl Marx** is the main venue for live shows by big-name rock and pop stars. Rock music is also played and danced to in the Playa's **Salón Rosado Benny Moré**.

Rio Club was the most famous rock venue in Havana in the 1970s, when it was called Johnny Club. People still refer to it by its old name.

Cubans love jazz, and Cuba's leading jazz musicians are popular the world over. An annual Jazz festival is held in venues throughout Havana. Among the best of these is **La Zorra y el Cuervo**, a cramped and smokey basement bar. Cuba's top performers, such as Chucho Valdés, play the spacious **Jazz Café**.

NIGHTCLUBS & DISCOS

Salsa is the staple of nightclubs and discos. Havana's hottest salsa venues are the twin **Casas de la Música** in Centro Habana and Miramar, where nightly events don't warm up until after midnight. The **Café Cantante**, in the Teatro Nacional, has inexpensive salsa sessions on Friday afternoons, as well as nightly live bands. The **Salón Turquino**, on the top floor of the Tryp Habana Libre hotel, is the classiest salsa spot. Like many Cuban nightclubs, no singles are allowed and foreigners are likely to be approached by potential partners hoping to have their entrance paid.

Café Concierto Gato Tuerto is famous as home of the blend of Cuban and North American music called *feeling*. This small venue fills quickly, so arrive early. Fans of the *bolero* should head to **Dos Gardenias**.

Among the best discos are the open-air **Macumba**, which allows couples only and draws Havana's equivalent of the jet set; and **Salón Rosado Benny Moré**, where live bands stir up some of the most sensuous dancing in town.

A live musical performance at one of Havana's many nightclubs

CABARET

The most exotic of venues, and a long-time Cuban tradition, *cabarets espectáculos* are famous for their extravagantly – and minimally – dressed female dancers in sequins and feathers. The music is first-rate, ranging from salsa to crooners performing traditional boleros.

The most famous is the Tropicana *(see p109)* featuring more than 200 performers. Though expensive, it offers a true spectacular with grandiose choreography, lavish costumes and legendary dancers. The **Cabaret Parisienne** is the most important of the hotel shows, while the **Cabaret Salón Rojo** and **Cabaret Copa Room** are among the better small shows.

BARS

The colourful bar-life of pre-revolutionary days is a mere memory today. Nonetheless, most upscale tourist hotels have classy bars (albeit filled with foreigners).

Three bars associated with Hemingway remain among the city's most colourful. La Bodeguita del Medio *(see p65)*, a cramped bar where the author popularized *mojitos*, features troubadors. The **Dos Hermanos** serves better *mojitos* and draws a local clientele. Famous for its daiquiris, **El Floridita** *(see p72)* exudes a fin-de-siècle ambience.

In Vedado, the Hotel Nacional's **Bar Vista del Golfo** has served cocktails to the rich and famous for decades.

Bartender preparing one of the famous daiquiris at El Floridita

Dancers at the Tropicana, Havana's most famous and colourful cabaret

CINEMA

Cuba has a thriving cinema industry. The annual December *Festival Internacional del Cine Latinoamericano*, a major international film festival, is organized by the **Instituto Cubano del Arte e Industria Cinematográfica** (ICAIC), which presides over the activities of the "seventh art" in Cuba *(see p29)* and also runs the **Cine Charles Chaplin**.

Most of the major cinemas are in the Vedado district. The main one is **Cine Yara**. **Cine Riviera** screens mostly Hollywood action movies, while **Cine La Rampa** shows mainly Cuban and Latin American films. Havana's largest cinema is the multi-screen **Cine Payret**, in Centro Habana; it has midnight shows at weekends.

CULTURAL CENTRES

For visitors interested in Cuban culture, the Casa de las Américas *(see p100)* has a good library, well-stocked book shop and a fine art gallery. It organizes literary and poetry festivals. High-level cultural events are also held at the **Fundación Alejo Carpentier**, dedicated to the work of the great Cuban writer, and the **Fundación Fernando Ortíz**, specializing in Afro-Cuban studies. The **Asociación Cultural Yoruba**, dedicated to African-derived religions, has a library, art exhibits, and lectures.

One of the most active centres is **UNEAC** (Writers and Artists' Union), which hosts musical and literary events at El Hurón Azul – the main spot for Havana's bohemians. The nearby **Casa de la Amistad** is a lively venue for music and dance. UNEAC's **Casa de la Poesía** has poetry readings.

CULTURAL TOURS

Week-long holiday packages are available from **Paradiso: Promotora de Turismo Cultural** *(see Ticket Agencies)*. The cost includes accommodation in a "4-star" hotel, lunch and dinner in typical Cuban restaurants, transport, guides, entrance to museums and theatres, meetings with Cuban artists and visits to schools and specialist educational centres.

The *"Cuba: Forma y Color"* programme focuses on art galleries, serigraphy (silk screen) workshops and artists' studios, while *"Cuba Paraíso de la Salsa"* features salsa classes, and *"Esta es mi Música"* educates visitors about Cuba's musical forms and traditions.

CHILDREN

Cubans adore children and the State takes good care of its young. However, entertainment venues for children are few. The **Aqvarium** displays tropical fish, and the Acuario Nacional *(see p109)* puts on dolphin shows. Donkey rides are offered at **Parque Luz Caballero** in Habana Vieja, and at Parque Lenin *(see p116)* and **Parque Metropoliano de La Habana**. The **Teatro Guiñol** hosts puppet shows and children's theatre.

A theme park with circus, miniature train and skate ring is under construction along the shorefront in Flores.

DIRECTORY

TICKET AGENCIES

Paradiso: Promotora de Turismo Cultural
Calle 19 560 esq. C. **Map 2** D3. *Tel (7) 832 6928.*

THEATRE

Café Teatro Brecht
Calle 13, esq. I. **Map 2** D2. *Tel (7) 863 1173.*

Casa de la Comedia
Calle Jústiz 18, esq. Baratillo. **Map 4** F2. *Tel (7) 863 9282.*

Teatro El Sótano
Calle K, e/ 25 y 27. **Map 2** E2. *Tel (7) 832 0630.*

Teatro Fausto
Paseo de Martí 201, esq. Colón. **Map 4** D2. *Tel (7) 863 1173.*

Teatro Hubert de Blanck
Calzada 657, e/ Calles A y B. **Map 1** C2. *Tel (7) 830 1011.*

Teatro Mella
Línea 657, e/ A y B. **Map 1** C2. *Tel (7) 833 5651.*

Teatro Trianón
Línea 706, e/ Paseo y A. **Map 1** C2. *Tel (7) 832 9648.*

CLASSICAL MUSIC & OPERA

Iglesia de San Francisco de Paula
Avenida del Puerto, esq. Leonor Pérez. **Map 4** F4. *Tel (7) 860 4210.*

Museo Nacional de la Música
Capdevila 1. **Map 4** E1. *Tel (7) 861 9846.*

Teatro Amadeo Roldán
Calzada y D. **Map 1** C2. *Tel (7) 832 4521.*

BALLET

Ballet Nacional de Cuba
Calzada 510 e/ D y E. **Map 1** C2. *Tel (7) 835 2948.*

FOLK & TRADITIONAL MUSIC

Asociación Cultural Yoruba de Cuba
Prado 615, e/ Dragones y Monte. **Map 4** D3. *Tel (7) 863 5953.*

Conjunto Folklórico Nacional
Calle 4 103 e/ Calzada y 5ta. **Map 1** B2. *Tel (7) 830 3060.*

Rumba del Callejón de Hamel
Callejón de Hamel, e/ Aramburo y Hospital. **Map 3** A2. *Tel (7) 878 1661.*

Salón de Ensayo Benny Moré
Neptuno 960, e/ Aguila y Galiano. **Map 3** C2. *Tel (7) 878 8827.*

RAP, ROCK & JAZZ

Casa de la Cultura Alamar
Calle 164, esq. 5taB, Zona 7, Alamar. *Tel (7) 65 0624.*

Jazz Café
Avenida 1ra esq. Paseo. **Map 1** B2. *Tel (7) 838 3556.*

La Madriguera
Avenida Salvador Allende, e/ Infanta y Luaces. **Map 2** F4. *Tel (7) 879 8175.*

La Zorra y el Cuervo
Calle 23, e/ N y O. **Map 2** F2. *Tel (7) 833 2402.*

Río Club (Johnny)
Calle A, e/3ra y 5ta, Miramar. *Tel (7) 209 3389.*

Teatro América
Avenida de Italia 253, e/ Concordia y Neptuno. **Map 3** C2. *Tel (7) 862 5416.*

Teatro Karl Marx
Avenida 1ra e/ 8 y 10. *Tel (7) 209 1991.*

NIGHTCLUBS & DISCOS

Café Cantante
Paseo, esq. 39. **Map 2** E6. *Tel (7) 878 4275.*

Café Concierto Gato Tuerto
Calle O 14, e/ 17 y 19. **Map 2** F1. *Tel (7) 838 2696.*

Casa de la Música
Galiano, e/ Concordia y Neptuno. *Tel (7) 862-4165.* Avenida 25 esq 20. **Map 3** C2. *Tel (7) 204 0447.*

Dos Gardenias
Complejo Dos Gardenias, Calle 7 y 26, Playa. *Tel (7) 204 2353.*

Macumba
Complejo La Giraldilla, La Coronela. *Tel (7) 204 4990.*

Salón Rosado Benny Moré
Avenida 41, esq. 48. *Tel (7) 206 4799.*

Salón Turquino
Calle L, e/ 23 y 25. **Map 2** F2. *Tel (7) 838 4011.*

CABARET

Cabaret Copa Room
Paseo y Malecón. **Map 2** B2. *Tel (7) 836 4051.*

Cabaret Parisienne
Calle O, esq. 21. **Map 2** F1. *Tel (7) 873 3564 ext 136.*

Cabaret Salón Rojo
Calle 21, e/ N y O. **Map 2** B2. *Tel (7) 833 3747.*

BARS

Bar Vista del Golfo
Calle O, esq. 21. **Map 2** F1. *Tel (7) 836 3564.*

Dos Hermanos
Avenida San Pedro 304, esq. Sol. **Map 2** F3. *Tel (7) 861 3514.*

El Floridita
Ubispo, esq. Monserrate. **Map 4** D2. *Tel (7) 867 1300.*

CINEMA

ICAIC
Calle 23 1155, e/10 y 12. **Map 1** C4. *Tel (7) 831 3145.*

Cine Charles Chaplin
Calle 23 1155, e/ 10 y 12. **Map 1** C4. *Tel (7) 831 1101.*

Cine La Rampa
Calle 23 111, e/ O y P. **Map 2** F2. *Tel (7) 836 6146.*

Cine Payret
Paseo de Martí 503, esq. San José. **Map 4** D3. *Tel (7) 863 3163.*

Cine Riviera
Calles 23 e/ H y G. **Map 2** E3. *Tel (7) 830 9564.*

Cine Yara
Calle 23 y Calle L. **Map 2** E2. *Tel (7) 832 9430.*

CULTURAL CENTRES

Asociación Cultural Yoruba
Paseo de Martí 615. **Map 4** D3. *Tel (7) 863 5953.*

Casa de la Amistad
Paseo 406, e/ 17 y 19. **Map 1** C3. *Tel (7) 830 3114.*

Casa de la Poesía
Calle Muralla 63, e/ Oficios y Inquisidor. **Map 4** F3. *Tel (7) 862 1801.*

Fundación Alejo Carpentier
Empedrado 215. **Map 4** E2. *Tel (7) 862 1801.*

Fundación Fernando Ortíz
Calle 27 160, esq. L. **Map 2** F2. *Tel (7) 832 6841.*

UNEAC
Calle 17 351, esq. H. **Map 2** D2. *Tel (7) 832 4551.*

CHILDREN

Aqvarium
Calle Brasil 9, e Mercaderes y Oficios. **Map 4** F3. *Tel (7) 863 9493.*

Parque Luz Caballero
Calle Tacón, Habana Vieja. Avenida 47, Miramar. **Map 4** E1.

Parque Metropolitano de La Habana
Avenida 47, Miramar.

Teatro Guiñol
Calle M, e/ 17 y 19. **Map 2** E1. *Tel (7) 832 6262.*

CUBA REGION BY REGION

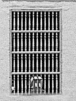
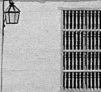

Cuba at a Glance

The lovely palm-fringed beaches of Cuba, such as those at Varadero and on Cayo Largo, are famous throughout the world, and justly so. But the interior of the island also offers a variety of unexpected experiences, from mountainous scenery to marshland and freshwater lagoons. The towns are full of interest, often with well-preserved architecture. Cuba really has two capitals. Havana is monumental and maritime, modern and Colonial, and represents the most European spirit of the country. The second, Santiago, embodies the Caribbean soul of Cuba. For the purposes of this guide, the island is divided into five regions – Havana, Western Cuba, Central Cuba – West, Central Cuba – East and Eastern Cuba. Each area is colour coded as shown here.

Varadero (see pp162–3), *known for its clear sea, is a popular holiday resort with sports centres and parks such as the Parque Josone.*

HAVANA

CENTRAL CUBA-WEST *(pp154–177)*

WESTERN CUBA *(pp132–153)*

Cayo Largo del Sur (see pp152–3), *a small island with splendid beaches on the shores of the Caribbean Sea, is a holiday paradise.*

The Valle de Viñales (see pp142–3) *has spectacular natural scenery with unique outcrops called* mogotes *and many cave formations. The most significant cave is the Cueva del Indio.*

Trinidad (see pp182–90) *is backed by the mountains of the Sierra del Escambray, which can be seen here beyond the Iglesia de San Francisco bell tower.*

◁ The church and monastery of San Juan de Dios in Camagüey

Cayo Coco *is a natural reserve for flamingos in the Jardines del Rey archipelago (see pp198–9). The coasts, mostly marshland, are dotted with mangrove swamps.*

Baracoa *(see pp242–3), the isolated, easternmost city in Cuba, is the only one with traces of the island's first inhabitants. Near the town are remnants of the tropical forest that covered the entire island when Columbus first landed here.*

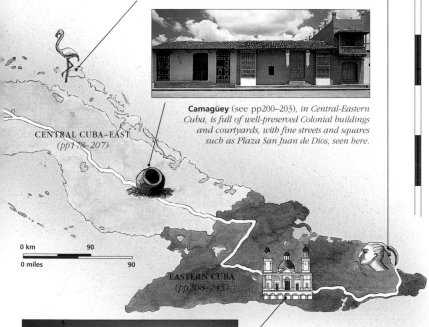

Camagüey *(see pp200–203), in Central-Eastern Cuba, is full of well-preserved Colonial buildings and courtyards, with fine streets and squares such as Plaza San Juan de Dios, seen here.*

CENTRAL CUBA-EAST
(pp178–207)

0 km 90
0 miles 90

EASTERN CUBA
(pp208–245)

Santiago de Cuba *(see pp222–31) is a fascinating town built around a bay, with its heart around the Catedral de la Asunción. Every summer Santiago plays host to the liveliest carnival in Cuba, in which the entire local population takes part.*

WESTERN CUBA

PINAR DEL RIO · ISLA DE LA JUVENTUD · CAYO LARGO DEL SUR

The western region of mainland Cuba is characterized by swathes of cultivated fields and at times extraordinarily beautiful scenery. The main attraction here is the Viñales valley, where unusual limestone outcrops (called mogotes*) loom over lush fields of tobacco. Off the coast, scattered islands with stunning white beaches offer a peaceful refuge from the bustle of Havana.*

According to the inhabitants of Santiago, Pinar del Río province is the least "revolutionary" part of Cuba. This, the island's most rural region, is populated by white farmers, who have never been known for their warlike passion, although western Cuba was the scene of several battles against the Spanish in the late 1800s, and in 1958 there was a revolutionary front here.

Pinar del Río was colonized in the 16th and 17th centuries by Europeans mainly from the Canary Islands. Historically Pinar has preferred to concentrate its efforts on producing what they claim is the best tobacco in the world. Tobacco fields are scattered among the Sierra del Rosario and Sierra de Organos ranges, which are barely 600 m (1,970 ft) above sea level – not high enough to be considered mountains yet high enough to create a breathtaking landscape. Palm trees mingle with pine trees, and delicate wild orchids thrive where the conditions are right. These low mountains provide excellent walking territory. The Sierra del Rosario is now a UNESCO world biosphere reserve, as is the Guanahacabibes peninsula in the far west. In both areas, the emphasis is placed on conservation-conscious ecotourism.

Ecotourism is less of a priority on Cayo Largo, a long-established island resort with lovely sea and sand, and numerous hotels. This island forms part of the Archipiélago de los Canarreos, in the Caribbean Sea, which is made up of 350 *cayos* or keys. All of these are uninhabited apart from Cayo Largo and Isla de la Juventud (Isle of Youth), a large island with a rich history and the best diving in Cuba.

Miles of white beaches and beautifully clear water at Playa Tortuga, Cayo Largo

◁ Bike riding in the peaceful Viñales valley; in the background is a typical *mogote*

Exploring Western Cuba

The extraordinary tranquillity and agreeable climate of Western Cuba make it a lovely area for a relaxing break. However, there is also plenty to do. Besides walking and horse riding, there is the provincial capital of Pinar del Río to explore, while tempting coral beaches are easily accessible off the north coast. More effort is required to reach remote María La Gorda, in the far west, but keen divers are attracted to this up-and-coming diving centre. Isla de la Juventud attracts divers and visitors interested in curious attractions, from painted caves to the one-time prison of Fidel Castro. The Valle de Viñales hotels make the best base for a stay in Western Cuba.

View of a street in Pinar del Río, "the city of capitals"

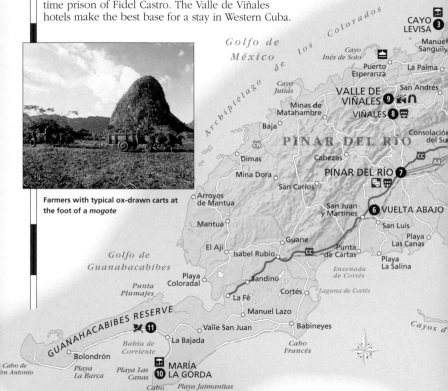

Farmers with typical ox-drawn carts at the foot of a *mogote*

Schools of tropical fish, easily spotted on the sea bed along the Los Canarreos archipelago

GETTING AROUND

The motorway *(autopista)* connects Havana and Pinar del Río (about a two-hour drive), and another slower, but more picturesque, road follows the northern coastline. From Pinar a road runs southwest to Guanahacabibes. There are one-day tours that start off from Havana and include Soroa, Pinar and Viñales, but not the beaches: information is available at tourist offices. The best way to get to Isla de la Juventud and Cayo Largo is by air from Havana (40 mins). There is also a catamaran service to the former from Batabanó; the trip takes two hours. Excursions can also be booked to the two islands; departures are from Havana or larger towns.

SIGHTS AT A GLANCE

SEE ALSO

- **Where to Stay** pp256–8
- **Where to Eat** pp279–80

KEY

━━ Motorway
━━ Major road
━━ Minor road
┈┈ Main railway
━━ Regional border

0 kilometres   20

0 miles   20

Soroa ❶

Candelaria (Pinar del Río). **Road Map**
A2. 🚇 *Candelaria*. 🏨 *Hotel Soroa,*
(48) 523 512, 523 556.

The Valley Road from Havana
to Soroa crosses a peaceful
area of cultivated fields and
rural villages. Soroa itself lies
250 m (820 ft) above sea level
in the middle of tropical
forest. It was named after two
Basque brothers, Lorenzo and
Antonio Soroa Muñagorri,
who, in around 1856, bought
various coffee plantations in
the area and soon became the
proprietors of the entire
territory. One of the estates
in the valley, Finca
Angerona, was in the 19th
century the setting for a
legendary love
story involving the
French-German
Cornelius Sausse, who
built the farm in 1813,
and a Haitian girl,
Ursule Lambert.
  Soroa, today, is a
small town and a
holiday village (Villa Soroa),
with a number of tourist
attractions. The most
photographed is the
Saltón, a spectacular waterfall

**A flower in the Soroa
orchid garden**

on the Manantiales river, a ten-
minute walk from the Villa
Soroa. But the major sight
here is the **Orquideario**, an
orchid garden which has been
declared a national monu-
ment. It has one of the largest
orchid collections in the
world, with more than 700
species, 250 of which are
endemic, in an area of 35,000
ha (86,500 acres). The park,
often visited by Hemingway,
was founded in 1943 by a
lawyer from the Canaries,
Tomás Felipe Camacho. He
had orchids sent here from all
over the world in memory of
his daughter, who had died at
the age of 20 in childbirth.
  Outside the town is the
Castillo de las Nubes, a
medieval-like
construction built in
1940 for Antonio
Arturo Sánchez
Bustamante, the land-
owner of this area.
The Castillo is
now a restaurant
with marvellous
views over the
Sierra del Rosario.

🌺 **Orquideario de Soroa**
Carretera de Soroa km 8. **Tel** (48)
522 558. 🕐 *daily.* 🈴 📷

**Bathing under the falls (saltón) of
the Manantiales river at Soroa**

Sierra del
Rosario ❷

Pinar del Río. **Road Map** A2.
🏨 *Las Terrazas, (48) 578 700.*

This area of 25,000 ha
(61,750 acres) of unspoilt
Cuba has been declared a
biosphere reserve by
UNESCO. Woods consisting
of tropical and deciduous
trees and plants cover the
Sierra del Rosario range,
which is crossed by the San

Beaches of the North Coast

An alternative route to the Pinar region from Havana
is the road that skirts the coastline at the foot of the
Guaniguanico mountain range. The drive from the
capital to Viñales, with fine panoramic views and
scenery, takes about five hours. From the northern
coast there is access to the splendid beaches on some
of the small islands in the Los Colorados Archipelago.
For the most part, the locals make their living by
fishing, but the islands have already attracted some
tourism. The sea can be rough and a general lack of
facilities makes this area more suitable for visitors
who love water sports rather than a place
for a relaxing beach holiday.

Cayo Jutías *is still unspoilt and
frequented more by Cubans than
by tourists. The island is an oasis
of peace and white sand,
populated by many species of
local and migratory birds.*

KEY

━ Motorway

─ Major road

⋯ Minor road

⛴ Ferry

Cayo Inès de Soto   Cayo Levis

Cayo Jutías

Puerto
Esperanza

Santa Lucía

Minas de
Matahambre

Around 3 km (2 miles) from Santa Lucía, which
has hotel facilities and connections, is a dam
connecting the mainland with Cayo Jutías.

For hotels and restaurants in this region see pp256–8 and pp279–80

Juan river with its small falls. The area is home to abundant, varied fauna: 90 species of bird as well as many different reptiles and amphibians. The walks here are lovely (permission is needed from the Bureau of Ecological Research), on paths lined with flowers, including wild orchids.

Most of the farmers in the Sierra live in communities founded by a government programme in 1968. The best-known is **Las Terrazas,** whose name derives from the terraces laid out for the pine trees that are now a characteristic feature of the area. The 1000 inhabitants make a living by maintaining the woods and from ecotourism, which has increased since the building of the environmentally friendly Hotel La Moka (see p257). The hotel makes a good starting point for walks in the reserve, all of which are fairly easy and take no more than two hours to cover. Also open is the old, recently restored Buena Vista coffee plantation, which has a restaurant.

For birdwatching, hike along the San Juan river as far as the Cañada del Infierno, a shady pool frequented by local birds such as the *zunzún* hummingbird, the *tocororo* and the *cartacuba* (see pp20–21).

The well-managed pine forest at Las Terrazas

Cayo Levisa ❸

Pinar del Río. **Road Map** A2.
🚢 from Palma Rubia (1 hr), departure 10am, return trip 5pm.
Excursions from Pinar del Río
ℹ Cubanacán Viajes, Calle Martí 109, esq. Colon, (48) 750 178.

This small island, with its white sand beaches, an offshore coral reef and mangroves, is the most geared up for tourists in the Los Colorados archipelago, and the only one with diving facilities. Despite this, it is still unspoilt and is home to several species of bird and the surrounding waters have an abundance of fish, especially marlin.

The artificial pool at the heart of the Las Terrazas rural community

Cayo Levisa, *the best-known island in the archipelago, has a fairly simple tourist village, 3 km (2 miles) of lovely beach, and a coral reef with splendid scuba-diving sites.*

Cayo Paraiso, whose name means paradise, was the setting for Hemingway's stories *Islands in the Stream*.

0 kilometres 15

0 miles 15

Marina Hemingway, 20 km (12 miles) from the heart of Havana, is a famous tourist spot known for hosting the annual marlin fishing tournament held in honour of the American author. Competitors come from all over the world to participate.

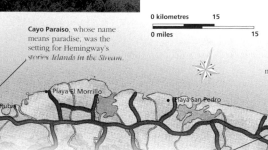

Playa El Morrillo

Palma Rubia

Playa San Pedro

Mariel

Mariel was the point of departure for the 1980 *Marielitos* boatlift (see p53).

Parque La Güira ❹

San Diego de Los Baños (Pinar del Río). **Road Map** A2. 👥 3,000. 🛈 La Güira Restaurant, (48) 812 611. ◯ daily. 📷

The former estate of the landowner Don Manuel Cortina, who was forced to leave Cuba in 1959, this was one of the first properties to be nationalized after Castro's revolution. The large park includes the ruins of a medieval-style residence and an English garden with a small Chinese temple and statues of mythological figures including sphinxes and satyrs.

About 5 km (3 miles) east of the Güira park is **San Diego de los Baños**, a peaceful village on the slopes of the Sierra de los Quemados, which has retained its original Colonial atmosphere. The village has always been a major tourist and therapeutic centre. The springs in the area produce sulphurous water that helps to cure rheumatism and skin diseases; it is available from the spa facility situated on a hill just outside town.

Don Manuel Cortina also owned a nearby cave, the **Cueva de los Portales**, discovered in the 19th century. This old hiding place was used by the natives as a refuge from the massacres that were waged by the Spanish in the early 16th

The lovely gardens in Parque La Güira

century. In more recent history, during the missile crisis, the cave became the headquarters of Che Guevara, some of whose personal belongings and mementoes are on display.

Maspotón ❺

Los Palacios (Pinar del Río). **Road Map** A3. 🛈 Ecotur, (48) 796 393.

The best-known of the many hunting reserves in Cuba, Maspotón includes three lagoons and 61 covers. Besides the endemic birds, migratory birds also come here to escape the cold in North America. Game includes ducks, snipe, pheasants and wild guinea fowl.

Hunting and fishing at Maspotón are regulated. Open season is from October to March, and hunters may not kill more than 40 birds per session. Each day includes two sessions. The hunting lodge hires out all necessary equipment, including everything needed for hunting on horseback, and will also provide hunters with expert guides. Maspotón is a 25-km (15-mile) drive from the Pinar del Río highway by dirt road.

Ecotur also offers another hunting area in Punta de

A Hoyo de Monterrey cigar band

Palma, with better options for hunters. Only 9 km (5.5 miles) away from Pinar del Río, hunters can stay at the recently renovated Rancho La Guabina.

Vuelta Abajo ❻

Pinar del Río. **Road Map** A3.

The small area between Pinar del Río, San Juan y Martínez and San Luís produces very high quality tobacco. Good growing conditions are the result of a series of factors: for example, the Sierra del Rosario protects the plants from heavy rainfall, and the sandy red soil in which the tobacco plants grow is well drained and rich in nitrogen. This is a unique environment; in fact, the former landowners who left Cuba in 1959 have tried in vain to reproduce the miracle in Nicaragua, Honduras, Santo Domingo and the US.

On the road from the provincial capital to San Juan y Martínez, the prestigious Hoyo de Monterrey plantations can be visited. Here plants are protected from the sun by cotton cloth in order to maintain the softness of the tobacco leaves. There are also the *ranchos*, windowless storehouses where the leaves are left to dry on long poles.

The entrance to the Cueva de los Portales

Cuban Tobacco

The tobacco plant *(Nicotiana tabacum)* grows from small, round, golden seeds. Cuban tobacco seeds are in demand throughout the world, because their quality is considered to be so good. The plant reaches its full height in the three or four months from November to February. Like cigar-making *(see pp32–3)*, tobacco growing is the result of age-old expertise handed down from generation to generation. Tobacco plants are quite delicate, and need skilful handling. There are two types: *Corojo*, grown in greenhouses, which has the prettiest leaves, selected for use as wrapper leaves for the cigars, and *Criollo*, which grows outdoors and provides the other leaves.

Criollo leaves *are separated into three grades:* ligero, seco *and* volado. *The first, which is the best, has the most aromatic leaves, which absorb most sun and are harvested only when completely mature.*

Floating cultivation *is a technique of experimental hydroculture in which the seeds germinate ten days earlier than those grown with traditional methods.*

Poles for transport and drying

Traditional cultivation in rows

TOBACCO HARVEST

Harvesting tobacco is a delicate and laborious operation. The leaves are tied in bunches, hung on horizontal poles and then transported to drying rooms. In the case of the *Corojo* plant, the harvest is carried out in various stages, at intervals of several days.

Drying *takes from 45 to 60 days. The leaves, hung on small poles in storehouses known as* casas del tabaco, *gradually turn from bright green to brown.*

Humidification *is a hydrating process carried out after the drying so that the leaves do not dry out and become brittle. Once sprayed, the bunches of leaves are suspended in order to eliminate excess water.*

By establishing a tobacco monopoly *in 1717, the Colonial authorities obliged farmers to sell all their tobacco to Spain. Now, although the Cuban government allows private tobacco growers to have 7-ha (17-acre) plots, the state is still the sole manufacturer and distributor of cigars.*

Pinar del Río ❼

Road Map A3. 🏠 *200,000.*
🛈 *Cubanacán, Calle Martí 109, esq.
Colón, (48) 750 178.* 🚌
from Havana.

In 1778, when the Cuban
provinces were founded, the
town of Nueva Filipina was
renamed Pinar because
of a pine grove in the vicinity,
on the banks of the Guamá
river. Nearby, General Antonio
Maceo fought a number of
battles in 1896–7 that were
crucial to the Cubans' victory
in the third war of Cuban
independence.

Today, the pines no longer
grow here, but the clean air
and Colonial atmosphere of
Pinar del Río are unchanged.
The town has long been a
centre for the cultivation and
industrial processing of
tobacco. The most striking
aspect about the historic
centre of this small, orderly
and peaceful town is the
abundance of columns:
Corinthian or Ionic, simple or
decorated. Not for
nothing is Pinar del
Río known as the
"city of capitals".

The most important
buildings lie on the
arcaded main street,
Calle Martí (or Real).
In the **Cultural
Heritage Fund** shop,
at the corner of Calle
Rosario, visitors can
buy local crafts as well as art
reproductions. In the evening,
the **Casa de la Cultura** (at No.
125) hosts shows and concerts
of traditional music such as

**A capital with bas-
relief decoration**

punto guajiro (from *guajiro*,
the Cuban word for farmer),
which is of Spanish derivation,
and is generally characterized
by improvisation.

At Nos. 172, 174 and 176 in
Calle Colón, there are three
unusual buildings
designed by Rogelio
Pérez Cubillas,
the city's leading
architect in the
1930s and 1940s.

🏛 **Palacio de Guasch**
Calle Martí, esq.
Comandante Pinares.
Museum Tel *(48) 753
087.* ⏱ *Tue–Sat, Sun
am.* ⬤ *1 Jan, 1 May, 26 Jul, 10 Oct,
25 Dec.* 📷

This somewhat extravagant
building is a mixture of
Moorish arches, Gothic spires
and Baroque elements. It was
built in 1909 for a wealthy
physician who had travelled
widely and who wanted to
reproduce in his new
residence the architectural
styles that had impressed him
the most. In 1979 the mansion
was transformed into a Museo
de Ciencias Naturales (natural
history museum) named after
Tranquilino Sandalio de
Nodas, a well-known land
surveyor in this region. The
museum illustrates the natural
and geological history of Pinar

One of the three eclectic-style buildings on Calle Colón

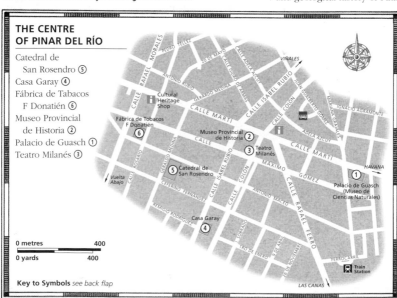

**THE CENTRE
OF PINAR DEL RÍO**

Catedral de
San Rosendro ⑤
Casa Garay ④
Fábrica de Tabacos
F Donatién ⑥
Museo Provincial
de Historia ②
Palacio de Guasch ①
Teatro Milanés ③

0 metres   400
0 yards   400

Key to Symbols *see back flap*

The unusual façade of the Palacio de Guasch, Pinar del Río

and has on display stuffed birds and animals, including the tiny Cuban *zunzún* hummingbird, and a crocodile more than 4 m (12 ft long), as well as rare plants and butterflies. In the inner courtyard are sculptures of prehistoric animals.

🏛 Museo Provincial de Historia

Calle Martí 58 e/ Colón y Isabel Rubio. *Tel* (48) 754 300. ◯ noon–4:30pm Mon, 8:30am–10pm Tue–Sat, 9am–1pm Sun. 🌑 1 Jan, 1 May, 26 Jul, 10 Oct, 25 Dec. ⬛ ⬛ ⬛

This museum illustrates the history of the province from the Pre-Columbian period to the present. On display is a major collection of 19th-century arms, Colonial furniture, works by local painters, including a huge landscape by Domingo Ramos (1955), and mementoes of the musician Enrique Jorrín, the father of the cha-cha-cha.

🎭 Teatro Milanés

Calle Martí y Colón. *Tel* (48) 753 871.

A Neo-Classical gem and the city's pride and joy, this theatre is named after the romantic poet José Jacinto Milanés. It started out as the Lope de Vega theatre, which first opened in 1845 and was then bought in 1880 by one Félix del Pino Díaz. He totally renovated it, modelling it on the Teatro Sauto in Matanzas *(see p158)*. Its name was changed in 1898.

This simple but functional structure has a rectangular plan, a linear façade and a portico with tall columns. Its opulent, three-level, U-shaped wooden auditorium has a seating capacity of about 500.

🎭 Casa Garay

Calle Isabel Rubio 189 e/ Ceferino Fernández y Frank País. *Tel* (48) 752 966. ◯ 8am–4:30pm Mon–Fri; Sat every other week. 🌑 1 Jan, 1 May, 26 Jul, 10 Oct, 25 Dec. ⬛ ⬛

Since 1892 the Casa Garay has produced Guayabita del Pinar, a famous liqueur based on an ancient recipe. It is made by distilling brandy from the sugar of the *guayaba* (guava), which is grown in this area.

Guided tours of the small factory finish up at the tasting area, where visitors can try the sweet and dry versions of this popular drink.

🎭 Fábrica de Tabacos Francisco Donatién

Calle Maceo 157 Oeste. *Tel* (48) 773 069. ◯ 9am–noon, 1–4pm Mon–Fri, 9am–noon Sat. 🌑 1 Jan, 1 May, 26 Jul, 10 Oct, 25 Dec. ⬛ ⬛ ⬛

This tiny cigar factory, housed in a former 19th-century jail, is open to the public. Visitors can watch the 70 or so workers making Trinidad cigars. These and other cigars are sold in the small shop. The factory is also a training school for *torcedores* (cigar rollers).

Viñales ❽

Pinar del Río. **Road Map** A3. 🏘 4,000. 🚌

Viñales, whose name derives from a vineyard planted here by a settler from the Canary Islands, was founded in 1607.

This small town, the economy of which has always been based on agriculture, is now the subject of government protection as an example of a perfectly preserved Colonial settlement. The main street, named after a 19th-century nationalist, Salvador Cisneros Betancourt, is lined with many Colonial houses with characteristic arcades, which make useful shelters from the hot sun and any sudden violent tropical rainstorms.

The town's most important architecture is in the main square, the **Parque Martí**, on which stand the Iglesia del Sagrado Corazón de Jesús (1888), and the former Colonia Española (diplomatic headquarters of the Spanish gentry). This is now the home of the Casa de la Cultura, which offers an interesting programme of cultural activities.

Viñales also boasts a minor architectural gem, the **Casa de Don Tomás**, built in 1887–8 for Gerardo Miel y Sainz, a rich merchant and agent for a shipping line. The building, designed by the Spanish architect Roger Reville, was restored in 1991 and turned into a good fish restaurant *(see p279)*.

The main street in Viñales, with its one-storey porticoed houses

Valle de Viñales **9**

A unique landscape awaits visitors to
the Viñales Valley. The *mogotes*, the
characteristic, gigantic karst formations
that resemble sugar loaves, are like stone
sentinels keeping watch over the corn
and tobacco fields, the red earth with
majestic royal palm trees and the
farmhouses with roofs of palm leaves.
According to legend, centuries ago some
Spanish sailors who were approaching
the coast thought the profile of the
mogotes they glimpsed in the fog looked
like a church organ. Hence the name,
Sierra de los Organos, given to the
network of hills in this area.

A storehouse for drying tobacco near a *mogote*

Mural de la Prehistoria
On the face of a mogote *the Cuban painter
Leovigildo González, a pupil of the famous
Mexican artist Diego Rivera, painted the history
of evolution (1959–62), from ammonites to
Homo sapiens. The mural, restored in 1980,
makes use of the cracks in the rock to create
special effects of light and colour.*

KEY

▲   Peak

═   Paved road

═   Path

═   River

▪▪▪   Underground river

Sierrita de San Vicente
is famous for its
hot springs.

San Vicente •

• Cueva
del Ruiseñor

*SIERRA
DE VIÑALES*

VALLE DE LA GUASASA

Mogote •
Dos Hermanas ▲   ▲ Mogote
Del Valle

Minas de Matahambre

Entrance to the
Santo Tomás Cavern

VALLE DE VIÑALES

Hotel Los Jazmines •

Pinar del R

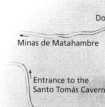

Gran Caverna de Santo Tomás
*This is the largest network of caves in Cuba
and the whole of Latin America. With its
18 km (11 miles) of galleries and up to five
levels of communicating grottoes, the Gran
Caverna is a speleologist's paradise. In the
19th century, the Cueva del Salón was used
by local farmers for festivals.*

Cueva del Indio

This cave, discovered in 1920, lies in the San Vicente Valley. The first part of the tour here is on foot through tunnels with artificial lighting. Then a small motorboat takes visitors up the underground San Vicente river for about a quarter of a mile.

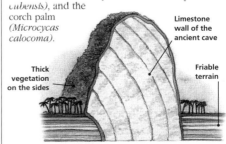

Palenque de los Cimarrones

In the depths of Cueva de San Miguel, past the bar at its mouth, is a spectacular cave that was once a refuge for runaway African slaves (cimarrones). It now houses a small museum and a pleasant restaurant.

THE STRUCTURE OF A MOGOTE

The *mogotes* are among the most ancient rocks in Cuba, and all that remains of what was once a limestone plateau. Over a period lasting millions of years, underground aquifers eroded the softer limestone, giving rise to large caverns whose ceilings later collapsed. Only the hard limestone pillars, or present-day *mogotes*, were left standing. *Mogotes* generally have only a thin covering of soil, but those in the Sierra de los Organos are covered with thick vegetation. Some endemic plant species have adapted to life on their craggy crevices; these include the mountain palm tree *(Bombacopsis cubensis)*, and the corch palm *(Microcycas calocoma)*.

Thick vegetation on the sides

Limestone wall of the ancient cave

Friable terrain

Viñales still has a Colonial feel *(see p141)*. It is a tranquil, pleasant little town, ideal for a short stay.

The jetty at María La Gorda, the departure point for boats taking people to dive sites

María La Gorda ⑩

Pinar del Río. ℹ️ *María La Gorda Diving Centre, La Bajada, (48) 778 131, 778 077.*

The best-known bathing spot on the southwestern coast owes its name to a sad legend. A few centuries ago, a plump *(gorda)* girl named María was abducted by pirates on the Venezuelan coast and then abandoned here. In order to survive, she was forced to sell herself to the buccaneers who passed by. The place still bears her name today.

The extraordinary beauty of the coral reefs – populated by sea turtles, reef sharks and other rare species of tropical fish – makes these 8 km (5 miles) of coastline with fine white sand and a warm, translucent sea a real tropical aquarium. The reefs are also easy to reach, lying just a short distance from the shore (the coral and fish can even be seen without swimming under water).

From the jetty opposite the diving area, a boat with a doctor on board takes divers twice a day to the various dive sites. Areas of particular interest include the so-called Black Coral Valley, a wall of coral over 100 m (328 ft) long, and the Salón de María, a sea cave at a depth of 18 m (60 ft), which is the habitat of rare species of fish.

A *cotorra*, a species of parrot seen in the reserve

Guanahacabibes Reserve ⑪

Pinar del Río. **Excursions** *from Pinar del Río.* ℹ️ *Cubanacán Viajes, Calle Martí 109, esq. Colón, Pinar del Río, (48) 750 178.* 🖥️

The peninsula of Guanahacabibes, named after a Pre-Columbian ethnic group, is a strip of land 100km (62 miles) long and 6–34 km (4–21 miles) wide. In 1985 it was declared a world biosphere reserve by UNESCO, to protect the flora and fauna. Access to the inner zone, in the vicinity of La Bajada, is therefore limited. Permission to visit is granted by the Pinar del Río forest rangers at the tourist offices in local hotels, and visits to the park are made in jeeps with a local guide.

The mixed forest of deciduous and evergreen trees contains about 600 species of plants and many animals, including deer, boar, reptiles and *jutías*, rodents similar to opossums that live in trees. Among the bird species are woodpeckers, parrots, hummingbirds, *cartacuba* and *tocororo (see p18)*.

Cabo San Antonio, the western tip of Cuba, is identifiable by the Roncalli lighthouse, built in 1849 by the Spanish governor, after whom it was named.

Cabo Corrientes at the southern end of the Guanahacabibes reserve

◁ **The Valle de Viñales with *bohíos*, farmers' houses characteristic of rural Cuba**

Diving in the Caribbean Sea

The Caribbean Sea beds off the island of Cuba offer some of the most exciting coral reef scenery imaginable. The coral formations lie at a maximum depth of 150 m (495 ft), at an average temperature of about 23° C (73 °F), and never less than 18° C (64 °F). The most fascinating areas for

A scuba diver surrounded by a school of grunts

divers are situated at María la Gorda, the Archipelago de los Canarreos, Playa Santa Lucía and Jardines de la Reina. Qualified scuba-diving centres *(buceo)* take visitors on trips out to the reefs. In some areas it is possible to see tropical fish and coral simply by snorkelling *(see p293).*

Sea plume is a type of gorgonia that looks much like a feather.

"Soft coral" results from an evolutionary process during which the hard skeleton turns into a flexible structrure.

The grouper, *with its unmistakable colouring, is one of the most common fish in the Caribbean, together with the queen triggerfish and the* Pomacanthus paru *angelfish. Other widespread species are the tarpon, with its silvery colouring, and the barracuda, with its powerful teeth. Sharks are less common.*

Sponge

The blue surgeon fish is born with bright yellow colouring that later turns blue.

Coral

THE SEA FLOOR

The coral reef is a rich and complex ecosystem. The Caribbean sea beds are home to numerous varieties of coral and a great many sea sponges and gorgonias, as well as tropical fish, sea turtles and various crustaceans.

Brain coral *is one of many types of coral common to the Cuban seas, along with black coral, iron wire coral with its rod-like structure, and elkhorn coral with its flat branches.*

Tubular sponges *vary in size, the largest ones being 2 m (6 ft) high. If they are squeezed or stepped on they emit a purple dye that will stain your skin for several days. There are also barrel- and vase-shaped sponges.*

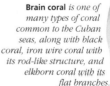

Gorgonian sea fans (Gorgonia ventalina) *are quite widespread on Caribbean sea beds. It is possible to see splendid examples of huge proportions.*

Isla de la Juventud

Billboard welcoming visitors to Nueva Gerona

The naturalist Alexander von Humboldt *(see p185)* described this island as an abandoned place, Robert Louis Stevenson called it *Treasure Island*, the dictator Batista wanted to turn it into a paradise for rich Americans, and Fidel Castro repopulated it with young people, and changed its name to the Isla de la Juventud (youth). With a surface area of 2,200 sq km (850 sq miles) and 86,000 inhabitants, this is the largest island in the Archipiélago de los Canarreos. Comparatively few tourists venture to the island, but there are a few interesting sights and the diving is excellent.

Ensenada de los barcos

La Demajagua

Atanagildo Cajig

Mina de Oro

0 km 5
0 miles 5

Hotel Colony

Ensenada de la Siguanea

Cocodrilo

Nuestra Señora de los Dolores, in Nueva Gerona

Nueva Gerona

The capital of the island is a small and peaceful town. Surrounded by hills that yield multicoloured marble, Nueva Gerona was founded in 1828 on the banks of the Las Casas river by Spanish settlers who, together with their slaves, had left countries on the American continent that had won their independence.

The town is built on a characteristic grid plan (intersecting and parallel streets, with a main avenue and a central square) and the modern outskirts are in continuous expansion.

A good starting point for a visit to Nueva Gerona is **Calle 39**, the graceful main street flanked by coloured arcades. Here can be found the local cinema, theatre, pharmacy (which is always open), post office, hospital, bank, Casa de la Cultura, tourist office and bars and restaurants.

This street ends at the Parque Central, Nueva Gerona's main square, where the **Iglesia de Nuestra Señora de los Dolores** stands. First built in Neo-Classical style in 1853, this church was totally destroyed by a cyclone in 1926 and rebuilt three years later in Colonial style.

South of the Parque Central, the former City Hall building is now the home of the **Museo Municipal**, or town museum. This has on display many objects and documents concerning pirates and buccaneers – the main protagonists in the island's history – as well as the inevitable photographs and mementoes of the revolution. There is another museum in town that is dedicated solely to the struggle against Fulgencio Batista's dictatorship: the **Casa Natal Jesús Montané**.

Lastly, another must for visitors is the **Museo de Ciencias Naturales**, the natural history museum. The geological and natural history of the island is illustrated and there is also a fine Planetarium, the only one in the world in which the North Star can be seen together with the Southern Cross.

The harbour at Nueva Gerona, where fishermen moor their boats

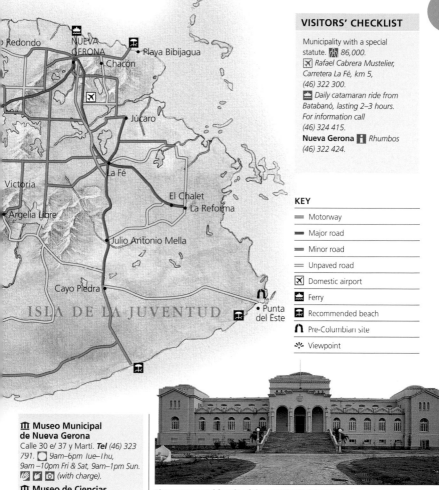

VISITORS' CHECKLIST

Municipality with a special statute. 🏘 86,000.
✈ *Rafael Cabrera Mustelier, Carretera La Fé, km 5, (46) 322 300.*
⛴ *Daily catamaran ride from Batabanó, lasting 2–3 hours. For information call (46) 324 415.*
Nueva Gerona 🛈 *Rhumbos (46) 322 424.*

KEY

━━ Motorway

━━ Major road

━━ Minor road

═══ Unpaved road

✕ Domestic airport

⛴ Ferry

🏖 Recommended beach

∩ Pre-Columbian site

☀ Viewpoint

The monumental façade of the Presidio Modelo prison

🏛 Museo Municipal de Nueva Gerona

Calle 30 e/ 37 y Martí. **Tel** (46) 323 791. ⏱ 9am–6pm Tue–Thu, 9am–10pm Fri & Sat, 9am–1pm Sun. (with charge).

🏛 Museo de Ciencias Naturales

Calle 41, esq.54. **Tel** (46) 323 143. ⏱ 9am–5pm Tue–Sat, 9am–1pm Sun. ⏱ 1 Jan, 1 May, 26 Jul, 10 Oct, 25 Dec. (with charge).

Strolling along the arcades on Nueva Gerona's Calle 39

🏯 Presidio Modelo

4 km southeast of Nueva Gerona, Reparto Delio Chacón. **Tel** (46) 325 112. ⏱ 8am–4pm Tue–Sat, 8am–noon Sun. (with charge).
On the road that connects the capital with Playa Bibijagua, a popular beach of black sand frequented by the inhabitants of Nueva Gerona, is Cuba's most famous penitentiary. Originally built by Machado, it was modelled on the famous one in Joliet, Illinois (US) and converted into a museum in 1967. The prison consists of tiny cells in the interior of four enormous multi-storeyed round cement blocks. In the middle of each stood a sentry-box from which guards could keep a close watch on all the prisoners. Guards and prisoners never came into contact with one another. Guards circulated in underground galleries, keeping constant watch over the prisoners above.

It was in the Presidio that the organizers of the attack on the Moncada army barracks in Santiago, led by Fidel Castro, were imprisoned in October 1953. They were liberated two years later, in May 1955.

At the entrance to the first pavilion is cell 3859, where Castro, despite his isolation, managed to reorganize the revolutionary movement, starting with the defence plea he made in court, *History Will Absolve Me (see p47).*

Exploring Isla de la Juventud

Unlike other islands in the Archipelago de los
Canarreos, there are no grand luxury hotels on the Isla
de la Juventud. As a result it seems to have a more
genuine Cuban atmosphere, and the tourist industry
works alongside other island activities without pressure.
The island is not new to habitation, unlike other *cayos*
which have only recently seen housing development,
and retains vestiges of five centuries of Cuban history.
The town of Nueva Gerona and its surroundings make a
good starting point for a visit, followed by the southern
coast. The main hotels are in the southwestern part of
the island, while the eastern tip has some fascinating
ancient cave paintings by Siboney Indians.

Coral formations on the island's
sea floor

🏛 Casa Museo Finca El Abra

Carretera Siguanea km 1.5
(5 km southwest of Nueva Gerona).
Tel (05) 219 3054. ⬚ 9am–5pm
Tue–Sat, 9am–1pm Sun. ⬤ Mon.
🖼 🔲 📷 (with charge).

On the edge of the Sierra de
las Casas is an elegant villa
where, in 1870, the 17-year-
old José Martí was held for
nine weeks before being
deported to Spain for his
separatist views. Part of the
building is now a museum
with a display of photographs
and documents relating to the
national hero's presence on
the island. The rest of the
villa is occupied by the
descendants of the original
owner, a rich Catalan.

Nearby is the vast Parque
Natural Julio Antonio Mella,
which has a botanical garden,
a zoo, an amusement park, an
artificial lake, and a viewpoint
overlooking the entire island.
To the south the Ciénaga de
Lanier is visible, a marshy
area in the middle of which is
the village of Cayo Piedra.

Hotel Colony

Tel (46) 398 181. 🚌 to the Centro
de Buceo, daily at 9am, return trip
at 4:30–5pm.

This low-rise hotel *(see p257)*
– a landmark for all scuba
divers on the island – blends
in well with the natural environment. The nearby sea is
green and translucent, with a
sandy floor that is often
covered with swathes of the
submerged marine aquatic
plant *Thalassia
testudinum.*

The hotel overlooks
Playa Roja, the large,
palm-shaded beach
where an important
diving centre, the
**Centro Inter-
nacional de Buceo**, is
also located.

In the mornings a van takes
guests from the Hotel Colony
to the diving centre, where all
kinds of diving equipment can
be rented (although it is
advisable to take a 3 mm
wetsuit and an oxygen tank
or bottle with you), and which

A hotel sign

provides boats to take visitors
to the dive sites. At noon,
lunch is served at the Ranchón,
a restaurant on a platform on
piles connected via a pontoon
to a beach at Cabo Francés.

The 56 dive sites, between
Cabo Francés and Punta
Pardenales, lie at the end of a
shelf which gently slopes
down from the coast
to a depth of 20–25 m
(65–82 ft), and then
abruptly drops for
hundreds of metres.
This vertical wall is a
favourite with passing
fish, which literally rub
shoulders with divers.

While dives on the
platform can be made
by beginners, those
along the shelf are more
difficult and suited to divers
with more experience.

Among the most fascinating
dives are: the one at La Pared
de Coral Negro, which has an
abundance of black coral as
well as sponges as much as
35 m (115 ft) in diameter; El
Reino del Sahara, one of the
most beautiful shallow dives;
El Mirador, a wall dive among
sponges and large madre-
pores; and El Arco de los
Sábalos, which is the domain
of tarpons. At Cayo Los Indios
shipwrecks can be seen on
the sea bed at a depth of
10–12 m (33–40 ft).

There are also two
wonderful boat trips that
can be made from the Hotel
Colony. One goes to the
Península Francés, which is
better known as **Costa de
los Piratas**. This is a paradise
for divers because of its
wonderfully colourful and

The Hotel Colony, surrounded by tropical vegetation

View of Punta del Este beach with its white sand and crystal-clear sea

varied underwater flora and fauna. A variety of other activities can also be enjoyed here, including water skiing, surfing, sailing, deep sea fishing and even horse riding.

The second excursion goes to **Cocodrilo**, formerly called Jacksonville. This traditional fishing village was founded in the early 20th century by a small community of emigrants from the British colony of the Cayman Islands. In fact, there are still a few inhabitants who speak English as their first language.

The settlers at Cocodrilo introduced a typical Jamaican dance known as the Round Dance, which blended with a variation of traditional Cuban *son* music (the *Son Montuno),* has resulted in the creation of a new and interesting dance which is highly popular among the locals, who call it the Sucu-Sucu.

Pre-Columbian drawings which may represent a calendar, in the Cuevas del Este

⋒ Cuevas de Punta del Este
59 km (37 miles) southeast of Nueva Gerona. ⬛ *Punta del Este, (46) 322 082; Ecotur, (46) 327 101.*

Punta del Este, on the south-eastern tip of the island, has a stunning white sand beach. It is however, most famous for its seven caves, which were discovered in 1910 by a French castaway who took refuge here. On the walls of the caves are 235 drawings made by Siboney Indians in an age long before the arrival of Christopher Columbus.

The drawings in the largest cave – a series of red and black concentric circles crossed by arrows pointing eastward – probably represent a solar calendar. The complexity of these drawings led the Cuban ethnologist Fernando Ortíz, who studied them in 1925, to call them "the Sistine Chapel of the Caribbean". Protect yourself against mosquitoes – the caves are full of them.

HISTORY OF THE ISLAND

The Taíno and Siboney peoples knew of the Isla de la Juventud *(see p38)* long before Columbus "discovered" it in 1494 on his second journey. The Spanish crown licensed the island to cattle breeders, but in practice handed it over to pirates. Because of the shallow waters, heavy Spanish galleons were unable to approach the island, while the buccaneers' light vessels could land there. This meant that such mythical figures as Francis Drake, Henry Morgan, Oliver Esquemeling and Jacques de Sores were able to exploit it as a hiding place for booty captured from Spanish ships.

The corsair Sir Francis Drake

After Nueva Gerona was founded (1828), the island was used as a place of detention for Cuban nationalists, including José Martí. Its use as a prison island continued for 50 years in the 20th century; construction of the Presidio Modelo began in 1926. In 1953 Batista turned the island into a free zone where money could be laundered. The dictator also wanted to turn it into a holiday paradise for rich Americans, but his plans failed. On New Year's night in 1958, as Castro's *barbudos* were entering Havana, a group of soldiers in the rebels' army took over the island during the opening ceremony of the Hotel Colony, and arrested the mafiosi in the hotel.

In 1966, after a devastating cyclone, the Cuban government decided to plant new citrus groves on the island which would be worked by students from Cuba and around the world. The idea was such a success that in ten years the island's population "grew from 10,000 to 80,000.

An old map of Isla de la Juventud from the Museo Municipal of Nueva Gerona

Cayo Largo del Sur ⑬

The Cayo Largo logo

This island is a wonderful holiday destination for those who love sun, sea and sand. It is 25 km (15 miles) long and has a surface area of 37.5 sq km (15 sq miles). There are no extremes of climate here. It rains very little, the temperature is 24° C (75° F) in winter and less than 30° C (86° F) in summer, the coast is flat, the sand as white and fine as talcum powder, and the sea is clear and calm. It is safe for scuba diving, and the island offers other sporting activities such as horse riding, sailing, tennis and surfing. And if you prefer not to swim, you can walk for miles in the shallow water. There are no villages except those built for tourists, with recently built, comfortable hotels, as well as restaurants, bars, discos and swimming pools.

View of Playa Tortuga

Marina Cayo Largo
is the point of departure for boat trips to several scuba diving sites. In shallow water there are coral gardens populated by multicoloured fish, and a black coral reef 30 km (19 miles) long. Fishing equipment can be hired in the water sports centre.

★ Playa Sirena
This 2.3-km (1.5-mile) beach is very tranquil: sheltered from the wind, the sea is calm all year round.

Combinado is a marine biology centre which is open to the public.

Isla del Sol

Las Piedras

Playa Paraíso is very secluded, making nude sunbathing possible.

Playa Lindamar is a shell-shaped beach, 5 km (3 miles) long, sheltered by white rocks, with many hotels, holiday villages and bathing facilities.

STAR SIGHTS
★ Playa Sirena
★ Playa Los Cocos
★ Playa Tortuga

Holiday Villages
Exclusive holiday resorts, with family bungalows and cottages, are concentrated on the southwestern coast.

VISITORS' CHECKLIST

Archipiélago de los Canarreos
(Isla de la Juventud).
Road Map B3. 🏘 *500.*
✈ *Vilo Acuña, (45) 248 141.*
🛈 *Cubatur, Hotel Isla del Sur
(45) 248 246 or (45) 248 258;
Havanatur (45) 248 215.*
Excursions *from Marina Cayo
Largo: departure in the morning,
return at sunset.*

★ Playa Tortuga

*This beach in the eastern part of the island is popular with
nature lovers: it is a nesting area for marine turtles and
has become a natural reserve for Chaelonidae (species of
marine turtle), which are also raised at Combinado.*

KEY

▬	Major road
▬	Minor road
═	Unpaved road
✈	International airport
🏖	Beach
⛴	Ferry

Playa
Los Pinos

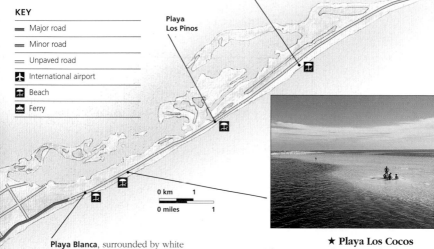

0 km   1

0 miles   1

Playa Blanca, surrounded by white
rocks, is the longest beach on the
island (7.5 km/5 miles). It also offers
some of the best tourist facilities.

★ Playa Los Cocos
*The coconut palms along the shore
provide some shade here and the shallow
water makes it ideal for children. The
nearby coral reefs and shipwrecks
attract scuba divers.*

An iguana in Cayo Iguana

VISITING THE NEARBY ISLANDS

The small *cayos* nearby offer many natural attractions. Cayo
Rico, an island surrounded by brilliant green water and
fringed with beaches of sand as fine as sugar, is only a few
minutes away by boat. The sea beds, which are especially
rich in lobsters and molluscs, are fascinating and can be
admired from glass-bottomed boats. While various species of
fish abound at Cayo Rosario, which is a scuba diver's dream,
the only inhabitants of Cayo Iguana, just off the western tip
of Cayo Largo, are the harmless iguanas, which can be as
much as 1 m (3 ft) long. Cayo Pájaro is the craggy habitat of
ocean birds, while Cayo Cantiles, rich in flowers, birds and
fish, is also home to several species of monkey.

CENTRAL CUBA – WEST

MATANZAS · CIENFUEGOS · VILLA CLARA

*T*he central-western provinces are the rural heart of Cuba, with cultivated fields and a gentle landscape, even where the plain gives way to the Sierra del Escambray. Apart from Varadero, the famous holiday resort, the main attractions in this region are two lively towns – Santa Clara and Cienfuegos – and the natural scenery of the Zapata peninsula and the Escambray mountains.

In 1509, while circling Cuba, the Spanish navigator Sebastián Ocampo caught sight of a bay on the northern, Atlantic coast inhabited by Siboney Indians. Their land was requisitioned almost immediately and assigned to settlers from the Canary Islands. The Indians opposed this injustice so fiercely that the city of Matanzas, which was built in that bay in the 1600s, probably owes its name to the memory of a massacre *(matanza)* of Spaniards by the natives.

Another bay, on the south coast, was sighted by Columbus in 1494. The Jagua Indians living there were later wiped out, but it wasn't until 1819 that Cienfuegos was founded by Catholic settlers from the former French colonies of Haiti and Louisiana, who were granted this territory to counterbalance the massive presence of African slaves. From the mid-1500s to the mid-1700s, both coasts in this region had to face the serious threat of pirate raids, against which the many redoubts, citadels and castles that are still visible along the coastline had very little effect. As a result, in 1689, 20 families from the village of Remedios, not far from the sea, decided to move to the interior, to be at a safe distance from the buccaneers' ships and cannons. In this way the city of Santa Clara was founded.

Santa Clara, capital of Villa Clara province, holds a special place in Cuban hearts since it was the setting for heroic acts by Che Guevara and his *barbudos*. On 28 December 1958, they captured the area after what was to be the last battle of the revolution *(see p48)* before Batista fled.

A typical wooden house along the Punta Gorda peninsula, Cienfuegos

◁ Varadero, extremely popular with international holidaymakers

Exploring Central Cuba – West

This part of Cuba boasts some exceptional attractions: the beaches of Varadero – perhaps the best and certainly the most well-equipped in Cuba – and the swamp *(ciénaga)* of Zapata, a nature reserve which is particularly good for birdwatching. Cienfuegos, Matanzas and Santa Clara are all appealing towns, this last a must for those interested in Che Guevara's life. A good route for a tour could begin with Matanzas and Varadero, before turning south to Cienfuegos, perhaps via the Península de Zapata. From there it is an easy ride to Santa Clara and beyond to Remedios.

Aerial view of Cayo Libertad, off the coast of Varadero

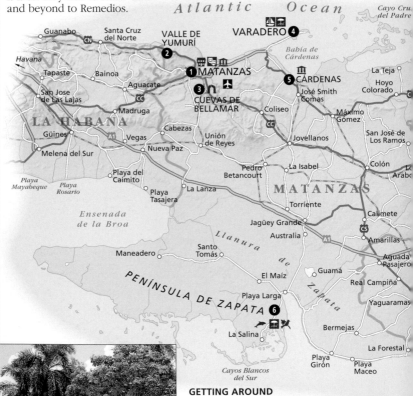

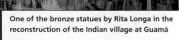

One of the bronze statues by Rita Longa in the reconstruction of the Indian village at Guamá

GETTING AROUND

The provinces of Central Cuba – West are traversed by the Carretera Central; although the motorway (Autopista Nacional) which links Havana and Santa Clara is a much faster (though less scenic) road. The railway line connecting Havana to Santiago passes through Matanzas and Santa Clara, while another links Havana and Trinidad via Cienfuegos. There are also daily return flights from Havana to Cienfuegos, Varadero and Santa Clara. For visitors with limited time, it may be best to go on an organized tour. These typically cover a province or a few cities, and include visits to parks.

For additional map symbols *see back flap*

SIGHTS AT A GLANCE

The arcades of the Prado with Corinthian columns in Cienfuegos

Iglesia de San Juan Bautista, the cathedral of Remedios

0 kilometres 30
0 miles 30

KEY

═══ Motorway
▬▬▬ Major road
═══ Minor road
▬▬▬ Regional border
╼╼╼ Main railway
△ Summit

Signpost at the entrance to the province of Villa Clara

Matanzas ❶

Stained-glass window, Triolet pharmacy

Situated on the shores of a large bay, Matanzas is the capital of the province of the same name. It is a major industrial town, with the fourth most important port in the world for sugar exports. Because of the many bridges over the Yumurí and San Juan rivers, linking the historic centre to the various quarters of Matanzas and its two suburban districts (Versalles and Pueblo Nuevo), the city has been called the "Creole Venice", a match for the no less ambitious "Athens of Cuba". These two names date back to the 19th century, when the artistic and cultural life of the city, the hub of a flourishing agricultural region, outshone that of Havana.

Teatro Sauto in Matanzas with its beautiful wood-panelling

The Centre of Matanzas

The streets in Matanzas are officially indicated by a number, but in practice their Colonial names are still commonly used.

The historic centre can be seen in a few hours. A good place to start is **Plaza de la Vigía**, connected to the outskirts by the Concordia and Calixto García bridges. In the square is the statue of an unknown soldier of the wars of independence, and around it stand several of the city's key sights: the Neo-Classical fire station (1898), the Palace of Justice (1826), the Museo Provincial, the Sauto Theatre and Ediciones Vigía.

🏛 Museo Provincial

Calle Milanés, e/ Magdalena y Ayllon. **Tel** *(45) 243 195.* ⏰ *9:30am–5pm Tue–Sat, 8:30am–noon Sun.* ◉ *Mon.* 📷 🎦 ◉
This museum occupies the Palacio del Junco, a bright blue porticoed building constructed in 1838. The

collection includes documents and objects concerning the history of the province from the Pre-Columbian period to 1959. The section devoted to the Colonial period, with documents on slavery and sugar cane farm tools, is of particular interest. Copies of *Aurora*, the most interesting Cuban periodical of the 19th century, are also on display.

🎭 Teatro Sauto

Calle Magdalena y Milanés. **Tel** *(45) 242 721.* ⏰ *Tue–Sun.* ◉ *20 Dec–5 Jan & 15 Aug–1 Sep.* 📷 🎦 ◉
The pride and joy of the city, this theatre was designed by the Italian architect Daniele Dell'Aglio, who was also responsible for the church of San Pedro in the Versalles district. On 6 April 1863 the auditorium was opened to the public as the Esteban Theatre, in honour of the provincial governor who had financed the construction. It was later renamed the Sauto Theatre because of the Matanzeros' affection for the local pharmacist, Ambrosio de la Concepción Sauto, a passionate theatre-goer. He was famous for having cured Queen Isabella II of Spain of a skin disease, using a lotion he had himself prepared.

A solidly built Neo-Classical structure with several Greek-inspired statues made of Carrara marble, the theatre has various frescoes of Renaissance inspiration, executed by the architect Dell'Aglio himself. The U-shaped interior is almost entirely covered with wood-panelling.

Because of its exceptional acoustics, the versatile theatre has been the chosen venue for all kinds of shows and great 19th- and 20th-century Cuban artists have appeared here. World-famous performers have included actress Sarah Bernhardt (in *Camille* in 1887), ballet dancer Anna Pavlova and the guitarist Andrés Segovia.

THE DANZON

In the 19th century two composers, José White and Miguel Failde, were born in Matanzas, which was at that time a major cultural centre. In 1879 the latter composed *Las Alturas de Simpson*, which introduced a new musical genre to Cuba, the Danzón. This Caribbean and Creole adaptation of European country dancing became the most popular dance on the island for about fifty years. It is still danced

Period print of people dancing the Danzón

in Matanzas, in the Casa del Danzón, the house where Failde was born, which is now a music museum.

Bookbinding at the Ediciones Vigía publishing house

◻ Ediciones Vigía

Calle Magdalena 1, Plaza de la Vigía.
Tel (45) 244 845, (45) 260 917. ◻
8:30am–4pm Mon–Fri. ● 1 Jan, 1
May, 26 Jul, 10 Oct, 25 Dec. ◻
This publishing house's
products are entirely hand-
crafted – duplicated, painted
and bound – on special
untreated or recycled paper.
Visitors can watch the various
stages of production and buy
books (on poetry, theatre and
history) by Cuban and foreign
authors, as well as periodicals.

Parque Libertad

Calle Milanés, an important
commercial street, leads to
the city's other large square,
Parque Libertad (formerly
the parade ground), where
military parades were held in
the 1800s. The square was
built on the site of the Indian
village of Yacayo. In the middle of the plaza is an impressive statue of José Martí, surrounded by some attractive
buildings: the Liceo Artístico y
Literario (1860); the Casino
Español, built in the early
1900s; the Palacio del
Gobierno; the **Catedral de
San Carlos**, dating from the
17th century but mostly rebuilt
in the 19th century; and, next
to Hotel El Louvre, the Museo
Farmacéutico de Matanzas.

�🏛 Museo Farmacéutico de Matanzas

Calle Milanés 49–51, e/ Santa Teresa
y Ayuntamiento. **Tel** (45) 243 179.
◻ 10am–5pm Mon–Sat, 10am–2pm
Sun. 🎦 🎦 📷 (with charge)
This fine example of a 19th-
century pharmacy, overlooking
Parque Libertad, was founded
on 1 January 1882 by Ernesto
Triolet and Juan Fermín de
Figueroa and turned into a
museum in 1964.

On the wooden shelves
stand the original French
porcelain vases decorated by
hand, others imported from
the US, and an incredible
quantity of small bottles with
herbs, syrups and elixirs. The
museum also has a collection
of three million old labels,
mortars and stills, and

advertising posters boasting
about the miraculous curative
powers of Dr Triolet's
remedies. The façade of the
pharmacy faces the square.

The shop also serves as a
bureau of scientific information, with more than a million
original formulae and rare
books on botany, medicine,
chemistry and pharmaceuticals,
in several foreign languages.

The wooden shelves at the Museo Farmacéutico de Matanzas

MATANZAS TOWN CENTRE

Catedral de
San Carlos ⑤
Ediciones Vigía ④
Museo Farmacéutico
de Matanzas ⑥
Museo Provincial ②
Parque Libertad ⑦
Plaza de la Vigía ①
Puente Concordia ⑧
Teatro Sauto ③

0 metres   300
0 yards   300

Key to Symbols see back flap

The Bacunayagua bridge, 110 m (360 ft) high, spanning the Yumurí river

Valle de Yumurí ❷

Matanzas. **Road Map** B2.

The Bacunayagua bridge, 7 km (4 miles) west of Matanzas, is a fine work of Cuban engineering. At 110 m (360 ft), it is the highest bridge in Cuba. Built over the Yumurí river in the early 1960s, it offers lovely views of the peaceful, wooded valley below, which can be reached via a road running parallel to the river.

This attractive area of undulating land dotted with royal palm trees is well known for its many centres and clinics specializing in treatments for stress, asthma and high blood pressure. From the Monserrat hill,

where the Nuestra Señora de Monserrat Sanctuary is located, there is a fabulous view of the bay of Matanzas.

Legends vary concerning the origins of the word "Yumurí". The most fantastic associates it with the lamentation of the Indians massacred by the

A huge limestone formation in the Cuevas de Bellamar

Spanish. Another version came in a letter written by the Swedish writer Fredrika Bremer, who visited Cuba in the late 19th century. According to her, in order to escape from slavery, Siboney Indians used to commit suicide by throwing themselves into the river while screaming "*Yo morí*" (I died).

Cuevas de Bellamar ❸

Carretera de las Cuevas de Bellamar, Matanzas. **Road Map** B2.
◯ *daily.*
🖼 🎥 📷 🛅 💺 🍴

Discovered by chance in 1861 by a slave who was surveying the terrain in search of water, the fascinating Bellamar caves lie just 5 km (3 miles) southeast of Matanzas.

Only the first 3 km (2 miles) of these extensive caves have been explored to date, and expert speleologists say there are still many surprises in store. Access to the public, with a specialist guide, is limited to the first 1,500 m (5,000 ft) of the caves. This stretch includes caves and galleries covered with crystal formations in intriguing shapes. The temperature is a constant 26° C (79° F), thanks to the continuous seepage of the cave walls. This impressive tour (available

THE HERSHEY TRAIN

The small Hershey electric train

The first stretch of the Hershey rail line, inaugurated in 1916, connected the Hershey sugar factory and the village of Canasí, both near the coast west of Matanzas. The electrical system was one of the first in Cuba. In 1924 there were 38 pairs of trains, though only four covered the full distance between Havana and Matanzas. Today, the Hershey train links Casablanca *(see p111)* and Matanzas *(pp158–9)* via beautiful scenery, covering 89 km (55 miles) in 3 hours 20 minutes, with frequent stops.

daily) goes 26 m (85 ft) below sea level, and visitors can see marine fossils dating from 26 million years ago. Trained speleologists are allowed to enter a cave that is 50 m (164 ft) below sea level.

At Varadero guided tours of the Bellamar caves can be booked at the larger hotels.

Varadero ❹

See pp162–3.

Cárdenas ❺

Matanzas. **Road Map** B–C 2.
🏛 100,000.

On arriving in Cárdenas, 50 km (31 miles) east of Matanzas and 18 km (11 miles) south of Varadero, visitors may feel they are entering another age. This is mostly due to the presence of gigs and one-horse carriages which, having regained popularity during the Periodo Especial *(see p53)*, circulate in their dozens through the streets.

The town, considered one of the most symmetrical on the island, was founded in 1828 as San Juan de Dios de Cárdenas. In the 19th century the town thrived thanks to the flourishing sugar industry. Today, however, except for a rum factory near the port, Cárdenas offers only two

The linear façade of the historic Dominica building at Cárdenas

possible areas of employment: work on a farm or a job of some kind in Varadero's important tourist industry.

A closer look at the squares and monuments allows visitors to appreciate the little hidden gems in this town. Parque Colón, one of the two main squares in Cárdenas, is dominated by the first statue of Christopher Columbus erected in Cuba, inaugurated in 1862 by Gertrudis Gómez de Avellaneda, the 19th-century Hispanic-Cuban author *(see p28)*.

Next to the Iglesia de la Inmaculada Concepción (1846) is a very important monument: the **Dominica** building. In 1850, when it was the headquarters of the Spanish government in Cuba, Cuban nationalist troops

led by Narciso López hoisted the Cuban flag here for the first time.

In the second major square, Parque Echevarría, is a fine Neo-Classical building, erected in 1862, which was once the city's district prison. It was turned into the **Museo Municipal Oscar María de Rojas** in 1900, making it the oldest town museum in Cuba. It houses a collection of coins, arms, shells, minerals, butterflies and stuffed animals.

Cárdenas is also famous for being the birthplace of José Antonio Echevarría (1932–57), the revolutionary who was president of the University Students' Federation in Havana. He waged an anti-Batista campaign and was assassinated by the police. The house he was born in is now a museum with an interesting historical survey of revolutionary Cuba; it also has on display items that once belonged to Echevarría.

🏛 **Museo Municipal Oscar María de Rojas**
Calzada 4, e/ José Antonio Echevarría y José Martí.
Tel (45) 522 417. ◯ 9am–6pm Tue–Sat, 9am–1pm Sun.
🔲 🔲 🔲 (with charge).

🏛 **Museo Casa Natal de José Antonio Echevarría**
Plaza José A Echevarría.
Tel (45) 524 145. ◯ 9am–6pm Tue–Sat, 9am–1pm Sun. ● 1 Jan, 1 May, 26 Jul, 25 Dec. 🔲 🔲 🔲

Cárdenas, the city of horse-drawn carriages

Varadero ④

Monument to the Indians

Cuba's top resort, which occupies the 19-km (12-mile) long Península de Hicacos, is connected to the mainland by a drawbridge, a sign of Varadero's exclusivity. When, in the late 19th century, some families from Cárdenas bought part of the land on the peninsula and built themselves summer residences on the north coast, Varadero became a fashionable beach for the wealthy. After Castro took power in 1959, the area was opened up to all kinds of people, and is now especially popular with Canadians and Europeans, drawn to the white, sandy beaches, clear blue water and good facilities.

The attractive home of Varadero's municipal museum

Exploring Varadero

The peninsula – which can be toured by hiring a bicycle, scooter or one-horse carriage – is a succession of hotels, restaurants, holiday villages, bars, discos, shops, cinemas, camping sites and sports centres, all set among lush greenery that includes bougainvillea, royal poinciana, coconut palms and seagrapes.

The main road along the northern side of the peninsula is Avenida Primera (1ra), the eastern part of which is named Avenida Las Américas. It is here that the main luxury hotels, the major yacht clubs and a golf course are located. The Autopista Sur (motorway) runs along the southern coast.

The Historic Centre

The old centre of Varadero, which has no significant historical monuments, lies around the Iglesia de Santa Elvira and the **Parque Central**, in Avenida 1ra between Calle 44 and 46. The oldest hotel of note is Hotel Internacional (at the western end of Avenida Las Américas), which was built in the 1950s, complete with a casino and extravagant swimming pool.

🌿 Parque Retiro Josone

Avenida Primera y Calle 56.
Tel (45) 667 228.
☐ *daily.*
This is a beautiful park, with elegant trees, tropical flowers and plants, three restaurants and a small lake where birds gather and tourists row boats. It was established in 1942 by José Uturrió, the owner of the Arrechabala *ronera*, the rum factory just outside Cárdenas. He named it Josone, a combination of the first syllable of his Christian name and that of his wife, Onelia.

The park is a hit with children, who can enjoy a miniature train and camel rides, among other attractions.

🏛 Museo Municipal

Calle 57 y Playa. *Tel (45) 613 189.*
☐ *10am–7pm Tue–Sun.* 🈲 🈲
📷 *(with charge).*
The Municipal Museum recounts the history of Varadero both as an urban and tourist centre and also has a collection of Indian tools on display. It is interesting primarily because of the building which it occupies.

The white and blue wooden chalet with French roof tiles is characteristic of the architectural style imported from the US and in fashion in Varadero and the Caribbean area in the early 1900s.

The architect Leopoldo Abreu, the original owner of this villa, landscaped splendid gardens which visitors to the museum can still enjoy. One side of the museum faces the sea, and the balcony on the first floor offers a fine view over the splendid beach and the coastline.

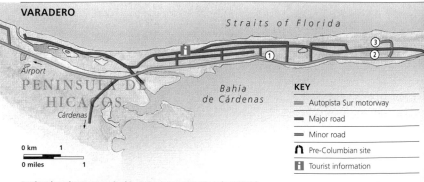

VARADERO

Straits of Florida

Airport

PENINSULA DE HICACOS

Cárdenas

Bahía de Cárdenas

0 km   1
0 miles 1

KEY

═══ Autopista Sur motorway
━━━ Major road
━━━ Minor road
∩ Pre-Columbian site
ℹ Tourist information

For hotels and restaurants in this region see pp258–63 and pp280–82

A stretch of the magnificent beach at Varadero

VISITORS' CHECKLIST

Matanzas. **Road Map** B2.
🏠 10,000. ✈ 🚌 Autopista Sur
y 36, (45) 612 626. ℹ Cubatur,
Ave 1ra y Calle 33, (45) 614 405;
Havanatur, Ave 2da y Calle 33,
(45) 667 027.

Upon request, golf players
can book accommodation
in the few luxury bedrooms
in the villa.

♨ Restaurante Las Américas (Mansión Xanadú)

Avenida Las Américas,
Reparto Las Torres. **Tel** (45) 667 750.
🔘 lunch and dinner.

During the years from 1920 to
1950 an American millionaire,
chemical engineer Alfred
Irénée Dupont de Nemours,
gambled a great deal of
money by purchasing most of
the beautiful Hicacos peninsula from the heirs of the
Spanish landowners. At that
time there were only a few
villas and one hotel here.
Dupont then parcelled the
land out to Cubans and
Americans who, within a few
years, had transformed
Varadero into a centre for
gambling and prostitution.

At the height of his
property dealings, Dupont
asked the two Cuban
architects Govantes and
Cabarrocas, who had
designed the Capitolio in
Havana *(see pp82–3)*, to
design a villa for the rocky
promontory of San
Bernardino, the highest point
in Varadero. This sumptuous
four-storey building,
completed in 1929 and
named Mansión Xanadú, was
dressed with Italian marble
and precious wood. The roof
was covered with green
ceramic tiles with thermal
insulation. The house was
surrounded by a huge garden
with rare plants and features
which included an iguana
farm and a golf course. This
extravagant construction cost
$338,000, an enormous sum
at the time.

In 1959, after the
Revolution, Dupont escaped
from Cuba, leaving the villa to
the Cuban government,
which, in 1963, turned it into
"Las Américas", the
most elegant restau-
rant in Varadero. It
specializes in French
cuisine, but can be
visited without any
obligation to eat
there. The dining
room still has its
original furniture,
and in the library
there are books and
photographs of the
Dupont family on
display. The large
terrace overlooking
the Varadero Golf
Club course is part
of the bar area.

♨ Punta Hicacos

For those interested in wildlife, the most fascinating part
of Varadero is the area near
Punta Hicacos, which has
become a nature reserve.
Here you can visit several
caves, including the Cueva
de Ambrosio, with Pre-
Columbian rock paintings,
a lagoon area (Laguna de
Mangón), and some quiet,
secluded beaches.

The peninsula is also an
attraction for scuba divers,
who have 23 dive sites to
choose from.

The former Mansión Xanadú, now a bar-restaurant, with its distinctive green roof

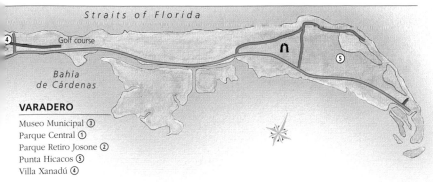

Straits of Florida

Golf course

Bahía de Cárdenas

VARADERO

Península de Zapata ❻

Pineapple plants, common here

This peninsula is named after the land-owner who was granted the land by the Spanish crown in 1636. It is one of the least populated areas of the island, and mostly consists of a huge swamp, partly covered by forest. In the past the inhabitants made their living by extracting peat and making charcoal. Zapata is one of the most complete wildlife reserves in the Caribbean, rich in birds and animals, and one part, the area around the Laguna del Tesoro, has been designated a national park, the Gran Parque Natural de Montemar. The Caribbean coast, with its sandy beaches, attracts scuba divers and fans of other water sports.

A mangrove swamp, characteristic of some tropical coastal areas

STAR SIGHTS

★ Guamá

★ Playa Larga

★ Playa Girón

Corral de Santo Tomás is a refuge and observation point for migratory birds. It can only be visited with an official guide (ask at the reception desk of the Villa Playa Larga Hotel).

Santo Tomás
Quemado Grande
Maneadero

ZAPATA

THE FAUNA OF THE ZAPATA SWAMP

This habitat supports about 150 species of bird, including the *zunzuncito (see p21)*, the Cuban Pygmy owl, the Zapata rail, a rare type of baldicoot, waterhen, various species of parrot, and heron. Along the coast manatees can be seen (the Caribbean species is over 4 m/13 ft long and weighs about 600 kg/1,320 lbs). The beaches and roads are invaded each spring by crabs leaving the water to mate.

The Laguna de las Salinas is the winter home of many species of migratory bird from November to May.

The local crocodile (Cocodrilo rhombifer) *has been protected since the 1960s.*

The Cuban Pygmy owl (Glaucidium siju) *is a small nocturnal raptor.*

The grey heron *lives in the mangrove swamps and feeds on small fish and amphibia.*

The zunzuncito (Mellisuga helenae) *is multi-coloured (male) or black-green (female).*

KEY

━ Major road

━ Minor road

✕ Aerotaxi

ℹ Tourist information

🏖 Recommended beach

✹ Nature reserve

✚ Medical centre

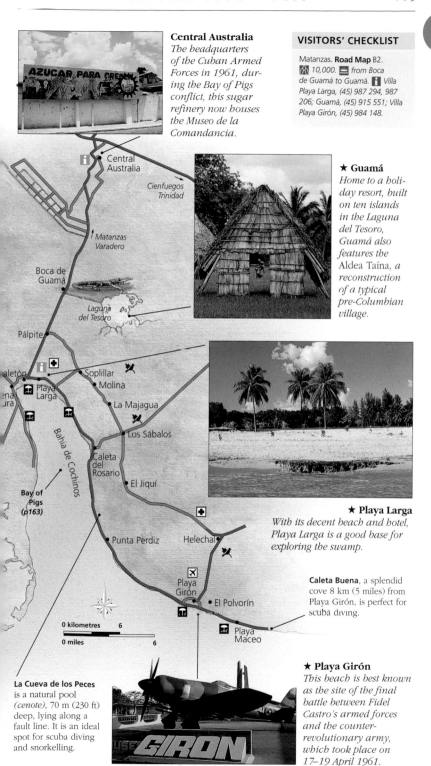

Central Australia
The headquarters of the Cuban Armed Forces in 1961, during the Bay of Pigs conflict, this sugar refinery now houses the Museo de la Comandancia.

★ Guamá
Home to a holiday resort, built on ten islands in the Laguna del Tesoro, Guamá also features the Aldea Taína, a reconstruction of a typical pre-Columbian village.

★ Playa Larga
With its decent beach and hotel, Playa Larga is a good base for exploring the swamp.

Caleta Buena, a splendid cove 8 km (5 miles) from Playa Girón, is perfect for scuba diving.

★ Playa Girón
This beach is best known as the site of the final battle between Fidel Castro's armed forces and the counter-revolutionary army, which took place on 17–19 April 1961.

La Cueva de los Peces is a natural pool *(cenote)*, 70 m (230 ft) deep, lying along a fault line. It is an ideal spot for scuba diving and snorkelling.

Exploring the Península de Zapata

A welcome sign at the Península de Zapata

The Península de Zapata is synonymous with unspoiled nature and luxuriant tropical vegetation. It is a place where visitors can walk among lianas, mangroves and swamp plants, lie in a hammock in the shade of palm trees, observe birds with multicoloured plumage, go fishing, or row a boat on the Laguna del Tesoro. The tranquil Gran Parque Natural de Montemar attracts lovers of wildlife and untouched habitats, rather than adventure seekers. In any case, there is nothing to be feared from the wildlife – there are no ferocious beasts or poisonous snakes on the island.

Statue of Manguanay by the Cuban sculptress Rita Longa, Guamá

Boca de Guamá

Arriving from the north, after passing through Jagüey Grande, which has the largest citrus groves in Cuba, and Central Australia *(see p165)*, you reach Boca de Guamá. Here a picturesque *ranchón*, a kind of rustic hut, converted into a restaurant, indicates that you are near the **Criadero de Cocodrilos**, or crocodile farm. Visitors can watch and photograph the crocodiles from an observation point overlooking the farm in the Zapata swamp.

Founded in 1962 to safeguard 16 endangered species of reptile, this is the largest crocodile farm in Cuba and includes about 100,000 animals kept in separate pools according to size, age and species.

Criadero de Cocodrilos
daily.

Guamá

This unusual holiday village *(see p260)* in the Laguna del Tesoro (Treasure Lake), measuring 16 sq km (6 sq miles), is named after Guamá, a Taíno warrior who resisted the Spanish conquistadors until he was killed in 1533.

The village consists of 18 huts standing on several small islands in the lagoon. Built of royal palm wood and thatched with palm leaves, the huts provide simple accommodation. However, they are equipped with modern amenities, including air-conditioning. Make sure you take adequate supplies of mosquito repellent if you plan to stay here.

The huts are supported on stilts and are connected to one another by hanging bridges or by canoe. In fact, the only way to reach this tourist village is by boat, which takes about 20 minutes to travel along the luxuriantly fringed canal to the lagoon from Boca de Guamá.

This unusual resort also includes a restaurant, a bar, and a small museum, Muestras Aborígenes, which has on display some finds dating back to the Taíno civilization, discovered in the Laguna del Tesoro area.

Also of interest is the reconstructed Taíno village of Aldea Taína, which occupies another of the islands in the lagoon. It comprises four earth *bohíos* (typical Indian huts), a *caney* (a larger round building), and 25 life-size statues of natives by the well-known Cuban sculptress Rita Longa. The figures form the Batey Aborigen, or native Indian square, and represent the few people who lived in the village: a young girl named Dayamí; a crocodile hunter, Abey; Cajimo, hunter of *jutías* (a type of rodent, *see p146*); Manguanay, the mother who is preparing *casabe* (cassava) for her family; Yaima, a little girl who is playing; and the key figure, Guamá, the heroic Taíno warrior.

One of the 18 thatched huts in the Laguna del Tesoro

Playa Larga

At the end of the Bay of Pigs is one of the better beaches along this part of Caribbean coastline, where thick vegetation usually grows down as far as the shore. The coral reef offshore offers magnificent dive sites. Playa Larga's resort area is a popular destination with Cubans and there are also enough facilities to attract international tourists.

Near the car park, a monument commemorates the landing of the anti-Castro troops in 1961, while along the road to Playa Girón there are numerous monuments honouring the Cuban defenders who died in the famous three-day battle.

Northeast of Playa Larga is an ornithological reserve, and the Centro Internacional de Aves (International Bird Centre) of Cuba.

Cueva de los Peces *(see p165)*, near Playa Larga, ideal for diving

Playa Girón

This beach was named in the 1600s after a French pirate, Gilbert Giron, who found refuge here. It became famous three centuries later, when it was the site of the ill-fated, American-backed landing in 1961. A large sign at the entrance to the beach reads: "Here North American imperialism suffered its first major defeat".

Situated on the eastern side of the Bay of Pigs, this is the last sandy beach in the area, ideal for fishing and diving and also equipped with good tourist facilities.

A must is a visit to the small **Museo Girón**, which covers the anti-Castro invasion using photos, documents, weapons, a tank and the wreckage of aeroplanes that took part in the last battle, as well as films taken during the invasion.

🏛 **Museo Girón**
Playa Girón, Península de Zapata. **Tel** (45) 984 122. ⬜ 8am–5pm daily. 🖼 🎫 📷 (with charge).

Playa Girón, the easternmost sandy beach in the Bay of Pigs

THE BAY OF PIGS INVASION

The long, narrow Bay of Pigs *(Bahía de Cochinos)* became known throughout the world in 1961. On April 14 of that year, at the height of the Cold War, a group of 1,400 Cuban exiles, trained by the CIA with the approval of the president of the United States, John F Kennedy, left Nicaragua for Cuba on six ships. The next day, six US B-26 aeroplanes attacked the island's three military air bases, their bombs killing 7 people and wounding 53.

On April 16 the group of counter-revolutionaries landed on the main beaches along the bay, Playa Larga and Playa Girón. However, they were confronted by the Cuban armed forces, headed by Fidel Castro

The hostages released by Cuba on their return to the US

himself, who were well prepared for the battle and had the support of the local population. The fighting lasted just three days and ended in the rapid defeat of the invaders. In order to avoid an international crisis, which could have escalated into an extremely serious situation, given the Soviet Union's support of Cuba, the US suddenly withdrew its aerial support, leaving the invading forces at the mercy of Cuban troops.

The abandoned invaders, many of whom were mercenaries, were taken prisoner and immediately tried. After 20 months in prison, they were allowed to return to the US in exchange for supplies of medicine, foodstuffs and equipment for Cuban hospitals.

Cienfuegos ❼

The triumphal arch (1902)

The capital of the province of the same name, Cienfuegos is a maritime town with a well-preserved historic centre and one of the most captivating bays in the Caribbean Sea, which helped earn the city the name "Pearl of the South" in the Colonial era. When Columbus discovered the gulf in 1494, it was occupied by Jagua Indians. In order to defend the bay from pirates, the Spanish built a fortress here in 1745. The first town was founded in 1819, and was named after the Cuban Governor General of the time, José Cienfuegos. The town was planned according to a geometric layout typical of Neo-Classicism.

The "zero kilometre" in the Parque Martí

Parque Martí

The "zero kilometre", the central point of Cienfuegos, is in the middle of Parque Martí, the former Plaza de Armas (parade ground). The vast square, a 200 x 100 m (655 x 330 ft) rectangle, has been declared a national monument because of the surrounding buildings and its historic importance. It was here that the foundation of Cienfuegos was celebrated with a solemn ceremony in the shade of a hibiscus tree, chosen as a marker for laying out the city's first 25 blocks.

Lions on a marble pedestal flank a monument to José Martí, erected in 1906. On Calle Bouyón stands the only triumphal arch in Cuba, commissioned by the local workers' corporation in 1902 to celebrate the inauguration of the Republic of Cuba. One side of the square is entirely

occupied by the **Antiguo Ayuntamiento**, now the home of the provincial government assembly, supposedly modelled on the Capitolio in Havana *(see pp82–3)*.

🎭 Teatro Tomás Terry

Ave. 56 No. 2703 y Calle 27. *Tel (43) 513 361.* 🔲 *daily.*
This theatre was built in 1886–89 to fulfil the last will and testament of Tomás Terry Adams, an unscrupulous sugar factory owner who had become wealthy through the slave trade and then became mayor. World-famous figures such as Enrico Caruso and Sarah Bernhardt performed here in the early 1900s.

The theatre was designed by Lino Sánchez Mármol as an Italian-style theatre, with a splendid U-shaped, two-tiered auditorium and a huge fresco by Camilo Salaya, a Philippine-Spanish painter who moved to Cuba in the

late 1800s. The austere, well-proportioned façade on the Parque Central has five arches corresponding to the number of entrances. The ceramic masks on the pediment, made by the Salvatti workshops in Venice, represent the Three Graces.

To the left of the theatre is the Neo-Classical Colegio de San Lorenzo, built thanks to a generous donation by the academic Nicolás Jacinto Acea to ensure that needy children in the town would be educated.

⛪ Catedral de la Purísima Concepción

Ave. 56 No. 2902 y Calle 29. *Tel (43) 525 297.* 🔲 *7am–2pm Tue–Fri, 7am–noon, 2–4pm Sat, 7–11:30am Sun.* ✝ *7:15am Mon–Sat, 7:30 & 10am Sun.*
The cathedral of Cienfuegos, which was constructed in 1833–69, is one of the major buildings on the central square. Its distinguishing features are the Neo-Classical façade with two bell towers of different heights, and stained-glass windows made in France depicting the Twelve Apostles.

🏛 Museo Provincial

Ave 54 No. 2702 esq. Calle 27. *Tel (43) 519 722.* 🔲 *10am–6pm Tue–Sat, 9am–1pm Sun.* ⬤ *1 Jan, 1 May, 26 Jul, 25 Dec.* 🈺 *(with charge).*
The Provincial Museum is in the former Casino Español, an eclectic-style building first opened on 5 May 1896. The furniture, bronze, marble and alabaster objects, crystal and porcelain collections, bear witness to the refined taste and wealth of 19th-century families in Cienfuegos.

The austere façade of the Teatro Tomás Terry

Palacio Ferrer, with its unmistakable blue cupola

⚍ Palacio Ferrer

Ave. 54 esq. Calle 25. *Tel (43) 516 584.* ◯ *for cultural events.*
The palacio that houses the Casa Provincial de la Cultura was built in the early 1900s by the sugar magnate José Ferrer Sirés. Enrico Caruso is said to have stayed here when he performed at the Teatro Tomás Terry.

This building stands on the western end of the plaza and is the most bizarre and eclectic in the square. It is distinguished by its cupola with blue mosaic decoration. It is worth climbing up the wrought-iron spiral staircase to enjoy the fine views over the city.

🏛 Museo Histórico Naval Nacional

Ave. 60 y Calle 21, Cayo Loco. *Tel (43) 519 143.* ◯ *10am–6pm Tue–Sat, 8am–1pm Sun.* ⬤ *1 Jan, 1 May, 26 Jul, 25 Dec.* 📷
A short walk northwest of Parque José Martí, on the Cayo Loco peninsula, is the most important naval museum in Cuba, featuring a series of documents concerning the anti-Batista insurrection of 5 September 1957, and an interesting display recording the history of the Cuban Navy.

VISITORS' CHECKLIST

Cienfuegos. **Road Map** C3.
🏘 *150,000.* ✈ *Carretera de Cajonao, km 3.5, (43) 551 328.*
🚉 *Ave. 58 y Calle 4, (43) 525 495.* 🚌 *Calle 49, e/ Ave. 56 y 58, (43) 525 898.* ℹ *Cubatur, Calle 37 e/n 54 y 56, (43) 551 242.*

Paseo del Prado

The liveliest street in town is known for its elegant, well-preserved buildings and the monuments honouring leading local figures. It crosses the historic centre and goes south as far as Punta Gorda. It was laid out in 1922.

Paseo del Prado, the main street in the historic centre of Cienfuegos

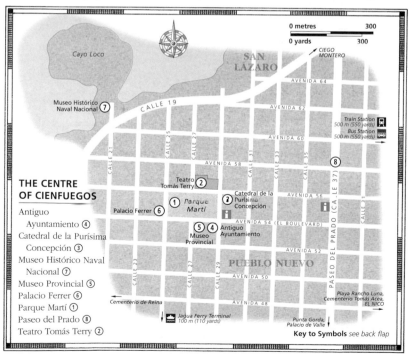

THE CENTRE OF CIENFUEGOS

0 metres 300
0 yards 300

Key to Symbols *see back flap*

Exploring Cienfuegos

The presence of the sea at Cienfuegos makes itself felt more and more the further you go from the historic centre towards the Reina and Punta Gorda districts, two narrow strips of land almost entirely surrounded by water. However, for a fuller taste of the sea, go to the mouth of the bay, which is dominated by the Castillo de Jagua fortress with the picturesque Perché fishing harbour. Southeast of Cienfuegos is one of Latin America's most spectacular botanic gardens.

The interior of Palacio de Valle, with its Neo-Moorish decoration

The characteristic wooden houses of Punta Gorda

Punta Gorda

At the southern tip of the bay of Cienfuegos lies Punta Gorda – the aristocratic quarter of the city in the early 1900s – which affords a lovely panoramic view of the bay. A short walk along the seafront takes you past many Art Nouveau villas. Various brightly coloured wooden houses can be seen towards the tip of the peninsula. They were modelled on the American prefabricated "balloon frame" homes that were so much in vogue in the early 20th century.

⚜ Palacio de Valle

Calle 37 e/ Ave. 0 y 2, Punta Gorda. *Tel* (43) 551 003 ext 830. ○ 10am–10pm daily. 🍴 🍸 📷

The most original building in the area, Palacio de Valle was designed by local and foreign architects engaged by the sugar merchant Acisclo del Valle Blanco, one of the wealthiest men in Cuba. It was built in 1913–17. This two-storey building, which is now a restaurant, is lavishly decorated with Gothic, Venetian and Neo-Moorish motifs, much in the Arab-Spanish style of the Alcázars in Granada and Seville. The façade has three towers of different design symbolizing power, religion and love. The terrace is open to the public.

⚜ Cementerio Monumental Tomás de Acea

Ave. 5 de Septiembre. *Tel* (43) 525 257. ○ daily. 📷 📷

This impressive monumental cemetery lies in the eastern suburb of Cienfuegos. Varied in stylistic influences, it was conceived as a large garden with paths and fruit trees. The entrance is a replica of the Parthenon in Athens.

Palacio de Valle, which Batista turned into a casino, now home to a restaurant

⚰ Cementerio General La Reina

Ave. 50 y Calle 7, Reina.
◯ *daily.* 🏛

The municipal cemetery of La Reina is located at the western end of the city, and has been declared a national monument. Laid out in the 1830s, this Neo-Classical cemetery includes a famous funerary statue of La Bella Durmiente (Sleeping Beauty).

The statue of Sleeping Beauty in La Reina cemetery in Cienfuegos

♣ Castillo de Jagua

Poblado Castillo de Jagua. 🚤
Tel (43) 965 402. ◯ 9am–5pm Tue–Sat, 9am–1pm Sun. 🏛 🚫 📷 (with charge).

Built by engineer José Tantete, following a design by Bruno Caballero, to protect the bay and the region from Jamaican pirates, the Castillo was the third most important fortress in Cuba in the 18th century and the only one in the central region of the island. The original moat and drawbridge are still intact. According to legend, the citadel was inhabited by a mysterious lady dressed in blue, who every night walked through the rooms and corridors, frightening the guards. It is said that one morning one of the guards was found in a state of shock while wringing a piece of blue cloth in anguish. The unfortunate man never got over this experience and ended up in an asylum.

At the foot of the Castillo is the fishing village of **Perché**, with picturesque wooden houses, in striking contrast to the majestic military structure above. Most visitors arrive by ferry from Pasacaballos hotel (29 km/18 miles south of Cienfuegos), from the dock in Cienfuegos, or on a boat from Punta Gorda.

Environs

Cienfuegos province is interesting to eco-tourists. Besides the **Ciego Montero** spa north of the capital, other noteworthy sights are **El Nicho**, to the southeast, which is famous for its waterfalls, and the conservation area of Aguacate.

However the main sight is the **Valle de Yaguanabo**, in the southern region, which is traversed by the river of the same name, which forms small waterfalls and clear freshwater pools. On the slopes of one of the mountains in this valley, populated by mammals such as boar, deer and opossums, is the entrance to the **Cueva de Martín Infierno**. This cave has been a national monument since 1990, because it has one of the largest stalagmites in the world (67 m/220 ft high) and other rare mineralogical sites such as Moonmilk and Flores de Yeso.

About 20 km (12 miles) south of Cienfuegos is **Playa Rancho Luna**, with golden sand and a hotel (*see p259*). It is popular with tourists and local families alike.

BENNY MORÉ

A great source of pride to Cienfuegos is the figure of Maximiliano Bartolomé Moré, better known as Benny Moré, who was born at nearby Santa Isabel de las Lajas on 24 August 1919. Moré inspired many generations of Cubans and foreigners with his supple, unique voice, which enabled him to interpret a variety of musical genres. For this reason the artist was nicknamed *el bárbaro del ritmo* (the barbarian of rhythm). He was self-taught, and when still quite young performed with famous orchestras such as those led by the Matamoros brothers and Pérez Prado (see *pp30–31*). He died in the early 1960s. For some time Cienfuegos – a city with a great musical tradition and the birthplace of cha-cha-cha – has paid tribute to him with the Benny Moré International Festival. The Cabildo Congo de Lajas in his home town puts on performances of Afro-Cuban popular songs and dances.

The Cuban singer, Benny Moré

Jardín Botánico Soledad ⑧

In 1912 Edwin Atkins, owner of the Soledad sugar works 15 km (9 miles) from Cienfuegos, transformed 4 ha (10 acres) of his estate into a sugar cane research centre, and filled the garden with a great number of tropical plants. In 1919 the University of Harvard bought the property and founded a botanical institute for the study of sugar cane and Caribbean flora. The botanical garden has been run by the Cuban government since 1961, and is one of the largest in Latin America, with a surface area of 90 ha (222 acres) and more than 1,500 different species of plant, including 210 palms. Besides the endemic species there are also huge bamboo trees. Guided tours, made partly on foot and partly by car, reveal the exceptional diversification of the garden.

★ Garden Drive
Lined with royal palm trees, the drive borders one entire side from the entrance to the glasshouse.

Leguminous plants

Laboratory

Ticket office, library

Medicinal plants, which are grown throughout the country, can be viewed in this small plot.

Forest plants

STAR SIGHTS

★ Banyan Tree

★ Garden Drive

Protected woodland

★ Banyan Tree
Among over 50 varieties of fig in the botanical garden, perhaps the most striking is a huge Ficus benghalensis *or banyan tree, a species with aerial roots (with a circumference of over 20 m/65 ft). The roots, trunks and branches form an impenetrable barrier.*

Cacti

Many species of cactus are housed in this glasshouse. They are young specimens, grown after the serious damage inflicted by hurricane Lilly (1996).

Water Lilies
The pool near the glasshouse is entirely covered with water lilies of different colours: bright pink, white, dark purple, violet, blue and yellow.

Mimosa
With its deeply divided leaves, the mimosa makes a very attractive ornamental plant.

Santa Clara ❾

See pp174–5.

Sierra del Escambray ❿

Villa Clara, Sancti Spíritus, Cienfuegos. **Map** C3. 🏨 *Hotel los Helechos, (42) 540 330.*

The Sierra del Escambray mountain range, with an average height of 700 m (2,300 ft) above sea level, covers a large part of southern Central Cuba, across three provinces: Villa Clara, Cienfuegos and Sancti Spíritus *(see p191)*. In the heart of the range is the **El Nicho** nature reserve, which is of great scientific and ecological value with its abundant mountain fauna and varied plantlife. **Pico San Juan** (1,156 m/ 3,790 ft), dotted with conifers and lichens as well as coffee plantations, is the highest mountain in the Sierra.

A long steep road leads from the northern side of the mountains up to stunning **Embalse Hanabanilla**, a large artificial lake overlooked by a hotel. The Río Negro path, which skirts the waterfall of the same name, leads to a belvedere viewing point from which one can see the entire lake.

In the village of Macagua is the **Comunidad Teatral del Escambray**, an international theatre school. The school was founded in 1968 by members of the Havana Theatre, who used to rehearse here before touring rural communities.

PALM TREES

For many Cubans, palm trees represent the power of the gods. A great variety of species, many of them native to Cuba, grow throughout the island: the royal palm *(Roystonea regia)*, the national plant; the bottle palm *(Colpothrinax wrightii)*, called *barrigona* (pregnant one), because the trunk swells in the middle; the sabal, whose fan-like leaves are used for roofing; the local coccothrinax *(C. crinita)*, with its unmistakable foliage; and the *corcho* *(Microcycas calocoma, see p139)*.

Royal palm

Bottle palm

Coccothrinax palm

Santa Clara ❾

The Teatro de la Caridad, where Enrico Caruso performed

Bust of Leoncio Vidal

Founded on 15 July 1689 by a group of inhabitants from Remedios *(see p177)*, who had moved away from the coast to escape from pirate raids, Santa Clara was for centuries the capital of the province of Las Villas, which included the present-day provinces of Cienfuegos, Sancti Spíritus and Villa Clara. One important historical event has made Santa Clara famous: in 1958 it was here that the last battle of the guerrilla war led by Che Guevara took place, the battle which marked the end of Batista's dictatorship. Santa Clara is now known as "the city of the heroic guerrilla". Today, it is a lively city and has several interesting sights.

Santa Clara's well-tended main square, Parque Leoncio Vidal

Parque Leoncio Vidal

The heart of the city, this charming square with its pristine flower beds, wrought-iron benches and period street lamps has retained its original 1925 atmosphere.

An obelisk stands here. It was commissioned by the rich heiress Martha Abreu de Estévez in honour of two priests, Juan de Conyedo and Hurtado de Mendoza. The heiress also financed the construction of the Teatro de la Caridad, the town's first four public bathhouses, the astronomical observatory, the electricity station, a hospital and a fire station.

There is also a bust of Leoncio Vidal, a colonel in the national independence army who died in battle in 1896, here in this square. There is also a fountain, and a sculpture entitled *Niño de la Bota* (child in boots), purchased by mail order from the J L Mott Company, an art dealer in New York.

Until 1894 the square was partly off limits to blacks, who could only walk along certain areas of the pavement.

🎭 Teatro de la Caridad

Parque Vidal 3. *Tel* (42) 205 548. ⬤ *closed for restoration until late 2009.*
Built to a design by the engineer Herminio Leiva y Aguilera for the heiress Martha Abreu de Estévez, this theatre was inaugurated in 1885.

An antique vase in a hall in the Museo de Artes Decorativas

The theatre offered many additional services – a barber shop, ballroom and gambling room, café and restaurant – with the aim of collecting money to be given to the poor in the city (hence its name, Charity Theatre).

The building has a simple, linear façade, in contrast to the ornate interior, with its profusion of chandeliers and painted panels and a stage with all kinds of mechanical gadgets and draped curtains. The auditorium itself, which has three tiers of boxes with wrought-iron balusters, had folding seats in the stalls right from the start – something completely new in Cuba at the time.

Perhaps the best feature of the theatre is the frescoed ceiling, executed by the Spanish-Philippine painter Camilo Salaya, representing the allegorical figures of Genius, History and Fame.

🏛 Museo de Artes Decorativas

Calle Martha Abreu esq. Luis Estévez
Tel (42) 205 368. ⬤ *9am–6pm Mon, Wed & Thu, 1–10pm Fri–Sat, 6–10pm Sun.* 📷 🎫 📷 *(with charge).*
The excellent Decorative Arts Museum, housed in a building dating from 1810, contains 17th-, 18th-, 19th- and 20th-century furniture, as well as furnishings and paintings that belonged to leading local families. Among the objects on display here, those donated by the Cuban poetess Dulce María Loynaz *(see p29)* are particularly elegant and delightful: five fans, eleven sculptures and two Sèvres porcelain jars, the largest of their kind in Cuba.

The Tren Blindado Monument, a work by José Delarra

VISITORS' CHECKLIST

Villa Clara. **Road Map** C3.
250.000. Luis Estévez 323.
Carretera Central km 2.5.
Havanatur, Calle Maximo
Gomez, (42) 204 002; Izla Azul,
Calle Lorda 6 (42) 217 338.

⛩ Tren Blindado Monument

Carretera Camajuaní, junction with railway line. **Tel** (42) 202 758.
9am–5:15pm Mon–Sat.

On 28 December 1958, with the aid of only 300 men, Che Guevara succeeded in conquering the city, which was fiercely defended by 3,000 of Batista's soldiers. The following day Guevara handed the dictator another severe setback by derailing an armoured train that was supposed to transport 408 soldiers and weapons of all kinds to the eastern region of Cuba in order to halt the advance of the rebels.

Cuban sculptor José Delarra commemorated this event by creating a museum–monument on the spot where it took place, in the northeastern part of Santa Clara, on the line to Remedios. The sequence of events is re-created using original elements such as four wagons from the armoured train, military plans and maps, photographs and weapons.

Also on show is the D-6 Caterpillar bulldozer that was used by the guerrillas to remove rails and cause the derailment. The episode ended with the surrender of Batista's men.

Parque Tudury

This square, in front of the Neo-Classical Iglesia di Nuestra Señora del Carmen (1756), is also known as Parque El Carmen. Here stands a monument commemorating the foundation of the town of Santa Clara. It was erected in 1951 around a tamarind tree, on the spot where, on 15 July 1689, the first mass was celebrated in the new city. The monument consists of 18 columns on which are carved the names of the first families in Santa Clara, crowned by a cross.

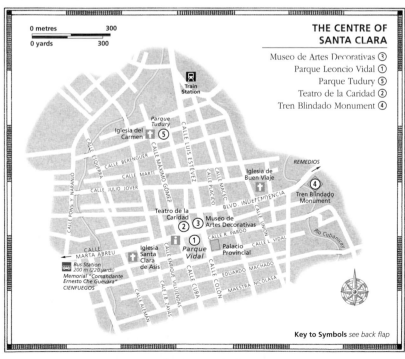

THE CENTRE OF SANTA CLARA

Museo de Artes Decorativas ③
Parque Leoncio Vidal ①
Parque Tudury ⑤
Teatro de la Caridad ②
Tren Blindado Monument ④

0 metres 300
0 yards 300

Key to Symbols see back flap

The group of sculptures in Santa Clara, dedicated to Che Guevara

🏛 Conjunto Escultórico "Comandante Ernesto Che Guevara"

Avenida de los Desfiles, Santa Clara.
Tel *(42) 205 985.* ◯ *9am–5pm Tue–Sat, 9am–1pm Sun.*
📷 🎦 📷 *(outdoors only).*

The monument in Plaza de la Revolución was built to commemorate the 30th anniversary of the battle of Santa Clara. It was designed by the architect Jorge Cao Campos and the sculptor José Delarra, and was unveiled on 28 December 1988.

The complex comprises a museum and memorial of Che Guevara. Dominating the monument is an impressive bronze statue of Che, with his arm in plaster (he had broken it in a previous battle). Beneath, a bas-relief depicts scenes from the battle, on which are carved the historic words that Che wrote in his farewell letter before leaving for Bolivia.

Under the monument (the entrance is at the back) is the museum, designed by the architect Blanca Hernández Guivernau, which has some of Che's personal belongings on display, together with a chronological reconstruction of his life, which clearly

reveals the evolution of his revolutionary ideas.

Che's personal effects include his pistol holster, his uniform, watch, pipe, the container from which he used to drink *mate* tea, his beret and the telephone he used during the campaign of Santa Clara, along with his binoculars, camera and radio.

The newest construction in the square is the memorial containing the remains of Ernesto Che Guevara and 38 other comrades, found in Bolivia 30 years after their death and transferred to Cuba beginning of July 1997. The tomb is in the shape of a cave and consists of numbers of niches with ossuaries as well as a central brazier where an eternal flame burns. Cubans flock here daily in order to pay their respects.

ERNESTO CHE GUEVARA

When Ernesto Guevara de la Serna was killed in Bolivia upon orders from the CIA, he was only 39 years old. In the summer of 1997 – while Cuba was celebrating the 30th anniversary of the death of the *guerrillero heroico* – the body of Che Guevara was returned to the island. He was one of only two foreigners in the history of Cuba (the other is the Dominican

The photographer Korda with his famous portrait of Che Guevara

general Máximo Gómez) to be proclaimed a Cuban citizen "by birth". Watching his coffin being lowered from the aeroplane to the sound of the *Suite de las Américas* served to remind everyone, especially young Cubans, that Che had died and had therefore really existed; he was not merely a 20th-century legend, but a reality for millions of people who had shared his ideas. Further testimony is given by his children, his widow Aleida March, many of those who fought with him on the Sierra and in the Congo, and also Alberto Granado, with whom Che made his first trips to Latin America and who, after the Revolution, moved to Cuba on his friend's invitation. Though Che suffered from asthma, he had an iron will, loved books as well as sports, and had a great spirit of sacrifice; he could appreciate beauty and was a perfectionist but had a sense of humour. He was a man of action who also found time to meditate on reality and to write.

SE ASIGNA AL COMANDANTE
ERNESTO CUEVARA LA MI-
SION DE CONDUCIR DESDE
LA SIERRA MAESTRA HASTA
LA PROVINCIA DE LAS VILLAS
UNA COLUMNA REBELDE

Part of the bas-relief memorial to Che Guevara

Interior of the Iglesia de San Juan Bautista, Remedios cathedral

Remedios ⓫

Villa Clara. **Map** C3. 🏙 50,000.
🚉 🚌 ℹ️ Hotel Mascotte, Calle Máximo Gómez 114, (42) 395 144.
🎉 Parrandas (24 Dec).

Founded around 1514 by Vasco Porcallo de Figueroa and given the name of Santa Cruz de la Sabana, this town was renamed San Juan de los Remedios del Cayo after a fire in 1578.

This peaceful place has a small, well-preserved Colonial historic centre in the area around Plaza Martí. Overlooking this square is the Iglesia de San Juan Bautista, the city cathedral, which is considered one of the most important churches in Cuba. What we see today is the result of restoration carried out in the 20th century thanks to the rich landowner Eutimio Falla Bonet, who revived its original Baroque splendour without touching the Neo-Classical bell tower. Most striking are the lavish Baroque altar and the magnificent decorative ceiling.

Behind the cathedral is the **House of Alejandro García Caturla**. Here, the musical instruments, photographs and some personal belongings of this talented 20th-century personality are on display. García Caturla was a composer, pianist, saxophone player, percussionist, violinist and singer, as well as a fine tennis player and rower, journalist and art critic. He caused a scandal by marrying a black woman, by whom he had 11 children. He defended the poor and was regarded as a fair and honest judge. His honesty was ultimately the cause of his assassination on 12 November 1940, at the age of 34, by a defendant who had tried to bribe him.

Also in the square are three other noteworthy buildings. The Mascotte hotel was the site of an important meeting between Generalissimo Máximo Gómez and a US delegation in 1899. The former Casino Español, now Casa de la Cultura, and the El Louvre café, founded in 1866, also stand here.

However, Remedios is probably most famous for the Parrandas, the local festival documented in the fascinating **Museo de las Parrandas Remedianas**. Here, photographs, musical instruments, costumes, sketches, carriages and *trabajos de plaza* – decorated wooden structures – bring to life Parrandas past and present.

🏛 **House of Alejandro García Caturla**
Calle Camilo Cienfuegos 5.
⬜ 8am–5pm Tue–Sat. ⬛ Sun.
🎫 ✔ 📷

🏛 **Museo de las Parrandas Remedianas**
Calle Máximo Gómez 71, esq. Andrés del Río. ⬜ Tue–Sat, Sun am.
⬛ 1 Jan, 1 May, 26 Jul, 25 Dec.
🎫 ✔ 📷

THE PARRANDAS

A 19th-century print showing people gathering in the square

In 1829 the parish priest of Remedios, Francisco Virgil de Quiñones, had the idea of getting some boys to bang on sheets of tin in order to get the lazier church members out of their homes to participate in the nighttime celebrations of the Advent masses (Dec 16–24).

In time this strange concert developed into a fully fledged festival, with music, dances, parades with floats and huge wooden contraptions *(trabajos de plaza)*. The festivity is a sort of cross between Mardi Gras and the Italian Palio horse race, based on the competition between two quarters of Remedios, San Salvador and Carmen.

The Parrandas begin on December 4 with concerts performed with various percussion instruments, and end with a great crescendo on Christmas Eve. The two *trabajos de plaza*, one per quarter, which are made during the year, are left in Plaza Martí during the festivities. They are illuminated at nine in the evening and may have a historical, patriotic, political, scientific or architectural theme. Later on there are fireworks to welcome the entrance of the floats *(carrozas)*, which never occurs before 3am. These *tableaux vivants* move among the crowd.

The most endearing aspect of the Parrandas, enlivened by songs, polkas and rumbas, is that all the inhabitants, of all ages, take part.

Plaza Martí, the tranquil central square in Remedios

CENTRAL CUBA – EAST

SANCTI SPIRITUS · CIEGO DE ÁVILA · CAMAGÜEY · LAS TUNAS

This area in the heart of the island presents two different facets. One is Colonial, with Spanish traits which are visible in the architecture and local customs and is best expressed in beautiful Baroque Trinidad, and fascinating, labyrinthine Camagüey. The other aspect is unspoilt nature, the coastline dotted with cayos, which has attracted visitors from abroad only in recent years.

Trinidad, Camagüey and Sancti Spíritus, the main cultural centres in this region, were three of seven cities founded in the 16th century by a small group of Spaniards led by Diego Velázquez. The 1600s and 1700s were marked by the threat posed to Cuba by England and by pirate raids such as that made by Henry Morgan at Camagüey (then Puerto Príncipe) in 1666. At that time Trinidad had political and military jurisdiction over the whole of central Cuba, where the economy was based solely on sugar cane cultivation and the sale of sugar. The great landowners resided in luxurious mansions in these three cities.

In the second half of the 19th century, a period of crisis began with the advent of new technology, for which there was no skilled labour. Slave revolts, the first of which broke out in Camagüey in 1616, became increasingly frequent and violent, while competition from Cienfuegos was becoming more intense. In the late 1800s the major landowners left the cities and as time went on they gradually ceded their sugar factories to American businessmen, who converted them into one large sugar-producing business. Camagüey concentrated on livestock raising, still an important resource in the province, while Trinidad had to engage in other activities such as handicrafts and cigar-making. It remained isolated from the rest of Cuba for a long time, since the railway was not extended to Trinidad until 1919 and the road to Cienfuegos and Sancti Spíritus was only laid out in the 1950s. One result of this isolation, however, is that the historic centres of Trinidad and Sancti Spíritus have preserved their Colonial atmosphere.

Aerial view of the causeway linking Cayo Coco to the mainland

◁ Calle Simón Bolívar in Trinidad, sloping down towards the plain

Exploring Central Cuba – East

From a cultural point of view, the most interesting place in the area is the delightful town of Trinidad. This small town also has a lovely beach nearby and makes a good base for tours to the Sierra del Escambray or for excursions to the Valle de los Ingenios. A transit town, Sancti Spíritus can seem disappointing after Trinidad, while Camagüey is appealing both for its fascinating Colonial architecture and as an authentic, vibrant Cuban city. The Atlantic coast in the province of Ciego de Ávila is good for swimming and diving, especially at Cayo Coco and Guillermo, where there are good tourist facilities.

Playa Prohibida at Cayo Coco, fringed by sand dunes

KEY

━━━ Motorway

━━━ Major road

┄┄┄ Minor road

┅┅┅ Main railway

━━━ Regional border

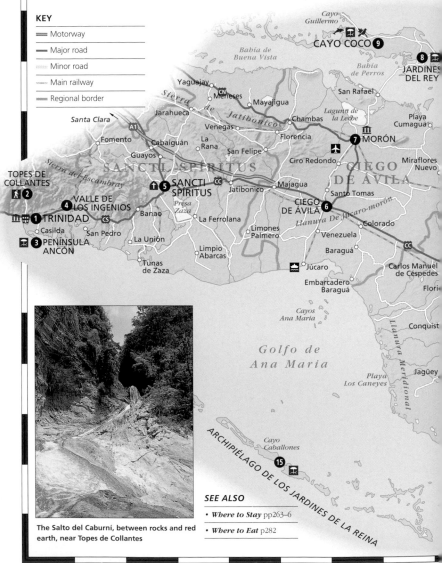

The Salto del Caburní, between rocks and red earth, near Topes de Collantes

SEE ALSO

- **Where to Stay** pp263–6
- **Where to Eat** p282

One of the Colonial houses around the peaceful pedestrian square of San Juan de Dios, in Camagüey

GETTING AROUND

There is at least one domestic airport in each province. The cities are linked by road and by trains bound for Oriente, while from Trinidad the Valle de los Ingenios can be toured on a delightful small steam train. Cayo Coco can be reached by car along the causeway, or by air. The most difficult area to travel around is the Sierra del Escambray *(see p173)*, although organized tours now include Topes de Collantes.

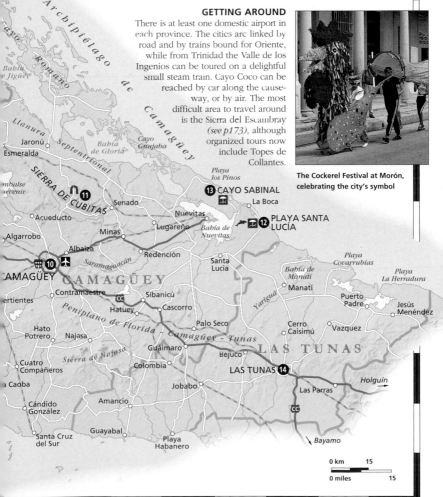

The Cockerel Festival at Morón, celebrating the city's symbol

0 km   15

0 miles   15

Trinidad ❶

A cannon used as a bollard

This city was founded by Diego Velázquez in 1514, and was declared a World Heritage Site by UNESCO in 1988. The original cobblestone streets and pastel-coloured houses give the impression that time has scarcely moved on since Colonial times. From the 1600s–1800s, the city was a major centre for trade in sugar and slaves, and the buildings around the Plaza Mayor, the heart of Trinidad, bear witness to the wealth of the landowners of the time. A long period of isolation from the 1850s to the 1950s protected the city from any radical new building and the original town layout has been left largely unchanged. The historic centre has recently been skilfully restored, down to details like the street lights.

★ **Palacio Brunet**
This mansion is now the Museo Romántico, with a collection of furniture and items that belonged to the wealthiest local families (p185).

★ **Iglesia y Convento de San Francisco**
The monastery is the home of the Museo de la Lucha contra Bandidos, while the church bell tower, the symbol of the city, offers fine views. The bell dates from 1853 (p189).

Casa de la Música

Nuestra Señora de la Popa *(see p190)*

SIMÓN BOLÍVAR

CALLE HERNÁNDEZ ECHERRI

CALLE PIRO GUINART

CALLE MARTÍNEZ VILLENA

Canchánchara
This typical casa de infusiones, housed in an 18th-century building, is known for its namesake cocktail canchánchara, made from rum, lime, water and honey. Live music is played here.

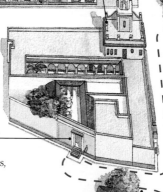

In Plazuela del Jigüe, where an acacia tree *(jigüe)* stands, Father Bartolomé de Las Casas celebrated the first mass in Trinidad in 1514 *(p189).*

The Museo de Arqueología Guamuhaya occupies an 18th-century building where the naturalist Humboldt once stayed *(see p185).*

STAR SIGHTS

★ Palacio Brunet

★ Palacio Cantero

★ Iglesia y Convento de San Francisco

KEY

– – – Suggested route

Iglesia Parroquial de la Santísima Trinidad

The church of the Holy Trinity was built in the late 1800s on the site of a 17th-century church that had been destroyed by a cyclone. It has an impressive carved wooden altar decorated with elaborate inlaid wood (p184).

The Casa de los Conspiradores, with a wooden balcony on the corner, was the meeting place of the nationalist secret society, La Rosa de Cuba.

La Casa de la Trova, a venue for listening to live music *(see p289)*, stands on the Plazuela de Segarte, a small square surrounded by 18th-century houses.

PLAZUELA DE SEGARTE

PLAZA MAYOR

Museo de Arquitectura Colonial

Housed in the beautifully restored Casa de los Sánchez Iznaga, this museum illustrates the main features of Trinidadian architecture (p184).

CALLE MARTÍNEZ VILLENA

CALLE JAVIER

Casa de la Cultura *(p189)*

Casa de Aldemán Ortiz

Besides being a fine example of 19th-century architecture, this building has an interesting art gallery with works by local artists, as well as handicrafts (p184).

CALLE SIMÓN BOLÍVAR

★ Palacio Cantero

This Neo-Classical gem was built in the early 19th century and is now the home of the Museo Histórico Municipal, which recounts the history of the region. The tower has a commanding view of the historic centre (p189).

0 metres 100
0 yards 100

Trinidad: Exploring Plaza Mayor

The museums and buildings facing the main square in Trinidad lend historic weight and depth to the "suspended-in-time" feel of this city. It is worth stopping in the town centre for at least half a day to see the museums, relax on the benches in the shade of the palm trees, enjoy a cocktail at the bar by the cathedral steps, or stroll around the stalls in the crafts market.

Decorative element in Plaza Mayor

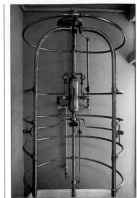

A 19th-century shower in the Museo de Arquitectura Colonial

🔒 Iglesia Parroquial de la Santísima Trinidad

Plaza Mayor.
🕐 *variable.*
Completed in 1892, this austere church with a Neo-Classical façade stands at the top of the sloping Plaza Mayor.

The four-aisle interior has a fine Neo-Gothic altar dedicated to the Virgin of Mercy, with a painting by the Cuban painter Antonio Herr on the rear wall. But the real attraction of this church is an 18th-century wooden statue made in Spain, the *Señor de la Vera Cruz* (Lord of the True Cross), which is associated with a curious story. The sculpture, made for one of the churches in Vera Cruz, Mexico, left the port of Barcelona in 1731, but three times in succession the ship was driven by strong winds to the port of

Casilda, 6 km (4 miles) from the city of Trinidad. While preparing to make a fourth attempt to reach Mexico, the ship's captain decided to leave behind part of the cargo, which included the huge chest containing the statue of Christ. The locals regarded the arrival of the sacred image as a sign from Heaven, and from that time on the *Señor de la Vera Cruz* became an object of fervent worship.

The Maundy Thursday procession, which was suspended in 1959 and revived again in 1997, is dedicated to this statue.

Bronze knocker, Museo de Arquitectura Colonial

🏛 Museo de Arquitectura Colonial

Calle Ripalda 83, e/ Hernández Echerri y Martínez Villena, Plaza Mayor.
Tel (41) 993 208. 🕐 9am–5pm Sat–Thu. 🌙 Fri. 📷 🎫 📷 *(with charge).*
The front of the 18th-century mansion of the Sánchez Iznaga family, now the home of the Museum of Colonial Architecture, features a lovely portico with slim columns, a wrought-iron balustrade and wooden beams. Originally, the building consisted of two separate houses, both of which belonged to sugar magnate Saturnino Sánchez Iznaga. The houses were joined during the 19th century.

The museum, the only one of its kind in Cuba, covers the different architectural

elements seen in Trinidad and illustrates the building techniques used during the Colonial period.

There is a collection of various locks, latches, doors, hinges, windows and grilles, as well as parts of walls and tiles. In one of the bathrooms facing the inner courtyard is a fine example of a 19th-century shower, with a complicated network of pipes supplying hot and cold water.

🏛 Casa de Rafael Ortiz (Galería de Arte)

Calle Rubén Martínez Villena y Bolívar, Plaza Mayor. **Tel** (41) 994 432. 🕐 8am–5pm daily.
This beautiful mansion with a long wooden balcony, reminiscent of the Colonial buildings in Habana Vieja, is evocative of the city's golden age. It was built in 1808 for Ortiz de Zúñiga, a former slave trader who later became the mayor of Trinidad. The house currently serves as an art gallery.

The first floor has paintings on display (and for sale) by contemporary Cuban artists, including Antonio Herr, Juan Oliva, Benito Ortiz, Antonio Zerquera and David Gutiérrez. Of interest in the gallery itself are frescoes, the great staircase, and, in the upper hall, a ceiling decorated with figures. From the balcony there is a fine view of the entire square.

The statue of Señor de la Vera Cruz (1731), in one of the chapels inside Santísima Trinidad

Museo de Arqueología Guamuhaya, seen from the Casa Ortiz; behind is Palacio Brunet

🏛 Museo de Arqueología Guamuhaya

Calle Simón Bolívar 457, e/ Fernando Hernández Echerri y Rubén Martínez Villena, Plaza Mayor. **Tel** *(41) 993 420.* ◯ *call ahead to check opening times.*

Alexander von Humboldt

HUMBOLDT IN CUBA

The German naturalist Alexander von Humboldt (1769–1859), the father of modern geography, made two trips to Cuba (1800–1, 1804), which are recorded in a museum at Calle Oficios 252 in Havana. The book that followed, *Political Essay on the Island of Cuba*, in which he described Cuba as "the land of sugar and slaves", illustrated its geography, rivers, population, economy, government and slave system. Because of its abolitionist ideas the book was soon banned.

The building that is now the home of the Archaeological Museum was constructed in the 18th century and was purchased in the 1800s by the wealthy Don Antonio Padrón, who added a portico with brick columns and Ionic capitals.

The Guamuhaya (the native Indian name for the mountainous Escambray area) collection includes Pre-Columbian archaeological finds as well as objects associated with the Spanish conquest and slavery in Cuba, and stuffed animals, including the *manjuari*, an ancient species of fish that still lives in the Zapata swamp.

In the courtyard is a bronze bust commemorating the German geographer and naturalist Alexander von Humboldt, who stayed here as Padrón's guest in 1801, during his travels in the New World.

🏛 Palacio Brunet (Museo Romántico)

Calle Hernández Echerri 52, esq. Simón Bolívar, Plaza Mayor. **Tel** *(419) 4363.* ◯ *9am–5pm Tue–Sun.* 🅿 📷 📷 *(with charge).*
Built in 1812 as the residence of the wealthy Borrell family, Palacio Brunet now contains the Museo Romántico. The decoration of the mansion blends in well with the objects on display, most of which once belonged to Mariano Borrell, the family

founder. They were inherited by Borrell's daughter, the wife of Count Nicolás de la Cruz y Brunet (hence the name Palacio Brunet), in 1830.

The museum's 14 rooms all face the courtyard gallery with its elegant balustrade. The spacious living room has a Carrara marble floor, a coffered ceiling, Neo-Classical decoration, furniture made of precious wood, Sèvres vases and Bohemian crystalware. There are also English-made spittoons, which reveal that the 19th-century aristocratic landowners were partial to smoking cigars. In the dining room the fan windows are a particularly attractive feature.

Other rooms of interest are the countess's bedroom, with a bronze baldachin over the bed, and the kitchen, which is still decorated with its original painted earthenware tiles.

One of the elegant frescoes decorating Palacio Brunet

The Houses of Trinidad

The historic centre of Trinidad has an extraordinarily dense concentration of old Colonial houses, many still inhabited by the descendants of old local families. The oldest, single-storey buildings have two corridors and a porch parallel to the street, with a courtyard at the back. In the late 1700s another corridor was introduced to the layout.

A mampara, an interior door with two leaves

In the 19th century, the houses formed a square around an open central courtyard. In general, the houses of Trinidad, unlike those in Havana, have no vestibule or portico. The entrance consists of a large living room that gives way to a dining room, either through an archway or a *mampara*, an inner, double door.

Barrotes, small turned wooden columns, characterize the 18th-century windows.

Red tile roof

Wooden supports

Wooden beams *support the two- or four-pitch sloping roof, which is covered with terracotta tiles. Inside, mudéjar-style coffered ceilings can often be found.*

TRINIDAD FAÇADES

The façade of the typical Trinidad house has a large central door, with a smaller door (or doors) cut in it for easy access. The windows, set slightly above ground level, are almost the height of the door. They have strong wooden shutters instead of glass. This house is in Plaza Mayor, next to the Casa Ortiz.

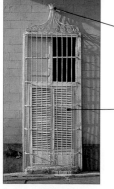

Wrought-iron ornamental motifs

Wooden shutters

The 19th-century iron grilles *replaced the wooden barrotes and typically have simple decoration at the top and bottom.*

The arched windows *so characteristic of Trinidad have radiating wooden slats instead of mediopunto windows. These allow the air to enter but keep out the sunlight.*

The wooden front door *is sometimes framed by plaster motifs: flattened pilasters, moulding, half-columns either with simple Tuscan capitals or with upturned bowls at the top.*

◁ The view from the San Francisco bell tower: in the foreground, Plaza Mayor, beyond, the coast

Trinidad: Around Plaza Mayor

Walking along the streets leading from Plaza Mayor is a fascinating experience even if you have no particular destination. A slow stroll allows time to observe the detail of a window, a small balcony, the irregular cobblestones, or the cannons used as bollards. The historic centre is more or less free of traffic. In the evening the houses glow in the warm hues of sunset, and music fills the streets: the Casa de la Trova *(see p183)* and Casa de la Música *(p182)* put on daily concerts by local bands.

The river cobblestones *(chinas pelonas)* used in Trinidad's streets

The frescoed entrance hall in Palacio Cantero and its Italian marble floor

🏛 Casa de la Cultura Trinitaria

Calle Zerquera 406. **Tel** *(419) 4308.*
During the day, the spacious, well-lit vestibule is used as permanent exhibition space by local artists (some of whom also have their studios here), who sell their paintings. In the evening, performances of various kinds of entertainment are held in the rear courtyard: theatre, dance, concerts and shows for children.

🏛 Palacio Cantero (Museo Histórico Municipal)

Calle Bolívar 423. **Tel** *(41) 994 460.*
⭘ *9am–5pm Sat–Thu.* ⬤ *Fri.* 📷 📷 *(with charge).*
This mansion, which belonged originally to Don Borrell y Padrón – one of the major figures in local sugar production – was purchased in 1841 by María de Monserrate Fernández, the widow of a sugar magnate. A year later she married the landowner Cantero, renaming the mansion and transforming it into a sumptuous Neo-Classical residence. The building is now the Museo Histórico Municipal.

From the grand entrance hall, with frescoed arches, the route takes in the dining room, the kitchen, the court-yard and an area for domestic servants.

The history of Trinidad can be traced through exhibits, maps, and monuments related to different themes: the Cantero family, piracy, the plantations in the Valle de los Ingenios, the slave trade and the wars of independence. There is a viewing platform atop the tower.

Plazuela del Jigüe

This peaceful little square, where a spreading acacia tree offers shady respite from the sun, is rich in history *(see p182)*. El Jigüe restaurant is housed in a lovely porticoed building decorated with panels of painted tiles.

🏛 Iglesia y Convento de San Francisco

Calle Hernández Echerri, esq. Guinart.
Museo de la Lucha contra Bandidos Tel *(41) 994 121.*
⭘ *9am–5pm Tue–Sun.* 📷 📷 📷
This elegant church was built in 1730 by Franciscan monks, but it was taken from them in 1848 in order for it to be used as a parish church. In 1895 the authorities transformed the monastery into a garrison for the Spanish army. Then in 1930, because of the lamentable state of the place, the monastery and part of the church were demolished. Only the bell tower was salvaged, along with adjacent buildings, which were used as a school until 1984, when the complex became the home of the **Museo de la Lucha contra Bandidos**.

The museum illustrates with documents, photographs and exhibits the struggle against the "bandits", the counter-revolutionaries who fled to the Sierra del Escambray after 1959. Fragments of a U2 plane, a boat, a militia truck and weapons are displayed in the former monastery's cloister.

The small Plazuela del Jigüe, with its handful of handicrafts stalls

Beyond Trinidad's Historic Centre

Away from the centre there are more interesting areas to explore. One spot to head for is Parque Céspedes, where locals, young and old, gather to listen and dance to live music in the evenings. Or, walking eastwards, lively Plaza Santa Ana draws people at all times of day. From the hill north of Plaza Mayor there are marvellous views over the valley, especially beautiful at sunset.

The Cabildo de San Antonio, with votive offerings and sacred drums

Façade of Nuestra Señora de la Candelaria de la Popa hermitage

🔒 Ermita de Nuestra Señora de la Candelari de la Popa

This small 18th-century church on a hill north of the centre is connected to Plaza Mayor by a narrow, steep street. The striking three-arch bell tower loggia was added in 1812, when work was done to the church to repair the damage done by a violent cyclone. Despite deterioration, the church is still intact. Even though it is closed, it is worth a visit because the location is so beautiful.

Plaza Santa Ana

A short walk from Plaza Mayor, in the eastern part of the city, this square is dominated by the 18th-century Iglesia de Santa Ana. It was partly rebuilt in 1800, and the bell tower was added 12 years later. The now decaying church is flanked by a royal poinciana tree.

The square is a popular place to gather, thanks to the cultural centre in the former prison. Set around a lovely courtyard, the centre includes a restaurant, café and art gallery.

🏛 Cabildo de los Congos Reales de San Antonio

Calle Isidro Armenteros 168.

In the picturesque working-class quarter of El Calvario, in the northern part of Trinidad, is the Cabildo de los Congos Reales, a temple founded in 1859 for the worship of Afro-Cuban divinities. In the 1800s Cuba witnessed the rise of many *cabildos*, cultural centres differentiated by ethnic group which aimed to preserve the spiritual and musical heritage of the slaves. The Cabildo in Trinidad, dedicated to Oggún – a warrior god whose Catholic equivalent is St Anthony of Padua – is for the followers of the Palo Monte religion *(see p23)*.

Environs

on a rise 1 km (half a mile) northeast of the centre, near Hotel Las Cuevas (*see p266*) is the **Museo Espeleológico**, opened on 20 May 1999. Located inside a cave of 3,700 sq m (4,440 sq yds), it can be visited with an expert guide as far as the Salón de las Perlas, a smaller cave where water drops "fall like pearls". According to legend, an Indian girl called Cacubu took refuge (and died) here, escaping from the lecherous Spanish conquistador Porcallo de Figueroa. Karstic fossils from caves near Matanzas are also on show.

Iglesia de Santa Ana, on the square of the same name, in eastern Trinidad

Topes de Collantes ❷

The unspoilt landscape of the Sierra del Escambray *(see p173)*, where pine and eucalyptus grow alongside exuberant trees, ferns and tropical plants, offers extraordinarily beautiful scenery that can best be seen by hiking from Topes de Collantes, a steep 30-minute drive north of Trinidad. Here, two itineraries are suggested, indicated by a letter and colour. Itinerary A consists of a walk of average difficulty through the tropical forest as far as the Caburní falls. Itinerary B is longer but easier and less tiring, and includes a detour to the Batata cave.

TIPS FOR HIKERS

Departure points: *Topes de Collantes.* 🛈 *Hotel Los Helechos, (42) 540 330, 540 117.*
Length: *Itinerary A: 3.5 km (2 miles); Itinerary B: 4.5 km (3 miles).*
Stopping-off point: *Hacienda Codina*

KEY

━━ Major road
══ Path
-- Itinerary A
▪▪ Itinerary B
🅿 Parking
✚ Hospital

0 kilometres 1
0 miles 1

La Batata ⑤
This cave is traversed by an underground river, with natural pools at a temperature which never rises above 20° C (68° F).

Santa Clara Manicaragua

Hacienda Codina ④
The Codina farm has orchid and bamboo gardens, a pool with mud baths, and fine views. The route continuesfor 1 km (half amile) among medicinal plants.

Topes de Collantes ①
At 800 m (2,625 ft) above sea level and with good clean air, this spot was chosen as the location for a sanitarium for lung diseases, now used as an anti-stress centre.

Trinidad

Salto del Caburní ③
After a two-hour walk you will come to a cliff with a steep, plunging water-fall. Water gushes over rocks and collects further down, forming a pool where it is possible to bathe.

The Forest ②
The path leading to Salto del Caburní crosses untouched tropical forest with curious rock formations.

Secluded La Boca beach, shaded by royal poinciana trees

Península Ancón ❸

Road Map C3.

About 10 km (6 miles) south of Trinidad is one of the first coastal areas in Cuba to be developed for tourism, the peninsula of Ancón, where foreign visitors have been coming since 1980. The fine white sand and turquoise water (not as clear here as along the north coast, though) make this promontory a miniature Varadero, with hotels, bars, restaurants and water sports clubs. However, unlike Varadero, this area is visited by visitors and locals alike. Cubans head mainly for **La Boca**, 6 km (4 miles) from Trinidad, near the neck of the peninsula, especially on warm Sundays and in summer.

At **Playa Ancón**, 5 km (3 miles) of white sand in the southern part of the peninsula, there are comfortable hotels, a splendid beach and a diving school. From the beach by Hotel Ancón, assorted boat excursions are available to take divers to snorkelling sites out on the coral reef.

For some fascinating dive sites, divers should take an excursion to **Cayo Blanco**, 8 km (5 miles) off the coast. At the western tip of this small coral island with white sand beaches, is the largest black coral reef in Cuba, where divers can choose from a number of different dive sites. On the rocky coasts near **María Aguilar**, on the other hand, there are pools where swimmers only need a mask to easily spot a great variety of tropical fish.

As with Varadero (see pp162–3), bicycles can be hired and make a pleasant way of getting around the Ancón peninsula.

Opposite the peninsula, across the bay, is the old port of **Casilda**, 6 km (4 miles) from Trinidad, where in 1519 Hernán Cortés recruited the troops that went on to conquer Mexico.

Once a prosperous port thanks to the sugar trade, Casilda has long since declined, and is now above all a place that people pass through on their way to the local beaches.

Valle de los Ingenios ❹

Road Map C3.
Excursions from Trinidad 🛈 at railway station, (41) 993 348; Cubatur, Calle Simón Bolívar 352, (41) 996 368.

The bell on the Iznaga bell tower

Leaving Trinidad and heading northeast, along the road to Sancti Spíritus, one can appreciate the beauty of the fertile plain, with the green hills of the Sierra del Escambray forming a backdrop. Only 12 km (7 miles) separate Trinidad from the Valle de los Ingenios, whose name derives from the sugar mills (ingenios, see pp42–3) built here in the

Valle de los Ingenios, from the Mirador de la Loma: green swathes of sugar cane at the foot of the Sierra

The Iznaga estate tower, with a commanding view of the valley

survives and has been converted into a bar and restaurant. Also still standing are the *barracones* (slaves' huts), and a monumental seven-level tower 45 m (147 ft) high. Each level is different from the next in shape and decoration: the first three are square, the top four are octagonal. The symbolic meaning of this tower is apparent. It was built in 1830 as an assertion of authority over the valley by Alejo Iznaga, a rival to his brother Pedro, who was also a major landowner and sugar producer. The tower also functioned as a lookout for supervising the slaves.

The top of the tower, which is reached via a steep wooden stairway, today offers lovely, wide-ranging views of the surrounding countryside. At the foot of the tower is the bell that once tolled the work hours on the plantation.

There are other estate mansions to be seen in this area, including one at Guachinango, which was built in the late 18th century in a dominating position over the Río Ay.

The village of **San Pedro** is an example of the urban settlements that developed in association with the sugar plantations and works.

early 19th century. Today, fields of sugar cane form a blanket of green, interrupted only by towering royal palms.

The valley is rich in history with ruins providing evidence of the time when the sugar industry was at its peak. These buildings also help visitors to understand the social structure that was the order of the sugar plantations. The whole zone, which has a surface area of 270 sq km (104 sq miles), includes more than 70 old *ingenios*. UNESCO has declared the valley a World Heritage Site.

A good way to visit the area is to take the steam train which departs from Trinidad and covers the entire valley. One of the places accessible only to those with a car is the **Mirador de La Loma del Puerto** (6 km, 4 miles east of Trinidad, on the road to Sancti Spíritus). This observation point *(mirador)*, 192 m (630 ft) above sea level, offers a magnificent view of the whole valley. There is also an outdoor café where you can sample the drink *guara-po*, sugar cane juice.

However, the most impressive destination is the **Manaca Iznaga Estate**, where about 350 slaves lived in the 1840s. The landowner's house

SUGAR PRODUCTION IN CUBA

For centuries, sugar cane *(Saccharum officinarum)*, which was introduced to the island in 1512 by Spanish settlers, has been the mainstay of the Cuban economy. Sugar extraction takes place in various phases: after being washed, the cane stalks are pressed by special mills and the juice *(guarapo)* is extracted from the fibrous mass *(bagassa)*, which is used as fuel and as livestock fodder. The juice is treated chemically, filtered and then evaporated so as to obtain a concentration of dark syrup that is then heated. This produces crystals of sucrose. The syrupy mass then goes into a centrifuge. Other by-products are obtained from sugar cane, including molasses, a residue of the syrup, which still contains 50 per cent sugar and is used as the basic ingredient in the production of rum *(see p75)*.

Ripe cane *is from 2–5 m (6–16 ft) tall with a diameter of 2–6 cm (1–3 in). Once cut, the plant shoots again and becomes ripe again in a year. Newly planted cane, grown from cuttings 30–40 cm (12–16 in) long, ripens in 11–18 months.*

The zafra (harvest) *takes place between December and June. Before harvest begins, the cane field is burned to remove the outer leaves, which obstruct harvesting. In the plains cutting is done with machines, while in the hills the machete is still used.*

Transport *has to be rapid to minimize the deterioration of the sucrose in the heat. To this end, in the late 1800s a special railway network was built and steam trains travelled between the cane fields and the sugar works. Some are still running.*

Sancti Spíritus ❺

The city of Sancti Spíritus, deep in the heart of fertile agricultural countryside, was founded by Diego Velázquez on the banks of the Tuinucú river in 1514. It was moved to its present site, near the Yayabo river, eight years later. In 1586 British pirates set fire to the town along with all the documents relating to its foundation. The political, economic and military centre of the area, Sancti Spíritus was embellished with elegant mansions throughout the 17th and 18th centuries. Today, its small, attractive Colonial centre receives few visitors, despite its "national monument" status.

Statue of Christ beside the cathedral

🀫 Yayabo Bridge

Its medieval appearance and large terracotta arches make this bridge, built in 1825, unique in Cuba, and for this reason it has been declared a national monument. According to one bizarre legend, in order to make the bridge more robust, the workmen mixed cement with goat's milk.

The Yayabo bridge is an important part of the city's street network: it is the only route into town for those coming from Trinidad.

Exploring Sancti Spíritus

The central part of the city can be explored on foot in a few hours. It is pleasant to simply stroll along the recently restored streets (many of which are for pedestrians only), where brightly coloured Colonial houses with wrought-iron balconies are characteristic. The most famous approach to the town is the southern one, across the lovely old bridge over the Yayabo river. The narrow, quiet streets leading up from the bridge to the city centre are the oldest in Sancti Spíritus. They are paved with irregular cobblestones and lined with one-storey houses with shingle roofs.

Calle Máximo Gómez, which leads to the main square, Parque Serafín Sánchez, is lined with 18th- and 19th-century monuments, museums and mansions. These include the **Teatro**

The Yayabo Bridge, leading to the Colonial centre

Principal, a bright blue porticoed construction built in 1876 and restored in 1980; a large 19th-century mansion that is now the Pensamiento bar; the **Casa de la Trova**; a typical bar-restaurant, Mesón de la Plaza; and the Placita, a small square with a statue of Dr Rudesindo Antonio García Rijo, an illustrious citizen.

🏛 Museo de Arte Colonial

Calle Plácido 74. *Tel (41) 325 455.* ⬤
9:30am–5pm Tue–Sat, 8am–noon Sun. ⬤ *Mon.* 🖼 ✔ 📷 *(with charge).*
This fine 18th-century building once belonged to the Iznaga family *(see p193).* It is now a museum with crystal, porcelain, furniture, paintings (many of them Spanish), and a splendid courtyard.

Recently restored Colonial homes, with their original colours, in one of the streets near the river

For hotels and restaurants in this region see pp263–6 and p282

The interior of the Parroquial Mayor during mass

🏠 Parroquial Mayor del Espíritu Santo

Calle Agramonte Oeste 58.
***Tel** (41) 324 855.* ⬜ *9–11am Tue–Sat, 8–11am Sun.* 🕆 *8pm Tue & Thu, 5pm Wed & Fri, 10am Sun.*
Using money donated by Don Ignacio de Valdivia, the local mayor, the present church was built of stone in 1680, over the original 16th-century wooden church that had been destroyed by pirates. It is one of Cuba's oldest churches. The simple and solid building is reminiscent of the parish churches of Andalusia, and still has its original, exquisitely worked wooden ceilings. The 30-m (100-ft) bell tower, with three levels, was added in the 18th century, and the octagon-al Cristo de la Humildad y la Paciencia chapel, built next to the church in the 19th century, has a remarkable half-dome.

Parque Serafín Sánchez

The heart of the city consists of a tranquil square with trees and a charming *glorieta* (gazebo), surrounded by Neo-Classical buildings. A national monument, the Parque is dedicated to Serafín Sánchez, a local hero in the wars of independence, whose house is open to the public in the nearby Calle de Céspedes. In the evenings, the plaza is a popular gathering place.

The most notable buildings here are the Centro de Patrimonio, with broad stained-glass windows and Seville mosaics, the large **Biblioteca** (library), and the **Hotel Perla de Cuba**, one of the most exclusive hotels in Cuba in the early 1900s. The **Hotel Plaza**, whose bar is popular with the locals, forms part of a Colonial building.

VISITORS' CHECKLIST

Sancti Spíritus. **Road Map** C3.
🏯 *100,000.* 🚌 *Carretera Central, km 2.* 🚉 *Avenida Jesús Menéndez.* 🛈 *Cubatur, Calle Máximo Gómez 7, (41) 328 518.*

Environs

Around 8 km (5 miles) east of Sancti Spíritus, in the direction of Ciego de Ávila, nature lovers and fans of fishing can enjoy **Presa Zaza**, an artificial lake well stocked with trout and black bass. Tours of the lake depart from the Zaza hotel, while the shores are ideal spots for birdwatching. Presa Zaza is Cuba's largest man-made lake and is the venue for a major international fishing competition every September.

Chatting in the Parque Serafín Sánchez in the evening, a popular pastime

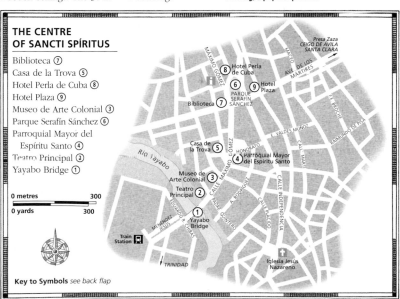

THE CENTRE OF SANCTI SPÍRITUS

Biblioteca ⑦
Casa de la Trova ⑤
Hotel Perla de Cuba ⑧
Hotel Plaza ⑨
Museo de Arte Colonial ③
Parque Serafín Sánchez ⑥
Parroquial Mayor del Espíritu Santo ④
Teatro Principal ②
Yayabo Bridge ①

0 metres   300
0 yards   300

Key to Symbols *see back flap*

Parque Martí in Ciego de Ávila, with a monument to José Martí

Ciego de Ávila ❻

Road Map D3. 🏘 *100,000.*
🚶 🚉 🚌 ℹ️ *Hotel Ciego de Ávila, Carretera a Ceballos, (33) 228 013.*

When Ciego de Avila was founded in 1538 by the conquistador Jácome de Ávila, it was just a large farm in the middle of a wood, a *ciego*. It only became a bona fide city in 1840. Today, it is a rural town with two-storey houses fronted with Neo-Classical columns, and streets filled with one-horse carriages.

The few visitors who come here are mostly on their way to the *cayos* in the Jardines del Rey archipelago.

Anyone who does stop off should visit the **Teatro Principal** (1927) and the **Museo Histórico Provincial**. This last has four rooms of documents and photographs concerning the history of the province, in particular the story of La Trocha. This line of defence was constructed in the 19th century. It was devised by the Spanish to block the advance of the Cuban nationalists *(mambises)* by cutting the island in half, from Morón, north of Ciego de Ávila, to Júcaro, on the Caribbean coast. Some surviving La Trocha towers, built about 1 km (0.6 mile) from one another, lie a short distance outside town and are open to the public.

One of La Trocha's redoubts

THE COCKEREL OF MORON

"Be careful not to end up like the cockerel of Morón, which lost its feathers as well as its crest". This Spanish saying dates back to the 1500s, when the governor of the Andalusian village of Morón de la Frontera, who lorded it over the local farmers and was known as "cockerel" *(gallo)* for his arrogance and presumptuousness, was punished with a good thrashing and thrown out of town by the angry citizens. The event became well known and to commemorate it, a statue of a plucked rooster was set up in the main avenue. When a community of Andalusians emigrated to Cuba in the 18th century and founded a city they called Morón, to maintain their traditions they put a statue of the rooster at the entrance to the town. It was taken down in 1959, and replaced in 1981 by a new bronze sculpture placed next to a tower. At 6am and 6pm daily, a recording of a cock crowing is played here.

The bronze statue (1981) of the legendary cockerel of Morón

The multi-ethnic character of the city means that visitors can enjoy both the rural festivals of Spanish origin *(parrandas)*, similar to those in Remedios *(see p177)*, and merengue and congo dance shows, especially in the quarter where Jamaican and Haitian immigrants live. Ciego de Ávila also has a cycling school which is attended by children from all over the island. At Epiphany the town is the starting point for the month-long Vuelta Internacional por la Paz, a cycle race much like the Tour de France.

Morón ❼

Ciego de Ávila. **Road Map** D3.
🏘 *45,000.* 🚌 ℹ️ *Cubanacán, Calle Colón 49, (33) 502 262/ 3.* 🗓
Cockerel of Morón: end of June.

Morón lies on the road that runs north from Ciego de Ávila (a town with a long-standing rivalry with Morón). The road is known for its occupation in 1896 by nationalist rebels *(mambises)* after they had managed to breach the Spanish defence.

Morón was founded as a villa in 1869 and retains a small, well-preserved Colonial centre. The **Museo Municipal** has more than 600 archaeological finds, brought to light

A street in Morón with pastel-coloured houses and arcades

Isla Turiguanó, the unusual "Dutch village" near Morón

in the 1940s a short distance from town, including a famous statuette, the Idolillo de Barro.

🏛 Museo Municipal
Calle Martí 374 e/ Antuña y Cervantes. *Tel (33) 504 501.*
◻ 8am–4pm Sun–Tue, 8am–9pm Wed–Sat. ● 1 Jan, 1 May, 26 Jul, 25 Dec. 🖼 🖪 🖾

Environs
North of Morón are two fresh-water lagoons: the **Laguna Redonda**, which owes it name to its almost circular form and is known for its great abundance of trout, and the **Laguna de Leche**. This latter is called the "Lagoon of Milk" because of its colour, caused by the limestone deposits in the water. It is the largest stretch of brackish water in Cuba, with a surface area of 67 sq km (26 sq miles). It abounds in carp and pike and is a refuge for herons and flamingos.

Immediately north of the Laguna de Leche is the **Isla Turiguanó**, a peninsula with a village of Dutch-style houses surrounded by grazing land for cattle. The animals are also Dutch, having been imported by Celia Sánchez (see p51).

Florencia, about 20 km (12 miles) west of Morón, is the starting point for hikes in the small **Sierra de Jatibonico**. This range can be explored on horse-back, along the route followed by Camilo Cienfuegos's column in 1958 (see p48).

The Canal Viejo de Bahamas is used for platform fishing for large tropical fish. There are also hunting reserves: the Coto de Caza de Morón and Coto de Caza Aguachales de Fala.

Jardines del Rey ❽

Ciego de Ávila, Camaguey.
Road Map D3.

In the Atlantic Ocean, north of the province of Ciego de Ávila, the Sabana and Camagüey archipelagoes, known collectively as "Jardines del Rey", include about 400 small islands, almost all of which are uninhabited.

The lighthouse at Cayo Paredón Grande

They were discovered in 1522 by the conquistador Diego Velázquez, who was so struck by them that he dedicated them to the king (rey), Carlos V. They later became a hiding place for pirates and, after the official abolition of slavery, a clandestine landing point for slaves.

A causeway 17 km (10 miles) long, built in 1988 as a link between the archipelago and mainland Cuba, makes it easy for visitors to get to the lovely beaches, the coral reef, and the holiday villages which are currently concentrated on Cayo Coco and Cayo Guillermo (see pp198–9). However, Cuban nationals themselves have limited access to the archipelago.

Cayo Paredón Grande, 6 km (4 miles) long, is the third largest island in the Jardines. Although there are no hotels, it is worth visiting for the lovely beaches, and the coral has some fine dive sites, too. There are good views of the distinctive black and yellow Diego Velázquez Lighthouse, built by Chinese immigrants in 1859.

Although part of the province of Camagüey, Cayo Romano belongs naturally to this archipelago. Its marshy coastline is the habitat of manatees.

The pristine white sandy beach of Cayo Paredón Grande, Jardines del Rey

Cayo Coco 9

A boat heading out to a coral reef

With 22 km (14 miles) of white sandy beaches and 370 sq km (143 sq miles) of partly marshy land abounding in mangroves and coconut palms, Cayo Coco is an important natural reserve for marine birds. Flamingos can be spotted easily in the lagoon areas near the coast. The name of the island derives from another rare species of bird that lives here: the white ibis, known to Cubans as the "coco". The island is peaceful, and tourist amenities have been built and organized with environmental concerns in mind. The beaches are lovely, with fine sand washed by clear turquoise water. The warm, shallow water makes Cayo Coco particularly suitable for families with children, but the island is also popular among diving and water sports enthusiasts, who can take advantage of the modern sports facilities here.

The *Coccothrinax litoralis* palm tree, common on Cayo Coco

Cayo Guillermo
Linked to Cayo Coco, this small island (13 sq km, 5 sq miles) is covered with mangroves and palms as well as mahogany, juniper and mastic trees. At Playa Pilar beach the dunes rise as high as 16 m (52 ft).

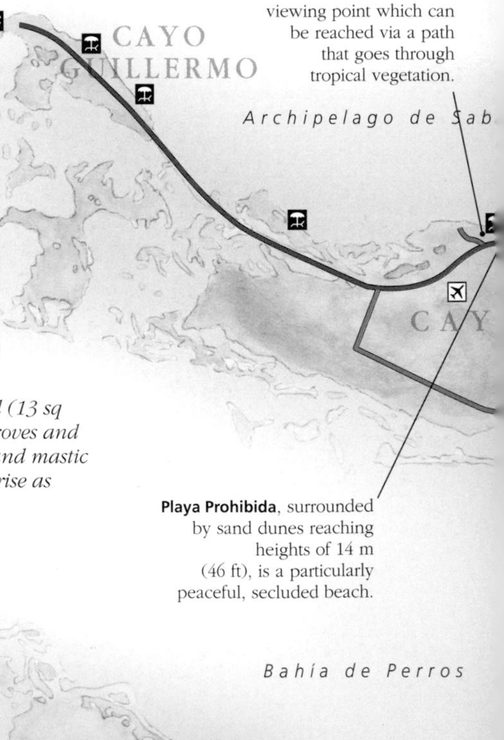

The Duna de la Loma del Puerto is a natural viewing point which can be reached via a path that goes through tropical vegetation.

Playa Prohibida, surrounded by sand dunes reaching heights of 14 m (46 ft), is a particularly peaceful, secluded beach.

KEY
- Major road
- Minor road
- Recommended beach
- Domestic airport

The Pedraplen
A major work of civil engineering, this causeway links the islands with the mainland. It has caused some concern to ecologists, since it blocks the tide and may disturb the ecosystem of the bay.

For hotels and restaurants in this region see pp263–6 and p282

★ Playa Flamencos
This beach, almost 3 km (2 miles) long, is regarded as one of the best on the island because of its lovely clear sea and fine sand. The shallow water is only knee-deep even 200 m (650 ft) from the shore.

Güira, a village founded in the early 1900s, still has its traditional houses. It is a starting point for horse riding excursions.

Cayo Paredón Grande *(see p197)*

Centro de Investigaciones de Ecosistemas Costeras

This centre for the environment studies the effects of tourism on local ecosystems. It is open to the public, and illustrates the bird species on the island, including the roseate spoonbill seen here.

Villa de los Trabajadores • Bautista

CAYO ROMANO

★ Parador La Silla
This is an ideal spot for viewing a spectacular array of pink flamingos, which flock here in great numbers during the wet season, from April to November, to breed.

STAR SIGHTS

★ Playa Flamencos

★ Parador La Silla

Camagüey ⑩

This city, declared a UNESCO World Heritage site in 2008, lies in the middle of a vast area of pastureland. It is nick-named "the Legendary" for its traditions of heroism and patriotism as well as for its Neo-Classical architecture. There is a large, rich Colonial-style historic centre and the city has an active cultural life. Founded in the bay of Nuevitas on the northern coast as Nuestra Señora de Santa María del Puerto Príncipe, the city was moved to the interior to escape from revolts by the Indians, who staunchly resisted Spanish domination in the 1500s, and from pirate attacks. The irregular, intricate street network that distinguishes Camagüey from other Cuban cities resulted from the need to protect itself from raids.

An example of 19th-century Neo-Classical architecture in Camagüey

Parque Agramonte: the equestrian statue and the Cathedral

1777 a bell tower was added, but it collapsed only a year later. Since that time, the church has been through several phases of reconstruction, taking on its present appearance in 1864. It now has a monumental façade surmounted by a pediment, and a bell tower on six levels, crowned by a statue of Christ.

Parque Ignacio Agramonte

The former Plaza de Armas is dominated by an equestrian statue of Agramonte, a Cuban independence hero, sculpted by the Italian artist Salvatore Boemi and inaugurated by Amalia Simoni, Agramonte's wife, in 1912. At the four corners of the small square stand royal palms, planted in memory of a group of nationalists executed here on 24 February 1851. As so often during the wars of independence, the palms were symbolic monuments to the rebels, as the Spanish would never have allowed real monuments to be built.

Buildings of interest on the square include the Palacio Collado (1942), Bar El Cambio, opened in 1909, a Colonial building housing La Volanta restaurant, the **Casa de la Trova Patricio Ballagas** in an 18th-century building with a courtyard, the Biblioteca Julio Antonio Mella and the cathedral. With its benches and shade

from the palm trees, the square is a natural gathering point for the people of Camagüey. During the day old people gather to watch life go by, and in the evenings the young are drawn to the square.

It is also a popular spot for tourists to see the town's famous *tinajones* up close.

🔒 Catedral de Nuestra Señora de la Candelaria

Calle Independencia 168, Parque Agramonte. **Tel** *(32) 294 965.* ◯ *8–11am & 2–5, 7–9pm Mon–Fri, 3–4:30pm Sat, 8–11am Sun.* 🔒 *8pm Mon–Fri, 9am Sun.*
Camagüey's cathedral, dedicated to Our Lady of Candelaria, the patron saint of the city, was designed by Manuel Saldaña and built in 1735. In

0 metres   250
0 yards   250

THE CENTRE OF CAMAGÜEY

Key to Symbols *see back flap*

The courtyard at Casa Agramonte, where concerts are performed

🏛 Casa Natal de Ignacio Agramonte

Calle Ignacio Agramonte 459,
e/ Independencia y Cisneros.
Tel *(32) 297 116.* ⟳ *9am–7:30pm Tue–Sat, 8:30am–noon Sun.*
🌣 *1 Jan, 1 May, 26 Jul, 25 Dec.*
📷 ▶ 📷 *(with charge).*

Near Plaza de los Trabajadores, where a large ceiba tree marks the middle of the old town, is the former home of Ignacio Agramonte. This famous local patriot died in battle in 1873 at the age of 31. The two-storey house dates from 1750 and has a beautiful inner courtyard with old *tinajones*.

The museum has documents concerning the war of independence, the hero's personal belongings, such as his 36-calibre Colt revolver from 1851, and family furniture, including the piano of his wife, Amalia Simoni, reputed to be one of the richest, loveliest, most virtuous women in the city.

A short walk away is another famous home. The **Casa Natal de Nicolás Guillén** *(see p28)*, birthplace of Cuba's poet laureate who died in 1989, is at Calle Hermanos Aguero 58.

Plaque on Nicolás Guillén's birthplace

VISITORS' CHECKLIST

Camagüey. **Road map** D3.
🏠 *300,000.* ✈ *Ignacio Agramonte, (32) 261 010.* 🚌
Ave Avellaneda y Finlay, (32) 288 744. 🚍 *Carretera Central km 3, (32) 270 394.* 🛈 *Islazul, Calle Ignacio Agramonte 448, (32) 292 550.* 🎭 *Jornadas de la Cultura Camagüeyana (first half of Feb); Carnival (26 Jul).*

🔒 Iglesia de la Merced

Plaza de los Trabajadores 4.
Tel *(32) 292 783.* ⟳ *8–11am, 3:30–6:30pm daily.* 🛈 *5pm Mon–Sat, 9am & 6pm Sun.*

The Iglesia de la Merced was built in 1601 but was rebuilt from 1748 to 1756, and now has a Baroque façade with a central bell tower. Inside are striking, almost Art Nouveau-style murals. The choir and catacombs are also of interest. Most famous, however, is the Holy Sepulchre with an 18th-century statue of Christ by the Mexican sculptor Juan Benítez Alfonso. It was cast from 23,000 silver coins collected from the faithful by Manuel Agüero, a citizen who, after his wife's death in 1726, became a monk in the Mercedarios order and devoted himself to restoring the church.

🎭 Teatro Principal

Calle Pedro Valencia 64.
Tel *(32) 293 048.*

First opened in 1850 and rebuilt in 1926 after a devastating fire, the local theatre is famous as the home of the Camagüey Ballet, one of the leading dance companies in Latin America *(see p288).*

THE *TINAJONES*

These symbols of the city can be seen everywhere – in parks and gardens and especially in the courtyards of the local Colonial houses. *Tinajones* are large jars, which may be as much as 2 m (6 ft) tall, made of clay from the nearby Sierra de Cubitas. The jars were introduced by Catalonian immigrants in the early 1700s, and are used today to collect rainwater and to store food.

A *tinajón* in the central square

Exploring Camagüey

The vast historic centre of Camagüey, a complex 16th-century labyrinth of winding alleyways, dead ends, forks and squares, is not easy to navigate. The centre consists mainly of two-storey houses without arcades, pierced by large windows protected by wooden grilles. Each house has an inner courtyard. There are numerous old churches, most of them well attended, whose bell towers jut above the red tile roofs of the Colonial houses. As with Trinidad, the well-preserved architecture is the result of the town's geographic isolation: the railway line only arrived in 1903, and the Carretera Central road in 1931.

The Cinco Esquinas (Five Corners), one of the town's more complicated junctions

Other City Centre Sights

Many interesting sights are just a short walk away from Parque Ignacio Agramonte.

Calle Martí runs west from the square up to Plazuela de la Bedoya, a delightful Colonial square in need of restoration. An old Ursuline convent stands here, as well as a church, the **Iglesia del Carmen**. Although not completed until 1825, it has a distinctly Baroque character.

Calle Cristo leads to Plazuela del Cristo, which is dominated by the Iglesia del Santo Cristo del Buen Viaje and the Cementerio General

Author Gertrudis Gómez de Avellaneda

(1814), the oldest cemetery in Cuba. Back near Parque Agramonte, there is a complex interchange, the **Cinco Esquinas** (five corners), near the top of Calle Raúl Lamar, which is a good example of the intricate layout of the city centre.

Another route to explore runs along or near Calle República, a narrow, straight street that crosses the entire city from north to south. At the northern end, beyond the railway line, is the Museo Provincial Ignacio Agramonte *(see p203)*.

Further south, a right turn at the Hotel Colón leads eastwards across to Calle Avellaneda. Here, at No. 22, is the birthplace of Gertrudis Gómez de Avellaneda, the 19th-century author of anti-slavery novels.

Further south stands the **Iglesia de Nuestra Señora de la Soledad**, built in 1776. It was here that local patriot Ignacio Agramonte was baptized and also got married. The façade features pilasters and moulding typical of early Cuban Baroque architecture, but the real attractions here are the decoratively painted arches and pillars and the wooden *alfarje* ceiling *(see p227)* inside.

By going south to the far end of this street you will reach Calle Martí, which will take you back to Parque Agramonte.

Plaza San Juan de Dios

This square is commonly called Plaza del Padre Olallo, in honour of a priest who is soon to be canonized because he dedicated his life to caring for the sick in the city hospital.

Today, the totally restored Plaza San Juan de Dios is a quiet, picturesque spot, but also a gem of Colonial architecture. Around it are 18th-century pastel buildings, two of which have been converted into restaurants. One whole side of the plaza is occupied by an important group of buildings that include a church and an old hospital, which is now the home of the Dirección

Plazuela de la Bedoya, dominated by the Iglesia del Carmen

Provincial de Patrimonio and the Oficina del Historiador de la Ciudad, a body that takes care of the province's cultural heritage. Construction of the building began in 1728.

Despite its small size, the **Iglesia de San Juan de Dios** is one of the most interesting churches in Camagüey. It still has its original floors, ceiling and wooden choir, and, most importantly, the high altar with the Holy Trinity and an anthropomorphic representation of the Holy Ghost, the only one in Cuba. The church façade is simple and rigorously symmetrical.

The old **Hospital** was used in the 20th century as a military infirmary, then a teacher training school, a refuge for flood victims, a centre for underprivileged children and, most recently, as the Instituto Tecnológico de la Salud (Technological Institute of Health). The square plan with two inner courtyards (clearly of *mudéjar* influence) was modelled on Baroque monasteries. The enclosure walls are thick and plain; in contrast the window grilles and wooden balustrades in the galleries are elegant and elaborate.

One of the cloisters in the old San Juan de Dios hospital

🏛 Museo Provincial Ignacio Agramonte
Avenida de los Mártires 2, esq. Ignacio Sánchez. **Tel** *(32) 282 425.* ◑ *closed for restoration until late 2009.* 📷 ✦ 📷 *(with charge).*

The only military building in town was the headquarters of the Spanish army cavalry in the 19th century. In 1905 it became a hotel, and since 1948 it has housed a large museum of the history, natural history and art of the city and its province. The prestigious art collection is second only to that in the Museo de Bellas Artes in Havana, and has three works by the famous Cuban artist Fidelio Ponce.

The museum also has an exceptional collection of books, including some manuscripts by the Canaries writer Silvestre de Balboa, author of

The Holy Trinity high altar

🛐 Iglesia y Hospital de San Juan de Dios
Plaza San Juan de Dios. ◑ *daily.* ◑ *1 Jan, 1 May, 26 Jul, 25 Dec.* 📷 ✦ 📷

Espejo de Paciencia, a poem (1608) regarded as the first literary work in Cuba *(see p28).*

🌿 Parque Casino Campestre
The largest natural park in any Cuban city, the Casino was for a long time used for agricultural fairs, and became a public park in the 19th century. The Hatibonico river flows through it. Besides the many statues of patriots and illustrious figures from Camagüey and Cuba, it has a monument to the Seville pilots Barberán and Collar, who on 10 June 1933 made a historic transatlantic flight from Seville to Camagüey in 19 hours 11 minutes.

Environs
The plains north of Camagüey are cattle country. **King Rancho**, a former cattle ranch, has a restaurant and rooms and offers horse-riding trips and rodeos. King Ranch is most easily accessed from Santa Lucia, 26 miles (16 km) to the north.

Plaza San Juan de Dios, known for its well-preserved Colonial architecture

A country road north of Camagüey, leading to Sierra de Cubitas

Sierra de Cubitas ⑪

Camagüey. **Map** D3.

The range of hills that lies 40 km (25 miles) north of Camagüey forms the largest local reserve of flora and fauna, with over 300 plant species. To date, however, this area has no tourist facilities on any scale.

The main attractions are caverns such as Hoyo de Bonet, the largest karst depression in Cuba, and the Pichardo and María Teresa grottoes, where cave drawings have been discovered. Expert speleologists, on the other hand, can visit the Cueva de Rolando, a cave 132 m (435 ft) long with a subterranean lake 50 m (165 ft) across, the bottom of which has not yet been explored.

In the neighbouring Valle del Río Máximo is the **Paso de los Paredones**, a long, deep ravine with holes caused by water erosion, some as much as 100 m (328 ft) deep and up to 1 km (0.6 mile) wide. The thick vegetation, through which sunlight penetrates for only a few hours, is home to a variety of native birds *(tocororo and cartacuba; see pp20–21)* and migratory birds, as well as harmless reptiles and rodents.

Playa Santa Lucía ⑫

Camagüey. **Map** D3. 🛈 *Cubatur, Ave. Turística, Playa Santa Lucía, (32) 336 291 or (32) 365 303.*

The most famous beach resort in the province offers 21 km (13 miles) of fine white sand lapped by turquoise waves. The large coral reef only 3 km (2 miles) from the shore is a scuba diver's paradise *(see p293)*. It shelters the coast from the currents of the Canal Viejo de Bahamas, thus safeguarding calm swimming conditions for adults and children alike, as well as creating a good area for practising all water

sports. There are more than 30 dive sites along the reef, which can be reached with the help of the international diving centres, while Virgen de Altagracia and Shark's Point offer dives full of romance, exploring the wrecks of pirate and Spanish vessels. For the brave there is also the chance to observe a special type of shark, the *Carcharinus leucas*, which is fed and trained and so can be viewed at close range.

At the bay of Nuevitas, 6 km (4 miles) west of Santa Lucía, near the tiny seashore village of La Boca, is **Playa Los Cocos**. This lovely unspoilt beach has fine white sand and clear water, and is a must for visitors to Santa Lucía.

A beach at Cayo Sabinal, accessible by car or catamaran

Cayo Sabinal ⑬

Camagüey. **Map** D3. 🚢

Together with Cayo Romano and Cayo Guajaba, this small island forms part of a protected area. It is the home of deer and the largest colony of flamingos in Cuba, as well as a nesting area for four

The pier at Playa Santa Lucía, departure point for boats going out to the coral reef

◁ **Playa Los Cocos, near Playa Santa Lucía**

species of sea turtle. Cayo Sabinal can be reached either via a causeway or by catamaran from Playa Santa Lucía.

In the past Cayo Sabinal was home to permanent residents: first the natives, then pirates and Spanish coalmen. Today, the key is visited mostly for its three beautiful beaches, Playa Bonita, Playa Los Pinos and Playa Brava.The Colón Lighthouse dates from 1894.

South of Cayo Sabinal is the Bay of Nuevitas, where the city of Camagüey was first founded. The three small islands in the bay, known as **Los Ballenatos**, are popular destinations for boat trips.

Las Tunas ⑭

Las Tunas. **Map** E3.
🏛 *100,000.* ✈ 🚌 🚐
🏨 *Hotel Las Tunas, Ave. 2 de diciembre, (31) 345 014.* 🎭 *Jornada Nacional Cucalambeana (end of Jun).*

Until 1975, Las Tunas was just one of the cities in the old Provincia de Oriente. Then administrative reform made it the capital of an autonomous province. The town was founded on the site of two native villages that were razed to the ground by the *conquistador* Alonso de Ojeda in the early 1500s. However, the town only really began to develop three centuries later, progressively taking on the character of a

frontier town between central and eastern Cuba and an obligatory transit point for anyone going to Santiago. The historic centre has some Colonial buildings but no major monuments of note. However, the city does have many artists' studios.

The **Museo Histórico Provincial**, in the town hall, has archaeological finds and documents relating to the history of the province. The Memorial a los Mártires de Barbados commemorates a terrorist act against Cuba carried out in 1976: a bomb exploded on a Cubana aeroplane headed for Havana, killing 73 passengers and the entire crew.

Every year Las Tunas springs to life on the occasion of the Jornada Nacional Cucalambeana, dedicated to Juan Cristóbal Nápoles Fajardo, known as El Cucalambé, a farmer and poet born here in 1829. Local and other Cuban artists, as well as foreign scholars, take part in this festival of music and folk traditions.

Environs
Near Las Tunas are many sites linked with the wars of independence.They include the **Fuerte de la Loma**, now a national monument, built by

The town hall of Las Tunas

the Spanish to halt the advance of the Mambí, and the city of **Puerto Padre**, the scene of major battles in the Ten Years' War (1868–78).

The best beach here is **Playa Covarrubias**, near Puerto Padre, on the Atlantic coast.

Jardines de la Reina ⑮

Ciego de Ávila, Camagüey. **Map** D4.
🚢 *Júcaro, Embarcadero Avalón, (33) 398 104 (may be closed due to hurricane damage, phone to check).*

This archipelago in the Caribbean Sea was discovered by Christopher Columbus and called Jardines de la Reina in honour of the queen *(reina),* Isabel of Castile. Currently, these islands can be reached by boat from the pleasant fishing village of Júcaro.

The great number of unspoilt *cayos*, the secluded pristine beaches, mangroves and palm groves with rich fauna consisting of crocodiles, iguanas, turtles and tropical birds, and a 200-km (125-mile) coral reef make this archipelago a paradise for nature lovers.

Near Cayo Anclita, only about 100 m (328 ft) from the coast, is a floating hotel reserved for fishermen, divers and photographers. The waters abound with groupers, snappers, barracudas and sharks, among many other fish. Traditional tours usually take place in daytime, departing from Cayo Blanco, an hour from the coast. Navigating the entire archipelago takes about 3 hours.

A scuba diver grasping a barracuda

EASTERN CUBA

GRANMA · HOLGUIN · SANTIAGO DE CUBA · GUANTANAMO

Cubans refer to the eastern part of Cuba as the Oriente, giving it an exotic, magical appeal. The landscape, stretching out towards Haiti and other Caribbean islands, is varied, with majestic mountains, magnificent coastlines and an area of arid desert, unusual in Cuba. The eastern cities, often rich in history, include Santiago de Cuba, host to one of Latin America's most famous carnivals.

From the 17th to the 19th centuries, thousands of black slaves were brought to Cuba from Africa, men and women who became the ancestors of the multi-ethnic mix visible in Eastern Cuba today, part African, but also part Spanish, part French and Chinese. In this cultural melting pot, African and European, Catholic and pagan traditions are blended, sometimes inextricably.

The area is full of apparent contradictions: there is the combative Oriente, rebellious and indomitable; and yet there is also the laid-back Oriente, an oasis of pleasure, and the sonorous Oriente, the cradle of great musicians. It is true that the people of Eastern Cuba have always fought with great fervour. One eloquent example is the Indian chief Hatuey, who was burned at the stake in the 16th century for organizing resistance against the Spanish. Then, in the 19th century, local nationalists led the wars of independence. The citizens of Bayamo even burned down their town rather than hand it over to the enemy. In the 20th century, there were the *rebeldes* (many of whom were from Eastern Cuba, including Fidel Castro himself), who launched the struggle against Batista's dictatorship by attacking the Moncada barracks in Santiago.

Yet the people of eastern Cuba also know how to have a good time, adore music, rhythm and dance of all kinds, and each year put on a colourful Carnival at Santiago de Cuba which rivals that of Rio de Janeiro, and is one of the most celebrated in Latin America.

Cacti growing along the Costa Sur, the only arid zone on the island, east of Guantánamo

◁ The steps on Calle Padre Pico, in the heart of Santiago de Cuba

Exploring Eastern Cuba

The classic starting point for touring the eastern
provinces is Santiago de Cuba, a city rich in history,
with lovely Colonial architecture and sites associated
with the revolution. To the west rises the majestic
Sierra Maestra, also with its own associations with the
guerrilla war of the 1950s. The Sierra is most easily
reached, in fact, from the north, near Bayamo. To the
east, the Parque Baconao has all kinds of attractions,
ideal for families with children, while more
adventurous souls can head further east, to the
province of Guantánamo, famous for its US naval
base, and Baracoa, Cuba's oldest city. The province
of Holguín, further north, has some fine beaches,
and Cuba's most interesting archaeological site.

The small islands of Bahía de
Naranjo, now a holiday village

SEE ALSO

- **Where to Stay** pp266–9
- **Where to Eat** p283

A group of musicians improvising a concert
in Parque Céspedes, Santiago de Cuba

KEY

- ▬▬ Motorway
- ── Major road
- ┈┈ Minor road
- ── Scenic route
- ┅┅ Main railway
- ▬▬ International border
- ── Regional border
- △ Summit

SIGHTS AT A GLANCE

The *azulejos* decoration in the
Colonia Española in Manzanillo

❹ GUARDALAVACA
❺ CHORRO DE MAITA
🏛 ❻ BANES
Antilla   El Ramón
Bahía de Nipe
Guatemala   ❽ CAYO SAETÍA
Playa Corinthia
Guaro   ❼ MAYARÍ
Pinares de Mayarí   *Sierra de Cristal*
Mensura   Mayarí Arriba
Sagua de Tánamo
Moa
Cupey
Caimanes Abajo
Chamarreta
Arroyo Bueno
Playa Maguaná
La Quijada   Felicidad
RÍO TOA ㉒   BARACOA
EL YUNQUE ㉑   ⓴
BOCA DE ㉓ YUMURÍ
La Ayúa   La Prueba
Zoológico de Piedra
GUANTÁNAMO
La Prueba   Carrera Larga
Jamaica
Maisí   *Punta Maisí*
Sabanilla
E CUBA
San Luis
Sierra del Purial
Puriales de Caujerí
Pico del Gato 1176
⓳ LA FAROLA
La Maya
⓱ GUANTÁNAMO
Cajobabo
Vilorio
San Antonio del Sur
Imías
SANTIAGO DE CUBA
⓲
⓮ 🏛
Caimanera
COSTA SUR
CASTILLO DEL MORRO
❺ ✈ Siboney   ⓰ PARQUE BACONAO
Tortuguilla
Guantánamo Naval Base (U.S.A.)
Mirador Los Malones
Sigua

GETTING AROUND

Although sights on the outskirts of Santiago can be reached by bus or taxi, by far the best way to get around Eastern Cuba is to hire a car. Some journeys are among the most picturesque in Cuba, especially the drive to Baracoa via "La Farola" *(see p239)*. Another option would be to fly to the main eastern towns. Various organized tours are also available, starting off from Santiago or from the beach resorts of Holguín province, especially Guardalavaca. These tours can be booked through travel agencies.

A perfectly restored Neo-Classical building
in the centre of Baracoa

Holguín ❶

Called the city of parks because of its many leafy squares, Holguín is a modern town built on a grid layout and situated between two hills, Cerro de Mayabe and Loma de la Cruz. The people of Holguín took an active part in the wars of independence under the leadership of Calixto García, the famous general who liberated the city from the Spanish in 1872. The house he was born in is now a museum; the square named after him marks the centre of the city and is dominated by a statue of the heroic general.

A peanut vendor in Parque García

San Isidoro Cathedral, in the spacious Parque Peralta

Exploring Holguín

Calle Maceo and Manduley – two parallel streets with shops, hotels, bars and clubs, including the Casa de la Trova – cross three squares: **Parque San José**, **Parque Calixto García** and **Parque Peralta**. Parque García, always buzzing with people, is the site of the town's chief monuments and museums including **Casa Natal de Calixto García**.

🏛 La Periquera (Museo Provincial de Historia)

Calle Frexes 198, e/ Manduley y Maceo. **Tel** (24) 463 395. ◯ 8am–4:30pm Tue–Sat, 9am–noon Sun. ● 1 Jan, 1 May, 26 Jul, 10 Oct, 25 Dec. 📷 📹 📷 (with charge).

This large Neo-Classical building with a court-yard overlooks Parque Calixto García. It was built in 1860 as a ballroom and casino for the local upper middle class. In 1868, at the beginning of the Ten Years' War *(see p44)*, the building was occupied by the Spanish army and converted into a barracks. Hence the building's nickname, *La Periquera*, which translates as "parrot cage", a reference to the brightly coloured uniforms of the Spanish army.

Today, the building is the home of the Museo Provincial de Historia, where five rooms illustrate the main stages of the cultural development of Holguín. Also on display are archaeological relics of the Taíno Indians, who lived here from the 8th to the 15th centuries. The most famous item in the collection is the Hacha de Holguín, a stone axe head carved as a human figure. It was discovered in the hills around Holguín, and has become the symbol of the city.

Hacha de Holguín

🏛 Museo de Historia Natural Carlos de la Torre y Huerta

Calle Maceo 129, e/ Martí y Luz Caballero. **Tel** (24) 423 935. ● closed for restoration until late 2009. 📷 📹 📷

One of the most interesting natural history museums in Cuba has 11 collections with many specimens of Cuban and Caribbean flora and fauna. There is an outstanding collection of birds and shells, including *Polymita* snails from the beaches of Baracoa *(see p245)*, and a 50 million year-old fossil fish, found in a quarry in the Sierra Maestra.

🏠 Catedral de San Isidoro

Calle Manduley, e/ Luz Caballero y Aricoches, Parque Peralta. **Tel** (24) 422 107 (may be closed due to hurricane damage, phone to check). ◯ 2:30–6:30pm Mon, 7am– noon & 2:30–6pm Tue–Sun. ✝ daily.

Consecrated as a cathedral in 1979, San Isidoro was built in 1720 on the site of the first mass held to celebrate the city's founding: Parque Peralta. It is also known as Parque de Flores because a flower market used to be held here.

The church contains a copy of the popular Madonna of Caridad, the original of which is in the Basilica del Cobre near Santiago de Cuba *(see p221)*. On 4 April there is a celebration in honour of the Virgin.

Loma de la Cruz

There are marvellous, far-reaching views from the top of the Loma de la Cruz (Hill of the Cross). The engineers who founded Holguín used this site to plan the layout of the town, but it was only much later (from 1927–50) that the 458-step stairway was built to the top. Every year on 3 May, the people of Holguín

Parque Calixto García, with La Periquera; behind, the Loma de la Cruz

For hotels and restaurants in this region see pp266–9 and p283

A panoramic view of Holguín from the top of the Loma de la Cruz

VISITORS' CHECKLIST

Holguín. **Road Map** E4.
🏠 200,000. ✈ 13 km (8 miles)
south. 🚌 Calle V Pita, (24) 422
331. 🚌 Carretera Central y
Independencia, (24) 422 111.
ℹ Cubatur, Guardalavaca, (24)
430 170, 430 171. 🎭 Romerías
de Mayo (3 May).

climb up the hill for the
Romerías de Mayo, a celebration of Spanish origin. The
top of Loma, about 3 km (2
miles) northwest of Parque
Calixto García, is marked by a
Spanish lookout tower and by
a cross placed there on 3 May
1790 by friar Antonio Alegría.

Plaza de la Revolución
Situated east of the city centre,
behind Hotel Pernik, this
vast square contains a
monument to the heroes of
Cuban independence, the
mausoleum of Calixto García
and a small monument to his
mother. The square is the
main venue for political rallies
and popular festivities.

Environs
Another, more distant viewing
point over the city is the
Mirador de Mayabe on the
Cerro de Mayabe, which is
about 10 km (6 miles)
southeast of the city centre.

From the mirador there is a
view of the valley with its
fruit orchards and of Holguín
in the distance. This spot is
also home to an *aldea
campesina* (country village),
with simple lodgings and a
restaurant, as well as an
open-air museum. This
illustrates the lives of Cuban
farmers living in a small
village, with various examples
of a *bohío real*, a typical rural
home with a palm-leaf roof

and earth floor, a hen-house
and a courtyard containing
jars for transporting water.

At No. 301 on the road
leading to Gibara, a mile or
so north of the centre, is the
small **Fábrica de Órganos**,
the only factory in Cuba that
manufactures mechanical
organs. The factory is open
to the public.

A mechanical organ made
in the Holguín factory

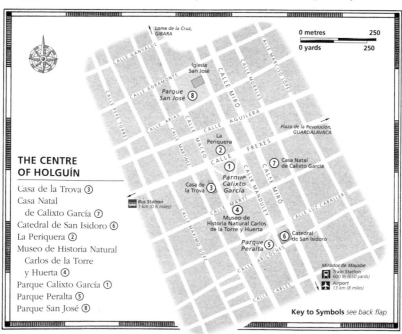

**THE CENTRE
OF HOLGUÍN**

Casa de la Trova ③
Casa Natal
   de Calixto García ⑦
Catedral de San Isidoro ⑥
La Periquera ②
Museo de Historia Natural
   Carlos de la Torre
   y Huerta ④
Parque Calixto García ①
Parque Peralta ⑤
Parque San José ⑧

0 metres 250
0 yards 250

Key to Symbols *see back flap*

View of Gibara, an appealing seaside town with a Colonial centre

Gibara ❷

Holguín. **Road Map** E3.
🏠 *100,000.* 🚌 *from Holguín.*

South of the bay that Columbus named Río de Mares (the river of seas) is the picturesque town of Gibara. In the 19th century this was the main port on the northern coast of the province of Oriente, and it has the most important Colonial architecture in the area. Gibara is sometimes known as "Villa Blanca" (white town) because of its white houses.

The shady Malecón (seafront) has a statue of Columbus shown gazing at the horizon, a ruined garrison and views of the small fishing harbour. From here, narrow streets lead to the main square, overlooked by the **Iglesia de San Fulgencio** (1854), and an old theatre. The **Museo de Ciencias Naturales** (Natural

Façade of the Iglesia de San Fulgencio at Gibara

History Museum) has one of the best butterfly collections in Cuba, and the **Museo de Artes Decorativas** (Decorative Arts Museum) is housed in a magnificent 19th-century mansion. This last contains fine examples of *mediopuntos (see p25)* and *mamparas (see p188)* as well as Cuban furniture and Art Nouveau objects.

🏛 Museo de Ciencias Naturales
Calle Maceo 131, e/ Martí y Luz Caballero. **Tel** (24) 423 935. ⏰ 8:30am–5pm Mon–Fri. ⬤ 1 Jan, 1 May, 26 Jul, 10 Oct, 25 Dec. 📷 🎫 📷 (with charge).

🏛 Museo de Artes Decorativas
Calle Independencia 19. **Tel** (24) 34407. ⏰ 9am–noon & 1–5pm Mon–Sat, 8am–noon Sun. 📷 🎫 📷 (with charge).

Bahía de Bariay ❸

Holguín. **Road Map** E3.

East of Gibara is a bay with a spit of land in the middle called Cayo de Bariay. Most historians (but not Baracoans, *see p242*) agree that Columbus first landed here in 1492. With its abundant flowers and trees laden with fruit, it looked like paradise to the explorer. In 1992, on the 500th anniversary of Columbus' landing in Cuba, a monument called *Encuentro* ("Encounter"), dedicated to the Taíno Indians, was erected here. The site is relatively remote if travelling by car, but boat trips can be arranged from Guardalavaca (*see p215*). East of Cayo de Bariay is the beautiful **Playa Don Lino**.

COLUMBUS IN CUBA

On 28 October 1492, when he first set foot on Cuban land, Columbus wrote in his travel journal: "I have never seen a more beautiful place. Along the banks of the river were trees I have never seen at home, with flowers and fruit of the most diverse kinds, among the branches of which one heard the delightful chirping of birds. There were a great number of palms. When I descended from the launch, I approached two

Christopher Columbus, explorer of the New World

fishermen's huts. Upon seeing me, the natives took fright and fled. Back on the boat, I went up the river for a good distance. I felt such joy upon seeing these flowery gardens and green forests and hearing the birds sing that I could not tear myself away, and thus continued my trip. This island is truly the most beautiful land human eyes have ever beheld."

Guardalavaca ❹

Holguín. **Road Map** F3.

Converted in the mid-1980s into a holiday resort, the beach of Guardalavaca is the most popular holiday destination in Cuba after Varadero *(see pp162–3)*. Although the resort is within easy reach of Holguín, 58 km (35 miles) to the southwest along a road through curious conical hills, the location still feels remote.

The 4-km (2-mile) crescent-shaped beach, enclosed at either end by rocks, is backed by abundant vegetation. The sea is crystal-clear, the sand is fine, and there is a coral reef quite close to the shore. Behind the beach is a modern tourist resort with the usual holiday facilities.

The name "Guardalavaca" (watch the cow) derives from the Spanish word for the cattle egret *(see p20)*, a bird which is common throughout Cuba, and especially prevalent here.

West of the beach is **Bahía de Naranjo**, a natural park that comprises 32 km (20 miles) of coastline and 1,000 ha (2,470 acres) of woods, with karst hills covered with thick vegetation. There are three small islands in the bay; on one, Cayo Naranjo, there is an aquarium featuring shows with sea lions and dolphins. Boat tours, diving and fishing trips are also organized here.

Skeletons found in the necropolis of Chorro de Maita

Chorro de Maita ❺

Cerro de Yaguajay, Banes (Holguín). **Road Map** F4.
⬜ *Tue–Sat.* ⬤ *1 Jan, 1 May, 26 Jul, 10 Oct, 25 Dec.* 📷 🎟 📷

Near the coast, just 5 km (3 miles) south of Guardalavaca, is Chorro de Maita, the largest native Indian necropolis in Cuba and the Antilles. At this unmissable site archaeologists have found 56 skeletons and a number of clay objects, bone amulets, funerary offerings and decorated shells.

All this material can be seen from a boardwalk inside the *aldea taína*, a reconstruction of a pre-Columbian rural village, built for entertainment, but historically accurate. Visitors can buy souvenirs and sample the food that the Amer-indians themselves used to eat. In front of the huts are some life-size statues of natives.

Banes ❻

Holguín. **Road Map** F4.

This country town, 32 km (20 m) southwest of Holguín, is located in the middle of a vast and rich excavation zone (the province of Holguín has yielded one-third of all archaeological finds in Cuba). Banes is the home of the **Museo Indocubano Bani**, Cuba's most important archaeological museum outside Havana. The museum has over a thousand objects on display, including axes, terracotta vases, flint knives and, most notably, a 4-cm (2-in) high figure of a woman in gold, known as the Idolo de Oro. It was found near Banes, and dates from the 13th century.

Ídolo de Oro, Museo Indocubano Bani

🏛 **Museo Indocubano Bani**
Calle General Barrero 305, e/ Martí y Céspedes. **Tel** (24) 802 487.
⬜ *9am–5pm Tue–Sat, 8am–noon Sun.* 📷 🎟 📷 *(with charge).*

The lovely clear turquoise sea at Guardalavaca, Eastern Cuba's Varadero

The coves at Cayo Saetía, known for their fine white sand

Mayarí **⑦**

Holguín. **Road Map** F4.
🏘 30,000.

Mayarí, 100 km (62 miles) southeast of Holguín, was founded in 1757 and, together with Gibara *(see p214)*, is the oldest city in the province. The small Colonial centre can be explored in a short time.

Nearby are the **Farallones de Seboruco**, caves where objects left by the Taíno people have been found. Nearby is an important eco-tourist site, the **Meseta de Pinares de Mayarí**, a large forest cloaking the hills up to an altitude of 1,000 m (3,280 ft).

Southwest of Mayarí is Birán, where Fidel Castro was born on 13 August 1926. His parents' house is still standing.

Cayo Saetía **⑧**

Holguín. **Road Map** F4.

Lying at the mouth of the Bay of Nipe, this small island covering 42 sq km (16 sq miles), with wonderfully fascinating coves, is connected to the mainland by a drawbridge. It was formerly a private hunting reserve, and in the woods and meadows, antelopes and zebra still live side by side with species native to Cuba. On safaris, led by expert guides, visitors travelling on horseback or in jeeps can observe and photograph the animals. The few tourist facilities on this island are for residents only and were designed with every care for the environment.

Bayamo **⑨**

Granma. **Road Map** E4. 🏘 130,000.
✈ 🚉 *Saco y Línea, (23) 423 012.*
🚌 *Carretera Central y Jesús Rabí (23) 424 036.* 🚹 *Islazul, Calle General García el Lora y Masó, (23) 426 989 (may be closed due to hurricane damage, phone to check).*

The second oldest town in Cuba after Baracoa, Bayamo was founded in 1513 by Diego Velázquez. Until

The statue of Carlos Manuel de Céspedes at Bayamo

1975 it was part of the large Oriente province, but after administrative reform it became the capital of a new province, Granma. It is a pasture and livestock breeding area, but has also been the home of nationalists and the cradle of political revolts and struggles.

In 1869, rather than surrender their town to Spain, the citizens burned Bayamo down. As a result, the centre is relatively modern. Daily life revolves around the **Plaza de la Revolución** (Parque Céspedes), the main square, dominated by a statue of local plantation owner and war of independence hero Carlos Manuel de Céspedes (1955). The square is home to almost all the important buildings in town: the Cultural Centre, the Royaltón Hotel, the offices of the Poder Popular, and the historic Pedrito café.

Adjacent to the main square is **Plaza del Himno** (Square of the Hymn). It gained its name after *La Bayamesa*, the Cuban national anthem, was first played in the church here on 20 October 1868. Marking this event is a sculpture that includes a bronze plaque on which are engraved the words and music by Perucho Figueredo. His bust stands next to the nationalists' flag.

Plaza de la Revolución, also known as Parque Céspedes, in Bayamo

BAYAMO "THE REBELLIOUS"

Bayamo has a long tradition of rebellion. In the early 1500s, the native Indians, led by their chief, Hatuey, fiercely resisted the Spanish (see p219). A few years later an African slave killed the pirate Gilberto Giron, displaying his head as a trophy in the central plaza. This episode inspired the epic poem *Espejo de Paciencia* by Silvestre de Balboa, the first major work of Cuban literature (see p28). But the most dramatic episode in the history of Bayamo concerns the struggles for independence, during which, on 10 October 1868, a group of local nationalists and intellectuals – Juan Clemente Zenea, Carlos Manuel de Céspedes (see p43), Pedro Figueredo, José Fornaris and José Joaquín Palma – organized an anti-Spanish revolt. They entered the town on 20 October, and declared it the capital of the Republic in Arms. On 12 January, faced with the fact that Bayamo would be recaptured by Colonial troops, the citizens decided to set fire to their own town, an act which later led to the choice of *La Bayamesa* as the national anthem.

The monument dedicated to the national anthem, *La Bayamesa*

Interior of the Parroquial Mayor de San Salvador

🔒 Parroquial Mayor de San Salvador

Plaza del Himno esq. José Joaquín Palma. **Tel** (23) 422 514.
⬜ 9am–noon & 3–5pm daily.

When the nationalists of Bayamo chose to burn down their own town rather than leave anything for the Spanish, they put the holy images kept in the Parroquial Mayor (the Cathedral) into safekeeping. That was the plan, at all events. Unfortunately, the only things spared by the fire were the font (which had been used for the baptism of Carlos Manuel de Céspedes) and the Capilla de los Dolores, a chapel built in 1740, which contained an image of the Virgin Mary and a Baroque altarpiece made of gilded wood. The altarpiece has a particularly fine frame decorated with tropical motifs and representations of local fruit and animals, an unusual and very Cuban element in the art of the 18th century.

In 1916, Bishop Guerra commissioned the re-construction of the old Parroquial Mayor, dedicated to Jesus the Saviour, the patron saint of Bayamo. The original building had been finished in 1613 and in the course of time had been transformed into a large three-aisle church with two choirs, nine altars and a finely wrought pulpit.

The new church was opened on 9 October 1919, with the old image of Jesus the Saviour salvaged from the fire, a new marble altar, a patriotic painting by the Dominican artist Luis Desangles, and plastered brick walls frescoed by Esteban Ferrer.

In the smaller **Parque Maceo Osorio**, formerly Parque de San Francisco, north of Plaza de la Revolución, is the Casa de la Trova Olimpio La O, one of the town's few 18th-century buildings. The courtyard is used by local groups for concerts.

🏛 Casa Natal de Carlos Manuel de Céspedes

Calle Maceo 57, e/ Marmol y Palma. **Tel** (23) 423 864. ⬜ 10am–5:30pm Tue–Fri, 10am–2pm & 8–10pm Sat, 10am–3pm Sun. 🖼 🎫 📷

The house where the leading figure in the first war against Spain in the 19th century was born on 18 April 1819 is a handsome, two-storey Colonial building facing Plaza de la Revolución. Architecturally it is the most important building in the city.

The rooms on the ground floor, which open onto a courtyard with a fountain, contain the heart of the collection, with Céspedes' documents and personal items, including his steel and bronze sword.

Upstairs are several furnished rooms, one of which has a bronze bed with mother-of-pearl medallions, a fine example of Colonial furniture. A gallery leads to the old kitchen, which still has its original ceramic oven.

Façade of the birthplace of Carlos Manuel de Céspedes

Manzanillo ⑩

Granma. **Road map** E4.
✈ *"Sierra Maestra", 8 km (5 miles)
south of town.* 🚉 🚌 *Bayamo,
Camagüey, Havana, Pilón, Yara.*

Built along the Caribbean Bay
of Guacanayabo, Manzanillo
is a charming seaside town. It
was founded as Puerto Real
in 1784, and reached its
apogee in the second half of
the 19th century, thanks to
sugar and the slave trade.
Memories are still strong
of the feats of Castro's rebel
forces in the nearby Sierra
Maestra, especially those of
Castro's assistant Celia
Sánchez, who organized a
crucial rearguard here. She
is honoured by a striking
monument in the town.
In Parque Céspedes, the
central square, a brickwork

The Glorieta Morisca de Manzanillo, where the municipal band plays

bandstand for concerts by
local bands was opened on
25 June 1924. The so-called
Glorieta Morisca gained its
name because of its Arab-
influenced decoration,
designed by José Martín del
Castillo, an architect from
Granada. Other monuments

in town, all near the Parque
Céspedes, include the Neo-
Classical Iglesia de la Purísima
Concepción, built in the
1920s; the atmospheric Café
1906, the 19th-century town
hall, now the Asamblea
Municipal del Poder Popular;
and the Colonia Española, a

Towards Santiago via Cabo Cruz ⑪

This fascinating route by road to Santiago skirts the
high slopes of the Sierra Maestra which, along the
south coast, almost force the road into the sea in
places. The surrounding scenery is unspoiled and at
times wild, and conceals several places of historical
significance. The route can be covered in a day, but
for a more relaxing drive visitors could consider
staying in Marea del Portillo.

La Demajagua ①
Céspedes's estate still has
sugar-making equipment,
such as these *calderas* used
for making molasses.

Playa Las Coloradas ③
It was here that 82 rebels
landed aboard the *Granma*
in December 1956 *(see p48)*.

Media Luna ②
This is the birthplace of
the revolutionary Celia
Sánchez *(see p51)*. The
house is now a museum.

El Guafe ④
This archaeological site has
pre-Columbian finds on
display in a small museum.

**Parque Nacional Desembarco
del *Granma*** ⑤
This park has few facilities but
is rich in local flora, including
some extraordinary orchids.
Interesting natural sights
include caves. There are also
various sites commemorating
the journey of the
revolutionaries following
their arrival on the *Granma*.

Niquero

Punto Nuevo

Bélic

Cabo Cruz

social club for Spanish immigrants that was completed in 1935. The club is located in a building with an Andalusian courtyard and a panel of painted tiles representing Columbus's landing in Cuba.

Environs

10 km (6 miles) south of Manzanillo are the remains of La Demajagua, the estate belonging to Carlos Manuel de Céspedes *(see pp42 & 217)*. On 10 October 1868, he freed all of his slaves, urging them to join him in fighting the Spanish.

Yara, 24 km (15 miles) east of Manzanillo, is where Céspedes proclaimed Cuban independence, and where the Indian hero Hatuey was burned at the stake. There is a small museum in the central square, Plaza Grito de Yara.

HATUEY'S SACRIFICE

Over the centuries, the sacrifice of Hatuey acquired great patriotic significance and gave rise to numerous legends, including *La Luz de Yara* (The Light of Yara), written by Luis Victoriano Betancourt in 1875. The author relates that from the stake on which the Indian hero was being burned, there arose a mysterious light that wandered throughout the island, protecting the sleep of the slaves who were awaiting their freedom. This light was the soul of Hatuey. Three centuries later, the wandering light returned to the site of the Indian's sacrifice, and in a flash all the palm trees in Cuba shook, the sky was lit up, the earth trembled, and the light turned into a fire that stirred Cubans' hearts: "It was the Light of Yara, which was about to take its revenge. It was the tomb of Hatuey, which became the cradle of independence. It was 10 October" – the beginning of the war of independence.

The Indian chief Hatuey being burned at the stake

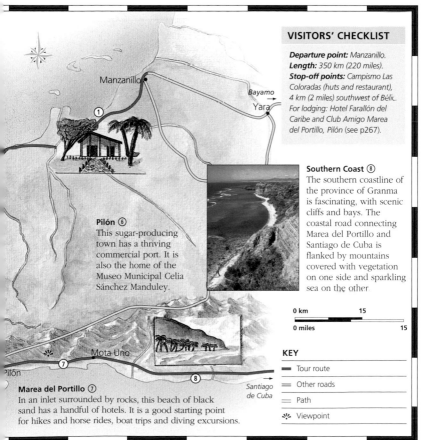

VISITORS' CHECKLIST

Departure point: *Manzanillo.*
Length: *350 km (220 miles).*
Stop-off points: *Campismo Las Coloradas (huts and restaurant), 4 km (2 miles) southwest of Bélic. For lodging: Hotel Farallón del Caribe and Club Amigo Marea del Portillo, Pilón (see p267).*

Manzanillo

Bayamo →
Yara

Southern Coast ⑧

The southern coastline of the province of Granma is fascinating, with scenic cliffs and bays. The coastal road connecting Marea del Portillo and Santiago de Cuba is flanked by mountains covered with vegetation on one side and sparkling sea on the other.

Pilón ⑥

This sugar-producing town has a thriving commercial port. It is also the home of the Museo Municipal Celia Sánchez Manduley.

0 km — 15
0 miles — 15

Mota Uno

Pilón

Marea del Portillo ⑦

In an inlet surrounded by rocks, this beach of black sand has a handful of hotels. It is a good starting point for hikes and horse rides, boat trips and diving excursions.

Santiago de Cuba

KEY

▬ Tour route
═ Other roads
= Path
⁂ Viewpoint

Gran Parque Nacional Sierra Maestra ⑫

Granma, Santiago de Cuba.
Road Map F4.
ℹ️ *Cubanacán, Santiago de Cuba, (22) 642 202, 641 752, 641 891; Cubanacán, Hotel Sierra Maestra, km 1.5 Carretera Santiago de Cuba, (23) 427 970.*

View from the Pico Turquino, the highest mountain in Cuba

This national park, which covers an area of 38,000 ha (95,000 acres), spans the provinces of Granma and Santiago de Cuba. This is where the major peaks of the island are found, including Pico Turquino (at 1,974 m/ 6,390 ft, the highest in Cuba), as well as sites made famous by the guerrilla war waged by Fidel Castro and the *barbudos*.

The main starting point for exploring the Sierra Maestra is **Villa Santo Domingo**, about 35 km (22 miles) south of the Bayamo–Manzanillo road (there is simple accommodation in Santo Domingo).

From Santo Domingo, you can make the challenging 5-km (3-mile) journey – on foot or in a good off-road vehicle – to the **Alto del Naranjo** viewpoint (950 m/3,120 ft). With a permit (obtainable from the forest rangers in Villa Santo

The *gavilán del monte*, common in the Sierra Maestra

Domingo), you can go on to **Comandancia de la Plata**, Castro's headquarters in the 1950s. Here there is a museum, a small camp hospital and the site from which Che Guevara made his radio broadcasts.

Comandancia de la Plata is accessible only on foot – an hour's walk through lovely, though often foggy, forest. The area was made into a national park in 1980, and is not only important historically. The dense, humid forest conceals many species of orchid and various kinds of local fauna. The mountains of the Sierra Maestra are excellent hiking territory, and also attract mountain climbers. The scenery is spectacular but be prepared for spartan facilities. A limited number of treks can

be organized in Villa Santo Domingo, where guides can be hired. Overnight accommodation in the mountains is available either at campsites or in simple refuges. Note however that since much of this area is a military zone, it is not always open to the public.

At present, it is possible to do a three-day guided trek across the park, beginning at Alto del Naranjo and ending at Las Cuevas, a small town on the Caribbean Sea. Hikers do not need to be expert mountaineers in order to take part in this walking tour, because the path is equipped with ladders, handrails and rock-cut steps. However, it is still advisable to do a certain amount of training beforehand. The final descent from Pico Turquino onwards is fairly strenuous and walkers need to be reasonably fit.

It is important to take proper mountain gear with you: walking boots, thick socks, a hat to protect you from the sun, as well as a sweater, a windproof jacket, perhaps even a waterproof groundsheet and a good tent. The humidity in the Sierra, which is often enveloped in mist, is very high, and showers are common.

The coast at the southern edge of the Sierra Maestra, known as the **Riviera del Caribe**, is spectacular. The coastal road runs close above the waters of the Caribbean Sea and offers excellent views of coastal stacks and coves.

View of the splendid coastline south of Sierra Maestra

For hotels and restaurants in this region see pp266–9 and p283

Basílica del Cobre 🔞

Santiago de Cuba.
Road Map F4. 🚌 *Carretera Central 21, (22) 346 118.* ⭕ *daily.* ✝ 📷 *procession (8 Sep).*

The village of El Cobre, about 20 km (12 miles) west of Santiago de Cuba, was once famous for its copper *(cobre)* mines. A great number of slaves worked here up until 1807. Nowadays the village is best known for Cuba's most famous church, the Basílica de Nuestra Señora de la Caridad del Cobre. Here the main attraction is a statue of the Virgen del Cobre. This black Madonna is richly dressed in yellow, and wears a crown encrusted with diamonds, emeralds and rubies, with a golden halo above. She carries a cross of diamonds and amethysts. The statue is kept in an air-conditioned glass case behind the high altar.

It is taken out every year on 8 September when a procession takes place to commemorate the Virgin's saint's day. The Virgen del Cobre was proclaimed the protectress of Cuba in 1916 and was blessed and crowned by Pope John Paul II during his visit to Cuba in 1998 *(see p64).*

The Basílica del Cobre, surrounded by tropical vegetation

This fine three-aisled church, built in 1926, stands on a hill, the Cerro de la Cantera, which is linked to the village by a flight of 254 steps. The elegant central bell tower

The austere interior of the Sanctuary of the Virgen del Cobre

and two side towers crowned by brick-red domes are a striking sight above the light-painted façade.

The basilica is the object of pilgrimages from all over the island. In the Los Milagros chapel, thousands of ex-votos left by pilgrims are on display. Some are rather curious, such as the Nobel Prize medal won by Ernest Hemingway, beards left by some of the rebels who survived the guerrilla war in the Sierra; an object belonging to Castro's mother; and earth collected by Cuban soldiers who fought in Angola.

THE VIRGEN DEL COBRE

The statue of the Virgen del Cobre

According to legend, in 1606 three slaves who worked in the copper mines of El Cobre were saved in the Bay of Nipe, off the north coast of Cuba, by the statue of a black Virgin Mary holding the Holy Child in her arms. They had been caught in a storm while out in a boat and would have drowned had not the Virgin, whose image was floating among the waves, come to their aid. In reality, it seems that the statue arrived in Cuba by ship from Illescas, a town in Castile, upon the request of the governor Sánchez de Moya, who wanted a Spanish Madonna for the village of El Cobre. Whatever the truth, in 1611 the Virgen de la Caridad was given a small sanctuary and immediately became an object of veneration for the locals, who continued to attribute miraculous powers to her. The devotion for this Madonna has always been very strong, even among non-practising Catholics. Her figure is associated with the Afro-Cuban cult of Ochún *(see p22)*, the goddess of rivers, gentleness, femininity and love, who is also always depicted as a beautiful black woman wearing yellow. Now that the *santería* religion is widespread in Cuba, the sacred image of the Virgin of El Cobre and the more profane, sensuous image of the beautiful African goddess are often combined in prayers and discussion, and set beside each other on rustic home altars, often without any apparent awareness of contradiction.

A group of ex-votos offered by the *barbudos*

Santiago de Cuba ⑭

Sign for the Rum Museum

This is perhaps the most African, the most musical and the most passionate city in Cuba. In 1930 the Spanish poet Federico García Lorca likened it to "a harp made of living branches, a caiman, a tobacco flower". Except for the cars and some modern buildings, Santiago has not altered much since those days. This is a city where the heat – and the hills – mean that people move to a slow rhythm. It is a lively, exciting place where festivities and dancing are celebrated with fervour, never more so than during Carnival. Santiago's citizens also take pride in the fact that Santiago is called the "Cradle of the Revolution". Sandwiched between the Sierra Maestra mountains and the sea, this is the second city in Cuba in population size.

A restored Neo-Classical building in the historic centre

Parque Céspedes

The city centre spreads out in chaotic fashion around Parque Céspedes in a maze of alleys and narrow streets. Any visit to the historic centre of Santiago must start in Parque Céspedes, the main square. From here visitors are inevitably drawn along **Calle Heredia**, the most famous, popular and festive street in the town. Every house bears signs of the city's great passions: music, dancing, carnivals and poetry. At certain times, including the first half of July when the Festival del Caribe is held, this street becomes a stage for amateur artists. Traditional *son* music, on the other hand, can be heard in the courtyard of the Casa de la

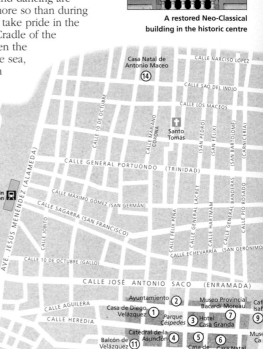

Calle Heredia, the liveliest street in Santiago de Cuba

UNEAC *(see pp 290–91)* at No. 266, while No. 208, the former "Cafetín de Virgilio", became the Casa de la Trova in 1968, and local and foreign bands can be heard playing here day and night. Photographs of great Cuban musicians past and present such as El Guayabero and Compay Segundo cover the walls.

West of Parque Céspedes

The picturesque area west of Parque Céspedes, called Tivoli, and the deep bay can be seen from the **Balcón de Velázquez**, a wonderful viewpoint situated at the corner of Calle Mariano Corona and Bartolomé Masó. The viewpoint was named after the Spanish conquistador Diego Velázquez, who founded the city in 1515. A small fort was built here in the 16th century

SIGHTS AT A GLANCE

Ayuntamiento ②
Balcón de Velázquez ⑪
Café La Isabelica ⑨
Casa de Diego Velázquez ①
Casa de la Trova ⑤
Casa Natal
de Antonio Maceo ⑭
Casa Natal de José María
Heredia ⑥
Catedral de la Asunción ④
Cuartel Moncada ⑮

Hotel Casa Granda ③
Museo de la Lucha
Clandestina ⑬
Museo del Carnaval ⑧
Museo del Ron ⑩
Museo Provincial
Bacardí Moreau ⑦
Parque Histórico
Abel Santamaría ⑯
Plaza de Marte ⑰
Steps of Padre Pico ⑫

VISITORS' CHECKLIST

Santiago de Cuba. **Road Map** F4.
🏠 400,000. ✈ 7 km (4 miles)
south of town. 🚌 Ave. Jesús
Menéndez, esq. Hechevarría. 🚍
Ave. de los Libertadores, esq.
Yarayó, (22) 623 050. 🛈 Havanatur, Hotel Santiago, Calle M y Ave
de las Américas, (22) 644 402;
Cubatur, Ave. Garzón e/ 3ra y 4ta,
(22) 652 560. 🎭 Festival del
Caribe (early Jul), Carnival (late Jul).

0 metres   200

0 yards   200

Key to Symbols see back flap

Calle Padre Pico seen from the top of the steps

to house artillery to be used
in the event of an attack.
Today, only fragments of the
original walls remain. Inside
the viewpoint area itself are
some attractive bronze tondos
(circular carvings in relief)
with portraits of Diego
Velázquez, Hernán Cortés,
Bartolomé de Las Casas and
the Indian Guamá. Cultural
events are sometimes held at
the Balcón de Velázquez.

South of Parque Céspedes

Around 100m
(330 ft) southwest
of the square, the
**Steps of Padre
Pico** lead to Tivolí, the
most authentic,
picturesque mixed quarter in
Santiago. Here, over the
centuries, various peoples
have arrived and stayed,
including Puerto Ricans,
Jamaicans, Arabs, Dominicans
and Chinese. In the 1700s a
colony of French people from
Haiti also settled here, setting
up shops, music schools,
theatres and hotels.

East of Parque Céspedes

To the east of the square, at
the corner of Calle Bartolomé
Masó and Calle Hartmann (San
Félix), is the **Museo del Ron**
(Rum Museum), housed in a
late 19th-century building.
Displays illustrate how rum is

distilled and matured (see
p75), alongside the history of
the Bacardí factory, with an
exhibition of labels from
bottles of rum, new and old.

Another place to visit is
Parque Dolores, a leafy square
surrounded by buildings
adorned with wrought-iron
balconies. A small old café
in the square, **La Isabelica**,
serves excellent coffee.

**Customers at La Isabelica, an
atmospheric historic café**

Street-by-Street: Parque Céspedes

The former Plaza de Armas in Santiago is the heart of the city, both geographically and spiritually. Renamed Parque Céspedes in honour of the nation's founding father *(see p44)*, whose statue stands in the middle, this square is a place for socializing, relaxing, chatting and celebrating. At all hours of the day and night, the benches are filled with people, young, old, women, children and visitors. No one is alone here for long. Everyone sooner or later gets involved in a conversation or entertainment of some kind, because this square's other role is as an open-air venue where music – live, recorded, or improvised – takes the leading role. Restored in Neo-Classical style in 1943, the square consists of four areas, each with fountains and greenery, divided by lanes.

Casa de la Trova
Live music is performed here daily.

The house where the poet José Heredia was born is a fine 18th-century building around a leafy courtyard *(p227).*

★ Museo Provincial Bacardí Moreau
The oldest museum in Cuba, housed in an elegant Neo-Classical building, is also the most eclectic. Items on display range from an Egyptian mummy to mementoes of the wars of independence and works by living artists (p228).

CALLE GENERAL LA
CALLE HARTMANN
CALLE HEREDIA
CALLE AGUILERA

KEY

– – – Suggested route

STAR SIGHTS

★ Casa de Diego Velázquez

★ Museo Provincial Bacardí Moreau

★ Catedral de la Asunción

Seafront

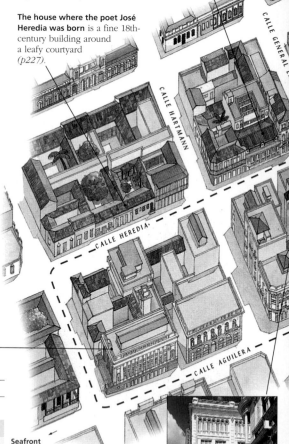

Hotel Casa Granda
One of Cuba's historic hotels (see p269), the Casa Granda opened in 1920. Graham Greene (see p87) described it in Our Man in Havana *as a hotel frequented by spies. Its terrace overlooks the square.*

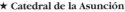

★ **Catedral de la Asunción**
The Cathedral façade is Neo-Classical, but the original church is four centuries old. It is believed that Diego Velázquez is buried somewhere beneath the building, but there is no proof of this (p227).

Paseo de Martí

CALLE BARTOLOMÉ MASÓ

CALLE FÉLIX PEÑA

CALLE HEREDIA

CALLE MARIANO CORONA

PARQUE CÉSPEDES

Balcón de Velázquez
This spacious viewing terrace, built over the site of a Spanish fortress, offers a magnificent view of the picturesque quarter of Tivolí, as well as the port and the bay of Santiago. There is an admission charge (p222).

★ **Casa de Diego Velázquez**
Built in 1516–30, the residence of the Spanish conquistador Diego Velázquez is considered by some to be the oldest building in Cuba. Restoration was carried out in 1965, and it is now the home of the Museo de Ambiente Histórico Cubano (p226).

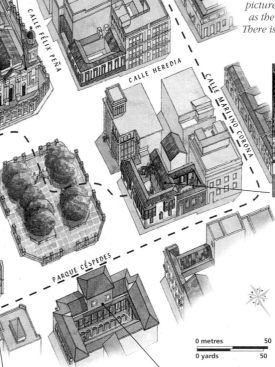

0 metres 50
0 yards 50

The Casa de la Cultura Miguel Matamoros, an eclectic building (1919) housing the sumptuous Salón de los Espejos, is a venue for artistic and cultural events.

Ayuntamiento
The Ayuntamiento (town hall), a symbol of the city, was built in 1950 according to 18th-century designs found in the Indies Archive. It was from this building's central balcony that Fidel Castro made his first speech to the Cuban people, on 1 January 1959.

Exploring Parque Céspedes

Ceramic plate, Casa de Velázquez

One of the liveliest squares in Cuba, Parque Céspedes is not only a place for socializing, but also has sites of cultural and architectural importance. Allow half a day to visit three of the most important monuments around the Parque: the house of Diego Velázquez, the impressive cathedral, and the residence of the great 19th-century poet José María Heredia.

The courtyard in the 19th-century wing of Diego Velázquez's house

A room with Colonial furniture in Diego Velázquez's house

The building now houses the Museo de Ambiente Histórico Cubano, covering the history of furniture in Cuba. It contains superb examples from all Colonial periods. Among the mostly austere Creole furniture, dating from the 16th and 17th centuries, are a splendid priest's high-backed chair and a finely wrought coffer – two excellent examples of Moorish-style objects.

The basement has 18th-century "Luis Las Casas" furniture, a style peculiar to Cuba which combines English

influences and French rococo motifs. These pieces of furniture are massive, lavish and intricately worked, often finished at the base with feet shaped like claws. The 19th-century section includes a dining room with stained-glass windows and French furniture, including rocking chairs, a console table and a Charles X mirror.

Another important item is a tapestry with the coat-of-arms of the Velázquez family, the only piece in the museum that is directly related to this Spanish *conquistador*.

🏛 Casa de Diego Velázquez (Museo de Ambiente Histórico Cubano)

Calle Félix Peña 612, e/ Heredia y Aguilera. *Tel* (22) 652 652. ☐ 9am–12:45pm, 2–5pm Mon–Sat, 9am–12:45pm Sun. ☀ Fri am. 🎟 ✗ 📷 (with charge).

This building, constructed in 1516–30 as a residence for the governor Diego Velázquez, is the oldest home in Cuba, according to architect Francisco Prat Puig, who restored the house in 1965. (Other scholars dispute this assertion, however, and not everyone has praised the restoration.) Whatever the truth, this splendid residence is still fascinating.

In the 1600s it was the so-called House of Transactions (the ground floor still has an old furnace in which gold ingots were made). In the 19th century it was joined to the building next door. The upstairs gallery facing the courtyard is closed off by a Moorish wooden blind, to screen residents from the eyes of strangers. Also upstairs, some of the original *alfarje* ceilings survive.

THE 16TH-CENTURY MUDEJAR-STYLE HOUSE

Considered the oldest private building in Cuba and declared a national monument because of its historic value, the 16th-century section of Velázquez's house is a fine example of the Cuban version of the *mudéjar* (Moorish) style – although much of what is there is the result of restoration.

The courtyard, *in* mudéjar *style, is narrow and long and runs around a central well.*

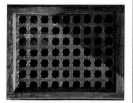

Wooden screens *protect the gallery and balconies from the sun and public gaze.*

Frescoes, *known as* cenefas, *decorate the lower part of the walls, but they are not original.*

Cedar ceilings *with geometric patterns, called* alfarjes, *were common in the 16th century.*

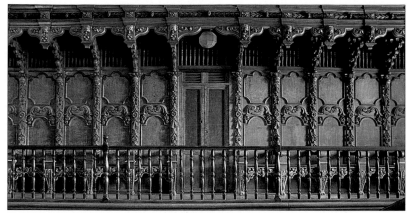

The lovely wooden inlaid choir in the Catedral de Nuestra Señora de la Asunción

ⓐ Catedral de Nuestra Señora de la Asunción

Calle Heredia, e/ Lacret y Félix Peña. **Tel** (22) 628 502 (may be closed due to hurricane damage, phone to check). ◯ 8:30am–1pm & 5–7pm Tue–Sat, 8–10:30am & 5–7pm Sun. 🔔 6:30pm Tue Fri, 5pm Sat, 9am & 6:30pm Sun.

The cathedral of Santiago has a basilica layout, with a central nave and four aisles, an apse and a narthex or vestibule at the back. The church has been rebuilt several times over the centuries. The original was built in 1522, but in the early 17th century a series of pirate raids caused so much damage that the church was rebuilt in 1666–70. In the 18th and 19th centuries it was further damaged by earthquakes.

Today the cathedral, which has been declared a national monument, displays a mixture of styles, the result of a series of changes made in 1922 by the architect Segrera, who added the bell towers, had the interior painted, and also re-worked the façade. A marble angel was set over the main entrance and statues of Christopher Columbus and Bartolomé de las Casas were placed in side niches.

The cathedral also has a museum, the **Museo Eclesiástico**, which displays frescoes by the Dominican friar Luis Desangles, liturgical objects, statues and an important collection of ecclesiastical music scores.

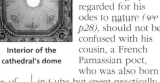

Interior of the cathedral's dome

� Casa Natal de José María Heredia

Calle Heredia 260, e/ Hartmann (San Félix) y Pío Rosado (Carniceria). ◯ Tue–Sat; Sun am. ● 1 Jan, 1 May, 26 Jul, 10 Oct, 25 Dec. 🖼 📷 📷

This is the modest but elegant 18th-century house where the nationalist poet José María Heredia (1803–39) was born. Heredia, highly regarded for his odes to nature (see p28), should not be confused with his cousin, a French Parnassian poet, who was also born in Cuba but spent practically all his life in Europe.

The well-preserved house contains period furniture and objects, wooden ceilings and tiled floors, and is well worth a visit. From the large entrance hall, with a coffered ceiling and paintings of the poet's ancestors on the walls, a large arch leads into the central peristyled courtyard. Here there are wooden columns, a stone well and abundant vegetation.

Other rooms in the house include Heredia's bedroom, which has an impressive mahogany bed and elegant antique lamps.

Cultural events and poetry readings are often held in the museum's large porticoes. In addition, every year literary seminars and workshops are held here as part of the Festival del Caribe, or Fiesta del Fuego. This summer cultural event takes over the entire city of Santiago (see p35).

Entrance hall of Heredia's house, its arch leading to the courtyard

Around Calle Heredia

This street is one of the liveliest in Cuba. It buzzes with music and activity, and the sound of guitars, maracas, percussion and voices can be heard at all hours of the day, not just in the Casa de la Trova or the Casa de la UNEAC, but also in the Museo del Carnaval, where concerts are held in the courtyard. The nearby Museo Bacardí is devoted to Cuban history.

Decorated *tumbadoras (see p31)* in the Museo del Carnaval

Techos *de Santiago de Cuba* by Felipe González, Museo Bacardí

🏛 Museo Provincial Bacardí Moreau

Calle Pío Rosado (Carniceria), esq. Aguilera. *Tel* (22) 628 402. ○
1–4:15pm Mon, 9–11:45am, 1–4:15pm Tue–Sat, 9am–noon Sun. 📷 🎫 📷 (with charge).

This is the oldest museum in Cuba. It was founded in 1828 and is a rich source of relics dating from the Spanish conquest to the wars of independence. The objects were collected and organized in the late 1800s and early 1900s by Emilio Bacardí, founder of the famous rum distillery. Bacardí was also a famous patriot and the first mayor of Santiago when Cuba became a republic. His aim was to display the origin and development of the Cuban nationalist movement from a cultural point of view, and he asked the architect Segrera to design a building for the objects and works of art he had collected.

The statue of Liberty in the foyer

The museum is housed in an eclectic building with a broad staircase and an atrium dominated by two large statues of Minerva and Liberty. On the ground floor is a large collection of arms used by nationalist generals and heroes such as Antonio Maceo, Máximo Gómez and José Martí. There is also an important collection of works by 19th-century Cuban painters, including Felipe López González, Juan Emilio Hernández Giro, José Joaquín Tejada Revilla and Buenaventura Martínez. Twentieth-century artists represented here are Wifredo Lam and René Portocarrero *(see pp26–7)*. The archaeology section is in the basement and includes the only Egyptian mummy in Cuba.

🏛 Museo del Carnaval

Calle Heredia 303, esq. Pío Rosado (Carniceria). *Tel* (22) 626 955. ○ 2–5pm Mon, 9am–5pm Tue–Sat, 9am–1pm Sun. 📷 🎫 📷 (with charge).

This lovely late 18th-century building was converted into an elementary school in the mid-1900s, then into an office building, and eventually became the offices of the Carnival Commission. The

Part of an elaborate float in the Museo del Carnaval

Museo del Carnaval was opened here on 7 June 1983. The six rooms contain photographs with explanatory captions, chronologies, banners, musical instruments, costumes and papier mâché masks – a well-documented survey of the Carnival festivities held in Santiago. Carnival here differs from the traditional Spanish model and combines many African and Franco-Haitian elements.

The courtyard is used for folk events and concerts, as well as for rehearsals by bands preparing to perform during Carnival.

🏛 Museo de la Lucha Clandestina

Calle Rabí 1, e/ San Carlo y Santa Rita. *Tel* (22) 624 689. ○ 9am–5pm Tue–Sun. 📷 🎫 📷

The Museum of the Clandestine Struggle overlooks a pleasant square in the district of Tivolí, southwest of Parque Céspedes. The building was the headquarters of Batista's police from 1951 to 1956. On 30 November 1956 it was burnt down by revolutionaries, led by Frank País *(see p50)*.

The four rooms in the restored building commemorate the activities of the Movimiento 26 de Julio, the movement headed in Santiago by Frank País up to 30 July 1957, when the young rebel leader was assassinated by Batista's police.

Carnival in Santiago de Cuba

The roots of the Carnival in Santiago are religious: since the end of the 17th century there have been processions and festivities from 24 June to 26 July in honour of the city's patron saint, Santiago Apostolo. At the end of the parade, slaves who were members of the *cabildos* – societies that kept alive African languages, traditions and beliefs – were allowed to go out into the streets, where they sang to the accompaniment of drums, rattles and other instruments. These were the forerunners of the *comparsas*, the soul of Carnival: groups of people wearing masks or costumes, dancing to the rhythm of the *conga* and carrying streamers, banners and *farolas* (brightly coloured paper street lamps). In the second half of July the whole town celebrates, every district taking part in the parades, each with at least one *comparsa*.

Playing the trompeta china

The young people *in each quarter meet every evening except Monday in the focos culturales, places where they prepare for Carnival by rehearsing the dances and music they will perform in July.*

Parades *go through the streets of Santiago. Some of the* comparsas, *such as the Carabalí Izuama (see p289), date from the 19th century.*

The type of tumbadora used in the conga

The musicians in each group are dressed alike. They are followed by a crowd swaying to the rhythm of the music.

THE CONGA
The chief dance for Carnival is the *conga* (also a genuine musical genre). People form a procession and dance through the streets, following a band playing various instruments, including different kinds of drums and the *trompeta china*, introduced to Cuba in the late 1800s.

The bombo, a drum with a deep sound

The Tropicana de Santiago *joins the procession with the other* comparsas, *and also presents open-air performances in lavish costumes.*

Papier mâché masks *are an essential part of a Carnival float. Huge and brightly coloured, they often represent animals or caricatures of human faces.*

Beyond Santiago's Historic Centre

Calle Saco (also known as Enramada), Santiago's main commercial street, links the heart of the old city with the port. After passing through a working-class quarter, with early 20th-century wooden houses, the street ends at Paseo Marítimo. Laid out in the Colonial era as a seafront promenade for the city's high society, this broad street retains echoes of its former beauty and still has its original 1840 paving, stretching out along the port, where cruisers and yachts are moored. An alternative route to explore is to go in the opposite direction, east of the centre, where there are important historic sites, including the Moncada barracks.

🏛 Casa Natal de Antonio Maceo

Calle Los Maceos 207, e/ Corona y Rastro. *Tel (22) 623 750.*
🕐 9am–5pm Mon–Sat. 📷 📹
📷 (with charge).

The house where this great general was born on 14 June 1845 (he died near Havana on 7 December 1896; *see p44*) is a modest place. Visitors can see some of the hero's personal belongings and family photographs, including one of his brother José, who was also a general, and one of his mother, Mariana Grajales.

🪦 Cementerio de Santa Ifigenia

Avenida Crombet. *Tel (22) 632 723.*
🕐 7am–5pm daily. 📷 📹
📷 (with charge).

This monumental cemetery (1868) is the second most important in Cuba after the Colón cemetery in Havana (*see pp104–5*). It was originally laid out with a Latin cross plan and divided into courtyards, the most important of which were

The mausoleum of Martí in the Santa Ifigenia Cemetery

reserved for those of higher social status. A visit to the Santa Ifigenia cemetery evokes two centuries of Cuban history, past the tombs of such illustrious 19th-century figures as José Martí, Carlos Manuel de Céspedes, Emilio Bacardí and the mother of Antonio Maceo, as well as the 20th-century revolutionaries of the Movimiento 26 de Julio such as Frank País, who was killed in 1957 (*see p50*).

The funerary monuments themselves are fascinating. The Neo-Classical tombs nearest the entrance are the oldest, followed by the eclectic and then Modernist tombs. The Rationalist tombs built from the mid-20th century on include Martí's large octagonal mausoleum.

🏛 Museo Histórico 26 de Julio – Cuartel Moncada

Calle General Portuondo (Trinidad), e/ Moncada y Ave de los Libertadores. *Tel (22) 620 157.* 🕐 9:30am–5:30pm Tue–Sat, 9:15am–12:30pm Sun.
📷 📹 📷 (with charge).

On 26 July 1953, at the height of the Carnival festivities, Fidel Castro led about 100 rebels in an attack on the Moncada barracks (*see p48*). Capturing Moncada, the second largest garrison in Cuba, built in the 19th century, would have meant securing a large stock of weapons and thus triggering a general revolt. Abel Santamaría was to attack the Saturnino Lora hospital, a strategic site on a promontory overlooking the barracks, and Raúl Castro was to capture the law courts building. This bold attempt failed, but it did succeed in increasing public awareness of the activity of the young revolutionaries. Eight of them died during the attack, while 55 were taken prisoner, tortured and executed.

Since January 1959 the barracks, which still bear bullet holes, have housed the Ciudad Escolar 26 de Julio school. Part of the building houses the Museo Histórico 26 de Julio, which in fact

The impressive façade of the former Moncada army barracks, now a school and museum

The monument to General Maceo in Plaza de la Revolución

illustrates the history of Cuba from the time of Columbus, but devotes most space to the guerrilla war of the 1950s. There is a model reproducing the attack on Moncada. There are also possessions which belonged to Fidel Castro, his brother Raúl and Che Guevara when they were waging war in the Sierra Maestra.

🏛 Museo Abel Santamaría Cuadrado – Parque Histórico Abel Santamaría

Calle General Portuondo (Trinidad), esq. Ave de los Libertadores. *Tel (22) 624 119.* ☐ *9am–5pm Mon–Sat.* 🖼 🚫 🚫

The Moncada barracks, Saturnino Lora hospital and law court buildings form part of the Parque Histórico Abel Santamaría. In the 1953 raid, the former hospital was the target of a group of rebels led by Abel Santamaría, who was captured and killed by the police after the failed attempt.

The hospital now houses a museum with documents and photographs relating to the trial of Fidel Castro and the other rebels, which was held a few days after the attack on the barracks in one of the rooms here.

Besides the photographs illustrating the difficult social and economic conditions in Cuba during the 1950s, there is the manuscript of Castro's landmark self-defence in court, later entitled *History Will Absolve Me (see p149).*

Plaza de Marte

East of Plaza Dolores is the third largest square in Santiago, laid out in the 19th century. It is of great historic importance: for here capital punishment was meted out both in the Colonial period and under General Machado. At its centre is a 20-m (65-ft) column (1902) celebrating Cuban independence.

🏛 Bosque de los Héroes

East of the centre, behind the unmistakable Hotel Santiago, lies a small, unobtrusive hill. A white marble monument was erected here in 1973 to honour Che Guevara and the comrades-in-arms who died with him in Bolivia. Their names are engraved here.

The column in Plaza de Marte

Plaza de la Revolución

In the northeastern part of Santiago, beyond the Moncada barracks, is Plaza de la Revolución, a large, rather soulless square at a crossroads of three major avenues. The square is dominated by a vast monument executed in the early 1990s by the Santiago sculptor, Alberto Lezcay, representing General Maceo *(see p44)* on horseback, surrounded by 23 stylized machetes.

Plaza de la Revolución marks the start of the modern, residential area of the city, where the architecture shows a marked Soviet influence.

Vista Alegre

The Vista Alegre quarter has fine eclectic-style buildings constructed in the 1920s and 1930s. The quarter also has two important institutions: the **Centro Africano Fernando Ortíz**, with African masks, statues and musical instruments on display, and the **Casa del Caribe**, which houses a historical archive, library, and centre for conferences, workshops and events *(see p290).* During the Festival del Caribe, the Casa del Caribe presents examples of Yoruba, Congo and voodoo rites.

Bosque de los Héroes, honouring Che Guevara and comrades

Castillo del Morro ⓫

At the entrance to the Bay of Santiago, 10 km (6 miles) southwest of the city centre, stands an imposing castle, declared a World Heritage site by UNESCO in 1997. The Castillo del Morro combines medieval elements with a modern sense of space, adhering nonetheless to classical Renaissance principles of geometric forms and symmetry. The fortress was designed in 1637 by engineer Giovan Battista Antonelli for the governor Pedro de la Roca, who wanted to defend the city against pirate raids. Construction of the citadel, large enough to house 400 soldiers, took from 1638 to 1700. The Castillo was converted into a prison in 1775, becoming a fortress once again in 1898 during the wars of independence, when the US fleet attacked the city.

A cannon, part of the old battery used to defend the bay

In the casemates
a display of prints illustrates the history of Santiago's forts.

Artillery area

★ **View of the Bay**
The parapets and lookouts on the upper parts of the fortress were used by the sentries to keep watch. Visitors today can appreciate the setting and enjoy a marvellous view over the bay.

Underground passageways
link the various parts of the castle. This one leads to the artillery area.

The stone stairway
on the side of the castle facing the sea is part of an open-air network of steps leading to the upper levels.

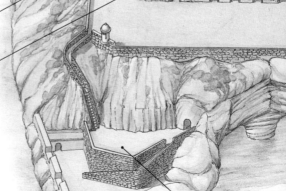

STAR SIGHTS

★ View of the Bay

★ Central Square

Plataforma de la Punta (*morrillo*, or bluff)

Triangular Lunette

Built in 1590–1610 as the main protection for the fortress gate, this structure originally stood separately from the castle. It was later incorporated into the main structure.

VISITORS' CHECKLIST

Santiago de Cuba.
Carretera del Morro, km 7,5.
Road Map F4.
Tel (22) 691 569.
🕐 8am–7pm daily.

Drawbridge

This bridge passes over a dry moat that runs alongside the fortification on the inland side. It is well preserved, and still has the original winch which was used to raise and lower the bridge.

Dry moat

★ Central Square

This square, the nerve centre of the castle, was used as an area for organizing daily activities. The square provides access to the chapel, barracks, garrison and underground rooms.

Three separate main structures, built on five different levels, form the skeleton of the castle. This unusual construction is a result of the uneven terrain of the headland.

THE BAY OF SANTIAGO

About 8 km (5 miles) southwest of the centre of Santiago, at the end of the Carretera Turística (which, despite its name, is a rather poorly maintained, traffic-filled road), is Marina Punta Gorda. From here ferries cross over to a small island in the middle of the bay. This is Cayo Granma, home to a picturesque fishing village made up of multicoloured huts and small houses built on piles. This island is a peaceful place off the beaten track, with only one restaurant and abundant greenery – a good place to relax in and round off a visit to Santiago de Cuba.

View of Cayo Granma from the Carretera Turística

Parque Baconao 16

Lying between the Caribbean Sea and the eastern fringes of the Sierra Maestra, and straddling the provinces of Santiago and Guantánamo, Parque Baconao has been declared a biosphere reserve by UNESCO. The largest and most original amusement park in Cuba (80,000 ha/197,600 acres) combines mountains and beaches with old coffee plantations and an unusual range of attractions. The park was developed in the 1980s thanks to the voluntary work of students and labourers, and has been updated periodically. Today, visitors can appreciate a wide range of cultural and outdoor activities and attractions, and there is plenty of hotel accommodation.

Gran Piedra
This is an enormous monolith, from the top of which, at an altitude of 1,234m (4,048 ft), you can even see Jamaica and Haiti on clear days (see p236).

The Cafetal La Isabelica, the oldest coffee plantation in the province, has been converted into a museum *(see p236)*.

Jardín Botánico (Botanic Garden)

Siberia

La Isabélica

Perseverancia

Tres Arroyos

Prado de las Esculturas
This sculpture garden, with 20 works by Cuban and foreign artists, was laid out in the late 1980s. The display extends for 1 km (0.6 mile) and can also be viewed by car.

Abel Santamaría

Las Guásimas

El Palenque

Damajayabo

El Oasis

Juraguá

Siboney

Museos y Exposiciones de la Punta, *(see p237)*

Granjita Siboney *(see p236)*

At the Oasis, a centre managed by artists, visitors can go horse riding and watch rodeo shows.

Playa Siboney is the favourite beach of the citizens of Santiago. Only 19 km (12 miles) from town, it can be reached by regular bus service.

KEY

━━ Major road

═══ Path

─── River

🏖 Recommended beach

☀ Viewpoint

🏛 Ruins of old *cafetales*

Valle de la Prehistoria
This children's park features huge sculptures of dinosaurs and there is also a Natural History Museum.

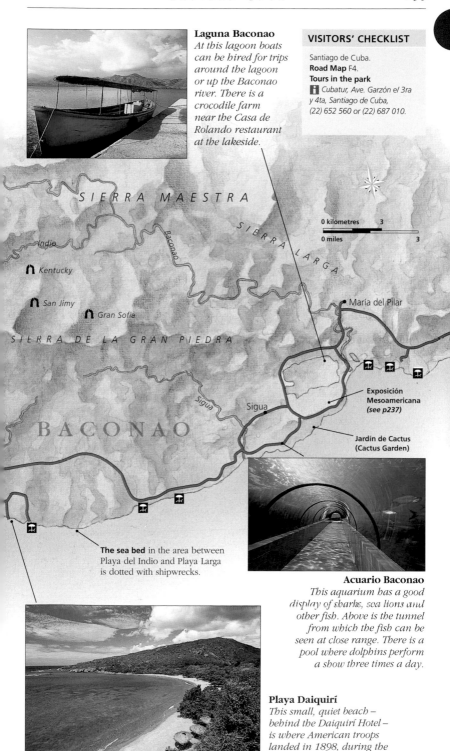

Laguna Baconao
At this lagoon boats can be hired for trips around the lagoon or up the Baconao river. There is a crocodile farm near the Casa de Rolando restaurant at the lakeside.

SIERRA MAESTRA

SIERRA LARGA

0 kilometres   3

0 miles   3

Indio

Kentucky

San Jimy   Gran Sofia

SIERRA DE LA GRAN PIEDRA

María del Pilar

Sigua

BACONAO

Sigua

Exposición Mesoamericana
(see p237)

Jardín de Cactus
(Cactus Garden)

The sea bed in the area between Playa del Indio and Playa Larga is dotted with shipwrecks.

Acuario Baconao
This aquarium has a good display of sharks, sea lions and other fish. Above is the tunnel from which the fish can be seen at close range. There is a pool where dolphins perform a show three times a day.

Playa Daiquirí
This small, quiet beach – behind the Daiquirí Hotel – is where American troops landed in 1898, during the US occupation (see p44).

Exploring the Parque Baconao

The 1960 Maya Cuba car, a museum piece

It is possible to explore the park by car or taxi in a day, although accommodation is available. Heading east from Santiago, along Avenida Raúl Pujol, you will pass the zoo (Parque Zoológico), and, nearby, the Arbol de la Paz (Tree of Peace), a ceiba tree beneath which the Spanish signed the surrender agreement in 1898. The entrance to Parque Baconao is not far beyond the confines of the city. Most of the attractions are suitable for families and can be reached by car, but the peak of the Gran Piedra and the easternmost beaches are only accessible on foot.

A strelitzia in flower at the Gran Piedra Jardín Botánico

The spectacular view from the Gran Piedra

🏠 Granjita Siboney

Carretera Siboney km 13,5.
Tel (22) 399 168.
◯ 9am–1pm Mon, 9am–4:45pm Tue–Sun. 🖼 🎫 📷 (with charge).
By the roadside 16 km (10 miles) east of Santiago, this is the farm rented by Abel Santamaría in 1953 as a base of operations in the run-up to the assault on the Moncada barracks. It was from here, on 26 July, that the young rebels drove into Santiago to launch the attack. Their attempt failed and Granjita Siboney itself was later attacked by Batista's men. The (reconstructed) bullet holes can be seen around the door.

Granjita Siboney is now a museum with the uniforms and some of the weapons that the revolutionaries wore and carried that day. Next door is the Generación del Centenario gallery, with paintings honouring the rebels who died during the attack on the barracks, as well as photographs, documents and the car Castro used in the attack.

🌿 Gran Piedra

Jardín Botánico ◯ daily.
🖼 📷
Heading west from Granjita Siboney, you come to a turn-off to Gran Piedra: this 12-km (7-mile) road with hairpin bends provides one of the best panoramas in Cuba and views of the intense green of the tropical and mountain forests. Beyond the Jardín Botánico, with its many

species of orchid and multi-coloured strelitzias (flowers more commonly known as bird of paradise), a flight of 459 steps leads up to the top of the Gran Piedra (1,234 m/4,048 ft asl). This gigantic, 25-m (82-ft) monolith rests on the crater of an extinct volcano.

It is best to make the climb in the morning, because the afternoon can bring foggy weather and you may not see far into the distance. However, on clear days the view is simply superb: it stretches from the mountains to the coast, and even as far as Haiti.

🏛 Cafetal La Isabelica

Carretera de la Gran Piedra km 14.
◯ daily. 🖼 📷 🎫
There are numerous old coffee plantations around the Gran Piedra, all of which were recently added to the World Heritage List by UNESCO. Almost all of the plantations are in ruins, but one exception is the Cafetal La Isabelica, which can be reached easily via a path from the foot of the Gran Piedra.

Granjita Siboney farm, showing the signs of the July 1953 attack

This plantation belonged to Victor Constantin, a French landowner who, together with many others, fled from Haiti in the late 1700s following a slave uprising there. He brought with him numerous slaves and his mistress, Isabel María, after whom he named his plantation.

The largest structure is the manor house. The ground floor was partly for the labourers and partly used to store tools and implements. The first floor consists of a bedroom, living room, dining room and studio, all with 18th-century furniture and furnishings.

The house overlooks a terrace where coffee beans were left to dry – actually the roof of a large storehouse.

Reproductions of pre-Columbian objects, Exposición Mesoamericana

Interior of the Cafetal La Isabelica owner's manor house

Nearby are the kitchens, behind which is the water tank; the whole area is surrounded by coffee plants. Visitors to the *cafetal* museum are offered a demonstration of how coffee is grown and processed for consumption.

The provincial authorities have approved a project to restore the Cafetal La Isabelica, which will then become the home of an ethnographic museum.

🏛 Conjunto de Museos y Exposiciones de la Punta

Carretera de Baconao.
⬜ *daily.* 🖼 📷
A cross between a museum and a trade fair, this collection of buildings contains displays of all kinds of things from stamps and dolls to ceramics

and archaeological finds. Of particular interest is the Salon de Historia del Transporte Terrestre por Carretera, which houses a fascinating collection of 2,000-plus miniature cars and an array of old vintage cars, including a local Maya Cuba – a tiny, one-cylinder car. The oldest is a 1912 Model T Ford. There are also vehicles of historical significance, including cars that once belonged to Fidel Castro and Benny Moré.

🏛 Exposición Mesoamericana

Carretera de Baconao.
⬜ *daily.* 🖼 📷
This series of sea caves along the road are showcases for reproductions of Central American pre-Columbian works of art.

THE ORIGINS OF COFFEE GROWING IN CUBA

Coffee was introduced to Cuba at the end of the 18th century, by which time it had been a fashionable drink among the European aristocracy and bourgeoisie for some time. The French coffee growers who had fled to Eastern Cuba from Haiti in 1791 were well aware of this: they were the ones who brought the "new" plant to the island. The hills around Santiago and the valleys between Baracoa and Guantánamo were ideal for coffee growing, because they offered both water and shade. Coffee was an immediate success, and demand increased so much that it was planted along the coast too. In 1803 there were 100,000 coffee trees; by 1807

this figure had increased to four million, cultivated on 191 plantations. The French growers became very wealthy, building palatial manor houses on their plantations. As the cultivation of coffee required plenty of manual labour, and there weren't enough workers from Haiti, there was a "boom" in the slave trade in the early 19th century. Cuban archives mention 7,654 "dead souls" at the beginning of the century, and 42,000 in 1820. While this immigration contributed to the economic fortune of the island, it proved to be the end of the landowners. It was not long before the slaves, increasingly numerous and organized, began to rebel against their condition (see p42).

Coffee growing beneath the trees in the mountains

Guantánamo ⑰

Guantánamo. **Road Map** F4.
🏃 200,000. ✈ 🚌 🏛

If it were not for the US
naval base and the famous
song *Guantanamera* (girl
from Guantánamo), this town
would probably only be
known to Cubans and music
experts. Its name, in fact, is
linked with the *changüí*, a
variation of *son* music that
developed in the coffee
plantations in the mountains,
music made famous by the
musician Helio Revé.

Guantanamera was
composed by Joseíto
Fernández in the 1940s
almost for fun, drawing
inspiration from a proud local
girl who had not reacted to a
compliment he paid her.
Later, some "literary" verses
from the *Versos Sencillos* by
José Martí were adapted to
the music.

The town of Guantánamo
was founded in 1796 to take
in the French fleeing from
Haiti and developed during
the 19th century. The capital
of a varied province where
desert areas studded with
cactus alternate with green
mountains, Guantánamo has
few sights of note. A tour of
the small historic centre is
little more than a walk around
Parque Martí, dominated by
the **Parroquial de Santa
Catalina de Riccis** (1868).

Opposite the church is a
statue of General Pedro A
Pérez, sculpted in 1928.

An interesting Colonial building facing the square is the
old Spanish prison, now the
home of the modest **Museo**

**Joseíto Fernández, composer of
the song *Guantanamera***

The Parroquial de Santa Catalina de Riccis in the Parque Martí

Provincial, which contains a
collection of documents, photographs and objects related to
the history of the province.

**🏛 Museo Provincial
de Guantánamo**
Plaza Martí, esq. Prado.
Tel *(21) 325 872.* ⬜ *2–6pm Mon,
8am–noon & 2–6pm Tue–Sat.*
⬤ *1 Jan, 1 May, 26 Jul, 10 Oct, 25
Dec.* 📷 🎥 📷 *(with charge).*

**A stone gorilla in the Museo
Zoológico de Piedra**

Environs
Around 20 km (12 miles) east
of Guantánamo, on the road to
Lomas de Yateras, a coffee-
growing area, is an unusual
open-air museum, the **Museo
Zoológico de Piedra**. It was
founded by Angel Iñigo, a
farmer and self-taught sculptor.
Since 1978 he has produced
sculptures of about 40 animals
in stone, including lions, boa
constrictors, tapirs, buffaloes,
rhinoceroses and gorillas. All
are on display.

At the mouth of Guan-
tánamo bay, some 20 km (12
miles) south of the city are two
Cuban ports, **Caimanera** and
Boquerón, both close to the
US naval base. The former is
within a Cuban military zone
and is off-limits to everyone

except those who live there
and those with a special pass.
There is a hotel in Caimanera
(*see p267*) but you need a
permit to stay.

The US naval base is not
open to the public. However,
it can be "spied" on from an
unusual viewing point (*mirador*), purpose built above an
existing military command post
by the Cuban authorities, who
now make the most of their
view over the base.

To visit the **Mirador Los
Malones**, situated on a hill off
the Baracoa road, about 15
miles (24 km) east of Guantánamo, make arrangements
either in Santiago, with the
Gaviota tourist agency, or in
Guantánamo, in the epony-
mous hotel.

After passing the main gate
of the Cuban military zone,
visitors proceed for about 10
km (6 miles) through forests
of cacti before reaching the
mirador. Firstly, the tour goes
into an underground museum,
where a Cuban military attaché
explains the reasons why Cuba
wants the US to give back this
territory. A detailed model of
the base is also on view here.
Stairs or a lift then take visitors
to the viewing point at the
top of the hill (where there is
also a small restaurant). A
telescope enables visitors to
have a good look at the base
and – unusually within a
military zone – it is permitted
to film and take photographs.

🏛 Museo Zoológico de Piedra
Boquerón de Yateras. ⬜ *Mon–Sat.*
⬤ *1 Jan, 1 May, 26 Jul, 10 Oct,
25 Dec.* 📷 📷

Costa Sur ⑱

Guantánamo. **Road Map** F4.

Travelling eastwards from Guantánamo, visitors will pass through the most barren part of Cuba, where the climate is desert-like because of the hot winds blowing here. This is a unique area on the island where cacti and succulents are the main vegetation. The coast road, tucked in between the mountains and the blue sea, is spectacular. The rocky coast has tiny coves with pebble beaches, home to an assortment of seashells and *Polymita picta* snails *(see p245).*

La Farola ⑲

Guantánamo. **Road Map** F4.

Cajobabo – a southern coastal town where José Martí and Máximo Gómez landed to begin the 1895 war against Spain – marks the beginning of La Farola, a spectacular 49-km (30-mile) road that wends its way upwards over the mountains to Baracoa, through vegetation that becomes more and more luxuriant as the coast is left behind.

Until 1959 Cajobabo could only be reached by ship. In order to connect it to the rest of the island, in the 1960s engineers excavated sections of mountainside in the Sierra del Purial in order to create a kind of "flying highway". The road acquired its name *(farola* means beacon) because in some stretches it looks like a beam, suspended in air. It is regarded as one of the great engineering feats of recent Cuban history.

This highway and the periodic viewing points offer incredible views of the peaks of the Sierra Maestra, lush valleys, tropical forests, pine groves, banana plantations, rivers, waterfalls and royal palm trees. The luxuriant vegetation seems to swallow up the road in places. Along the road, people sell local produce such as coffee, red bananas and tangerines.

THE AMERICAN NAVAL BASE

In 1903 the US – the victors, together with the Cubans, in the war against Spain – obliged the Cuban Republic to accept the Platt Amendment *(see p45),* whereby the latter had to grant the US Navy the right to install a naval base in the bay of Guantánamo. The US was granted a lease of a minimum of 99 years in 1934. For this occupancy, the American government pays $2,000 per year, though it is said that the Cuban government has regularly returned this sum to the US since 1959. In the past the situation has taken on the dramatic overtones of the Cold War and highlighted a difficult state of co-existence. Inside the base, the menial jobs are done by Puerto Ricans, the wives of the servicemen do their shopping in supermarkets stocked with food flown in from the US, and there are two English-language radio stations and one TV station. The base, US territory in Cuba, covers 110 sq km (43 sq miles), and has two runways for military planes. The whole area is surrounded by 27 km (17 miles) of fence.

Mirador Los Malones: a telescope looking over the American base

View from one of the observation points along La Farola road

Baracoa ⑳

Cocoa fruit, a local crop

The oldest city in Cuba lies at the far eastern tip of the island. Its name in the Arauaca language, spoken by the former inhabitants of the area, means "the presence of the sea". Nuestra Señora de la Asunción de Baracoa villa was founded on 15 August 1511, on a curved bay that had been discovered some 20 years earlier by Columbus, and immediately became the political and ecclesiastical capital of Cuba. However, this status was short-lived. In 1515, the city founder Diego Velázquez transferred his residence to Santiago, marking the beginning of a long period of social and economic isolation for Baracoa.

The Cruz de la Parra, perhaps brought to Cuba by Columbus

🏠 **Catedral de Nuestra Señora de la Asunción**
Calle Maceo 152. *Tel (21) 643 352.*
⭘ 9am–noon & 2–6pm Mon– Sat, 9am–noon Sun. 🕯 7:30am Tue–Wed, 5:30pm Thu–Fri, 8pm Sat, 10am Sun.
This modest church, built in 1512 and restored in 1833, is most famous as the home of the Cruz de la Parra, a wooden cross that is said to be the oldest symbol of Christianity in the New World. According to legend, the cross was brought to Cuba by Columbus on his first voyage to America, and on 1 December 1492 it was placed on the spot where Baracoa was later founded. It is said that the cross disappeared one day and was then miraculously found under the climbing vine *(parra)* in a settler's garden, hence its name. The four tips of the cross are now covered with metal sheets, because in the past worshippers used to pull off splinters and keep them as relics.

The cathedral is not always open, but if you want to see the Cruz de la Parra and want information about it, or about the city in general, just ask for the sacristan and he will try to help you.

A street in Baracoa, dominated by lush vegetation

Exploring Baracoa

"Baracoa means nature", the Cubans say, and it is certainly true: enclosed by tropical forest and the sea, for four centuries this town has managed to live by fishing, cultivating cocoa, coconuts and bananas, and by gathering wood. While the isolation has created inconveniences, it has also allowed the locals to maintain their traditions and preserve the ecosystem.

The historic centre of Baracoa is not Colonial, but a mixture of styles, with some Neo-Classical and French influences. Thick vegetation towers over the buildings and has even invaded some houses, many of which are built of wood.

The best view of the town is seen from the terrace of an 18th-century fortress on a hill above the town: the **Castillo de Seboruco**, now El Castillo hotel *(see p267)*. From here you can see the roofs and the bay of Baracoa, dominated to the west by the rock of El Yunque *(see p244)*.

Parque Independencia

In the main square, overlooked by the cathedral, is a famous bust of the Indian leader Hatuey *(see p219)*. Nearby are the **Casa de la Trova**, the **Fondo de Bienes Culturales**, which exhibits works by local painters, sculptors and craftsmen, and the **Casa de la Cultura**, an eclectic building with Colonial elements that hosts evening performances and events.

At No. 123 Calle Maceo is the **Casa del Chocolate**, which serves excellent hot chocolate. Baracoa cocoa is famous throughout Cuba.

A typical single-storey wooden house in Baracoa

◁ **The bay of Baracoa viewed from the Castillo de Seboruco**

🏛 Fuerte Matachín (Museo Municipal)

Calle Martí y Malecón. *Tel (21) 642 122.* ◻ 8am–noon & 2–6pm daily. 🎦 🎫 📷 (with charge).

This small museum, which provides an interesting overview of local history, is housed in a military fortress built during the Colonial period to defend the city from pirates. (Piracy was particularly active in the 18th and 19th centuries.)

The displays start with archaeological finds of the pre-Columbian era, and are followed by documents, maps, paintings and prints related to Spanish domination, pirates, slaves and the plantations.

There is an interesting natural history section with specimens on display, including the *Polymita* snails (see p245). The museum is also a historical and geographical research centre and fosters initiatives to preserve and develop local culture.

Along the fort walls is a battery of cannons facing seawards, and a small garden.

Statue of Columbus, Museo Municipal garden

El Malecón

This is the seafront that connects the two 19th-century forts in Baracoa: Fuerte Matachín, to the east, and **Fuerte de la Punta**, to the west, now a restaurant. The Malecón is ideal for a quiet stroll during the week. On Saturdays a bustling food market is held here in the morning, and in the evening the road is prepared for the *noche baracoesa*, a lively folk festival during which people eat, drink and dance along the seafront.

Hotel La Rusa

Halfway along the Malecón is Hotel La Rusa, a historic hotel that once belonged to the Russian princess Magdalena Rowenskaya, who fled her country with her husband in 1917 after the October Revolution. She eventually settled in Baracoa, where she ended up opening a restaurant and giving singing lessons. Much later,

VISITORS' CHECKLIST

Guantánamo. **Road Map** F4. 🏠 50,000. ✈ 4 km (2 miles) west of town, (21) 645 376. 🚌 Ave. Los Mártires, esq. Martí, (21) 643 880. ℹ Cubatur, Calle Maceo 149 esq. Pelayo Cuervo, (21) 645 306. 🗓 Sat.

she became active in the 26 July Movement and entertained Castro, Che and other revolutionaries.

The hotel foyer has photographs and relics belonging to this eccentric figure, who was later immortalized by the novelist Alejo Carpentier (see p29) in his work *The Consecration of Spring*.

The rundown exterior of the Hotel La Rusa

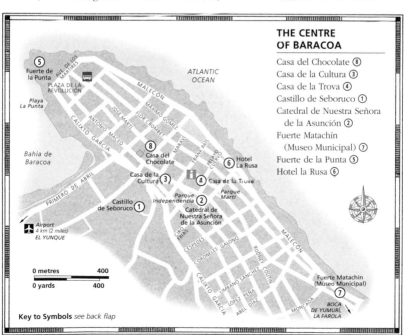

THE CENTRE OF BARACOA

Key to Symbols see back flap

The mountain of El Yunque, dominating the bay of Baracoa

El Yunque ㉑

Guantánamo. **Road Map** F4.
🛈 *Buró de Turismo, Hotel El Castillo, Baracoa, (21) 642 103.*

A limestone formation, 575 m (1,885 ft) high, covered with thick vegetation, El Yunque was a sacred site for the Taíno Indians for many centuries. Later it became a natural landmark for navigators about to land at the port of Baracoa. The Spanish called it "El Yunque" (the anvil) because of its unmistakable outline. The outcrop's shape has led to local misapprehension that this was the rock that Columbus described as "a square mountain that looks like an island" in 1492. In fact, he was referring to a similarly shaped rock at Bariay near Gibara *(see p214)*.

The slopes of the mountain, which has been declared a biosphere reserve by UNESCO, are home to botanical rarities, including two carnivorous plants and *Podocarpus*, one of the oldest plant species in the world, as well as an endemic palm tree, *Coccothrinax yunquensis.*

El Yunque is also the habitat for some endangered species of bird such as the *carpintero real (Campeophilus principalis)* and the *caguarero* hawk *(Chondrohierax wilsonii)*, as well as for the smallest amphibian in the world, the *Sminthillus limbatus,* less than 1 cm (0.4 inch) long, and another very ancient species, the *almiquí (Solenodon cubanus),* a mammal similar to a rat.

Río Toa ㉒

Road Map F4.

The valley fed by the Río Toa, Cuba's biggest river, was recently made a nature reserve, the **Parque Natural Río Toa**. Still lacking in roads and facilities, this park is part of a wide-ranging project to create refuges and camping sites that will not interfere with the local ecosystems.

Local farmers still use an old-fashioned craft to travel upstream – the *cayuca,* a flat canoe of Indian origin. From the river, visitors can admire the majestic Pico Galán (974 m/3,200 ft) and the great waterfalls that cascade into the river from steep cliffs. Enquire in Baracoa if you are interested in exploring the area.

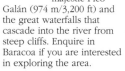

Going up the Río Toa in a rowing boat

Environs
Northwest of Baracoa, 21 km (12 miles) past the mouth of

Playa Maguaná, one of the unspoilt beaches near Baracoa

Río Miel, flowing through virtually virgin tropical forest between Baracoa and Boca de Yumurí

the Río Toa, is **Playa Maguaná**, the most beautiful beach in the province, with dazzling white sand. The beach's Indian name refers to the presence of a nearby archaeological site. A 2-km (1-mile) coral reef lies only 500 m (1,640 ft) from the shore. Be warned though that the sea can often be rather choppy in this area.

There is a modern holiday village hidden among the coconut palms, where villas can be rented, but this place is still delightfully unspoilt.

Boca de Yumurí ㉓

Road Map F4.

Around 30 km (18 miles) east of Baracoa, this village of *bohíos* (traditional dwellings with palm-leaf roofs) takes its name from the Yumurí river, which flows into the sea here. Its inhabitants live by fishing, but earn a little extra by taking tourists on boat rides on the river (and by selling *Polymita* shells).

A short boat ride across the Yumurí river will take you to an enchanting beach. Another interesting trip is to go upstream, where the river course reaches an impressive canyon with walls as much as 180 m (590 ft) high.

The Río Yumurí flows through an area interesting for its ecology. Colourful tropical birdlife abounds, including the *zunzún*, the *tocororo* and the *cartacuba* (*see pp20–21*).

Environs
East of Boca de Yumurí, also accessible from Cajobabo, is the tiny, isolated village of **Maisí** and beyond is the easternmost tip of Cuba, Punta Maisí. On clear days it is possible to see as far as Haiti from the headland. This area has been turned into the Parque Natural Terrazas de Maisí and the building of further roads and facilities is planned.

POLYMITA SNAILS

A genus endemic to the Baracoa area, the *Polymita* is a snail with a brilliantly coloured shell. According to the colour, six species of *Polymita* can be identified: *P. picta, P. muscarum, P. sulphurosa, P. versicolor, P. venusta* and *P. brocheri*. All these species live on trees and plants, and feed on mushrooms and lichens, contributing to the health of the plants, especially coffee trees. *Polymita* snails can be easily recognized, because the shell with coloured stripes looks as though it has been painted, and stands out clearly against the bright green vegetation. Legend has it that the snail acquired its colours from a young Indian who had no pearls or jewels to give to his beloved. He painted a snail shell with the yellow of the sun, the green of the woods, the red of the flowers, and the white from the foam of the waves. But when he decided to take the blue from the sky, it was too late in the day, and he had to be content with the black of night. Today this snail, highly prized for its shell, is an endangered species. Although selling or gathering *Polymita* is not illegal, both locals and visitors are urged to leave them alone.

Patterned
Polymita shells

Viewing Haiti from Punta Maisí, at the eastern-most tip of Cuba

TRAVELLERS' NEEDS

WHERE TO STAY

Since 1980, when Cuba decided to open its frontiers to foreign visitors, the growth in tourism has obliged the government to invest heavily in the hotel industry. Some of the old historic hotels have been restored and equipped with international standards of comfort, and new infrastructure has been created, often through joint ventures involving the Cuban Ministry of Tourism and foreign companies. Today, visitors can choose from a variety

Carro de la Revolución, ceramic piece by Sosabravo (see p25) Habana Libre hotel, Havana

of accommodation, with choices ranging from modern luxury hotels with swimming pools and good sports facilities to Colonial, city centre hotels and all-inclusive holiday villages on small uninhabited islands. The cheapest hotels are still decidedly spartan and rarely meet international standards. Since 1996, Cubans have been allowed to let out rooms in their own homes or even entire apartments, an increasingly popular arrangement with tourists.

Airy hotel interior in Havana

HOTEL CHAINS

Most visitors to Cuba come on package holidays and a number of hotel chains cater for this type of tourism. All hotels are state-owned, although some are managed by joint venture agencies.

One upmarket chain is the Cuban **Gran Caribe**, whose hotels include the historic Hotel Nacional in Havana *(see p98)*, an architectural gem built in 1930, the Hotel Plaza and the Hotel Inglaterra *(see pp81–2)* in Havana's Parque Central, and the elegant Casa Granda in Santiago.Gran Caribe also manages several more modern hotels, such as the Habana Riviera in Havana and the Hotel Jagua in Cienfuegos, and well-equipped residences in seaside resorts such as the Hotel Internacional in Varadero and the Hotel Pelícano at Cayo Largo.

High standards are also guaranteed by the **Cubanacán** and **Sol Meliá** chains, both of which have built hotels throughout Cuba. Cubanacán manages good hotels of its own and others affiliated to international chains,

The foyer in the Hotel Meliá Cohiba, Varadero, seen from the glass lift

including several good-value 3-star hotels, such as the Versalles in Santiago and the Faro Luna in Cienfuegos. The Sol Meliá chain manages the elegant Meliá Cohiba in Havana and the modern Hotel Santiago in Santiago de Cuba.

Gaviota, which specializes in ecological tourism *(see p250)*, offers comfortable accommodation in the main coastal resorts, on the *cayos* and in mountain areas. Gaviota runs the only holiday village at Cayo Saetía.

The hotels forming the **Islazul** chain are of a lower standard, but are still on an international level, offering basic levels of comfort at lower prices.

Another quite different style is offered by **Habaguanex**, a Cuban company founded under the auspices of the Oficina del Historiador de la Ciudad in Havana, which restores old buildings in the Habana Vieja quarter, converting them into shops, cafés and hotels. Habaguanex hotels include historic buildings such as the Hostal Conde de Villanueva, a converted 17th-century mansion; the new San Miguel; the Hotel Ambos Mundos, a Hemingway favourite; and the Santa Isabel, in a splendid Colonial building facing the Plaza de Armas *(see p67)*.

◁ **Interior of the historic Floridita bar-restaurant in Havana**

GRADING

Cuban hotels are classified according to the international star system, from one star rising to five stars. However, visitors are likely to find that standards within a particular star rating can vary considerably. Some mid-range hotels may have been good quality in the 1950s, but have since become rundown and not brought into line with modern needs. One-star hotels are generally to be avoided; a better choice would be a private house.

The Meliá Cohiba in Havana, a five-star luxury hotel

PRICES

Hotel rates in the capital and in the more famous seaside resorts such as Cayo Largo, Varadero, Cayo Coco and Playa Guardalavaca, are higher than in the rest of the country and correspond more or less to international levels.

The terrace at the Casa Granda hotel in the heart of Santiago de Cuba

Whatever the star rating of a hotel, prices will be higher in peak season, which runs from Christmas to 1 April, and from the beginning of July to the end of August.

BOOKING

It is best to book accommodation well ahead of your visit through a travel agency in your home country to ensure that you will get a room and date to your liking. Your tour operator may also be able to offer special package deals that are rarely to be found in Cuba itself. In high season, in particular when there are special events such as Carnival in Santiago, or one of the many local and cultural festivals in Havana, it may be difficult to find a room.

Visitors taking part in trade events such as the Convención del Turismo (Tourism Fair), held in May, or the February Book Fair, will find there are special pricing agreements with hotels in Havana.

TIPPING

It is customary to leave a tip (propina) for the hotel staff at the end of your stay. The amount of the propina is at your discretion and will vary according to the type of hotel, how long you stay and the type and quality of service. It is, however, useful to remember that a tip in convertible pesos or euros may amount to the equivalent of a month's salary in Cuban pesos (see p306).

A percentage of the tips is often donated to charities. The national fund for cancer research is one of the main causes to benefit in this way.

HOLIDAY VILLAGES

These are ideal for people who want a relaxing, sunny holiday by the beach or surrounded by unspoiled landscape, with comfortable rooms and all meals and facilities provided.

All-inclusive packages offer a complete deal, with lodging in bungalows or apartments with bathroom, phone, air conditioning and TV. The price typically includes breakfast, lunch and dinner (usually buffet), and all drinks. Plus, sports activities of all kinds (sailing, snorkelling, scuba diving, swimming, surfing) are provided. Other options include a snack bar and pool bar; games rooms, playgrounds and babysitting services; freshwater pools for children and adults; car rental service; shops and beach equipment. In some parts of Cuba, these all-inclusive holiday villages are the only hotel option available.

The pool and tennis courts at the Hotel Sol Palmeras in Varadero

The Hotel La Moka, in the Sierra del Rosario reserve, a favourite with "eco-tourists"

CAMPING

Besides some very modest camping sites reserved for Cubans, there are other sites (campismos) run by **Cubamar Viajes**, located in or near nature reserves and along the coast. Despite being categorized as camping sites, accommodation is in fact in bungalows (cabañas). The sites also usually have a restaurant and a pool.

The quality of the cabañas varies, but they are usually simple and clean. However, this type of accommodation does not suit everyone. These camping sites often operate more like a holiday village, with daytime and evening recreational activities.

Casual tent-pitching or sleeping out on beaches is not permitted in Cuba.

SPECIALIST HOLIDAYS

Many tour operators specializing in holidays in Cuba also offer specialist tours for those interested in a particular activity. Many all-inclusive resorts offer diving lessons for beginners, but qualified divers have a wider range of options. People planning more advanced diving need to provide proof of their qualifications and must take out fully comprehensive travel insurance. Many operators recommend that divers should be able to demonstrate a minimum of ten logged dives. Some dive sites such as María La Gorda (see p146) and Isla de la Juventud (see p150) require skill and experience.

Keen divers can stay in hotels and tourist villages near dive sites or in some of the marinas (particularly those belonging to the Marinas Marlin chain). All-inclusive packages usually include the dives as well.

The best place to learn salsa is of course in Cuba, and UK-based **Dance Holidays** arranges all-inclusive holidays with salsa tuition by expert teachers and visits to the best dance venues.

Conservation-conscious holidays in unspoiled landscape are available from a few hotels that operate as ecological tourism centres. These are found in the Pinar del Río area and in the Sierra del Rosario, near Marea del Portillo (in the Sierra Maestra) and Baracoa. Many centres also organize excursions, such as birdwatching trips.

There are also health farms, combining relaxation and medical or beauty treatments. The modern, comfortable clinics and beauty centres are run by well-trained staff. Health provision for foreign visitors is provided in these centres by **Servimed**, while accommodation is organized by **Cubanacán Turismo y Salud**.

The Gaviota and Islazul chains also run a number of spa hotels; two of these are the Kurhotel at Topes de Collantes and the Hotel Elguea at Corralillo.

A cabin in pinewoods in Las Terrazas village

DISABLED TRAVELLERS

Only the more recently built hotels have rooms purpose-built for disabled people, including bathrooms with wheelchair access. Unfortunately, the majority of Cuban hotels are not equipped with such facilities. Nonetheless, in general hotel staff will do everything they can to be of help to disabled clients.

Accommodation in the María La Gorda holiday village, particularly popular with divers

PRIVATE ROOMS

Renting rooms in private homes *(casas particulares)* is a good arrangement for visitors who want to experience everyday Cuban life at first-hand and meet local people. Hosts will respect privacy, but you should be prepared to become involved in the family's everyday life. It will help to have a smattering of Spanish.

Besides single rooms, you can also rent small apartments. Sometimes you can even find very comfortable living quarters in historic buildings, particularly in old cities like Trinidad.

The proverbial Cuban hospitality makes this type of accommodation particularly pleasant: after all, living in a private home is the simplest and best way to feel part of the place. Another advantage is that the home owners and their families can provide ideas about what to see, where to eat and how to spend the evening.

If you are interested in this type of arrangement, it is best to get addresses from someone you know who has already done this. On the whole, avoid taking advice from strangers – above all, do

Interior of a private home in Gibara, in Holguín province

not allow someone you have met casually on the street to take you to a private home, as he/she may simply be an unreliable "hustler". These people usually receive a commission of your room rent from the owners, which is added to the room price.

If you are pleased with the accommodation in a private home, ask the owners for recommended addresses in other places that you intend to visit: this should provide some guarantee of similar standards. Houses legally authorized to let out rooms can be recognized by the sticker on the door.

The sticker used for *casas particulares* licensed for rental

When you take up your room, the owners will request a passport or some identification, as they are obliged by law to register your personal data with the Immigration Police.

The taxes paid for room rental in the *casas particulares* are used by local authorities to build homes for young couples.

The amenities, cleanliness and charm of these homes will of course vary and there are no cut-and-dried standards. This type of accommodation is relatively new, and as yet there are no official lists of home owners offering rooms. Some information can be had by visiting: www.geocities.com/ Paris/Parc/6851/habana.htm.

DIRECTORY

HOTEL CHAINS

Cubanacán Hoteles
Calle 23 #156 e/n N y O,
Vedado,
Havana.
Tel (7) 833 4090.
Fax (7) 834 4277.
www.cubanacan.cu

Gaviota
Edificio La Marina,
Ave. del Puerto 102,
Havana.
Tel (7) 866 6777.
Fax (7) 866 2780
or *(7) 866 1879.*
www.gaviota-grupo.com

Gran Caribe
Calle 7 no. 4210, e/42 y
44, Miramar, Havana.
Tel (7) 204 0575.
Fax (7) 204 0238.
www.grancaribe.cu

Habaguanex
Calle Oficios 110,
e/ Lamparilla y
Amargura, Havana.
Tel and Fax (7) 8609 761.
www.habaguanex.com

Islazul
Tel (7) 8325 152
or *(7) 8320 571.*
Fax (7) 833 3458
www.islazul. cu

Sol Meliá
Ave. 5 no. 2008,
Miramar,
Havana.
Tel (7) 204 0910.
Fax (7) 204 0912.
www.solmeliacuba.com

CAMPING

Cubamar Viajes
Calle 3e/ 12y
Malécon,
Vedado,
Havana.
Tel (7) 833 2524
or *(7) 832 1116.*
Fax (7) 831 2891.
www.cubamarviajes.cu

SPECIALIST TOURISM

Dance Holidays
Tel (01206) 577 000 (UK).
Fax (01206) 570 057 (UK).
www.danceholidays.com

Servimed – Cubanacán Turismo y Salud
Ave. 43 no. 1418,
esq.18, Miramar,
Havana.
Tel (7) 204 4811.
Fax (7) 204 1630.

Choosing a Hotel

The hotels in this guide have been selected across a wide price range for their character, facilities and location. The prices at many establishments, particularly the national hotel chains and the big beach resort hotels, are subject to frequent change. Entries are listed by region, beginning with Havana. For details of restaurants, see pages 276–83.

PRICE CATEGORIES (IN CUBAN CONVERTIBLE PESOS – CUC$)

Standard double room per night, with breakfast and all taxes included.
Ⓢ Under 50 CUC$
ⓈⓈ 50–100 CUC$
ⓈⓈⓈ 100–150 CUC$
ⓈⓈⓈⓈ 150–200 CUC$
ⓈⓈⓈⓈⓈ Over 200 CUC$

HAVANA

HABANA VIEJA Casa de Amalia　Ⓢ

Prado 20, 7mo piso, e/ San Lázaro y Cárcel **Tel** *(7) 861 7824* **Rooms** *2*　　**Map** *4 D1*

There are fantastic views out over the ocean and across to the lighthouse and fortress complex on the eastern side of the bay from this seventh-floor flat. One of the guest rooms is very small, and the furnishings are quite basic, but the hosts are attentive.

HABANA VIEJA Casa de Humberto Acosta　Ⓢ

Compostela 611, 2do piso, e/ Sol y Luz **Tel** *(7) 860 3264* **Rooms** *2*　　**Map** *4 E3*

The Casa de Humberto Acosta's large first-floor terrace is the highlight here, but the common rooms of the whole house are a delight, with bags of colonial character. Conversely, the guest rooms are rather basic. **johnyterroni@yahoo.es**

HABANA VIEJA Casa de Sergio y Miriam　Ⓢ

Luz no.109, apto 5, e/ Inquisidor y San Ignacio **Tel** *(7) 860 8192* **Rooms** *2*　　**Map** *4 F3*

This is deep in southern Habana Vieja and provides an authentic taste of old town life away from the tour groups. Both rooms here have two single beds (one with en suite bathroom), and both are a bit cramped but very clean. Breakfast is charged at 4 CUC$ per person. **mirysergio@yahoo.es**

HABANA VIEJA Chez Nous　Ⓢ

Brasil (Teniente Rey) 115 esq. Cuba **Tel** *(7) 862 6287* **Rooms** *2*　　**Map** *4 E3*

An exceptional *casa particular* and one of the most distinctly furnished in the city. There's genuine original colonial-era furniture all over the high-ceilinged house and an extraordinary Romanesque bathroom. One of the rooms is on the roof, accessed via a spiral staircase and, in contrast to the rest of the house, is very modern. Lots of comfort.

HABANA VIEJA Hostal Mesón de la Flota　ⓈⓈ

Mercaderes 257 e/ Amargura y Brasil (Teniente Rey) **Tel** *(7) 863 3838* **Fax** *(7) 862 9281* **Rooms** *5*　　**Map** *4 E2*

The least expensive hotel in Habana Vieja and one of the most rustic with a distinct tavern character and a vague Spanish theme. Don't expect any early nights here as the tapas restaurant has nightly flamenco performances with amplified music. **www.habaguanex.com**

HABANA VIEJA Hostal Valencia　ⓈⓈ

Oficios 53 esq. Obrapía **Tel** *(7) 867 1037* **Fax** *(7) 860 5628* **Rooms** *14*　　**Map** *4 E2*

Rural chic and rustic charm characterize this down-to-earth hostel. There's an excellent paella restaurant whose tables spill out from its intimate interior onto the central patio, rich in potted plants. All rooms are located up the wide staircase on the first floor and are very comfortable. **www.habaguanex.com**

HABANA VIEJA Hotel Park View　ⓈⓈ

Colón 101 esq. Morro **Tel** *(7) 861 3293* **Fax** *(7) 863 6036* **Rooms** *55*　　**Map** *4 D2*

The most modern of Habana Vieja's recently renovated hotels, with a character distinct from all the others. The lobby area with its small bar is smart and shiny but also down-to-earth with comfy cushioned armchairs. There are great views from the seventh-floor restaurant and rooms are homely with curtains and small TVs. **www.habaguanex.com**

HABANA VIEJA Hostal del Tejadillo　ⓈⓈⓈ

Tejadillo 12 esq. San Ignacio **Tel** *(7) 863 7283* **Fax** *(7) 863 8830* **Rooms** *32*　　**Map** *4 E2*

An intimate, refined hotel but the least distinct of the colonial conversions in Habana Vieja. The restaurant is very small, though it spills onto a tiny, walled-in patio. Rooms are of the same high standard as all the hostels, and some are gathered around a second patio brimming with potted plants. **www.habaguanex.com**

HABANA VIEJA Hostal Los Frailes　ⓈⓈⓈ

Brasil (Teniente Rey), e/ Oficios y Mercaderes **Tel** *(7) 862 9383* **Fax** *(7) 862 9718* **Rooms** *22*　　**Map** *4 F3*

Something of a novelty hotel, the staff in this moody little place all dress as monks. This seems to have engendered an appropriately subdued vibe. The communal areas, such as the lobby lounge with its low wood-raftered ceiling and the intimate patio with a quietly flowing fountain, are deliberately dark and shady. **www.habaguanex.com**

Key to Symbols *see back cover flap*

HABANA VIEJA Hotel Armadores de Santander

$$$

Map 4 F3

Luz esq. San Pedro **Tel** *(7) 862 8000* **Fax** *(7) 862 8080* **Rooms** *32*

This is the only Habana Vieja hotel right on the harbour with views out across it from the first-floor restaurant. With little else of note in the immediate vicinity it feels a touch isolated, but this is a good thing for those looking to avoid the hustle and bustle surrounding most hotels in this neighbourhood. There is also a pool table. **www.habaguanex.com**

HABANA VIEJA Hotel Florida

$$$

Map 4 E2

Obispo esq. Cuba **Tel** *(7) 862 4127* **Fax** *(7) 862 4117* **Rooms** *25*

A magnificent colonial conversion with an enchanting central patio surrounded by Neo-Classical stone arches and pillars. The guest rooms are excellent – very large and sumptuously furnished in a colonial style with wrought-iron beds. The hotel is located on Habana Vieja's busiest street, but once inside you barely feel it. **www.habaguanex.com**

HABANA VIEJA Hotel San Miguel

$$$

Map 4 E1

Cuba 52 esq. Peña Pobre **Tel** *(7) 862 7656* **Fax** *(7) 863 4088* **Rooms** *10*

Set on a wide avenue with traffic passing by (as opposed to the narrow, historic streets characteristic of most of the old town's hotels), there are great views from the rooftop bar of the fortifications across the bay. San Miguel is also one of the few hotels in this area with a solarium. The guest rooms are large and comfy. **www.habaguanex.com**

HABANA VIEJA Hotel Ambos Mundos

$$$$

Map 4 E2

Obispo esq. Mercaderes **Tel** *(7) 860 9530* **Fax** *(7) 860 9532* **Rooms** *52*

Hotel Ambos Mundos is famous for counting Ernest Hemingway among its guests. His room, still much as he left it, is now a tourist attraction. The spacious lobby and its refined bar is a classic Habana Vieja hangout, as is the lovely rooftop-garden restaurant and bar. The original cage-elevator is a great touch. **www.habaguanex.com**

HABANA VIEJA Hotel Palacio O'Farrill

$$$$

Map 4 E2

Cuba 102-108 esq. Chacón **Tel** *(7) 860 5080* **Fax** *(7) 860 5083* **Rooms** *38*

Another impressive colonial restoration, this stylish hotel is located on a street in a residential neighbourhood. Though just a couple of blocks from the cathedral and close to the most touristy sections of the city, it feels strangely removed from them. The highlight here is the jazz-club bar, where live music is performed at weekends. **www.habaguanex.com**

HABANA VIEJA Hotel Raquel

$$$$

Map 4 E2

Amargura esq. San Ignacio **Tel** *(7) 860 8280* **Fax** *(7) 860 8275* **Rooms** *25*

The superbly stylish lobby with its ornate ceiling, marble pillars and stained-glass skylight roof, is a great place to sit and read, drink and generally relax. Cordoned off in one corner is the city's only Jewish-themed restaurant. The rooms upstairs, gathered around a set of interior balcony corridors, are really top-notch. **www.habaguanex.com**

HABANA VIEJA Hotel Santa Isabel

$$$$$

Map 4 F2

Baratillo 9 e/ Obispo y Narcisco López **Tel** *(7) 860 8201* **Fax** *(7) 860 8391* **Rooms** *27*

At the foot of the Plaza de Armas, this refined colonial building is larger than most hotels in Habana Vieja. It is a shrine to "high art", with Neo-Classical furniture and evocative paintings all around. The guest rooms really stand out, their furnishings beautifully and authentically in keeping with this historic building. **www.hotelsantaisabelcuba.com**

CENTRO HABANA AND PRADO Casa de Miriam y Sinaí

$

Map 3 C2

Neptuno 521, e/ Campanario y Lealtad **Tel** *(7) 878 4456* **Rooms** *2*

A fabulous first-floor flat with a surprisingly large central patio full of rocking chairs. The two spacious rooms, one with streetside balcony, are spotlessly clean and have top-drawer en suite bathrooms. The hosts are extremely friendly and Sinaí speaks English, German and Italian. **sinaisole@yahoo.es**

CENTRO HABANA AND PRADO Casa de Ricardo Morales

$

Map 3 C3

Campanario 363, apto 3, e/ San Miguel y San Rafael **Tel** *(7) 866 8363* **Rooms** *1*

A great option for those who want complete independence, since the owner is often out working and allows guests the run of this entire first-floor flat. Tastefully furnished, neat and compact, the living room is particularly fetching, with a little dining table, a large comfy sofa and artwork from Mexico. There's also a balcony. **moralesfundora@yahoo.es**

CENTRO HABANA AND PRADO Hotel Lincoln

$

Map 3 C2

Virtudes 164 esq. Avenida de Italia (Galiano) **Tel** *(7) 862 8061* **Rooms** *134*

The cheapest hotel in Centro Habana, on the edge of one of the most residential and untouristy of the borough's neighbourhoods. The building itself dates from 1926 but the decor inside is pure 1970s kitsch, with flowered curtains and garish three-piece suites in the lobby. Certainly not lacking in character. **www.islazul.cu**

CENTRO HABANA AND PRADO Hotel Caribbean

$$

Map 4 D2

Prado 164, e/ Colón y Refugio **Tel** *(7) 860 8233, 860 8210* **Fax** *(7) 860 9479* **Rooms** *35*

A small hotel on the promenade section of the Prado, but with more of a backstreet flavour. Rooms are half the price of what you'd pay up the road on the Parque Central. Ask for a room facing the street as the others are quite dingy. Internet access available. **www.islazul.cu**

CENTRO HABANA AND PRADO Hotetur Deauville

$$

Map 3 C2

Avenida de Italia (Galiano) esq. Malecón **Tel** *(7) 866 8812* **Fax** *(7) 866 8148* **Rooms** *144*

A plain, unexceptional high-rise hotel but the only one in Centro Habana located on the Malecon, a fact which enhances its appeal considerably, as does the small second-floor swimming pool. There's a basement nightclub and a standard issue restaurant. **www.hotetur.com**

VEDADO Hoteles C Presidente
$$$

Calzada 110 esq. Avenida de los Presidentes **Tel** *(7) 838 1801 to 04* **Fax** *(7) 833 3753* **Rooms** *158* **Map** *1 C1*

Recently renovated, this classy hotel stands in its own secluded corner of residential Vedado, with a dashing, gentlemanly look and feel. The marble-floored lobby is accented with elegant colonial furniture and antiques, and the pool is flanked by balaustraded terraces. Comfortable rooms, many with ocean views. **www.hotelesc.com**

VEDADO Habana Libre Tryp
$$$$

Calle L e/ 23 y 25 **Tel** *(7) 838 4011, 834 6100* **Fax** *(7) 834 6365, 834 6177* **Rooms** *572* **Map** *2 F2*

Life in this part of the city revolves around this swish hotel, a Havana landmark known as the Havana Hilton before the Revolution. Its guest rooms are some of the largest in the city, many with unbeatable views. The small pool is on a first-floor terrace, and there are several excellent restaurants, including the rooftop Sierra Maestra. **www.hotelhabanalibre.com**

VEDADO Hotel Nacional de Cuba
$$$$

Calle O esq. 21 **Tel** *(7) 836 3564* **Fax** *(7) 836 5054* **Rooms** *426* **Map** *2 F1*

No other hotel presents regal elegance and grace on such a grand scale as the palatial Nacional, built in the 1930s. Among the highlights are a swanky banquet-hall restaurant divided by arches, two more restaurants in the moody basement, sweeping lawns on low cliffs above the Malecon and a nice garden-terrace bar. **www.hotelnacionaldecuba.com**

VEDADO Meliá Cohiba
$$$$$

Avenida Paseo e/ 1ra y 3ra **Tel** *(7) 833 3636* **Fax** *(7) 834 4555* **Rooms** *462* **Map** *1 B2*

Melía Cohiba is a sleek ultra-modern high-rise, a block from the seafront. One of the best equipped hotels in the city, it has five restaurants, nine meeting rooms for business guests, squash courts, a jacuzzi and sauna and one of the ritziest clubs in the city – the Habana Café. A large, two-part pool caps it all off. **www.melia-cohiba.com**

GREATER HAVANA (KOHLY PLAYA) Hotel Kohly
$$

Calle 49 esq. 36A **Tel** *(7) 204 0240 to 42* **Fax** *(7) 204 1733* **Rooms** *136*

Less attractive but better equipped than its sister hotel, the Hotel El Bosque, this parkside building features a small pool, a tennis court, a diminutive gym and a sauna. The enclosed, terraced pool has a relaxing aura of privacy and you can wander directly into the wooded park from the hotel grounds. Bright rooms. **www.gaviota-grupo.com**

GREATER HAVANA (KOHLY-PLAYA) Hotel El Bosque
$$

Calle 28A e/ 49A y 49C **Tel** *(7) 204 9232 to 35* **Fax** *(7) 204 5637* **Rooms** *62*

Perched just above the Parque Almendares, Havana's only archetypal big-city park, this location is pleasantly green and suburban You don't get the kind of luxury found at many of Miramar's hotels, but the more down-to-earth, intimate vibe will better suit some tastes. Shares facilities with its neighbour, the Hotel Kohly. **www.gaviota-grupo.com**

GREATER HAVANA (MARINA HEMINGWAY) Hotel y Villas Marina Hemingway
$$

Residencial "Marina Hemingway", Calle 248 y 5ta **Tel** *(7) 204 1150 to 55, 204 7628* **Fax** *(7) 204 4379* **Rooms** *22*

Few places in Cuba feel more like the opposite side of the Florida Straits than this international yachting community and its small hotel district, made up of a variety of houses, villas and a three-storey main building with a huge pool. The restaurant specializes in Italian food. **jrecep@hmar.mh.cyt.cu**

GREATER HAVANA (MIRAMAR) Casa de Mauricio Alonso
$

Calle A no.312, apto 9, e/ Ave. 3ra y Ave. 5ta **Tel** *(7) 203 7581* **Rooms** *1*

Just over the river from Vedado, this *casa particular* is much closer to the livelier parts of the city than most accommodations in Miramar. The spacious accommodation, in a penthouse apartment, is well equipped and there are great views both of the city and of the ocean. **mauricioydiana@gmail.com**

GREATER HAVANA (MIRAMAR) Residencia Miramar
$

Avenida 7ma no.4403, e/ 44 y 46 **Tel** *(7) 202 1075* **Rooms** *2*

A delightful *casa particular* in a classic Miramar residence à la 1950s suburban Miami. Room facilities include phone and fridge, and the whole house is kept spotlessly clean. There's a lovely patio garden and the hosts are very friendly, with plenty of experience in the room-renting business. **www.habanasol.com**

GREATER HAVANA (MIRAMAR) Chateau Miramar
$$$

1ra y 62, Miramar **Tel** *(7) 204 1951 to 57* **Fax** *(7) 204 0224* **Rooms** *50*

Right on the waterfront, this hotel looks like a cross between a castle and a multi-storey car park. It's aimed at the business market and this shows in the shiny, well kept but essentially soulless environment here which pervades the rooms as well as the restaurant and bars. **www.hotelescubanacan.com**

GREATER HAVANA (MIRAMAR) Occidental Miramar
$$$

5ta e/72 y 76 **Tel** *(7) 204 3584* **Fax** *(7) 204 8158* **Rooms** *427*

This upmarket hotel looks a bit like a conference centre but has sports and activity facilities unrivalled in the city. Six tennis courts, an indoor squash court, a fitness centre, sauna, jacuzzi and even tennis lessons on offer as well as outdoor and indoor playgrounds for children. Generic but very comfortable rooms. **www.occidental-hoteles.com**

GREATER HAVANA (MIRAMAR) Meliá Habana
$$$$$

3ra. e/ 76 y 80 **Tel** *(7) 204 8500* **Fax** *(7) 204 3902, 204 3905* **Rooms** *397*

A swish, top-class business hotel in the heart of Miramar's commercial district with a knockout lobby, a huge curving corridor of polished floors, rising columns and an army of sofa suites. There are 12 meeting rooms and offices for rent, plus 3 pools and 4 restaurants. **www.solmeliacuba.com**

Key to Price Guide *see p252* **Key to Symbols** *see back cover flap*

CENTRO HABANA AND PRADO Hotel Inglaterra

Prado 416 esq. San Rafael, Parque Central **Tel** *(7) 860 8594 to 97* **Fax** *(7) 860 8254* **Rooms** *83*   **Map** *4 D2*

A focal point for this part of Havana, the pavement-porch café of this austere building, founded in 1875, is always alive with chatter. The interior is a model of elegant austerity, particularly in the large restaurant with its columned arches. Rooms vary in size but are all decorated with the restrained refinement. **www.hotelinglaterracuba.com**

CENTRO HABANA AND PRADO Hotel Plaza

Ignacio Agramonte 267 **Tel** *(7) 860 8583* **Fax** *(7) 860 8592* **Rooms** *188*   **Map** *4 D2*

This grand old hotel near the Parque Central has touches of grandeur, although the communal areas lack character. The main restaurant is a kind of Neo-Classical cafeteria and the lobby is quite elegant but feels like a waiting room. There's a cheap pizza restaurant. **www.gran-caribe.com**

CENTRO HABANA AND PRADO Hotel Telégrafo

Prado 408 esq. Neptuno **Tel** *(7) 861 1010* **Fax** *(7) 861 4844* **Rooms** *63*   **Map** *4 D2*

Brought back from the dead at the start of the millenium, having originally opened in 1911, this newest of the Parque Central hotels has combined modern and colonial-style architecture to great effect, particularly in the ground-floor bar with its brick arches and in the top-floor glass ceiling. **www.habaguanex.com**

CENTRO HABANA AND PRADO Hotel Saratoga

Prado 603 esq. Dragones **Tel** *(7) 868 1000* **Fax** *(7) 868 1002* **Rooms** *96*   **Map** *4 D3*

Outlandishly posh, with resplendently stylish interiors and jaw-dropping colonial details, this is the classiest hotel in this part of the city. A rooftop pool, restaurant and bar, solarium and gym and rooms with DVD players, internet connection, satellite tv and minibar reflect the levels of comfort all over this amazing hotel. **www.hotel-saratoga.com**

CENTRO HABANA AND PRADO Hotel Parque Central

Neptuno, e/ Prado y Zulueta, Parque Central **Tel** *(7) 860 6627* **Fax** *(7) 860 6630* **Rooms** *278*   **Map** *4 D2*

The least historically authentic of the old hotels on the Parque Central, but by far the best equipped and most luxurious. There's a swimming pool on the roof, a business centre and a gym, and the classy lobby bar is encircled by a balaustraded interior balcony, all bathed in a warm glow from the skylight. **www.nh-hotels.cu**

CENTRO HABANA AND PRADO Hotel Sevilla

Trocadero 55, e/ Prado y Zulueta **Tel** *(7) 860 8560* **Fax** *(7) 860 8075* **Rooms** *178*   **Map** *4 D2*

Uniquely for this part of the city, Sevilla has a garden terrace outside the hotel itself, the site of its swimming pool. The majestic building also possesses a spectacular top-floor restaurant serving up some of the fanciest cuisine in Havana. Fitness centre, sauna and solarium. Very comfortable rooms, with mock colonial furniture. **www.hotelsevillacuba.com**

VEDADO Casa de Melida Jordán

Calle 25 no.1102, e/ 6 y 8 **Tel** *(7) 8335219* **Rooms** *2*   **Map** *1 C4*

Surrounded by a wealth of plant life, this magnificent two-floor house has distinguished black railings on the exterior and a gorgeous interior. Both guest rooms are very comfortable, with good beds. One even has its own separate entrance for complete privacy.

VEDADO Casa de Mercedes González

Calle 21 no.360, apt. 2A, e/ G y H **Tel** *(7) 8325846* **Rooms** *2*   **Map** *2 E2*

On the second floor of a 1950s building, this spacious apartment has two very well-equipped, large rooms with fridge, tv and en suite bathrooms. The house has a library of books for guests to use, and a lovely terrace balcony where you can sit and read. **mercylupe@hotmail.com**

VEDADO Hotel Saint John's

Calle O e/ 23 y 25 **Tel** *(7) 833 3740, 834 4187* **Fax** *(7) 833 3561* **Rooms** *86*   **Map** *2 F2*

There's always a buzz, day or night, outside Saint John's, on one of the busiest corners in the city and sharing the same space as a trendy jazz club. The restaurant has a slight canteen feel about it, though the food isn't bad. There's a simple cafeteria bar on the roof with great views along the seafront. **www.gran-caribe.com**

VEDADO Hotel Vedado

Calle O 244 e/ 23 y 25 **Tel** *(7) 836 4072* **Rooms** *203*   **Map** *1 C1*

Though a somewhat tired-looking tower block in the heart of Vedado, lacking in character, this is more affordable than almost all the other hotels in the district, with a cosy, private pool area. A nice touch is the series of photos of Havana landmarks and architecture spread around the hotel. There's also a fitness centre. **www.gran-caribe.com**

VEDADO Hotel Victoria

Calle 19 esq. M **Tel** *(7) 8333510* **Fax** *(7) 833 3109* **Rooms** *31*   **Map** *1 C1*

One of Vedado's smallest hotels, the charming, unpretentious Hotel Victoria is the area's best lower-end option. The communal areas are intimate and quite chic, with a handsome and cosy bar, wood-panelled restaurant room and a miniature pool. Rooms are on the small side. Not far from restaurants and nightspots. **www.hotelvictoriacuba.com**

VEDADO Hotel Riviera

Avenida Paseo e/ Malecón y 1ra **Tel** *(7) 836 4051* **Fax** *(7) 833 3739, 834 4225* **Rooms** *352*   **Map** *1 B2*

A classic from the pre-Revolution years, this upmarket seafront high-rise hotel was once controlled by the US Mafia. There's a wealthy 1950s-chic look about the place, in the rooms and particularly in the Art Deco lobby. The pool is one of the largest in urban Havana, and the Copa Room Cabaret is one of the city's most renowned. **www.gran-caribe.com**

GREATER HAVANA (PLAYAS DEL ESTE) Aparthotel Las Terrazas   ⑤

Avenida de las Terrazas el 10 y Rotonda **Tel** *(7) 797 1344* **Fax** *(7) 797 1316* **Rooms** *247*

Though there are three restaurants on site, the apartments are sufficiently equipped for self-caterers, with cookers and fridges, and some with three bedrooms. There's a grocery store but you'll need to go further afield to buy enough provisions for a proper meal. Large, split-level pool. **www.islazul.cu**

GREATER HAVANA (PLAYAS DEL ESTE) Mirador del Mar   ⑤

Calle 11 el 1ra y 3ra **Tel** *(7) 797 1354 to 55, 797 1284* **Rooms** *79*

Spread around a hillside looking down onto the beach, this hotel neighbourhood is made up of houses of varying sizes, some of them bungalows, some with first floor balcony terraces, some sleeping as many as five people. There are two small pools, two restaurants, three bars and a modest nightclub. **www.islazul.cu**

GREATER HAVANA (PLAYAS DEL ESTE) Villa Mégano   ⑤⑤

Km 22 1/2, Santa María del Mar, Habana del Este **Tel** *(7) 797 1610* **Fax** *(7) 797 1624* **Rooms** *103*

Surrounded by a grassy field, this is a modest concrete-cabin complex with little that marks it out from the competition. There's a rectangular, medium-sized pool, a games room and a daily entertainment programme. Not all the cabins have sea views. **www.hotelescubanacan.com**

GREATER HAVANA (PLAYAS DEL ESTE) Hotel Atlántico   ⑤⑤⑤

Avenida de las Terrazas 21, Santa María del Mar **Tel** *(7) 797 1085, 797 1532* **Fax** *(7) 797 1263* **Rooms** *92*

An old shell but a newer, renovated interior with upbeat colours make this one of the smarter hotels in the Playas del Este, operating as an all-inclusive resort. There are two tennis courts, an entertainment programme which includes a cabaret, a buffet restaurant and a pizza parlour. **reservas@complejo.gca.tur.cu**

GREATER HAVANA (PLAYAS DEL ESTE) Villa Los Pinos   ⑤⑤⑤⑤

Avenida de las Terrazas 21, Santa María del Mar **Tel** *(7) 797 1361* **Fax** *(7) 797 1263* **Rooms** *70*

Here you will find roomy two- and three-bedroom houses, some with their own pool and all with their own kitchen (including microwave ovens and all the usual mod cons) while one house even has its own squash court. This is the most upmarket accommodation in this area, and is located on a good section of beach. **www.villalospinos.com**

GREATER HAVANA (SIBONEY, PLAYA) CIS La Pradera   ⑤⑤⑤

230 el 15A y 17 **Tel** *(7) 273 7467 to 84* **Fax** *(7) 273 7202* **Rooms** *164*

Set in the leafy outskirts of the city, the Centro Internacional de Salud de "la Pradera" is as much a health centre as a hotel. From obesity and stress to MS, there is a huge variety of treatments on offer, with 17 rooms designed for guests with disabilities. A games room, gym, sauna and beauty salon are among the facilities. **www.cuba.cu/PRADERA**

GREATER HAVANA (MIRAMAR) Comodoro   ⑤⑤⑤

3ra y 84, Miramar **Tel** *(7) 204 5551* **Fax** *(7) 204 0319* **Rooms** *132 (plus 322 bungalows)*

Featuring Havana's largest shopping mall and a series of pastel two-storey apartment buildings, this hotel has the feel of a wealthy suburb. The grounds extend down to a tiny artificial beach on the otherwise rocky shoreline, with various water sports facilities. The all-inclusive package includes daily bus service to the city centre. **www.hotelescubanacan.com**

WESTERN CUBA

CAYO LARGO DEL SUR Villa Marinera Cayo Largo del Sur   ⑤⑤

Marina Cayo Largo del Sur, Isla de la Juventud **Tel** *(45) 248 212* **Fax** *(45) 248 213* **Rooms** *12*

An attractive wood-cabin complex on a great patch of beach. The roomy cabins have porches and a natural feel inside with wood-panelled walls and subtle furnishings. They all face the sea, just a few metres from the shore. The small pool, simple restaurant and marina all enhance this lovely little complex, which is in tune with its surroundings.

CAYO LARGO DEL SUR Barcelo Cayo Largo   ⑤⑤⑤

Cayo Largo del Sur, Archipiélago de los Canarreos, Isla de la Juventud **Tel** *(45) 248 080* **Fax** *(45) 248 088* **Rooms** *306*

The majestic lobby is vaguely reminiscent of Tony Montana's mansion lobby in the film *Scarface*, with staircases on either side leading up to indoor balconies. From here a walkway lined with palms leads to one of the two pools. Dotted around are paintings and sculptures by local artists. Rooms are gracefully decorated. **www.barcelo.com**

CAYO LARGO DEL SUR Hotel Isla del Sur   ⑤⑤⑤⑤

Cayo Largo del Sur, Archipiélago de los Canarreos, Isla de la Juventud **Tel** *(45) 248 111* **Fax** *(45) 248 160* **Rooms** *59*

This is the reception building for four neighbouring complexes – Isla del Sur, Villa Coral, Villa Soledad and Villa Lindamar – that share the same contact and booking details. Facilities at all hotels are open to guests, and include tennis courts, swimming pools, and fitness facilities. **www.cayolargodelsur.cu**

CAYO LARGO DEL SUR Villa Coral   ⑤⑤⑤⑤

Cayo Largo del Sur, Archipiélago de los Canarreos, Isla de la Juventud **Tel** *(45) 248 111* **Fax** *(45) 248 160* **Rooms** *60*

Part of the Isla del Sur complex *(see above)*, this slightly rag-tag collection of garish pink blocks with minimal landscaping doesn't really form a cohesive single complex, but the pool area provides a focus and is pleasantly encircled by low trees. The round pool is small but has a swim-up bar. **www.cayolargodelsur.cu**

Key to Price Guide *see p252* **Key to Symbols** *see back cover flap*

CAYO LARGO DEL SUR Villa Soledad 🔲🅿️🗺️ $$$$

Cayo Largo del Sur, Archipiélago de los Canarreos, Isla de la Juventud **Tel** *(45) 248 111* **Fax** *(45) 248 160* **Rooms** *24*

With no pool or restaurant it's just as well that guests here have access to the facilities of all the other Isla del Sur member hotels (see Hotel Isla del Sur) . The rooms, in brightly coloured bungalows and semi-detached houses, have tv and mini-bar and each has its own porch or balcony. A good place for undisturbed tranquility. **www.cayolargodelsur.cu**

CAYO LARGO DEL SUR Hotel Sol Cayo Largo 🍴🏊🛎️📺🅿️ $$$$

Cayo Largo del Sur, Archipiélago de los Canarreos, Isla de la Juventud **Tel** *(45) 248 260* **Fax** *(45) 248 265* **Rooms** *296*

On a great stretch of beach and featuring a magnificent swimming pool, a well equipped fitness centre, a beach-front restaurant and two other indoor restaurants. This hotel specializes in weddings and honeymoons, with lovely romantic spaces like the gazebo overlooking the beach and the raised, poolside arbours. **www.sol-cayolargo.com**

CAYO LARGO DEL SUR Hotel Sol Pelícano 🍴🏊🛎️📺🅿️ $$$$$

Cayo Largo del Sur, Archipiélago de los Canarreos, Isla de la Juventud **Tel** *(45) 248 333* **Fax** *(45) 248 265* **Rooms** *304*

Looking a bit like a Wild West village outpost (but painted pastel blue), this unusual luxury resort has slightly haggard, sandy grounds and two- and three-storey concrete ranch-house buildings. There's a ranchon beach eatery, an intimate gourmet restaurant and a large buffet restaurant. The large pool has a fountain in the centre. **www.sol-pelicano.com**

CAYO LEVISA Hotel Cayo Levisa 🛏️🍴📋🗺️ $$

Carretera a Palma Rubia, La Palma, Pinar del Río **Tel** *(48) 756 501, (48) 756 505* **Rooms** *33*

Hidden from the mainland behind the thick scrub that covers the low island (cay) on which it nestles, this offshore cabin retreat can't be beaten for peace and tranquility. Watersports provide the only entertainment, with excursions to more remote cays. Closed for rennovation due to 2008 hurricanes, phone to check. **www.hotelcayolevisa-cuba.com**

ISLA DE LA JUVENTUD Hotel Rancho del Tesoro 🍴📋🅿️ $

Carretera La Fe Km 2 1/2 **Tel** *(46) 323 085, 323 035* **Rooms** *34*

This is a very basic countryside hotel consisting of a box building with a three-storey turret tower and a simple restaurant and bar. It is an unfussy, restful place to stay but don't expect to be pampered here. Guest rooms have satellite tv and mini-bar.

ISLA DE LA JUVENTUD Villa Isla de la Juventud 🍴🏊📋🅿️ $

Carretera La Fé Km 1 1/2 **Tel** *(46) 321 739* **Rooms** *20*

In a pleasant natural setting with a hilly backdrop, just outside Nueva Gerona, this place is popular with locals who come from the town at weekends to use the medium-sized pool. Rooms, with tv, radio and mini-bar, have a 1970s kitsch look about them and are all gathered around the pool. **leida@ranchoij.turisla.co.cu**

ISLA DE LA JUVENTUD Villa Marisol 📋📋🅿️ $

Calle 24 no.5107, e/ 51 y 53, Nueva Gerona **Tel** *(46) 322 502* **Rooms** *2*

A few blocks from the centre of town on a leafy street with a hillside backdrop is this well-maintained *casa particular*. Both rooms have small double beds and a simple, airy uncluttered feel. The shady terrace with its table and chairs is a nice spot for relaxation, and the house as a whole has a laid-back, homely ambience.

ISLA DE LA JUVENTUD Villa Mas 📋📋🅿️ $

Calle 41 no.4108, apto. 7, e/ 8 y 10, Nueva Gerona **Tel** *(46) 323 544* **Rooms** *1*

This *casa particular* in a dusty apartment complex away from the centre may not look like much from the outside but the accommodation here is sprucely decorated and well equipped, featuring tv and fridge. There's a homemade bar on the inviting rooftop terrace.

ISLA DE LA JUVENTUD Hotel Colony 🍴🏊📋🅿️🗺️ $$

Carretera Sigüanea Km 42 **Tel** *(46) 398 282* **Fax** *(46) 398 420* **Rooms** *24*

The closest hotel to the beach on the Punta Francés peninsula, this modest coastal resort is aimed predominantly at scuba divers (dive packages can be arranged from here). There are rooms in the original, rather plain 1950s building and slightly better ones in the bungalows. The highlight is the bar and grill at the end of a long pier. **carpeta@colony.turisla.co.cu**

LAS TERRAZAS Hotel La Moka 🍴🏊🛎️📺🅿️ $$$

Las Terrazas, Autopista Nacional Habana-Pinar del Río Km 51, Candelaria **Tel** *(48) 578 600* **Fax** *(48) 578 605* **Rooms** *31*

Few hotels in Cuba are as harmonious with their environment as this superb hillside sanctum. Shrouded in woodland, the graceful main building, with its outdoor corridors, has a lobby built around a large tree that rises through the roof. Paths and staircases wind through the trees to the village below. Comfortable rooms. **reservas@commoka.get.tur.cu**

PENÍNSULA DE GUANAHACABIBES Hotel María La Gorda 🛏️🍴📋🗺️ $$

María La Gorda, Península de Guanahacabibes, Pinar del Río **Tel** *(48) 778 131* **Fax** *(48) 778 077* **Rooms** *55*

A real end-of-the-line beach resort, this is Cuba's most isolated mainland hotel. Rooms are in comfortable wood cabins on the edge of a forest thicket or in concrete villas on the beach. There's an excellent dive club for the world-class scuba diving here. Buffet breakfast and dinner are included. The whole resort is cash only. **www.gaviota-grupo.com**

PINAR DEL RÍO CITY Casa de Maribel Pérez Madera 📋📋 $

Isabel Rubio 4 (bajos), e/ Martí y Adela Azcuy **Tel** *(48) 753 217* **Rooms** *1*

Located right in the heart of Pinar del Río City is this freshly furnished, pocket-size ground-floor flat with one guest room. It is clean, cosy and comfortable, with a homely atmosphere. Although basic and small, the flat has a snug rather than cramped feel to it.

PINAR DEL RÍO CITY Hotel Pinar del Río

Martí y Final **Tel** *(48) 755 070 to 74* **Fax** *(48) 771 699* **Rooms** *149*

Though much better equipped than the city's other hotel, this unattractive building is past its prime. Guest rooms are small, and the furnishings are old-fashioned. It does, however, possess the only pool in Pinar del Río and the best nightclub in the city. **www.islazul.cu**

PINAR DEL RÍO CITY Hotel Vueltabajo

Martí 103, esq. Rafael Morales **Tel** *(48) 759 381 to 83* **Rooms** *39* .

Right in the centre of town, on the bustling main street, this recently renovated small-scale hotel is in a handsome balconied two-storey building fronted by simple high arches. The lobby, bar and rooms are all smart, small and refined but the restaurant lacks character and its food is unremarkable. **www.islazul.cu**

SAN DIEGO DE LOS BAÑOS Hotel Mirador

Calle 23 y Final, San Diego de los Baños, Los Palacios **Tel/Fax** *(48) 778 338* **Rooms** *30*

Tucked away in the corner of tiny San Diego de los Baños village, just over a river from dense woodlands, is this picturesque two-storey hotel with canopied corridor balconies. It has well-tended terrace gardens with a pretty little pool, complete with its own mini-bridge. The hotel offers health programmes at the spa across the road. **www.islazul.cu**

SOROA Villa Soroa

Carretera de Soroa Km 8, San Cristóbal **Tel** *(48) 523 534, 523 556, 523 512* **Rooms** *49*

Surrounded by looming hills in its own compact valley, this villa complex has a wonderful natural setting. With modest facilities but a large pool, it is a real chillout spot and popular with package tourists. There's a hilltop restaurant nearby. The reasonably comfortable villas surround the pool. **www.cubanacan.cu**

VIÑALES Villa El Isleño

Carretera a Viñales Km 26 **Tel** *(48) 793 107* **Rooms** *2*

The first house in the village on the road from Pinar del Río, this very well-kept *casa particular* has a backyard with great views of the Mogote hills. With tv and fridge and sparkling new bathrooms, these are among the most comfortable guest rooms in Viñales, especially the one in its own block out the back.

VIÑALES La Ermita

Carretera La Ermita Km 1.5 **Tel** *(48) 796 071, 796 100, 796 122* **Fax** *(48) 796 069* **Rooms** *62*

Up a small hill from the village, this neat and tidy cabin complex is the most relaxing place to stay in Viñales. The panoramic views of the valley can be enjoyed equally from the balcony restaurant, the pool, the well-trimmed lawns or the rooms themselves – in villas or in the graceful two-storey buildings with red-tile roofs. **www.hotelescubanacan.com**

VIÑALES Los Jazmines

Carretera a Viñales Km 23 **Tel** *(48) 796 205, 796 123, 796 124* **Fax** *(48) 796 215* **Rooms** *78*

Most photos of Viñales are taken from the lookout platform of this magnificently situated hotel. The main building is a splendid 1950s pink neo-colonial provincial mansion, where the average-quality restaurant is housed, and there are modern blocks housing the most comfortable rooms. **www.hotelescubanacan.com**

VIÑALES Rancho San Vicente

Carretera Puerto Esperanza Km 33 **Tel** *(48) 796 201, 796 221, 796 222, 796 111* **Fax** *(48) 796 265* **Rooms** *54*

Down in the valley, set on wooded, grassy slopes leading down to the quiet road, this wood-cabin refuge is a well-priced option. The delightful cabins, in their natural setting, have porches and glass-panelled front walls. There's also a pretty pool and an arched restaurant building. **www.hotelescubanacan.com**

CENTRAL CUBA – WEST

CAIBARIÉN Brisas del Mar

Carretera Playa final, Caibarién **Tel** *(42) 351 699* **Rooms** *12*

Brisas del Mar is a good budget alternative to the resorts on the nearby cays, and well placed for day trips. Right at the end of town on a secluded little jut of land, this low-key hotel has rooms facing out to sea and its own small patch of beach. Guest rooms are kept in good condition with the standard modern conveniences. **www.islazul.cu**

CAYO ENSENACHOS Royal Hideaway Ensenachos

Cayo Ensenachos, Villa Clara **Tel** *(42) 350 300* **Fax** *(42) 350 301 to 03* **Rooms** *506*

This enormous resort is awesomely well equipped and its setting jaw-droppingly gorgeous. Split into three sections, the Royal Suite area features garden villas on their own peninsula at the far end of the hotel's two private beaches. State-of-the-art spa, four restaurants, six bars and CD/DVD players in all rooms. **www.royalhideawayensenachos.com**

CAYO LAS BRUJAS Villa Las Brujas

Cayo Las Brujas, Villa Clara **Tel** *(42) 350 199* **Rooms** *24*

The least expensive place to stay on Villa Clara's north coast cays is hidden away at the end of a road cutting through the island scrub. The comfortable cabin accommodation faces the sea, and there's a simple rustic restaurant next to the beach in a circular wooden building where a spiral staircase leads to a viewing platform. **www.gaviota-grupo.com**

Key to Price Guide *see p252* **Key to Symbols** *see back cover flap*

CAYO SANTA MARÍA Meliá Cayo Santa María 🍴🏊🛎🗐🄾🈳 $$$$$
Cayo Santa Maria, Villa Clara **Tel** *(42) 350 500* **Fax** *(42) 350 505* **Rooms** *358*

Beautifully built into and around the cay's dense vegetation, this high-class resort counts three swimming pools, an amphitheatre, and Mediterranean, Italian and buffet restaurants among its extensive facilities. Guest rooms are exquisitely furnished and quite homely, with balconies or terraces. **www.solmeliacuba.com**

CAYO SANTA MARÍA Sol Cayo Santa María 🍴🏊🛎🗐🄾🈳 $$$$$
Cayo Santa Maria, Villa Clara **Tel** *(42) 350 200* **Fax** *(42) 350 205* **Rooms** *300*

Of the three all-inclusive resorts on the cays, this is the smallest yet still boasts two tennis courts, a gym, three bars and three restaurants. Standard double rooms in one- and two-storey villas are brightly furnished with ceiling fans, satellite tv, mini-bar, hair dryer and breakfast table and chairs. **www.solmeliacuba.com**

CIENFUEGOS Casa de la Amistad 🗐 $
Avenida 56 no.2927, e/ 29 y 31 **Tel** *(43) 516 143* **Rooms** *2*

Run by an old couple whose set of guestbooks attest to both their friendliness and the popularity of this eclectic old house near the centre. A spiral staircase to the roof, a little bar installed in the entrance hall, stained-glass windows and period furnishings makes this place a fascinating and enjoyable place to stay. **casamistad@correodecuba.cu**

CIENFUEGOS Casa de Luis y Odalys 🗐🗐🄾 $
Avenida 16 no.4702, e/ 47 y 49, Punta Gorde **Tel** *(43) 515 864* **Rooms** *1*

A couple of blocks from the baseball stadium in the laid-back, open-plan district of Punta Gorda, there's a shady bijou backyard patio with tables and chairs just outside the dining room with its mounted deer head. The guest rooms are large, with attractive built-in closets and en suite bathrooms.

CIENFUEGOS Casa Piñeiro 🗐🄾 $
Calle 41 no.1402, e/ 14 y 16, Punta Gorda **Tel** *(43) 513 808* **Rooms** *2*

An enthusiastic cook and an astute host, Jorge Piñeiro runs one of the best-known *casas particulares* in the city and is a great source of information for visitors. The house has a spacious outside eating area with a banquet-length picnic table and a built-in brick barbecue. Rooms are large and come equipped with tvs. **www.casapineiro.com**

CIENFUEGOS Palacio Azul 🗐🍴🗐🄾🈳 $
Calle 37 e/ 12 y 14, Punta Gorda **Tel** *(43) 555 828* **Rooms** *7*

Standing proudly on its own modest patch of bayside real estate, this pastel blue 1921 mansion has a down-to-earth atmosphere and is a great place to stay if you're looking for character. The guest rooms are well equipped and very spacious, some with bay views. The restaurant is only open for breakfast. **www.hotelescubanacan.com**

CIENFUEGOS Club Amigo Rancho Luna 🍴🏊🛎🄾🈳 $$
Carretera Rancho Luna Km 15 **Tel** *(43) 548 012, 548 020, 548 026* **Fax** *(43) 548131* **Rooms** *225*

Hogging the only decent section of beach on this stretch of coastline, this patchy resort has a huge rectangular pool and a family atmosphere. Scuba diving lessons are offered, as are various other watersports. The long buildings accommodating guest rooms have a weathered look; about half of them have sea views. **www.hotelescubanacan.com**

CIENFUEGOS Hotel Faro Luna 🍴🏊🗐🄾🈳 $$
Carretera de Pasacaballo Km 18 **Tel** *(43) 548 030* **Fax** *(43) 551 686* **Rooms** *46*

A cosy little complex with a small main building and pool, and an attractive set of cabins lined up above and along the rocky shore. This is a good place for divers, with an excellent dive-club on site as well as a dolphinarium, located in a natural pool, a short walk away. Rooms are comfortable but nothing special. **www.hotelescubanacan.com**

CIENFUEGOS Hotel Unión 🖥🍴🗐🄾🈳 $$
Calle 31, esq. 54 **Tel** *(43) 551 020* **Fax** *(43) 551 685* **Rooms** *49*

This 19th-century building has been wonderfully restored to its former Neo-Classical glory and is now the best hotel in Cienfuegos. Luxury and style combine comfortably, so that the sleek glass elevator and the pool, which is intimately enclosed within the hotel walls, blend in with the Old World decor and ambience. **www.hotelescubanacan.com**

CIENFUEGOS Hotel Jagua 🖥🍴🏊🗐🄾🈳 $$$
Calle 37, e/ 0 y 2, Punta Gorda **Tel** *(43) 551 003* **Fax** *(43) 551 245* **Rooms** *149*

With the most attractive setting in town, at the tip of the peninsula reaching out into the bay waters, is this unremarkable block building containing a well-appointed four-star hotel. The interior is easier on the eye, with a light and airy lobby, and a pool area looking out over the bay. **www.gran-caribe.com**

LAGO HANABANILLA Hotel Hanabanilla 🖥🍴🏊🗐🄾🈳 $
Salto del Hanabanilla, Manicaragua, Villa Clara **Tel** *(42) 208 550, 208 461* **Fax** *(42) 203 506* **Rooms** *125*

A hulk of a main building in a glorious natural setting in lush green hills and by the side of a large, twisting lake, this hotel attracts a large number of fishing enthusiasts. It is well set up for making the most of what the lake has to offer, with daily boat trips and water sports facilities. Rooms are basic and the rate does not include breakfast. **www.islazul.cu**

PENÍNSULA DE ZAPATA Hotel Playa Girón 🍴🗐🄾🈳 $$
Playa Girón, Península de Zapata, Matanzas **Tel** *(45) 984 110* **Rooms** *123*

The peninsula's largest resort is spread around a grassy patch of land. Guest rooms are housed in simple concrete bungalows, some quite large, and are comfortable and reasonably well equipped. The beach here is somewhat spoiled by a concrete wave-breaker, which obscures the view out to sea. **www.hotelescubanacan.com**

PENÍNSULA DE ZAPATA, MATANZAS Batey Don Pedro   🗺 🍴 👤 $

Península de Zapata, Matanzas **Tel** *(45) 912 825, 913 224* **Rooms** *12*

This rustic set of wooden lodges offers excellent value – the most affordable on the peninsula, though the coast is a 20-minute drive away. The farmland setting is a bit rough and ready, but the lodges are spacious, comfortable and have satellite tv, mini-bar, ceiling fans, porches and rocking chairs. Great place to relax. **www.hotelescubanacan.com**

PENÍNSULA DE ZAPATA. MATANZAS Guamá   🍴 🏊 📋 👤 🖼 $

Laguna del Tesoro, Península de Zapata, Matanzas **Tel** *(45) 915 551* **Rooms** *44*

Wonderfully isolated out on the huge Laguna del Tesoro lake on a series of interconnected little islands, this mini-complex is modelled on a pre-Columbian Taino settlement. Guest rooms are housed in round, wooden lodges hovering over the lake on stilts. **www.hotelescubanacan.com**

PENÍNSULA DE ZAPATA MATANZAS Hotel Playa Larga   🍴 🏊 📋 👤 🖼 $

Playa Larga, Península de Zapata, Matanzas **Tel** *(45) 987 294* **Fax** *(45) 987 294* **Rooms** *60*

At the foot of the bay and at the edge of the nature reserve, this is the best located hotel on the peninsula for those wanting to combine scuba diving, bird watching and nature trailing. Accommodation is in bungalows facing the sea on somewhat tired-looking landscaped grounds. **www.hotelescubanacan.com**

REMEDIOS Hotel Mascotte   🍴 📋 $

Máximo Gómez 114, e/ P Margal y A del Río, Plaza Martí **Tel** *(42) 395 144* **Fax** *(42) 395 327* **Rooms** *10*

A plain yet refined and tastefully refurbished colonial period building, the town's only hotel is the focal point for most visitors whether or not they're staying here. Hotel Mascotte is a lovely, uncomplicated and comfortable place to stay for a few days. Rooms have satellite tv and mini-bar. **www.hotelescubanacan.com**

SANTA CLARA Casa de Consuelo Ramos Rodríguez   🗺 📋 👤 $

Independencia 265, apto 1, e/ Pedro Estevez (Unión) y San Isidro **Tel** *(42) 202 064* **Rooms** *2*

This ground-floor flat looks small and ordinary from the outside, so the wide corridors and large double rooms come as quite a surprise. The sizeable patio in the back garden is embellished with trees, shrubs and a green canopy shading the benches. There's a piano in the dining room, which is flanked by two more tiny patios. **marielatram@yahoo.es**

SANTA CLARA Casa de Martha Artiles Alemán   🗺 📋 👤 $

Martha Abreu 56 (altos), e/ Villuendas y Zayas **Tel** *(42) 205 008* **Rooms** *4*

A large first-floor flat with a half-colonial, half-modern look and feel. There are two three-piece suites in the cavernous, pristinely furnished living room with its streetside balcony. A huge roof terrace with table and chairs provides sweeping views of Santa Clara. Impressive rooms, one with leather couch, tv and video. **musicauvc@cenit.cult.cu**

SANTA CLARA Casa Mercy   🗺 📋 👤 $

Eduardo Machado (San Cristóbal) 4, e/ Cuba y Colón **Tel** *(42) 216 941* **Rooms** *2*

Just one block from the central square, there's an unpretentious family vibe at this well-run house. Both rooms are located upstairs, with their own terrace area overlooking the tiny central patio. Rooms have well-stocked mini-bars, and one has a small balcony. Mercy is a fantastic cook and does everything with a smile. **isel@uclv.edu.cu**

SANTA CLARA Florida Center   🗺 📋 👤 $

Maestra Nicolasa (Candelaria) 56, e/ Colón y Maceo **Tel** *(42) 208 161* **Rooms** *2*

This stunning house has an almost overwhelming number of notable features. The spellbinding central patio is a jungle of potted plants, palms and bushes; the bedrooms are an original mix of Colonial-era and Art Deco furniture with modern, spotless bathrooms; and the front room is crammed full of Colonial furniture and pictures. A unique option.

SANTA CLARA Santa Clara Libre   📶 🍴 📋 👤 🖼 $

Parque Leoncio Vidal 6, e/ Tristá y Padre Chao **Tel** *(42) 207 548* **Fax** *(42) 202 771* **Rooms** *143*

An undistinguished high-rise hotel in a great location, right on the lively Parque Leoncio. Most rooms are small, but many have fantastic panoramic views of the city. There's a roof-top bar and nightclub, but the other communal areas are unremarkable. This is the best budget option if you don't want to stay in a *casa particular.* **www.islazul.cu**

SANTA CLARA Hotel Los Caneyes   🍴 🏊 📋 👤 $$

Avenida los Eucaliptos y Circunvalación **Tel** *(42) 204 513, 218 140* **Fax** *(42) 218 140* **Rooms** *96*

Just beyond the southern outskirts of the city, a three-peso can ride from the centre, this hotel nestles in its own woodlands and feels isolated and tranquil, though the peace is occasionally disturbed by the hotel's entertainment programme. Good buffet restaurant in a reconstructed traditional Taino circular lodge. **www.hotelescubanacan.com**

SANTA CLARA Villa La Granjita   🍴 🏊 📋 👤 $$

Carretera de Malezas Km 2.5 **Tel** *(42) 218 190* **Fax** *(42) 218 149* **Rooms** *71*

A large ranch in the middle of farmland beyond the city limits, this wooden cabin complex has an organic feel, the extensive grounds only partly landscaped, with a lot of it left in a natural state. The unusual accommodation units are multi-sided, two-storey, matted-roof huts with satellite tv, minibar and balcony or terrace. **www.hotelescubanacan.com**

VARADERO Villa La Mar   🍴 🏊 📋 👤 $

Avenida 3ra, e/ 28 y 30 **Tel** *(45) 614 515* **Fax** *(45) 612 508* **Rooms** *264*

This is the least expensive but certainly not the worst hotel in Varadero. Though it's firmly rooted in the old school of Cuban beach architecture, it has more soul than some of the alternatives elsewhere, thanks in part to its large gardens. There is also a games room, two restaurants and a discoteque. **www.islazul.cu**

Key to Price Guide *see p252* **Key to Symbols** *see back cover flap*

VARADERO Hotel Acuazul
Avenida 1ra y 13 **Tel** *(45) 667 132* **Fax** *(45) 667 229* **Rooms** *78*

Hotel Acuazul is an apartment block high-rise with little architectural merit, but lending great views to most rooms, which are surprisingly spacious. Guest rooms come equipped with satellite tv, balcony and bath tub and have a 1970s look about them. **www.hotelacuazul.com**

VARADERO Hotel Dos Mares
Calle 53, esq. Avenida 1ra **Tel** *(45) 612 702* **Rooms** *34*

One of the most likeable budget options, this is not a classic beach-resort hotel at all. A pastel-yellow and white building looking something like a large and expensive Meditteranean townhouse, the rooms here are on the small side, but there's a cool and cosy sunken bar, just below street level. **www.islazul.cu**

VARADERO Hotel Herradura
Avenida de Playa, e/ 35 y 36 **Tel** *(45) 613 703* **Fax** *(45) 667 496* **Rooms** *75*

A semi-circular building that couldn't be any closer to the beach, with steps down from the terrace area leading virtually into the ocean. Guest rooms come in twos, and each pair shares a communal living room and blacony, all of which face the sea. The hotel restaurant is not recommended. **www.islazul.cu**

VARADERO Hotel Ledo
Avenida de Playa y 43 **Tel** *(45) 613 206* **Rooms** *19*

Just across the road from the beach, this is a miniscule hotel by Varadero standards, but its small size lends it an endearing cuteness. Hotel Ledo is a good option if you like peace and quiet at budget prices, but don't expect anything more than the bare minimum of facilities.

VARADERO Hotel Mar Del Sur
Avenida 3ra y 30 **Tel** *(45) 612 246* **Fax** *(45) 667 881* **Rooms** *366*

Closer to the main road than to the beach, this dated-looking complex has a reasonable set of facilities for the price and, unlike most hotels, receives as many Cuban visitors as foreign tourists. The gardens linking it all together help to soften the look of the clumsily designed concrete blocks. **www.islazul.cu**

VARADERO Hotel Pullman
Avenida 1ra, e/ 49 y 50 **Tel** *(45) 612 702* **Rooms** *16*

Sister hotel of the Hotel Dos Mares *(see above)* and of a similar down-to-earth character with more of a town than a beach feel. A single castle-like turret gives it a toytown look, and there's a simple garden terrace around which the rooms are located. It's worth paying the extra 10 CUC$ for one of the larger rooms with a balcony. **www.islazul.cu**

VARADERO Hotel Varazul
Avenida 1ra y 13 **Tel** *(45) 667 132* **Fax** *(45) 667 229* **Rooms** *69*

Guests here have access to all the facilities at the Acuazul next door, including the pool. Like its neighbour, this is a high-rise hotel with little charm but its apartments have large guest rooms with balconies and are set up for self-catering. Fourteen of the rooms are available for long stays. **www.islazul.cu**

VARADERO Villa Sotavento
Avenida 1ra y 13 **Tel** *(45) 667 132* **Fax** *(45) 667 229* **Rooms** *36*

Blending into the local neighbourhood, Villa Sotavento consists of a variety of different houses, no different in outward appearance to local domestic residences, split into two or three units each and spread around a five- or six-block area. Guests have access to the facilities at the Hotel Acuazul *(see above)*. **www.islazul.cu**

VARADERO Club Amigo Tropical
Avenida 1ra, e/ 21 y 22 **Tel** *(45) 613 915* **Rooms** *173*

One of the better-looking and better-equipped town hotels, Club Amigo Tropical is arranged in a u-shaped four-storey building on the beach side of the peninsula. This mid-range hotel offers two restaurants, a daily entertainment programme, a bar and snack bar plus a medium-sized pool. **www.hotelescubanacan.com**

VARADERO Cuatro Palmas
Avenida 1ra, e/ 60 y 64 **Tel** *(45) 667 040* **Fax** *(45) 667 208* **Rooms** *312*

A town hotel with optional all-inclusive plans, bridging the gap between the mega resorts up the road and the budget hotels down the other way. Facilities are good, with a gym and sauna, a large buffet restaurant and a more intimate Cuban cuisine restaurant. **www.accorhotels.com**

VARADERO Hotel Los Delfines
Avenida 1ra, e/ 38 y 39 **Tel** *(45) 667 720* **Fax** *(45) 667 727* **Rooms** *103*

One of the only all-inclusives in the town section of Varadero, this is made up of a set of modern apartment blocks. The compact landscaped grounds and small circular pool are modest by the standards of all-inclusives on the peninsula, but this is one of the few places you can get the all-in treatment without being completely isolated. **www.islazul.cu**

VARADERO Hotetur Sun Beach
Calle 17, e/ Avenida 1ra y Avenida 3ra **Tel** *(45) 667 490* **Fax** *(45) 614 994* **Rooms** *272*

Two towering blocks, dominating the immediate surroundings, make up this hotel. Among the several high-rise hotels in this part of town, Hotetur Sun Beach has by far the best set of facilities and the largest communal areas, though there are more attractive alternatives in the same price category. **www.hotetur.com**

VARADERO Club Kawama

Avenida Kawama, e/ 0 y 1 **Tel** *(45) 614 416 to 20* **Fax** *(45) 667 334* **Rooms** *336*

Hugging a long stretch of beach, this is one of the more interesting all-inclusives, thanks to the grey stone, fort-like buildings which were the original resort buildings. It's in one of these that a marvellous basement restaurant-cabaret is housed. In a separate section of the complex, along the beach, are newer holiday mansions. **www.gran-caribe.com**

VARADERO Hotel Barlovento

Avenida 1ra, e/ 10 y 12 **Tel** *(45) 667 140* **Fax** *(45) 667 218* **Rooms** *296*

This smart and stylish (though relatively small) all-inclusive is framed around pseudo-colonial architecture that underwent refurbishment in late 2006. It lies within walking distance of the western end of the town and a number of local restaurants. Rooms have a balcony or terrace, kitchenettes and all the usual gadgets. **www.gran-caribe.com**

VARADERO Palma Real

Avenida 3rd y 64 **Tel** *(45) 614 555* **Fax** *(45) 614 550* **Rooms** *466*

Only a couple of blocks from the beach but backing onto the main road of Varadero, the location of Palma Real is not as good as that of the other upmarket area hotels. It has two large pools, and rooms are of a good standard, though many are in an older but freshly painted building that predates the rest of the complex. **www.hotetur.com**

VARADERO Puntarena

Avenida Kawama y Final **Tel** *(45) 667 125, 667 667, 667 129* **Fax** *(45) 667 074* **Rooms** *255*

At the western extreme of the peninsula, lying between the ocean and the Laguna de Paso Malo, the two nine-storey buildings that form the corner pieces of this compact resort offer views stretching up almost the entire length of the peninsula. Basketball, minigolf and of course watersports are among the activities available. **www.gran-caribe.com**

VARADERO Villa Cuba

Avenida Las Américas Km 3 **Tel** *(45) 668 280* **Fax** *(45) 668 282* **Rooms** *365*

The multi-level lobby area, a network of platforms and staircases with a bar at the halfway point, is one of the most captivating hotel interiors in Varadero. From here the grounds stretch down to the beach and feature small groups of villas, each with their own little pools. Two restaurants, a gym, sauna and jacuzzi. **www.gran-caribe.com**

VARADERO Arenas Blancas

Calle 64, e/ Avenida 1ra y Autopista del Sur **Tel** *(45) 614 450* **Fax** *(45) 614 490* **Rooms** *358*

A family all-inclusive at the very top of the town, Arenas Blancas is the most luxurious hotel in town. The huge main building is otherwise unremarkable but the pool is one of the largest in Varadero, snaking its way around a large part of the landscaped gardens. The guest rooms are very large, with all modern conveniences. **www.gran-caribe.com**

VARADERO Barcelo Solymar Beach Resort

Avenida Las Américas Km 3 **Tel** *(45) 614 499* **Fax** *(45) 668 791* **Rooms** *525*

This bright and colourful all-inclusive is within walking distance of the eastern end of the town. It packs a whole host of facilities into an area smaller than many of the mega resorts further along the peninsula. On-site are five restaurants, six bars, two pools, two tennis courts, a gym and a children's playground. **www.barcelosolymar.com**

VARADERO Mansión Xanadú

Autopista del Sur Km 8.5 **Tel** *(45) 667 388* **Fax** *(45) 668 481* **Rooms** *6*

This unique hotel is housed in the millionaire mansion that belonged to the Dupont Family before they abandoned it with the Revolution (*see p163*). The guest rooms are huge, the restaurant is one of Varadero's finest and there are special deals for guests using the golf course next door. **varaderogolfclub@enet.cu**

VARADERO Meliá Las Americas

Autopista del Sur Km 7 **Tel** *(45) 667 600* **Fax** *(45) 667 625* **Rooms** *336*

Run in conjunction with the golf course that stretches out either side of this superb hotel, Meliá Las Americas is one of the few all-inclusives where most of the rooms are in the main building and the area occupied by the complex is comparatively small. The gardens are fabulous, with undulating paths up to the split-level pool. **www.solmeliacuba.com**

VARADERO Meliá Paradisus Varadero

Punta Francés **Tel** *(45) 668 700* **Fax** *(45) 668 705* **Rooms** *429*

An 'ultra all-inclusive' in the parlance of the Meliá chain that run this staggeringly extensive and expensive complex, with no less than eight restaurants as well as two pools, tennis courts, gym, sauna, and jacuzzi. if you want your own pool, sauna and jacuzzi you can pay the extra for the Garden Villa, which also comes with a butler. **www.solmeliacuba.com**

VARADERO Meliá Cohiba Varadero

Autopista del Sur Km 7 **Tel** *(45) 667 013* **Fax** *(45) 667 012* **Rooms** *490*

This sumptuous shrine to holiday architecture has an unforgettable lobby patio, with hanging vines dropping down six storeys of balconies to encircle a little maze of waterways and plantlife. One of its four restaurants is located on a small clifftop with waves lapping down below. **www.solmeliacuba.com**

VARADERO Riu Las Morlas

Avenida Las Américas y A, Reparto La Torre **Tel** *(45) 667 230* **Fax** *(45) 667 215* **Rooms** *148*

One of the most intimate all-inclusives, here almost everything is on a smaller scale, lending Las Morlas an endearing appeal. The pool (more of an artificial stream forming a figure of 8) is enclosed by the semi-circular main building, making the main outdoor area feel something like a secret hideaway. Guest rooms are also small. **www.riu.com**

Key to Price Guide *see p252* **Key to Symbols** *see back cover flap*

VARADERO Sandals Royal Hicacos Resort and Spa $$$$$

*Carretera de las Morlas Km 15 **Tel** (45) 668 844 **Fax** (45) 668 851 **Rooms** 404*

On one of the most secluded sections of the peninsula, this resplendent resort has some of the best rooms in Varadero, each with a king-size bed, a living room and bacony or patio all decked out in gentle colours. The impressive facilities include squash courts, a fitness centre, a mini basketball court and three tennis courts. **www.sandalshicacos.com**

VARADERO Sol Palmeras $$$$$

*Autopista del Sur Km 8 **Tel** (45) 667 009 **Fax** (45) 667 008 **Rooms** 407 (plus 200 bungalows)*

Dense in plantlife and trees, the grounds around the pool and the various sports courts invite exploration, with paths weaving around the vegetation from the main four-storey building. There are different types of rooms, with standard doubles in the large main building, and over a hundred bungalows and four grades of suites. **www.solmeliacuba.com**

VARADERO Sol Sirenas Coral $$$$$

*Avenida Las Américas y K, Reparto La Torre **Tel** (45) 668 070 **Fax** (45) 668 075 **Rooms** 660*

Sol Sirenas Coral was once two separate resorts, and there are two distinctly different sections that feel quite remote from one another (one in need of an injection of life and colour). It also means there are twice the number of facilities as at most comparable hotels, including three swimming pools. **www.solmeliacuba.com**

VARADERO SuperClubs Breezes Varadero $$$$$

*Avenida Las Américas Km 3 **Tel** (45) 667 030 **Fax** (45) 667 005 **Rooms** 265*

At this over-18s only resort all rooms are suites, with a high level of comfort and lots of space. The usual amenities (plus CD players, irons and ironing boards) come as standard in all suites, while those in the eleven two-storey buildings have separate living rooms. Extensive grounds, fitness centre and three restaurants. **www.superclubs.org**

VARADERO Tryp Península Varadero $$$$$

*Punta Hicacos **Tel** (45) 668 800 **Fax** (45) 668 805, 668 808 **Rooms** 591*

The top choice for families, this massive resort has a fabulous kids' zone with its own pool that features a little castle on an island, and various other facilities for the under 12s. The standard double rooms would be considered suites in most hotels, with walk-in closets, couch and coffee table, as well as Internet access. **www.solmeliacuba.com**

CENTRAL CUBA – EAST

CAMAGÜEY Casa de Alfredo Castillo $

*Cisnero 124 esq. Raúl Lamar **Tel** (32) 297 436 **Rooms** 2*

A few blocks away from the centre, this is one of the city's more modern *casa particulares* with two spacious rooms offering an above-average level of comfort within the private home market. Casa de Alfredo Castillo is astutely well run, and the owners speak English and French. **allan.carnot@gmail.com**

CAMAGÜEY Casa Lucy $

*Alegría 23, el Ignacio Agramonte y Montera **Tel** (32) 283 701 **Rooms** 2*

This reassuringly clean house has a delightful patio garden with a fountain, seven bird cages and even a little bar counter. The rooms are large, one of them actually more of a mini-apartment with a living room and cooking facilities. Good food here, too.

CAMAGÜEY Hotel Colón $

*República 472 el San José y San Martín **Tel** (32) 283 346, 251 520, 254 878 **Fax** (32) 254 878 **Rooms** 47*

This medium-sized town hotel is in a beautifully restored 1920s gem of a building. The majestic lobby, with its shiny dark wood, marble and tiled surfaces, is a highlight and sets the tone for the rest of the classy interior spaces, including a lovely central patio and bedrooms which are a bit small – ask for one of the matrimonial rooms. **www.islazul.cu**

CAMAGÜEY Hotel Plaza $

*Van Horne 1, Camagüey **Tel** (32) 282 457, 282 413, 282 435 **Rooms** 67*

The oldest and least refined of Camagüey's three neo-colonial hotels, this is still a smart-looking place and certainly doesn't lack character. Guest rooms vary considerably in size and are located either around the central patio or looking onto the street outside. There are two bars in the lobby and a stylish restaurant. **www.islazul.cu**

CAMAGÜEY Gran Hotel $$

*Maceo 67 el Ignacio Agramonte y General Gómez **Tel** (32) 292 093, 292 094 **Fax** (32) 293 933 **Rooms** 72*

Built in 1939, this is a real classic and has maintained the look and feel of refined decadence that would have characterized it prior to the Revolution. There's a rooftop bar and top-floor restaurant, both with great views, and a dimly atmospheric piano bar. Throughout the building are hallmarks of this marvellous hotel's vintage. **www.islazul.cu**

CAYO COCO Villa Gaviota $$$

*Jardines del Rey, Cayo Coco, Ciego de Ávila **Tel** (33) 302 180 **Fax** (33) 302 192 **Rooms** 48*

On a different scale to the majority of the hotels in the Jardines del Rey cays, this down-to-earth little resort provides a pleasant, affordable alternative to the all-inclusives. Wooden communal buildings and one- and two-storey chalets sit nicely with the informal atmosphere. Small pool, gym and beauty parlour. Good for couples. **www.gaviota-grupo.com**

CAYO COCO Hotel Blau Colonial $$$$$

Jardines del Rey, Cayo Coco, Ciego de Ávila **Tel** *(33) 301311* **Fax** *(33) 301384* **Rooms** *286*

Following a thorough renovation, this distinctive all-inclusive reopened in 2005. The arch-laden main building is modelled on classic colonial Cuban architecture and centres around a beguiling garden patio. The elegant rooms feature wrought-iron beds and refined wooden furniture in keeping with the colonial theme. **www.blau-hotels.com**

CAYO COCO Hotel Playa Coco $$$$$

Jardines del Rey, Cayo Coco, Ciego de Ávila **Tel** *(33) 302 250* **Fax** *(33) 302 255* **Rooms** *307*

Not as impressive as other resorts on Cayo Coco, the colonial theme here could have been taken much further. Nevertheless there are three pools, two jacuzzis (one large enough for 20 people), numerous sporting facilities and Japanese and Italian restaurants. **www.gaviota-grupo.com**

CAYO COCO Meliá Cayo Coco $$$$$

Jardines del Rey, Cayo Coco, Ciego de Ávila **Tel** *(33) 301 180* **Fax** *(33) 301 195* **Rooms** *250*

This exceptional all-inclusive resort, aimed at couples (over 18s only), goes for quality over quantity with its facilities. Most outstanding are the 62 rooms suspended over a saltwater lagoon on stilts. Three excellent restaurants include the airy Arena Real, perched just over the water's edge with serene views. **melia-cayococo@solmelia.com**

CAYO COCO NH Krystal Laguna Villas Resort $$$$$

Jardines del Rey, Cayo Coco, Ciego de Ávila **Tel** *(33) 301 470, 301 070* **Fax** *(33) 301 498* **Rooms** *690*

An imaginatively designed jumbo resort, the most remarkable feature of which is the set of cabins built on a natural lagoon. Linked together by wooden gangways, these are top-notch accommodations with living rooms and balconies. Seven restaurants, four pools and three tennis courts are among a huge number of other facilities. **www.nh-hotels.com**

CAYO COCO Sol Cayo Coco $$$$$

Jardines del Rey, Cayo Coco, Ciego de Ávila **Tel** *(33) 301 219, 301 036* **Fax** *(33) 301285* **Rooms** *270*

The most family-oriented resort on Coyo Coco has all sorts of facilities for kids, including a playgroup centre and a kids' pool area. There's an impressive list of watersports, such as water basketball, canoeing and water polo while the excellent nautical club has numerous catamarans, sailing boats and pedal boats. **www.solmeliacuba.com**

CAYO COCO Tryp Cayo Coco $$$$$

Jardines del Rey, Cayo Coco, Ciego de Ávila **Tel** *(33) 301 300* **Fax** *(33) 301 386* **Rooms** *508*

A family all-inclusive with an enormous sprawling pool and extensive ocean front grounds smothered in palm trees. There's a playground, babysitting services and a kids' club for 5-13 year olds. Adults wanting to escape can enjoy the smaller "ecological pool" with a jacuzzi . Four restaurants, gym and night-lit tennis courts. **www.solmeliacuba.com**

CAYO GUILLERMO Villa Cojimar $$$

Jardines del Rey, Cayo Guillermo, Ciego de Ávila **Tel** *(33) 301 712, 301 725* **Fax** *(33) 301 727* **Rooms** *212*

The oldest resort on Cayo Guillermo, Villa Cojimar is a little past its best given the more luxurious, modern neighbouring hotels but it's also one of the least expensive. The guest rooms, in concrete houses, are better looking on the inside and are well equipped. Facilities include a gym, sauna, jacuzzi and games room. **www.gran-caribe.com**

CAYO GUILLERMO Iberostar Daiquiri $$$$$

Jardines del Rey, Cayo Guillermo, Ciego de Ávila **Tel** *(33) 301 650* **Fax** *(33) 301 645* **Rooms** *312*

Iberostar Daiquiri is not as widely spread out as some of the other all-inclusive on the cays, though it is still a large resort. The rooms here are arranged in several long three-storey buildings enveloping the pool area. There are four restaurants, a beach barbecue grill, gym, tennis courts and indoor soccer. **www.iberostar.com**

CAYO GUILLERMO Meliá Cayo Guillermo $$$$$

Jardines del Rey, Cayo Guillermo, Ciego de Ávila **Tel** *(33) 301 680* **Fax** *(33) 301 685, 301 684* **Rooms** *301*

Though it isn't a couples-only resort, Meliá Cayo Guillermo specializes in romance with a wedding gazebo, hammocks in their own hut suspended over the water and a long wooden walkway extending into the sea where covered platforms offer seclusion and tranquility. Four restaurants, fitness centre and two tennis courts. **www.solmeliacuba.com**

CAYO GUILLERMO Sol Cayo Guillermo $$$$$

Jardines del Rey, Cayo Guillermo, Ciego de Ávila **Tel** *(33) 301 760* **Fax** *(33) 301 748* **Rooms** *268*

There's a relaxing, harmonious feel around this neatly designed hotel complex. The scattered bungalows and two-storey villas blend in with the palm-shrouded gardens, all with traditional red brick-coloured roofs, polished tile floors and pastel interiors. There's an attractive pool and decent stretch of beach. **www.solmeliacuba.com**

MORÓN Casa de Juan Carlos Espinosa $

Cristóbal Colón 39, e/ Carretera de Patria y Linea de Ferrocarril **Tel** *(33) 504 177* **Rooms** *2*

A remarkable *casa particular* given that it has a swimming pool and a matted-roof bar in the back garden. Right next to the train station, this elegant neo-colonial residence contains two simple but comfortable rooms and is run by the biographer and friend of *Buena Vista Social Club*'s Pio Leiva, a musician who died in March 2006.

MORÓN Hotel Morón $

Avenida Tarafa, Morón, Ciego de Avila **Tel** *(33) 502 230* **Fax** *(33) 502 133* **Rooms** *143*

This is a conveniently located transit hotel and although the building isn't attractive it is one of the province's largest hotels outside of the cays, making it a reliable place to get a room if you're driving through Cuba or out to Cayo Coco. There is a decent sized, clean swimming pool, too. **www.islazul.cu**

Key to Price Guide *see p252* **Key to Symbols** *see back cover flap*

PENÍNSULA ANCÓN Club Amigo Ancón 🏨🏊♨📋🅿🌐 $$

Playa Ancón, Península Ancón, Trinidad, Sancti Spíritus **Tel** *(41) 996 120, 6123 to 29* **Fax** *(41) 996 121* **Rooms** *279*

At the tip of the peninsula, on the best section of beach, recent renovations have brightened up this multi-storey building. There's plenty to do here, with a large swimming pool, hidden from the beach behind the hotel, two tennis courts, pool tables and bicycles for rent. **www.hotelescubanacan.com**

PENÍNSULA ANCÓN Hotel Costasur 🏨🏊📋🅿🌐 $$

Playa María Aguilar, Península Ancón, Trinidad, Sancti Spíritus **Tel** *(41) 996 174* **Fax** *(41) 996 173* **Rooms** *131*

The beach here is inferior to those found nearer the other hotels on the peninsula, but the attractive bungalows lining the seafront lawn are as appealing a place to stay as anywhere else on this stretch of coastline. There's an airy lobby bar, a tennis court and standard pool. **www.hotelescubanacan.com**

PENÍNSULA ANCÓN Brisas Trinidad del Mar 🏨🏊♨📋🅿🌐 $$$$

Península Ancón, Trinidad, Sancti Spíritus **Tel** *(41) 996 500 to 07* **Fax** *(41) 996 565* **Rooms** *241*

The newest and most upmarket resort on the peninsula is dotted with architectural touches meant to mimic the colonial buildings up the road in Trinidad. These touches do add some character to what is otherwise a standard all-inclusive with all the usual comfort and facilities, such as tennis courts and a gym as well as a kids' club. **www.hotelescubanacan.com**

PLAYA SANTA LUCÍA Club Amigo Mayanabo 🏨🏊📋🅿🌐 $$

Avenida Turística de Tararaco, Playa Santa Lucía, Camagüey **Tel** *(32) 336 184* **Fax** *(32) 365 295* **Rooms** *225*

This hotel is a mixed bag. The landscaped grounds are a tad patchy in places and the main buildings a little dated but it does have the biggest pool in Santa Lucía and there's a captivating water-bound beach bar at the end of a mini-pier. Guest rooms are clean but would improve with refurbishment. **www.hotelescubanacan.com**

PLAYA SANTA LUCÍA Gran Club Santa Lucía 🏨🏊♨📋🅿 $$$

Avenida Turística de Tararaco, Playa Santa Lucía, Nuevitas, Camagüey **Tel** *(32) 336 109* **Fax** *(32) 365 147* **Rooms** *252*

The rooms here and the resort in general are as well equipped as any hotel in the area. There are several restaurants, tennis courts, a beauty parlour, a gym and a games room. Be sure to ask for a room away from the road (some rooms are disappointingly close to the road) or pay extra for a suite. **aloja@clubst.stl.cyt.cu**

PLAYA SANTA LUCÍA Hotel Brisas Santa Lucía 🏨🏊♨📋🅿 $$$

Avenida Turística, Playa Santa Lucía, Nuevitas, Camagüey **Tel** *(32) 336 317* **Fax** *(32) 365 142* **Rooms** *400*

Admittedly there is a long list of facilities here, among which are five bars, tennis courts, a gym and a host of water sports apparatus, but the hotel really qualifies as a 3-star rather than a 4-star facility. Some of the rooms are in need of refurbishment **www.hotelescubanacan.com**

SANCTI SPÍRITUS Casa de Martha Rodríguez Martínez y Miguel 📋🅿 $

Plácido 69, e/ Calderón y Tirso Marín **Tel** *(41) 323 556* **Rooms** *2*

One of the most professionally run *casas particulares* in the city. Its guest rooms, which have ceiling fans as well as a/c, tv and top-quailty en suite bathrooms, are cleaned daily and the owner produces a menu for meal times. There's an intimate terrace where food is served, and a roof terrace with modest views over the city.

SANCTI SPÍRITUS Hotel Zaza 🏨🏊📋🅿🌐 $

Finca San José Km 5.5, Lago Zaza **Tel** *(41) 237 035* **Fax** *(41) 328 359, 325 490* **Rooms** *77*

Another of Cuba's shrines to concrete, this heavy-set four-storey hotel is completely out-of-sync with its natural surroundings and the man-made reservoir (the largest of its kind in Cuba) stretching before it. Hunting and particularly fishing are the focus here, and though there's a pool most visitors bring a rod rather than a swimsuit. **www.islazul.cu**

SANCTI SPÍRITUS Los Richards 📋🅿 $

Independencia 17 (altos), Plaza Serafín Sanchez **Tel** *(41) 326 745* **Rooms** *2*

Of all the houses renting rooms in the city, this is the most centrally located. There's a huge space exclusively for the use of guests with a living-room, bedroom and bathroom as well as a balcony looking out onto the plaza. Up on the roof the owners have contructed their own *bohio*-roof open-air dining area.

SANCTI SPÍRITUS CITY Hostal del Rijo 📋🏨 $

Honorato del Castillo 12 **Tel** *(41) 328 588* **Fax** *(41) 328 577* **Rooms** *16*

Considerably underpriced compared to numerous other town hotels in Cuba, this delectable little colonial conversion on a tiny square in the heart of the city is a wonderful place to stay. Rooms are surprisingly spacious, well equipped, subtly decorated with dark-wood furnishings and high-quality bathrooms with marble touches. **www.hotelescubanacan.com**

SANCTI SPÍRITUS CITY Hostal Plaza 📋🏨 $

Independencia 1, esq. Avenida de los Mártires, Plaza Serafín Sánchez **Tel** *(41) 327 102* **Fax** *(41) 326 940* **Rooms** *27*

Right on the main square, this is the city's other excellent-value hotel. All the spaces are full of character, from the graceful lobby with its wicker furnishings to the intimate restaurant and the attractive rooms with colonial-style furnishings, many with balconies looking over the square. Recently refurbished. **www.hotelescubanacan.com**

SANCTI SPÍRITUS CITY Villa Los Laureles 🏨🏊📋🅿 $

Carretera Central Km 383 **Tel** *(41) 327 016* **Fax** *(41) 323 913* **Rooms** *76*

This roadside villa complex on the outskirts of the city on the island-wide Carretera Central is used predominantly by weary motorists. The basic layout, with inoffensive-looking bungalows gathered around a medium-sized, oblong pool, adds to the straightforward appeal of the place. Rooms have satellite tv, radio and minibar. **www.islazul.cu**

SANCTI SPÍRITUS CITY Rancho Hatuey ⬛🏤📋0🔳 $$
Carretera Central Km 383 **Tel** *(41) 328 321* **Fax** *(41) 328 830* **Rooms** *74*

Spread thinly around its spacious, grassy, gently undulating grounds, this simple hotel complex melts into the surrounding countryside to the extent that you can't really see the joint. Rooms are in boxy, two-storey concrete cabins and there's a pool area in the centre. The best place in town for peace and relaxation. **www.islazul.cu**

TRINIDAD Casa de Azalea y Alfredo 📋 $
Frank País 504, e/ Piro Guinart y Fidel Claro **Tel** *(41) 993 845* **Rooms** *2*

Run by two middle-aged teachers (one of history, the other of maths), this simple house, built in 1840, has some nice touches, like the colonial-era doorway shutters and the more modern crazy-paving on the walls in both bedrooms. There's a roof terrace and a diminutive patio. **ugaaza@yahoo.es**

TRINIDAD Casa Margely 📋📋0 $
Piro Guinart 360, e/ Fernando Hernández Echerri y Juan M Márquez **Tel** *(41) 996 525* **Rooms** *2*

The rooms in this fairly opulent colonial residence are walled off at the back of the central patio in a private little section of the house with its own garden gate and dining room. Both rooms have two double beds, but only one has an en suite bathroom; the other bathroom is at the end of the leafy outdoor corridor linking it all up.

TRINIDAD Casa Santana 📋0 $
Maceo 425, e/ Fco. J. Zerquera y Colón **Tel** *(41) 994 372* **Rooms** *1*

Casa Santana is run by an enthusiastic host who hands you a book on the history of Trinidad when you arrive. The whole of the upstairs of the house, three rooms in all, is given over to guests. The backyard patio is spacious, and the well is one of the many original colonial artifacts found all over the house. **www.particuba.net/villes/trinidad/santana**

TRINIDAD Hostal Las Mercedes 📋📋0 $
Camilo Cienfuegos 272, e/ Maceo y Francisco Cadahia **Tel** *(41) 993 107* **Rooms** *1*

On one of the busier streets just outside the historic centre of Trinidad, the room here looks onto the open backyard patio full of plants and trees, including a huge cactus. The high-ceiling guest room has a huge colonial style bathroom, a bronze bed and an imposing wardrobe. Run by an exuberant owner and her son. **ezequiel@cimex.com.cu**

TRINIDAD Hotel Las Cuevas ⬛🏤📋0🔳 $$
Finca Santa Ana **Tel** *(41) 996 133, 6434* **Fax** *(41) 996 161* **Rooms** *109*

Laid out on a hillside just above the town, there are great views wherever you are in this very relaxing and secluded cabin complex. The serenity is disturbed only by the nightly shows of traditional Cuban music and dance that take place on the terrace outside the restaurant. The unique hotel disco is in a cave deep in the hillside. **www.hotelescubanacan.com**

TRINIDAD Iberostar Grand Hotel Trinidad 🔲⬛📋📋 $$$$$
José Martí 262, e/ Lino Pérez y Colón, Parque Céspedes **Tel** *(41) 996 073, 6074, 6075* **Fax** *(41) 996 077* **Rooms** *40*

Opened in 2006 this sumptuous small-scale five-star hotel has an enchanting central patio and some great touches, like the giant pineapple lampshade and the memorabilia encased in the glass-topped lobby coffee tables. The restaurant is the best and most expensive in Trinidad. Rooms have either a balcony or terrace. **www.iberostar.com**

EASTERN CUBA

BARACOA Casa de Clara Carratalá 📋📋0 $
Mariana Grajales 30 **Tel** *(21) 643 361* **Rooms** *2*

Run by a chatty former doctor, this laid-back spick-and-span house features rooms centred around a pleasant little patio. The cooking here is of a high standard and the speciality of the house is fish cooked in coconut milk. Casa de Clara Carratalá is located five blocks from the seafront.

BARACOA Casa de Nancy Borges Gallego 📋📋 $
Ciro Frías 3 esq. Flor Crombet **Tel** *(21) 643 272* **Rooms** *3*

An agreeable place run by friendly owners, one of whom – René Frometa – is the adopted son of local legend La Rusa, an immigrant Russian who gave shelter to the rebel army during the Revolution. One of the rooms here is set up as a kind of museum in homage to the lady. Rooms are clean and comfortable.

BARACOA Hostal La Habanera 📋⬛📋0 $
Los Maceos 124 e/ Maravi y Frank Pais, Baracoa, Guantánamo **Tel** *(21) 645 273* **Rooms** *10*

Occupying a beautifully refurbished Colonial residence built in 1867, this charming hotel is right in the heart of Baracoa. For the price, rooms are of an excellent standard: spacious with high ceilings and smart, tiled floors. The hotel runs a programme of relaxation therapies, including a variety of massages. **www.hostallahabanera.com**

BARACOA Hotel la Rusa ⬛📋📋🔳 $
Máximo Gómez no.161 e/ Pelayo Cuervo y Ciro Frías, Baracoa, Guantánamo **Tel** *(21) 643 011* **Rooms** *12*

On the seafront, this simple, three-storey building has small rooms, modestly furnished, with tiny bathrooms. Some have pleasant sea views. The restaurant tables are lined up along a narrow terrace. The former owner was a Russian immigrant (hence the name) who gave refuge to Fidel and his men during the Revolution. **www.hotellarusa.com**

BARACOA El Castillo 🍽 🏊 📋 🛈 📶 $$

Loma de Paraíso, Baracoa, Guantánamo **Tel** *(21) 645 194, 645 165* **Fax** *(21) 645 339* **Rooms** *34*

The best place to stay for postcard views of Baracoa and the bay, this laid-back hotel is part-housed in a converted 18th-century fort. The historic theme extends to the rooms, which are furnished in a smart, refined colonial style. The whole hotel is imbued with a soothing sense of calm. Great views from the small pool. **www.gaviota-grupo.com**

BARACOA Porto Santo 🍽 🏊 📋 🛈 📶 $$

Carretera del Aeropuerto, Baracoa, Guantánamo **Tel** *(21) 645 106* **Fax** *(21) 645 339* **Rooms** *60*

Secluded and right on the edge of the bay, the location is where Columbus is said to have planted the Cruz de Parra, a cross declaring the European arrival in the Americas. The hotel has its own private patch of beach and is gracefully spread around neatly trimmed lawns. Guest rooms are average. **www.gaviota-grupo.com**

BAYAMO Hotel Escuela Telégrafo 🍽 📋 $

José Antonio Saco no.108, e/ General García y Donato Mármol, Bayamo **Tel** *(23) 425 510* **Fax** *(23) 427 389* **Rooms** *12*

An excellent-value hotel, originally opened in 1925 but remodelled in recent years, is now a training school for the hotel trade. Rooms are furnished with differing styles of beds and contrasting colour schemes, some of them a little garish, but all have minibar and satellite tv. They're also managed to squeeze in two restaurants and two bars. **www.ehtgr.co.cu**

BAYAMO Hotel Royalton 🍽 📋 📶 $

Antonio Maceo no.53, e/ General García y José Palma, Bayamo **Tel** *(23) 422 290* **Fax** *(23) 424 792* **Rooms** *33*

The smartest hotel in town, dating from the 1940s, is located on the main square. Its restaurant is one of the best in the city, with a veranda overlooking the square. All rooms have been decorated and furnished with a well-ordered restraint, featuring dark wood, tv and small but pristine bathrooms. Four of them have views of the square. **www.islazul.cu**

CAIMANERA Hotel Caimanera 🍽 🏊 📋 🛈 📶 $

Loma Norte, Caimanera, Guantánamo **Tel** *(21) 499 414 to 16* **Fax** *(21) 499 649* **Rooms** *19*

This small, simple hotel has a unique claim to fame: it's as near as most people are allowed to get to the controversial US naval base at Guantánamo Bay and even has a designated lookout from where guests view the base through binoculars. Rooms are slightly cramped. Booking in advance is obligatory. **caimanera@enet.cu**

CAYO SAETÍA Villa Cayo Saetía 🍽 📋 🛈 $$

Cayo Saetia, Mayari, Holguín **Tel** *(24) 516 900, 516 901* **Rooms** *12*

A chilled-out, unpretentious little cabin complex on the coast, perfect for relaxation. The well-equipped wooden cabins are thoughtfully and harmoniously furnished, combining perfectly a good level of comfort with a rustic decor neatly in tune with the natural surroundings. Breakfast is not included in the rate. **www.gaviota-grupo.cu**

GRANMA PROVINCE Club Amigo Marea del Portillo 🍽 🏊 🍴 📋 🛈 $

Marea del Portillo Km 12 1/2, Pilón, Granma **Tel** *(23) 597 008, 597 102* **Fax** *(23) 597 080* **Rooms** *140*

A serene natural setting between the mountains and the sea make this three-star all-inclusive a perfect place to escape. From the pool area, with its mountain views, sloping lawns lead down to lovely, shrub-lined beach. There are programmes of entertainment, including showcases of traditional Cuban culture. **www.hotelescubanacan.com**

HOLGUÍN CITY Villa Formell 🏊 📋 🛈 $

Morales Lemus 189, e/ Frexes y Martí **Tel** *(24) 422 547* **Rooms** *1*

Just a couple of blocks from central Parque Calixto García, this large house is run by Deisy Formell, cousin to Juan Formell – founder of the world-famous Cuban salsa group, Los Van Van. The comfortable guest room has its own bathroom, and communal areas include a pleasant little leafy patio.

HOLGUÍN CITY Hotel Pernik 📶 🍽 🏊 📋 🛈 $$

Avenida Jorge Dimítrov y Plaza de la Revolución, Nuevo Holguín, Holguín **Tel** *(24) 481 011* **Fax** *(24) 481 158* **Rooms** *200*

From the 1970s school of Russian-influenced hotel architecture, this relatively well equipped but unspectacular town hotel has a large oblong pool, three restaurants and several bars. More uniquely, there are eight "gallery rooms" dedicated to personalities from the world of Cuban culture. **www.hotelpernik.cu**

HOLGUÍN PROVINCE Villa Mirador de Mayabe 📶 🍽 🏊 📋 🛈 📶 $$

Altura de Mayabe Km 8.5, Holguín **Tel** *(24) 422 160, 423 485* **Fax** *(24) 425 498* **Rooms** *24*

Perched on a hillside covered in flourishing dense woodlands and overlooking a valley surrounding the city of Holguín, the view from this hotel is a large part of the attraction of staying here. A smaller part is witnessing the resident beer-drinking donkey! **www.islazul.cu**

PARQUE BACONAO Villa Gran Piedra 🍽 📋 🛈 📶 $

Carretera Gran Piedra Km 14, Santiago de Cuba **Tel** *(22) 686 393, 686 147, 686 395* **Rooms** *22*

At over 1,200 m (3,940 ft) above sea level, this is Cuba's highest hotel. The breathtaking views from this mountainside resort, woven into the ruins of a colonial coffee plantation, make it a very special place to stay, even though the amenities and facilities here are only average. Rooms are in stone and brick cabins. **www.islazul.cu**

PARQUE BACONAO Club Amigo Carisol Los Corales 🍽 🏊 🍴 📋 🛈 $$

Carretera de Baconao Km 31, Santiago de Cuba **Tel** *(22) 356 122* **Fax** *(22) 356 177* **Rooms** *310*

The Club Amigo Carisol Los Corales has its own section of beach and accommodation is spread out around attractive tree-studded grounds. Decent pool and a lively entertainment schedule, but the standard of food is average. There's a kids' club, and water sports facilities include catamarans, kayaks and aqua bikes. **www.hotelescubanacan.com**

PARQUE BACONAO Hotel Costa Morena $$

Carretera de Baconao Km 24 1/2, Sigüa, Santiago de Cuba **Tel** *(22) 356 135* **Fax** *(22) 356 160* **Rooms** *115*

Overlooking the Caribbean and surrounded by the hills of the Parque Baconao, this is a great place to stay if you like the outdoors. There's a natural swimming pool as well as a standard man-made one, and all rooms have sea views. Hiking and trekking around the park can be arranged from here. **www.islazul.cu**

PLAYA COVARRUBIAS Villa Covarrubias $$$

Playa Covarrubias, Puerto Padre, Las Tunas **Tel** *(31) 515 530* **Fax** *(31) 515 352* **Rooms** *180*

This waterfront all-inclusive with landscaped grounds leading down to the beach is located close to a fantastic coral reef. There are facilities for snorkelling and diving, while other available activities range from billiards, table tennis and bingo to basketball, archery and exercises in the aqua gym. **www.hotelescubanacan.com**

PLAYA ESMERALDA Paradisus Río de Oro $$$$$

Carretera Guardalavaca, Playa Esmeralda, Rafael Freyre, Holguín **Tel** *(24) 430 090* **Fax** *(24) 430 095* **Rooms** *300*

This ultra all-inclusive set on a bayfront nature reserve has an exclusive feel and is aimed predominantly at the couples market, with facilities for weddings and honeymoons. All rooms are luxurious and tasteful and the two Garden Villas have 300 sq m (3,230 sq ft) of private grounds and their own pools and gardens. **www.solmeliacuba.com**

PLAYA ESMERALDA Sol Río de Luna y Mares $$$$$

Playa Esmeralda, Rafael Freyre, Holguín **Tel** *(24) 430 030* **Fax** *(24) 430 065* **Rooms** *465*

On a fantastic, broad stretch of beach backing onto wooded, palm-dotted grounds, this family resort has a lively, upbeat feel. Rooms are colourful and all feature either a terrace or a balcony. Six restaurants, two pools and two tennis courts, plus a beach disco. It is also the site of the only certified dive centre in the area. **www.solmeliacuba.com**

PLAYA GUARDALAVACA Club Amigo Atlántico-Guardalavaca $$$

Playa Guardalavaca, Banes, Holguín **Tel** *(24) 430 180 to 82, 430 121* **Fax** *(24) 430 200* **Rooms** *747*

A vast all-inclusive complex with a variety of different accommodation choices, some in the large main building, others in villas of varying shapes and sizes. Dance and Spanish classes are offered alongside all sorts of sporting facilities with football, basketball, tennis, volleyball and archery all catered for. **www.cubanacan.cu**

PLAYA GUARDALAVACA Hotel Brisas Guardalavaca $$$$

Calle 2 no.1, Playa Guardalavaca, Banes, Holguín **Tel** *(24) 430 218, 430 162* **Fax** *(24) 430 418* **Rooms** *437*

A hotel village made up of attractive tiled-roof apartment blocks. The under-12s are well-catered for here with a kids' club, games area and a full programme of entertainment. Adults don't do badly either, and all doubles come with king-sized beds. The all-inclusive package includes tours of a historic Amerindian village. **www.brisasguardalavaca.com**

PLAYA PESQUERO Blau Costa Verde Beach Resort $$$$

Playa Pesquero, Rafael Freyre, Holguín **Tel** *(24) 433 510* **Fax** *(24) 433 515* **Rooms** *309*

At the heart of this luxury resort is the impressive and alluring pool, snaking around trees and buildings and featuring a poolside bar and restaurant. Other facilities include a beauty parlour, jacuzzi, gymnasium, a diving centre, a disco and a cigar shop. There's also a baby-sitting service. **www.blau-hotel.com**

PLAYA PESQUERO Hotel Playa Pesquero $$$$$

Playa Pesquero, Rafael Freyre, Holguín **Tel** *(24) 433 530* **Fax** *(24) 433 535* **Rooms** *944*

A staggeringly large all-inclusive hotel complex on the beach. The endless list of facilities includes three swimming pools, three jacuzzis, seven restaurants, six bars and three tennis courts with spotlights for night-time games. Rooms are luxurious and feature Internet access as well as all the mod cons you would expect. **www.gaviota-grupo.com**

PLAYA PESQUERO Playa Costa Verde $$$$$

Playa Pesquero, Rafael Freyre, Holguín **Tel** *(24) 433 520* **Fax** *(24) 433 525* **Rooms** *480*

A beachfront mega-resort featuring a great selection of outdoor areas including a huge pool, a set of four tennis courts and a multi-purpose sports pitch all linked together by immaculately landscaped gardens. Indoors there's an extremely well-equipped gym as well as Japanese, Italian and Cuban restaurants. **www.gaviota-grupo.com**

SANTIAGO DE CUBA Casa Colonial Maruchi $

Hartmann (San Félix) 357, e/ Trinidad y San Germán **Tel** *(22) 620 767* **Rooms** *2*

One of the most professionally run and characterful *casas particulares* in the city. The front rooms are furnished with Colonial period furniture, and the delightful central patio has plants everywhere and a peacock roaming around. Gregarious Maruchi runs the place. **maruchib@yahoo.es**

SANTIAGO DE CUBA Casa de Leonardo y Rosa $

Clarín (Padre Quiroga) 9, e/ Aguilera y Heredia **Tel** *(22) 623 574* **Rooms** *2*

This early 20th-century residence offers two guest accommodations – a small double room with a large bathroom, and located at the back of the house beyond the patio with its attractive water feature is a separate little apartment with its own garden gate, kitchenette with classic 1950s fridge and stone steps leading up to the airy bedroom.

SANTIAGO DE CUBA Casa de Sra Vilma Herrero $

Avenida Garzón 332, e/ 2da y 3ra, Reparto Santa Bàrbara **Tel** *(22) 656 981* **Rooms** *2*

One of the few *casas particulares* in this part of town, halfway between the historic centre and the outer suburban neighbourhoods. It is an eclectically furnished and decorated 1920s bungalow with a roof terrace and a higgedly-piggeldy back yard. The elderly owners have a Chevrolet 53 parked in the tiny driveway. **vilma@film.cineclubes.com**

Key to Price Guide *see p252* **Key to Symbols** *see back cover flap*

SANTIAGO DE CUBA Casa Mundo

Heredia 308, e/ Pío Rosado (Carnicería) y Porfirio Valiente (Calvario) **Tel** *(22) 624 097* **Rooms** *2*

A colonial house right in the historic centre of the city. Though there is no single definable style, inside there is a genuine sense of the past and some great pieces of furniture, like the ornate early 20th-century dresser in one of the bedrooms. Both rooms have their own bathroom, but only one is en suite. **co8kz@yahoo.es**

SANTIAGO DE CUBA Gran Hotel

José Antonio Saco (Enramada) 312, esq. Hartmann (San Félix) **Tel** *(22) 653020* **Rooms** *15*

An everyday town hotel and the least touristy in Santiago de Cuba. Located on one of the main shopping streets, a couple of blocks from Parque Céspedes, this budget option is surrounded by hustle and bustle. Rooms are basic but clean and comfortable, and some have small balconies. **www.granhotelstgo.cu**

SANTIAGO DE CUBA Hostal San Basilio

Bartolomé Masó 403 e/ Carnicería y Porfirio Valiente (Calvario) **Tel** *(22) 651702* **Fax** *(22) 687069* **Rooms** *8*

Tucked away on an old, narrow street a few blocks from the main square, this pleasant, tiny hotel is housed in a graceful colonial residence. It's the kind of place where you can't help getting to know the staff, with the receptionist doubling up as the waiter and the dinky kitchen and dining area occupying the same room. **www.hotelescubanacan.com**

SANTIAGO DE CUBA Hotel Libertad

Aguilera 652, Plaza de Marte **Tel** *(22) 627710* **Rooms** *17*

On the least touristy of the three central squares, this neo-colonial conversion has bags of character and is more stylish and refined than its price band might suggest. A dignified, columned, arched lobby leads onto wide corridors and a broad staircase ascending to the roof-terrace bar and sweeping vistas of the east of the city. **www.islazul.cu**

SANTIAGO DE CUBA Versalles

Carretera al Morro Km 1, Altura de Versalles **Tel** *(22) 691016* **Fax** *(22) 686039* **Rooms** *72*

From this good-value cabin complex near the historic El Morro castle, beyond the southern edge of Santiago, there are fabulous views back over the city and out to the Sierra Maestra mountains. Facilities include tennis, basketball and volleyball courts. There is also easy access to the airport. **www.cubanacan.cu**

SANTIAGO DE CUBA Hotel Las Américas

General Cebreco y Avenida de las Américas **Tel** *(22) 642011* **Fax** *(22) 687075* **Rooms** *70*

The location on the aristocratic side of the city, with its broad, tree-lined avenues, provides what was formerly one of Santiago's most prestigious hotels with attractive enough surroundings to take the less attractive edge off this now dated-looking apartment hotel. As well as two restaurants and two bars, the hotel has its own cabaret. **www.islazul.cu**

SANTIAGO DE CUBA Hotel San Juan

Carretera de Siboney Km 1 1/2 **Tel** *(22) 687200* **Fax** *(22) 687237* **Rooms** *110*

Right at the city limits, this is a laid-back place to stay set in attractive, verdant grounds with a large swimming pool around which many of the cabins housing the rooms are centred. The rooms themselves are nothing special but well equipped with satellite tv, radio, safety deposit box and en suite bathrooms. **www.sanjuan.co.cu**

SANTIAGO DE CUBA Villa Gaviota Santiago de Cuba

Avenida Manduley 502, e/ 19 y 21, Reparto Vista Alegre **Tel** *(22) 641368* **Fax** *(22) 687166* **Rooms** *54*

Dotted around this enchanting neighbourhood that was home to the city's wealthy before the Revolution, the guest rooms here are in converted mansions, which have been divided into two or three apartments each. Some rooms share bathrooms. A purpose-built central building houses the pool and restaurant. **www.gaviota-grupo.com**

SANTIAGO DE CUBA Hotel Casa Granda

Heredia 201 esq. San Pedro **Tel** *(22) 686600* **Fax** *(22) 686035* **Rooms** *58*

A magnificent colonial building on the main square in the heart of the city, this is ideal for anyone wanting to stay in the thick of the action without sacrificing comfort. Rooms are of a high standard and there is a roof terrace where you can eat and drink with sweeping views down to the bay. **www.gran-caribe.com**

SANTIAGO DE CUBA Meliá Santiago de Cuba

Calle M e/ 4ta y Avenida Las Américas **Tel** *(22) 687070* **Fax** *(22) 687170* **Rooms** *302*

On a pleasant, leafy avenue away from the centre, this is the flashiest, most upmarket hotel in Santiago. The main building is a quirky, colourful high-rise block from which most rooms with stunning views. There are three good restaurants, and the impressive grounds feature a fantastic split-level pool, a basketball court and football pitch. **www.solmeliacuba.com**

SIERRA MAESTRA Brisas Los Galeones

Carretera Chivirico Km 72 **Tel** *(22) 326160* **Rooms** *34*

The sister hotel of the Brisas Sierra Mar (below), this is the more intimate version of the impressive all-inclusive. All rooms have mountain and sea views. A minibus links the two hotels, 12 km (7.5 miles) apart, and guests can use the facilities at either, which include massage, jacuzzi, sauna, gym and tennis courts. Over 16s only. **www.hotelescubanacan.com**

SIERRA MAESTRA Brisas Sierra Mar

Carretera Chivirico Km 60 **Tel** *(22) 329110* **Fax** *(22) 329116* **Rooms** *200*

A beach-front hotel in its own beautiful little woody enclave with the Sierra Maestra mountains as a backdrop. A great option for families with young children, as this all-inclusive has a play area and a series of entertainment programmes designed for 4- to 12-year olds. Many rooms have balconies with uninterrupted sea views. **www.hotelescubanacan.com**

WHERE TO EAT

In traditional Cuban cooking, rice and beans are the staples rather than bread, and the most common dishes are meat-based. Seafood also features heavily with shrimp, lobster and fish dishes found on a large proportion of restaurant menus. Different influences can be seen in Cuban cooking and there are local variations, especially on the eastern side of Cuba. Food is rarely hot and spicy. Besides international

The neon sign at the historic La Zaragozana restaurant

dishes, local menus generally feature some specialities of *comida criolla* (Creole cuisine; *see p272*). Places offering food range from state-run restaurants and hotel restaurants, which are usually comfortable and elegant, to informal *paladares* serving inexpensive home cooking. In Havana there are also Chinese and Arab restaurants, and pizzerias are everywhere. Vegetarian restaurants are a rarity.

RESTAURANTS AND CAFES

State-run restaurants have for years had a bad reputation. However, in recent years a great effort has been made to improve them (partly due to competition from private *paladares*). Now, standards in some cases, for example in branches of the **Palmares** chain run by Cubanacán, are very good.

Some of Havana's most delightful restaurants are housed in well-restored Colonial buildings with period furnishings. Many have a view or a garden of some kind. Live music is often performed and makes for a lively atmosphere.

The restaurants in luxury hotels are usually high-quality and feature international dishes along with a good wine list. As an alternative to formal, à la carte dining, many hotels offer buffets, which in Cuba are called *mesa sueca* (smorgasbord), where, for a fixed price, you can eat

The inviting dining room of the Tocororo restaurant in Havana

anything from pasta to roast suckling pig with rice and black beans.

Some of Havana's most famous bars have a separately managed restaurant. Examples are the Bodeguita del Medio and El Floridita in Havana, and the Terraza de Cojímar. These are open all day serving snacks and cocktails, and offer a full menu for lunch and dinner.

PALADARES

The cheapest places offering Cuban cooking are called *paladares*. These are small private restaurants with a handful of tables, offering a fixed price or à la carte menu. Dishes are often simple but can be surprisingly good – and often better quality than their state-run equivalents. *Paladares* are subject to all kinds of government restrictions that don't affect state restaurants – in some areas they are forbidden from providing chairs for customers (effectively making them takeaways), and they are banned altogether from major beach resorts.

However, be wary of people who accost you in the street and offer to show you a *paladar*: once there, your helpful guide will receive a commission from the proprietor and your bill will cost a few dollars more. Furthermore, your new friend will probably also ask you to treat him to dinner!

In the *paladares* people usually drink cold beer with their food, but mineral water and soft drinks are also normally available. The price shown for a dish includes service and side dishes such as beans, salad and fried plantains or yucca.

Dining out at La Campaña de Toledo restaurant in Camagüey

Inside a typical *paladar*, which has traditional cuisine and live music

PRIVATE HOMES

It often happens that private homes offering rooms to let *(see p251)* also provide main meals as well as breakfast. Since the food normally eaten by the home owners is plainer than the food offered to guests, you will be asked to let them know in advance whether you intend to eat in or out. In general, the standards of cleanliness in authorized private homes are good. The quality of the food varies quite a lot: you may be lucky and eat extremely well, feasting perhaps on fresh lobster or prawns.

SNACKS AND FAST FOOD

All kinds of snacks are widely available in Cuba. Virtually all *cafeterías*, inside and outside hotels, sell the classic Cuban sandwich, with cheese and ham, or hot dogs with mustard, ketchup and chips, to eat in or take away.

There is also an American-style fast food chain, **El Rápido**, where for a few convertible pesos you can get fried chicken with a side dish of *papitas fritas* (chips), beer or *refresco* (soft drink). These places also offer *perritos calientes* (hot dogs), *hamburguesas* (hamburgers), pizza and ice cream.

Coppelia®

Sign of the Coppelia ice cream chain

People eat either at tables or at the counter. This chain is comparatively new and standards of hygiene are usually high.

Along the major roads and on the motorways you will find the equivalent of motorway cafés selling soft drinks, beer, fruit juice, pizza, ice cream and, sometimes, sandwiches. Some kiosks are set among trees, perfect for a relaxing stop in the shade.

The best ice cream is sold at the **Coppelia** parlours, which are found in many Cuban cities (the one in Havana is an institution, *see p98*). They are highly popular so be prepared to wait in a queue.

Lastly, you can buy food along the road from people who run small stalls in front of their homes. Food on offer may include pizza, sandwiches, fritters of corn or

malanga (a local root vegetable), coconut sweets and peanut nougat. Around noon *cajitas*, cardboard boxes containing rice, beans, salad, pork or chicken, are served.

The same foods can be found on sale in the fruit and vegetable markets *(agros)* throughout the island. However, standards of hygiene may vary considerably *(see p302)*.

PAYING

In many restaurants and *paladares*, expect to pay in cash with convertible pesos. Only the better restaurants and hotels accept credit cards. At markets or on the road you can pay in Cuban *pesos*, although convertible pesos would also be accepted (change will be given in *pesos*). Restaurant bills should include a tip; add more to show appreciation.

WHEN TO EAT

Breakfast (desayuno) is served from 6 or 7am and usually consists of a buffet offering fresh fruit, bread, butter, ham, cheese and eggs, yoghurt, milk, coffee and at times jam. Lunch is served from noon to 1:30pm, but many restaurants and *paladares* have adapted to tourists' needs and serve food well into the afternoon.

Dinner is eaten from 7 to 9pm. Don't expect to find a restaurant willing to serve you a meal after 10pm, except perhaps in Havana.

A branch of the fast-food chain, El Rápido, at Sancti Spíritus

The Flavours of Cuba

Cuba's *mercados agropecuarios* (farmers' markets) are a cornucopia of fruits and vegetables fresh from the fields. Tomatoes, cucumbers and squash are staples, along with ripe *plátanos*, the humble yet ubiquitous plantain (a relative of the banana). Exotic fruits enliven stalls with their distinctive bouquets and hues. Poultry run around freely until ready for the pot, while home-fed pigs provide pork – the main meat. The government maintains a monopoly on the sale of beef, prawns and lobster, making them hard to find outside the state-run restaurants.

Guava paste and white cheese

A young Cuban farmer displays his harvest of plantains

COMIDA CRIOLLA

Traditional Cuban *comida criolla* (creole cuisine) is the main cuisine, based mainly on the frying pan and using simple ingredients, with little regional variation – not least due to national shortages of everything. It is a melding of Spanish, African and indigenous, pre-Columbian Indian influences. Local produce such as *calabaza* (a squash), yucca (cassava) and maize (sweetcorn), tomatoes, potatoes and bell peppers are combined with pumpkin and cabbage introduced by the Spanish. African vegetables include *malanga* (a root vegetable with a delicate flavour), *platano vianda* (a variety of plantain that is eaten cooked) and *quimbombó* – okra, often called ladies' fingers.

Typically flavoured with peppers, onion, oregano and cumin, *criolla* dishes are usually served with boiled potatoes or other root vegetables *(viandas)*. Simple salads vary according to the time of year: in winter they might well feature lettuce, tomatoes, white cabbage and, at times, beets; in the summer they may include green beans, carrots, cucumber and avocado.

Custard apple   Plantains   Limes   Watermelon   Pineapple
Mango
Papaya
Some of the tropical fruits that add flavour and colour to Cuban cuisine

CUBAN DISHES AND SPECIALITIES

Cuba's zesty cultural mix has produced some superb national dishes, although visitors are often hard-pressed to find dishes such as aromatic *ropa vieja*. Pork *(cerdo)* is a Cuban favourite, especially smoked loin *(loma ahumado)* roasted on a spit. The main accompaniment is white rice with black beans, often cooked together to form *moros y cristianos*, known as *congrí* or *congrí oriental* when the beans are red. Another common accompaniment is fried plantains, which are sometimes mashed and re-fried in patties *(tostones)*. Rice dishes, and even succulent roast chicken cooked in orange sauce, are often enlivened with *mojo*, a zesty sauce of garlic, oil and bitter orange. Main meals are usually followed by a fruit plate, or a relatively simple dessert such as flan or a fruit preserve served with cheese.

Black beans

Filete de pescado grillé *may be any grilled fillet of white fish, here served with* tostones *and white cabbage salad.*

Fruit and vegetable stall at a Havana farmers' market

The most ubiquitous meat on the island is ham; pork is also served roasted *(cerdo asado)* or as thin fillets *(chuletas)*. Chicken is usually coated with flour and fried in oil *(pollo frito)*, although it is also occasionally served fricasséed, accompanied by French fries. Fish and seafood, notably lobster and shrimp, is typically served in a tomato sauce *(enchilada)* or fried, grilled or baked with butter and garlic, as with sea bass and mahi mahi, which is almost always grilled. *Camarones* (meaty prawns) are served in many different ways – stewed, grilled, baked or boiled and garnished with mayonnaise. Breakfasts are usually limited to simple omelettes and a fruit plate, perhaps with bread and local white cheese (similar to Greek féta) plus yoghurt.

BARACOAN SPECIALITIES

Baracoan fare, from the far eastern side of the island, revolves around the use of coconut and cocoa, cultivated since pre-Columbian times

Cubans fishing in the evening on the Malecón in Havana

by the indigenous peoples. Coconut milk flavours *bacán*, a tortilla of baked plantain filled with spiced pork and cooked wrapped in a banana leaf. It is also used as a base in which to simmer spinach-like *calalú*. Red plantains, known as *plátanos manzanos*, are mashed with coconut milk to make *rangollo*. Cocoa forms the base of Baracoa's delicious chocolate and is the key ingredient of *chorote*, an ambrosial drink thickened with cornflour. Mixed with copious amounts of sugar (sometimes with the addition of grated orange peel and nuts), shredded coconut makes a delicious sweet.

ON THE MENU

Coco rallado Grated coconut in syrup, served with cheese.

Cucurucho Shredded coconut with orange, fruits, nuts and syrup, pressed in a palm leaf.

Empanada Turnover pastries filled with minced meat, potatoes and other vegetables.

Filete uruguayano Pork or fish cutlet stuffed with ham and cheese, then baked.

Potaje Thick soup made from black or red beans with garlic, onions and herbs and spices.

Ropa vieja Shredded beef marinated and cooked with spices and onion, served with white rice.

Ajiaco *consists of vegetables, including plantains, which are simmered with meat and herbs to form a rich stew.*

Cerdo asado *is roast pork, usually served quite simply with rice and beans and often an orange sauce.*

Flan de huevos *appears on most menus. It is a typically Spanish dessert, similar to crème caramel but sweeter.*

What to Drink in Cuba

A wide range of drinks, both alcoholic and non-alcoholic, is available in Cuba, although wine tends to be available only in restaurants and is almost always imported. Tap water is drinkable in many places but to avoid any health problems it is better to keep to bottled water. Visitors should be careful, too, about buying drinks such as fruit juice or fruit shakes from street or market stalls. In bars and cafés not up to international standards – especially in Eastern Cuba – avoid ice in drinks like cocktails. In such places stick to pre-packaged drinks, draught beer or rum.

Preparing refreshing *guarapo*, or sugar cane juice

BEER

Beer *(cerveza)* is the most widely seen and popular drink in Cuba. It is drunk very cold and at all hours of the day, as well as during meals. There are excellent bottled and canned Cuban lager beers, such as Cristal, Lagarto, Mayabe and Bucanero (the latter is also sold in a *fuerte* version, which is stronger and drier). A drink similar to beer is *malta*, a very sweet, fizzy malt-based drink that is popular with Cuban children. *Malta* is some-times mixed with condensed milk to be used as an energizer and tonic.

Beer: Bucanero (strong) and Cristal (light)

PACKAGED SOFT DRINKS

Soft drinks – lemon, orange and cola – called *refrescos*, either Cuban or imported, are sold canned, bottled or in cartons. The Tropical Island range of fruit juices is excellent. All kinds of fruits are used: mango, *guayaba* (guava), pineapple, apple, pear, orange, grapefruit, banana with orange, tropical cocktail, tamarind, peach and tomato. The most common brand of water sold, still *(sin gas)* or sparkling *(con gas)*, is Ciego Montero.

Tropical Island *guayaba* juice

HOT DRINKS

Hotel bars serve Italian espresso coffee or American coffee. The coffee served in private homes or sold on the streets is usually strong and has sugar already added. It is served in a tiny coffee cup. For a dash of milk, ask for a *cortado*; order a *café con leche* for a more milky coffee. *Sin azúcar* means "without sugar". Camomile tea *(manzanilla)* is also easy to find.

SPIRITS

The most widespread and popular spirit in Cuba is, of course, rum. There are several different types *(see p75)*: the youngest – *silver dry* and *carta blanca* – are used in cocktails, while the aged rums *(carta oro*, five years old, and *añejos*, at least seven years old) are drunk neat. Besides Havana Club and Varadero, which are known worldwide, there are many other different brands of rum in Cuba. Among the best are Matusalém, an upmarket, aged rum from Santiago with a smooth flavour; and Mulata, which is very popular.

A "poor relation" of rum is *aguardiente*, which is stronger and quite sour, and drunk mainly by locals. *Guayabita* is a speciality of Pinar del Río, made from rum and guava fruit *(see p141)*. In addition, a range of very sweet flavoured liqueurs (such as coconut, mint, banana and pineapple) is available, usually served with ice or in cocktails.

A bottle of aged rum

FRUIT SHAKES AND SQUASHES

The most common fruit squash is lemonade, made with lime, sugar, water and ice. More nutritious drinks are the *batidos*, which are shakes made from fresh fruit, often mango and papaya. Milk, sugar and *guanábana*, not an easy fruit to find, make a drink called *champola*. Coconut juice with ice is a delicious, refreshing drink. Another typical Cuban drink is *guarapo*, which is made by squeezing fresh sugar cane stalks with a special crusher. It makes for a refreshing and energizing drink, and is not as sweet as you might expect. Even so, to tone down the sweetness, Cubans add a few drops of lime or a dash of rum.

Coconut juice served in the shell

Cuban Cocktails

Cuba has been famous for its rum since the 1500s, although the rum the pirates loved so much was not the same as today's, but a bitter and highly alcoholic drink, at times sweetened with sugar and *hierba buena*, a variety of mint common in Latin America. This explosive mixture, jokingly called *draguecito* or "little dragon", is probably the ancestor of the *mojito*, one of the most famous Cuban cocktails. In the early 1900s a Cuban

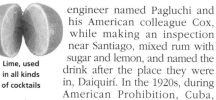

Lime, used in all kinds of cocktails

engineer named Pagluchi and his American colleague Cox, while making an inspection near Santiago, mixed rum with sugar and lemon, and named the drink after the place they were in, Daiquirí. In the 1920s, during American Prohibition, Cuba, which had become an "off limits" paradise for drinkers, developed and refined these early cocktails and went on to create others. In parallel, the role of the professional barman *(cantinero)* acquired increasing importance.

Daiquirí frappé *is served in a chilled cocktail glass. White rum is placed in an electric blender and mixed with one teaspoon of sugar, five drops of maraschino, lime juice and crushed ice. Hemingway liked to drink this cocktail at El Floridita (see p277).*

Mojito *comes in a highball glass. White cane sugar is mixed with lime juice and a crushed stem of mint. To this is added white rum, and the glass is then filled with sparkling mineral water and chopped ice and the drink is stirred. The "temple" of mojito is the Bodeguita del Medio (see p276).*

Cuba Libre *is made from rum and Coca-Cola mixed with ice and lime juice. The drink was supposedly invented by US soldiers who took part in the Cuban wars of independence (1898). The name, Free Cuba, comes from the nationalists' motto.*

Havana Especial *is made with pineapple juice, silver dry rum, a dash of maraschino and crushed ice, mixed and served in a tall, slim glass. This cocktail has a very delicate flavour.*

THE *CANTINEROS'* CLUB

This club for professional barmen *(cantineros)* was founded in Havana in 1924 and sponsored by a group of Cuban distilleries and breweries. By the early 1930s the club had a central office on the Prado. The club's aims remain unchanged today: defence of the interests of its members, professional training for young people (who are required to learn the recipes for at least 100 cocktails), and English lessons. The club also currently promotes the Havana Club International Grand Prix.

The Bodeguita del Medio barman with a *mojito*

Canchánchara *is made by the bar of the same name in Trinidad (see p182) with rum, lime, honey and water. It is served in an earthenware cup.*

Choosing a Restaurant

These restaurants have been selected across a wide range of price categories for their good value, quality of food and good atmosphere. In parts of Cuba, where there are no particularly recommendable restaurants, places that offer at least good value have been included. Alternatives are hotel restaurants *(see pp248–69)* and *paladares (see p270)*.

PRICE CATEGORIES (IN CUBAN CONVERTIBLE PESOS – CUC$)

For a three-course meal for one including a cocktail, tax and service:

$ Under 10 CUC$
$$ 10–15 CUC$
$$$ 15–20 CUC$
$$$$ 20–25 CUC$
$$$$$ Over 25 CUC$

HAVANA

HABANA VIEJA Gentiluomo
$

Obispo esq. Bernaza **Tel** *(7) 867 1300 ext.134*   **Map** *4 D2*

This is the most conveniently located Italian restaurant in this part of town – you will almost certainly pass this place at some point, at the top of Habana Vieja's busiest street. It serves average-quality pasta but generously topped pizzas, and at as little as 3 CUC$, this is an inexpensive if somewhat soulless place to re-fuel.

HABANA VIEJA Hanoi
$

Brasil (Teniente Rey) esq. Bernaza **Tel** *(7) 867 1029*   **Map** *4 D3*

Without doubt the least expensive restaurant in Habana Vieja, this seemingly Cuban-Vietnamese place serves standard-fare meat and seafood dishes, all cooked in the usual Cuban way. Paella and lobster, both at half the price you'd pay elsewhere, also feature on the menu. A series of plain but intimate rooms make up the dining area.

HABANA VIEJA Al Medina
$$

Oficios no.12, e/ Obispo y Obrapía **Tel** *(7) 867 1041*   **Map** *4 F2*

The key to making the most of this Lebanese restaurant, whether in the lovely canopied courtyard or under the brick arches inside, is to not expect authentic Arabic food. *Pollo Musukan* or *Samac Libanes* might sound like exotic dishes but are actually simply prepared meat and fish, grilled or fried without spices or sauces but with perfectly fresh ingredients.

HABANA VIEJA La Bodeguita del Medio
$$

Empedrado no. 207, e/ San Ignacio y Cuba **Tel** *(7) 866 8857*   **Map** *4 E2*

The most famous restaurant in the city, this is definitely a tourist trap but at the same time has retained much of the alluring character that made it so popular in the first place. Always packed, this grotto of narrow corridors and intimate corners is never short on sociable atmosphere. The Cuban meat and seafood dishes are good but don't quite match the ambience.

HABANA VIEJA La Dominica
$$

O'Reilly 108 esq. Mercaderes **Tel** *(7) 860 2918*   **Map** *4 E2*

There's a seafood slant at this decent Italian restaurant with smoked salmon on the starters menu, shrimp and lobster pasta among the specials and a number of shrimp and squid dishes. The laid-back pavement café is in contrast to the chandeliers and polished floors of the refined, rather formal interior. There's a good wine list here.

HABANA VIEJA La Julia
$$

O'Reilly no.506a, e/ Bernaza y Villegas **Tel** *(7) 862 7438*   **Map** *4 D2*

This stalwart Habana Vieja *paladar* has been dishing out specialist pork dishes for years. Not much variety, but satisfying portions and good-quality cooking. You step off the street directly into the dining room, so the less-than-private eating experience, with people constantly poking their head around the door, won't suit everyone, but is idiosyncratically Cuban.

HABANA VIEJA La Mina
$$

Oficios esq. Obispo, Plaza de Armas **Tel** *(7) 862 0216*   **Map** *4 E2*

At the heart of the tourist circuit, this place is always buzzing with foreign clientele and is a lively place to experience Cuban creole cooking. The fish, pork and chicken meals are surprisingly well priced given the touristy location and there are seven dining areas to choose from, including the terrace on the square and a superior central courtyard.

HABANA VIEJA La Torre de Marfil
$$

Mercaderes, e/ Obispo y Obrapía **Tel** *(7) 867 1038*   **Map** *4 E2*

This Chinese restaurant in the most spruced-up section of the old city has a red and black colour scheme and some hearty, good-value chop sueys, including a vegetarian option. Soups are one of the specialities here, and all dishes are served up on fine Oriental china. There's an indoor pagoda and a simple central patio.

HABANA VIEJA El Baturro
$$$

Egido no.661, e/ Merced y Jesús María **Tel** *(7) 860 9078*   **Map** *4 E4*

The waiters at this rustic restaurant usually offer a set-meal menu featuring a cocktail, blackbean or chickpea soup, a main dish of lobster, shrimp, beef or chicken with *viandas*, rice and salad, dessert and coffee. Though not overpriced, you will be obliged to spend more than you would otherwise pay if you coax the *à la carte* menu out of them.

Key to Symbols *see back cover flap*

HABANA VIEJA El Jardín del Edén

Hotel Raquel, Amargura esq. San Ignacio **Tel** *(7) 860 8280* **Map** *4 E2*

The only Jewish restaurant in the city. In the captivatingly elegant lobby of this fantastic hotel, this semi-formal place offers a distinctive eating experience. Beetroot soup and Milanese eggplant stand out among the starters, with *shashliks* (kebabs) featuring heavily in the main dishes. Unusual accompaniments like sweet and sour cabbage complete the picture.

HABANA VIEJA El Santo Ángel

Brasil (Teniente Rey) esq. San Ignacio, Plaza Vieja **Tel** *(7) 861 1626* **Map** *4 E3*

There are original uses of standard Cuban ingredients at this highly respectable restaurant, producing dishes like spiced grilled chicken in peppermint and lemon sauce, or fish with toasted almonds. Choose from a table on the plaza, the pleasant central patio or the graceful dining rooms in this historic building. The 20 CUC$ set meal is good value.

HABANA VIEJA El Patio

San Ignacio no.54, Plaza de la Catedral **Tel** *(7) 867 1035* **Map** *4 E2*

A seemingly endless succession of bands keep the only restaurant on the Plaza de la Catedral lively day and night. This is a good place to try top-quality Cuban classics. The grilled lobster is expensive but very good, and the *Ropa Vieja* (shredded beef) and *Lonjas de pierna* (slices of pork) are faithfully prepared. A choice of 11 rooms and a wonderful leafy patio.

HABANA VIEJA El Templete

Avenida del Puerto no.12-14 esq. Narcisco López **Tel** *(7) 866 8807* **Map** *4 F2*

This seafood specialist facing the harbour offers the best cuisine in Habana Vieja. Significantly, the head chef is Basque and breaks all the Cuban norms with plenty of flavours and variety. From an impressive set of starters, like octopus *a la gallega*, to simple mains like grilled sardines or fancier dishes like eel *a la vasca*, it's all top quality.

HABANA VIEJA El Floridita

Avenida de Bélgica (Monserrate) esq. Obispo **Tel** *(7) 867 1299* **Map** *4 D2*

One of the plushest restaurants in this part of the city, beyond the classic bar where Hemingway famously used to drink, has soft furnishings and soft lighting but hard prices. Fancy dishes like shrimp in orange cream sauce or thermidor lobster characterize the menu, while the cocktail list is perhaps the most comprehensive in the city.

CENTRO HABANA AND PRADO Casa de Castilla

Neptuno no.519, e/ Campanario y Lealtad **Tel** *(7) 862 5482* **Map** *3 C2*

The simple creole cuisine on offer at this restaurant in the heart of Centro Habana is fresh, well prepared and tasty, offering outstanding value for money. A sliding door at the back of a large entrance hall seals the dining room off from the noise and heat of the busy street.

CENTRO HABANA AND PRADO Chan Li Po

Campanario no.453, e/ Zanja y San José **Map** *3 C3*

The hybrid menu at this characterful place, popular among the locals and off the beaten track near Chinatown, includes pizzas, chop suey dishes and traditional Cuban cuisine. The staircase up from the street takes you into the comfortable dining rooms, usually humming with chatter. The pizzas are huge.

CENTRO HABANA AND PRADO A Prado y Neptuno

Paseo del Prado esq. Neptuno **Tel** *(7) 860 9636* **Map** *4 D2*

Some of the best, most authentic pizzas in the city are served up here on large wooden plates at this popular, down-to-earth Italian eatery. There are some seafood main dishes and 14 pastas, but the real focus is on the 19 different pizzas. Dimly lit, with a clubby vibe, this place is almost always bustling, even when neighbouring restaurants are dead.

CENTRO HABANA AND PRADO El Fénix

Animas no.273, e/ Aguila y Amistad **Tel** *(7) 863 6334* **Map** *3 C2*

Tucked away on the first floor of a typical neo-colonial Centro Habana building, this simple restaurant has a private, almost exclusive feel. The food is above average for a *paladar* in both quality and price. Pork, fish, chicken and lobster are all on the menu and come with well-prepared classic side dishes like *congri* and *tostones*.

CENTRO HABANA AND PRADO La Guarida

Concordia no.418, e/ Gervasio y Escobar **Tel** *(7) 863 7351, 866 9047* **Map** *3 B2*

This *paladar* is special. Its original claim to fame as the top-floor apartment where the film *Fresa y Chocolate* was shot has now been superceded by the reputation of its food and ambience. Whether the succulent mutton marinated in papaya juice or the tuna à la sugar cane, every dish is imaginative and flavourful. Three cosy, eclectically decorated rooms.

CENTRO HABANA AND PRADO Roof Garden

Hotel Sevilla, Trocadero no.55, e/ Paseo del Prado y Agramonte **Tel** *(7) 860 8560 ext.164* **Map** *4 D2*

This ritzy gourmet restaurant on the ninth floor of the Hotel Sevilla owes its sense of occasion to the regal decor and furnishings, featuring an ornately crafted high ceiling and panoramic views through its huge windows. The offerings are vaguely French but definitely out-of-the-ordinary by Cuban standards, like rum lobster. Open from 7pm.

VEDADO El Conejito

Calle M esq. 17 **Tel** *(7) 832 4671* **Map** *2 E1*

A red-brick lodge with a chimney stack and a mock-Tudor interior is not the usual Vedado edifice, and this isn't the usual Cuban restaurant, with a menu dominated by rabbit dishes. They have found a surprising variety of ways to cook the little critter, from roasting or grilling to serving it in garlic or mushroom sauce. Other meats and seafood are also available.

VEDADO La Casona de 17
🈯📋🕭🎵🎴🍴 $ $

17 no.60, e/ M y N **Tel** *(7) 838 3136* **Map** *2 E1*

Located in a freshly painted neo-colonial building with a grand, columned terrace and first-floor balcony, the food here is mostly Cuban, though there is a house paella made with shrimp, pork, chicken and fish. The *Arroz con Pollo* (rice with chicken topped with peas) starter, another house speciality, is recommended.

VEDADO El Hurón Azul
🈯📋🕭🍴 $ $ $

Humboldt 153, e/ O y P **Map** *2 F2*

Rated highly by locals, the setting of this *paladar* – a ground-floor flat on a block of uninspiring apartment buildings – is fairly ordinary, but the menu is very impressive. A fantastic array of fish, chicken, rabbit, pork, lamb and rice options, many in rich sauces, and a small selection of Italian-style dishes are followed by one of the best dessert selections in Havana.

VEDADO La Roca
🈯📋 $ $ $

21 esq. M **Tel** *(7) 834 4501* **Map** *2 E2*

The food here is good – the grilled fillet of fish is a good choice, as is the better-than-average-value lobster, and beef is prominent on the international and Cuban menu – but more of a draw is the distinctive environment. Formal black-tie service in an Art Deco dining space with coloured-glass panels that give off a soothing light.

VEDADO El Polinesio
📋🍴 $ $ $ $

Calle 23, e/ L y M **Tel** *(7) 834 6131* **Map** *2 F2*

Below the lobby of the Habana Libre hotel, but accessed from the street outside, there is a distinct basement flavour to this moody, low-ceiling, bamboo-bedecked establishment that supposedly specializes in Polynesian food (Cuban-Asian would be more accurate). Barbecued chicken is the house speciality.

VEDADO La Torre
📋🍴 $ $ $ $

Edificio Focsa, 17 e/ M y N **Tel** *(7) 832 7306, 838 3089* **Map** *2 E1*

There are spectacular views from this restaurant at the top of this vast apartment block. On offer is a broad selection of good-quality Cuban and international fare, including seafood dishes like flame-grilled shrimp and various roasted or grilled meats. The chocolate profiteroles are delicious. You can also just have a drink at the bar – the bar food isn't bad, either.

VEDADO 1830
🈯📋🕭🎵🎴🍴 $ $ $ $ $

Malecón no.1252 esq. 20 **Tel** *(7) 838 3090 to 92* **Map** *1 A3*

At this magnificent mansion in its own private corner of Vedado on the waterfront near Miramar, a delectable selection of cosmopolitan dishes is served, including duck in orange sauce and beef in blue cheese. The formal, attentive staff match the sumptuous dining rooms, but the mood lightens on the terrace during the nightly music and dance shows.

GREATER HAVANA (COJÍMAR) La Terraza de Cojímar
🕭🎴🍴 $ $ $

Real no.61, Cojímar **Tel** *(7) 766 5151*

This restaurant is renowned for its Ernest Hemingway associations, and held more allure when it was frequented by the late Gregorio Fuentes – on whom the author based the protagonist in *The Old Man and the Sea*. You can still enjoy seafood soup, shrimp and various fish dishes surrounded by photos of both men and some big local catches.

GREATER HAVANA (HABANA DEL ESTE) Los XII Apóstoles
📋🕭🎵🎴🍴 $ $ $ $

Castillo del Morro, Parque Morro Cabaña **Tel** *(7) 863 8295*

From the terrace of this restaurant at the foot of the El Morro fortress, there are pleasant views of Habana Vieja on the other side of the bay. Traditional Cuban food is served behind a battery of 12 cannons (the 12 "apostles" in the restaurant's name). Somewhat at odds with the relaxing atmosphere, a karaoke bar-cum-nightclub operates nightly 'til 3am.

GREATER HAVANA (HABANA DEL ESTE) La Divina Pastora
🕭🎵🎴 $ $ $ $ $

Avenida Monumental, Parque Morro Cabaña **Tel** *(7) 860 8341*

Get a table out on the terrace from where you can enjoy the fantastic views of the city and bay – the main reason for making the trip here. The Cuban cuisine is reasonable but pricey. There's a lobster tank here, so if you like your shellfish fresh, this is a good option. The excellent live traditional music also makes a visit worthwhile.

GREATER HAVANA (JARDÍN BOTÁNICO NACIONAL) El Bambú
🈯🕭🎴🍴 $ $

Jardín Botánico Nacional, Carretera Rocío Km 3.5, Calabazar **Tel** *(7) 643 7278*

Looking down onto the beautifully landscaped Japanese section of the Botanical Gardens, outside the city proper, this excellent organic, vegetarian outdoor restaurant has one of the most serene settings in the whole of Havana. They operate a buffet service, with herbs from the gardens flavouring the salads, rices and soups. Open lunchtime only, Wed–Sun.

GREATER HAVANA (LA LISA) La Giraldilla
📋🎵🎴🍴 $ $ $

Calle 222 esq. Avenida 37, Reparto La Coronela **Tel** *(7) 273 0568*

On the western outskirts of the city, on a magnificent country estate, are the delightful dining areas of swanky La Giraldilla. You can enjoy top-quality Cuban delicacies in the splendid dining hall where arched floor-to-ceiling windows create a lovely light, on the fantastic leafy patio, or in the candle-lit wine cellar. There's a cigar shop and nightclub here, too.

GREATER HAVANA (MIRAMAR) Don Cangrejo
📋🕭🎵🎴🍴 $ $ $

Avenida 1ra, e/ 16 y 18 **Tel** *(7) 204 3837*

This waterfront restaurant with outdoor tables right by the ocean is one of Havana's finest seafood specialists. The large variety of dishes includes crab cooked in several styles, shrimp, lobster and its Gran Mariscada house special – a huge mixed seafood platter. It is run by the Ministry of Fisheries, guaranteeing that the fish here is as fresh as possible.

GREATER HAVANA (MIRAMAR) El Aljibe $$$

Avenida 7ma, e/ 24 y 26 **Tel** *(7) 204 1583*

With a reputation for up-to-the-mark creole cooking going back many years, this top-class ranch-style restaurant is a great place to sample some classic national dishes like *Picadillo de Res* (minced beef), *Masas de Cerdo* (hunks of pork) and the house special, *Pollo Asado El Aljibe* (roast chicken in citrus juices). Plenty of rustic charm.

GREATER HAVANA (MIRAMAR) La Cecilia $$$

Avenida 5ta, e/ 110 y 112 **Tel** *(7) 204 1562*

Surrounded by and entwined with tropical plants, this is a subdued place to enjoy the mostly Cuban menu, except when there's a tour group visiting. As well as a fine selection of typical pork, beef, chicken and fish dishes, the rarely seen house special, *Tamal en Cazuela*, is a simple but delicious creamy maize soup. There's a good wine list, too.

GREATER HAVANA (MIRAMAR) Tocororo $$$$$

Avenida 3ra y 18 **Tel** *(7) 204 2209*

This smart but laid-back eatery in a fabulously decorated Miramar mansion is a good place for foodies as there's no fixed menu and the chefs will do their best to accommodate all requests. Effectively two restaurants in one, the emphasis is mainly on creole ingredients, including live lobster, with a smaller Japanese section serving sushi and tempura.

GREATER HAVANA (PLAYA) La Ferminia $$$$$

Avenida 5ta no.18207 esq. 184, Reparto Flores **Tel** *(7) 273 6786, 273 6555*

In the decadent surroundings of what was once a residential mansion, there are four elegant private dining rooms with windows onto the beautiful garden patio, which holds more tables. Topping the list of exquisitely prepared international and Cuban food is *La Espada Corrida*, a full-on mix of six different tasty meats.

WESTERN CUBA

ISLA DE LA JUVENTUD El Cochinito $

José Martí esq. 24, Nueva Gerona **Tel** *(46) 322 809*

Cubans and foreigners alike are charged in normal *pesos* here, so the creole cuisine works out extremely cheap. Right in the centre of Nueva Gerona, this is one of the best-known restaurants round these parts but don't assume this translates to top-end cookery. Like at most *peso* restaurants the food is basic, but good value.

ISLA DE LA JUVENTUD La Insula $

José Martí esq. 22, Nueva Gerona **Tel** *(46) 321 825*

The only place in Nueva Gerona that can justifiably claim to have a bit of class, this is the most popular restaurant with tourists and has the most reliable meals in town. Their take on traditional Cuban dishes includes *Pollo Insula*, a chicken dish in a sweet and sour sauce with butter, and *Lomo Ahumado* – smoked loin of pork.

PINAR DEL RÍO Nuestra Casa $

Colón no.161, e/ Ceferino Fernández

A meal here in one of the city's only two *paladares* feels like eating in a giant tree house, with several tables set out on a roof terrace in the shadow of overhanging trees. Set meals of simply prepared chicken, fish or pork make up the limited selection here. This is a basic operation but it still offers better food than in all the state restaurants in town.

PINAR DEL RÍO Rumayor $$

Carretera a Viñales Km 1, Pinar del Río city **Tel** *(48) 763 007, 763 051*

The best state restaurant in the provincial capital of Pinar del Río is out of the way, on a woody patch of land on the northern outskirts of the city. The smoked chicken is the best dish on a short menu, but the rustic surroundings of this wooden lodge and its tribal imagery give it character. Ring ahead, as opening hours are sporadic.

SIERRA DEL ROSARIO Casa del Campesino $$

Comunidad de Las Terrazas, Las Terrazas **Tel** *(48) 578 555, 578 700*

For a traditional farm meal, surrounded by animals, fruit trees and beehives, visit this farmer's countryside house where guests can help with the cooking, share with the family, walk around the house, or even ride on horseback while waiting for the roast pork or chicken to be served. A nice experience.

SIERRA DEL ROSARIO El Romero $$

Comunidad de Las Terrazas, Las Terrazas **Tel** *(48) 578 555 ext.129*

This organic, predominantly vegetarian restaurant perched over the back of the village in an apartment block is a rarity in Cuba, offering a comprehensive menu of genuinely tasty, imaginatively prepared and presented non-meat dishes. Purées, soups, salads, pastas, pâtes, egg dishes and more. Each dish comes in large, medium or small portions.

VIÑALES El Palenque de los Cimarrones $

Cueva de San Miguel, Carretera a Puerto Esperanza Km 36 **Tel** *(48) 796 290*

You can drive or walk around the outside of the *mogote* hill, behind which are the *bohío* roofs of this tour-group lunch-only stop, but it's more fun to go through the rock itself to the hideout location on the other side. Juicy chicken dishes and other creole food make up the menu. Coincide with a tour group and you'll get an Afro-Cuban show of music and dance.

VIÑALES Casa de Don Tomás 🟦🎵🎴🔲 ⑤⑤

Salvador Cisnero, e/ Adela Azcuy y Carretera a Pinar del Rio **Tel** *(48) 796 300*

The only proper restaurant in the village at Viñales, and one of few places open after dark, this ranch building surrounded by attractive gardens is always full of guests. The house special, the *Delicias de Don Tomás* – a weighty combination of meats and rice – is not for the faint-hearted. For more delicate palates there's good-value lobster, fish, pork and chicken.

VIÑALES Las Terrazas 🟦🟦🔵🎵🎴🔲 ⑤⑤

Hotel La Ermita **Tel** *(48) 796 071 ext.216*

The best-located restaurant in Viñales is on a hillside balcony terrace at the back of this hotel complex, with stunning views of the valley. There are a number of pricey but worthwhile lobster options on the Cuban menu and plenty of cheaper dishes, most of them following the same grilled-meat formula so prevalent across the country.

CENTRAL CUBA – WEST

CIENFUEGOS Dinos Pizza 🟦🟦🔵 ⑤

Calle 31, e/ 54 y 56 **Tel** *(43) 552 020*

This plain, straighforward pizzeria right in the heart of the historic town centre offers great value medium-crust pizzas and a few Cuban staples like chicken, pork and shrimp. Choose between a small and family-sized base and add your own toppings for between 50 c and 4 CUC$ a pop. The small size is easily enough for one person.

CIENFUEGOS Café Cienfuegos 🟦🟦🔲 ⑤⑤

Club Cienfuegos, Paseo del Prado, e/ Ave. 8 y Ave.12 **Tel** *(43) 512 891 ext.112*

In the palatial Club Cienfuegos building is this refined seafood restaurant with a classic saloon bar and high ceilings. It's one of the best restaurants in Cienfuegos, if you want a sense of occasion. Fish, shrimp and lobster dominates the menu but there's also vegetarian paella and several meat dishes. The 3 CUC$ entrance fee will be taken off your bill.

CIENFUEGOS El Criollito 🟦🟥🟦🔵 ⑤⑤

Calle 33 no. 5603, e/ 56 y 58 **Tel** *(43) 525 540*

Another menu-less *paladar*, the waiter will offer you chicken, pork or fish cooked to your requirements, each accompanied by copious amounts of fried plantain chips, rice and salad. One of only two legal *paladares* in the whole of Cienfuegos, and the more reliably open of the two thanks to the central location of this colonial house.

CIENFUEGOS Palacio del Valle 🟦🎵🔲 ⑤⑤

Paseo del Prado esq. Ave. 0 **Tel** *(43) 551 003*

The ornate dining room in the magnificent Palacio del Valle is in keeping with the intricate Moorish architecture that characterizes the whole building. The food isn't quite magnificent, but the seafood platter or the lobster are good bets. Climb the spiral staircase to the delightful rooftop bar for views of the bay and city.

CIENFUEGOS 1869 🟦🔵🔲 ⑤⑤⑤

Hotel Unión, Calle 31 esq. 54 **Tel** *(43) 551 020 ext.318*

There are touches of refinement in this hotel restaurant, but it stops short of real elegance. Four central arches divide the room in two, and there are examples of colonial-era furnishings. There's a wide choice of traditional Cuban dishes from *picadillo* and grilled meats to the *La Unión* Seafood Special of fish, shrimp, lobster and squid.

PENÍNSULA DE ZAPATA Punta Perdíz 🟦🎴🔲 ⑤⑤

Carretera de Playa Larga a Playa Girón Km 24

On a patchy section of secluded coastline, this boat-themed restaurant stands out like a sore thumb but serves up some reasonable (if slightly overpriced) seafood dishes and, more notably, crocodile meat. One of the peninsula's many tour-group stop-offs, the quality of food here is at least as good as that of the local hotel restaurants.

PENÍNSULA DE ZAPATA Rancho Benito 🟦🎴🔲 ⑤⑤⑤

Caleta Buena, Playa Girón **Tel** *(45) 915 589*

Some 8 km (5 miles) down a bumpy track beyond the Playa Girón hotel resort is this seafront ranch-style restaurant on a plot of land known as Caleta Buena. It's a wonderfully secluded and tranquil place for a seafood lunch. The open-air grill sits just above a lovely, clear natural pool. The entrance fee to Caleta Buena will be deducted from your bill.

SANTA CLARA El Marino 🟦🟥🟦🔲 ⑤

Carretera Central esq. Ave. Ramón González **Tel** *(42) 205 594*

This canteen-like restaurant on a main road is known as a seafood specialist, but in reality there are just as many meat dishes on the limited menu here. The real draw here is the low prices. Though the menu is priced in Cuban *pesos*, you can pay the equivalent cost in convertibles.

SANTA CLARA La Concha 🟦🔵🔲 ⑤

Carretera Central esq. Danielito **Tel** *(42) 218 124*

Consistently recommended by locals as the best state restaurant in the city, this billing is accurate but very much relative to the low standards set by the competition. Here you will find basic pastas, pizzas and reasonable *comida criolla* (creole food). A large school-style dining room with a tiled mural provides the basic setting.

Key to Price Guide *see p276* **Key to Symbols** *see back cover flap*

SANTA CLARA Los Taínos

Hotel Los Caneyes, Avenida los Eucaliptos y Circunvalación **Tel** *(42) 218 140*

The 8 CUC$ buffet in a reconstructed Taíno lodge setting at this hotel is worth the trip to the low hills beyond the southern outskirts of the city. With dishes based around pasta, traditionally prepared meat or plates for vegetarians from the modest salad counter, it offers a selection of food way beyond anything on offer in the city centre.

SANTA CLARA Sabor Latino

Esquerra no.157, e/ Julio Jover y Berenguer **Tel** *(42) 224 279*

As the only official sit-down *paladar* in the city, they can afford to charge a little above the market rate here but it's worth the extra cost for the finest cooking in the city centre. Thoughtful presentation and extra touches mark out the creole dishes here, for example by adding shrimp and cheese to their lobster dish and pineapple to the chicken.

VARADERO Albacora

Calle 59 y Playa **Tel** *(45) 613 650*

One of the better beachfront eateries in the centre of Varadero. This basic outdoor patio with plastic chairs and tables and steps leading onto the sand offers simple, fresh Cuban food under the shade of a couple of trees. The pricier dishes are lobster and a mixed seafood grill, while you can enjoy pork, beef and chicken selections at a quarter of the cost.

VARADERO Chong Kwok

Avenida 1ra esq. 55 **Tel** *(45) 612 460, 613 525*

The floor-cushion seating and low tables at this Chinese restaurant are more authentic than the food, but there are at least some chop suey dishes and a choice of stir-fried rice, all of it very reasonably priced. On the menu alongside these are some remarkably Cuban-looking dishes, including grilled lobster at just under 20 CUC$.

VARADERO Dante

Parque Josone, Ave. 1ra, e/ 56 y 58 **Tel** *(45) 667 738*

Unusually for an Italian restaurant in Cuba, the pasta dishes here are superior to the pizzas. That said, there are some sauces to be avoided, like the carbonara which has a very odd kick to it, and others which are much more dependable, like the bolognese. Ask for a table on the balcony over the lake for a wonderfully relaxing meal.

VARADERO El Bodegón Criollo

Avenida de Playa esq. 40 **Tel** *(45) 667 784*

With more character than most other restaurants in the town, this grey and red fairytale-style cottage with a small collection of intimate spaces has more than a passing resemblance to the famous Bodeguita del Medio in Havana, with walls full of scribbled signatures. Good-quality classic Cuban dishes.

VARADERO Esquina Cuba

Avenida 1ra esq. 36 **Tel** *(45) 614 019*

An open-air venue by the side of the road serving standard tasty *comida criolla*, this place suffers slightly from its unexotic location but regains a little lost ground with the 1950s memorabilia scattered around, including a genuine white and pink Oldsmobile and an old jukebox. Dine *à la carte* or go for the excellent value all-you-can-eat buffet at 12 CUC$.

VARADERO Guamairé

Avenida 1ra, e/ 26 y 27 **Tel** *(45) 611 893*

A humble little wooden bungalow with a veranda facing the road and a set of very reasonably priced *comida criolla* dishes. Along with lobster, chicken and pork dishes, you can order crocodile steak, a rare dish anywhere in Cuba – Guamairé this is the only place in the town where you can find it.

VARADERO La Fondue (Casa del Queso Cubano)

Avenida 1ra, e/ 62 y 63 **Tel** *(45) 667 747*

La Fondue offers a unique menu by Cuban standards, based loosely on French-Swiss cuisine. The simple formula here is to cook everything with cheese. There are also less experimental dishes based on more familiar Cuban recipes. The restaurant itself is in a pleasant roadside building with a Mediterranean villa interior.

VARADERO Mallorca

Avenida 1ra, e/ 61 y 62 **Tel** *(45) 667 746*

The reputation of Mallorca as a Spanish restaurant is owed almost exclusively to the fact that its trademark dish is paella, but the rest of the menu is Cuban. The excellent-value paellas come with either vegetables, shrimp, squid, chicken or, for the house special, a mixture of all four. A smart but homely interior in a handsome villa.

VARADERO Pizza Nova

Plaza América, Autopista del Sur Km 7 **Tel** *(45) 668 585*

A pizza chain restaurant in a shopping mall might not sound like a great place to eat, but with a lovely view of the sea over tree tops from the balcony, and a good selection of appetizing thin-crust pizzas, this is actually a great option. There's a decent range of pastas, too, including the experimental *Rigatoni à la Vodka*.

VARADERO Antigüedades

Avenida 1ra esq. 59 **Tel** *(45) 667 329*

The marvellous interior decoration of this seafood specialist is an Aladdin's Cave of antiques, furniture, pictures and all sorts of curiosities hanging from the walls and ceiling. The cheapest dish at this eye-catching place to eat is 10 CUC$, making it relatively expensive but the quality of food is good.

VARADERO El Retiro $$$

Parque Josone, Ave. 1ra, e/ 56 y 58 **Tel** *(45) 667 316*

Housed in what was once the residence of wealthy financiers, there's still a slight air of class about this place, though the staff are approachable and friendly. The speciality here is lobster, served whole or on skewers, garnished with garlic or lemon or, in the case of the *Gran Grillada*, cooked and served with shrimp, beef and pork.

VARADERO La Campana $$$

Parque Josone, Ave. 1ra, e/ 56 y 58 **Tel** *(45) 667 224*

Inside this restaurant with its rustic interior and large fireplace, there's a sense of being in an alpine lodge rather than in the middle of Parque Josone, with the sweeping, wooded grounds laid out before it. It's also one of the better purveyors of authentic creole cooking in Varadero. The house speciality is the Cuban classic, *Ropa Vieja* (shredded stewed beef).

VARADERO Steak House Toro $$$

Avenida 1ra esq. 25 **Tel** *(45) 667 145*

Meat lovers will not be disappointed at this Canadian-Cuban joint venture offering North American-sized steaks. Lying cellar-like, a few feet below street level, this is a stereotypical steak house with a wagon wheel and beer barrel central to the decor. From six-ounce filets to 24-ounce chateaubriand at 38 CUC$, all appetites and wallets are catered for.

VARADERO Las Américas $$$$$

Mansión Xanadú, Autopista del Sur Km 7 **Tel** *(45) 667 750, 667 877*

A high-class establishment in the refined antique-furniture dining rooms of what was once a millionaire's mansion, the Mansión Xanadú (*see p262*). Nowadays it's an exclusive hotel and one of the best restaurants on the whole peninsula, serving Cuban and international *haute cuisine* and with a fantastic wine list.

CENTRAL CUBA – EAST

CAMAGÜEY Don Ronquillo $

Ignacio Agramonte no. 406 esq. República **Tel** *(32) 285 239*

In the touristy Galería Colonial complex, a bar, shops and cabaret share an immaculately restored colonial residence with this attractive restaurant where you can sample a number of traditional Camagueyan recipes. The local *Bistec Mayoral* stands out – sautéed kidney served on toast in an onion and red wine sauce, a welcome break from the Cuban norm.

CAMAGÜEY La Campaña de Toledo $

Plaza San Juan de Dios **Tel** *(32) 286 812*

An 18th-century townhouse typical of the plaza where it's found, with a large and leafy courtyard out back where there are several tables. Chicken, pork and fish feature on one of the better menus in the city but for something a bit different there's *Boliche Mechado* – beef garnished with bacon served with fries and *congrí*.

SANCTI SPÍRITUS Mesón de la Plaza $$

Máximo Gómez no.34 y Honorato **Tel** *(41) 285 46*

This rustic restaurant reminiscent of a Spanish *taberna* has long wooden tables with benches, a wooden raftered ceiling with wrought-iron hanging lamps and earthenware bowls at each table. The food is Cuban with a Spanish twist; the house tipple is *sangría* and there's a delicious chickpea soup. The selection of main dishes features beef stewed with corn.

TRINIDAD Vía Reale $

Rubén Martínez Villena, e/ Piro Guinart y Ciro Redondo **Tel** *(41) 996 476*

It would be wrong to label Vía Reale an Italian restaurant, but it is the only pizza specialist in Trinidad. A diminutive, canopy-covered patio provides an alternative to the street-side main dining room in what is, by local standards, a run-of-the-mill though well-restored colonial building. Grilled shrimp, lobster and steak dominate the menu.

TRINIDAD Estela $$

Simón Bolívar no.557, e/ Juan Manuel Márquez y José Mendoza **Tel** *(41) 994 329*

Though this pleasant backyard *paladar* may not be the most sophisticated home-run restaurant in the city, many locals regard it as among the best Cuban food. In the cobbled historic centre with a split-level patio, the ambience is delightfully tranquil. Accompanying the pork, chicken or fish mains are mountainous side orders of *viandas*, *congrí* and salad.

TRINIDAD Trinidad Colonial $$

Maceo esq. Colón **Tel** *(41) 996 473*

Located in the most aristocratic colonial building in the city to have been converted into a restaurant, here you will find one of Trinidad's most extensive selections of creole cuisine. Shrimp in hot sauce stands out from the other classic Cuban and creole dishes. Antique dressers and cabinets are dotted about the several grand dining rooms.

TRINIDAD Restaurante de Iberostar $$$$$

Iberostar Grand Hotel Trinidad, José Martí 262, e/ Lino Pérez y Colón **Tel** *(41) 996 073*

The finest and most expensive food in the town by a country mile is found in the fantastically plush restaurant at the Grand Hotel Trinidad. The buffet dinner is the biggest treat – an opportunity to feast on international food simply unheard of elsewhere such as beef carpaccio, salade niçoise, serrano ham, smoked salmon and tiramisú.

Key to Price Guide *see p276* **Key to Symbols** *see back cover flap*

EASTERN CUBA

BARACOA Duaba

⊜⚠♫▦⋈ ⑤⑤

Hotel El Castillo, Loma de Paraíso **Tel** *(21) 645 165*

Not to be confused with Finca Duaba in the nearby countryside, this restaurant in the wonderfully located Hotel El Castillo, gazing over the town, is arguably the finest in Baracoa and one of the best places for local variations on traditional Cuban cooking. Among these are chicken with maize and bacon or the fish and coconut speciality, *Pescado a la Santa Bárbara*.

GUARDALAVACA Pizza Nova

⊜♫▦⋈ ⑤⑤

Near Club Amigo Atlántico Guardalavaca hotel, Playa Guardalavaca, Banes **Tel** *(24) 430 137*

This pizza chain does a decent job of giving each of its restaurants a look and feel of its own, in this case a smart interior and a broad half-covered outdoor terrace backing onto sweeping, lawns with trees. The usual selection of good-quality, thin-crust pizzas is available as well as numerous pastas and a few Cuban dishes, too.

HOLGUÍN Salón 1720

⊟⊜⚠♫▦⋈ ⑤⑤

Frexes esq. Miró **Tel** *(24) 468 150*

This standout restaurant in a magnificently refined colonial building offers the tastiest food in Holguín, a mixture of international and Cuban delicacies. The plush surroundings enhance the experience, as do the names of the dishes, such as *Tesoros del Mar* (Sea Treasures), a lobster, shrimp and fish combination, or *Tres Reyes* (Three Kings) a mixed meat grill.

SANTIAGO DE CUBA La Taberna de Dolores

⊟▦ ⑤

Aguilera esq. Mayía Rodríguez, Plaza Dolores **Tel** *(22) 623 913*

The sombre, shadowy interior lends this place a distinct character. Downstairs is a bar and café from where a hidden staircase leads up to the restaurant on the first floor. The balcony seats, looking down on the Plaza Dolores, are the nicest place to sit and order from the limited pork and chicken menu. Prices are officially in *pesos*, but check to be sure.

SANTIAGO DE CUBA Don Antonio

⊟⊜⚠♫⋈ ⑤⑤

José Antonio Saco, e/ Porfirio Valiente y Mayía Rodríguez, Plaza Dolores **Tel** *(22) 652 307*

Classic *comida criolla* in the smartest restaurant on Plaza Dolores, with wide-open shutters providing views across the square from this single-floor colonial building. Compared to its neighbours, this joint also has the best selection of dishes. As an alternative to the usual lobster, pork and chicken offerings, there is a tasty beef casserole.

SANTIAGO DE CUBA Las Gallegas

⊟⚠▦ ⑤⑤

San Basilio no. 305 altos, e/ General Lacret y Hartmann **Tel** *(22) 624 700*

Just round the corner from Parque Céspedes is this first-floor *paladar* in a colonial house, now divided into apartments. The house special is lamb in a subtle tomato sauce flavoured with spices and beer, and fried chicken and a couple of pork variations can also be found on the menu. The best tables are squeezed onto the narrow balcony.

SANTIAGO DE CUBA Salón Tropical

⊟⚠⊜▦⋈ ⑤⑤

Fernández Marcané no. 310 (altos), e/ 9 y 10 **Tel** *(22) 641 161*

The tables at this impressive, professionally run *paladar* in suburban Santiago occupy a plant-filled rooftop patio from where there are splendid views of the city; there's also a cosy indoor dining room. The unusually long menu includes seven different pork variations, a couple of liver dishes, fish and chicken, all cooked with care and subtly garnished.

SANTIAGO DE CUBA El Morro

⊟⚠♫▦ ⑤⑤⑤

Carretera al Morro Km 7.5 **Tel** *(22) 691 576*

This outdoor restaurant, nesting on the edge of green cliffs by the fortress of the same name, has a truly spectacular setting outside Santiago at the mouth of the bay. It's worth eating here for the superb mountain and sea views alone. There's a wide choice of seafood, chicken and pork and there are 10 CUC$ three-course set meals.

SANTIAGO DE CUBA Zunzún

⊟⊜♫▦⋈ ⑤⑤⑤

Avenida Manduley no.159 esq. 7, Reparto Vista Alegre Viejo **Tel** *(22) 641 528*

On a broad, tree-lined avenue, in what used to be a very rich neighbourhood before the Revolution, is the 1940s mansion housing this classy restaurant. Divided into five compact and well appointed dining rooms, the same restraint shown in the decor characterizes the menu which has just six main courses, all original takes on traditional creole cooking.

SANTIAGO DE CUBA La Casona

⊜⚠♫⋈ ⑤⑤⑤⑤

Meliá Santiago de Cuba, Calle M e/ 4ta y Avenida Las Américas **Tel** *(22) 687 070*

If you're looking for good-quality international food, head for La Casona, the buffet restaurant in the city's most luxurious hotel. In a huge dining hall, the choice is outstanding, with everything from raw meats ready to be cooked to your taste to a well-stocked salad bar. The buffet costs 20 CUC$, excluding drinks. You pay in advance at the hotel reception.

SANTIAGO DE CUBA La Isabelica

⊜⚠⋈ ⑤⑤⑤⑤

Meliá Santiago de Cuba, Calle M e/ 4ta y Avenida Las Américas **Tel** *(22) 687 070*

An intimate and formal little *comida criolla* restaurant on the edge of the central garden court in the Meliá Santiago de Cuba. Despite the high prices at the top end of the menu, you don't actually have to break the bank to eat here. The curried chicken breast with plum and pineapple, for example, is only just over the 10 CUC$ mark.

SHOPS AND MARKETS

Tourists do most of their shopping in state-run shops, often in the hotels. However, the legalization of limited private enterprise has given a boost to the handicrafts and food markets *(mercados agropecuarios)*. Until a few years ago there wasn't much to buy, but now an improving range of souvenirs is available. All the same, Cuba is

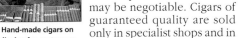

Hand-made cigars on display for customers

not the place to look for designer outlets. State-run shops offer goods at fixed prices, which tend to be on the high side, whereas market prices are lower and may be negotiable. Cigars of guaranteed quality are sold only in specialist shops and in hard currency shops. Be very wary of buying cigars – or anything else for that matter – on the black market.

Handicrafts for sale at La Rampa market in Havana *(see p98)*

OPENING HOURS

Opening hours in Cuba are erratic but as a guideline *tiendas* (convertible pesos shops) are open 10am–7pm in the summer and 9am–6pm in the winter, while small shops open 9am–6pm all year round. On Sundays, shops close at 1pm. The fruit and vegetable markets are open on Sunday mornings, closed on Mondays, then open Tuesday to Friday from 8am to around 6pm. Fast food chains – El Rápido, Di Tú, Burgui, and Rumbos *(see p271)* – are open 24 hours a day.

HOW TO PAY

Most tourists will not use the local currency, the *peso* *(see p307)*, at all during their stay. Most goods that tourists want to buy, from rum to CDs, are only available in hard currency shops (most of which accept credit cards). In the food markets, the locals use mainly *pesos* but stall holders will happily accept convertible pesos (change may be in

pesos). To buy *pesos*, go to one of the bureaux de change, called CADECA, found in most city centres and often near the entrance to major food markets.

WHERE TO GO

In the cities and tourist resorts, *tiendas* and supermarkets sell everything from cosmetics and clothes to tinned food, but do not carry the range of items seen in European supermarkets. Tourist resorts and larger towns often have shops

The logo of a popular *tiendas* chain

specializing in clothes (though not designer ranges). Tourist *tiendas*, especially in hotels, sell T-shirts printed with Cuban images including the inevitable portraits of Che, as well as *guayaberas*, typical Caribbean cotton shirts.

In the El Rápido and Rumbos *(see p271)* chains, and in the Fotoservice shops where film is sold and processed, visitors can buy soft drinks, rum, biscuits, sweets, butter and milk, as well as small household utensils and articles normally found in perfume shops.

Fresh fruit, vegetables and fresh meat are to be found only in the food markets.

SPECIALIST SHOPS

Cigars should be purchased either in the *tiendas* in hotels or at the airport, or in the specialist shops, often known as **La Casa del Habano**, which sell cigars direct from the cigar factories (and which may, in fact, be attached to a factory), and keep them at the right temperature and humidity level. It is best not to buy cigars from people

An outlet of the hard-currency Tiendas Panamericanas chain

on the street, as they are almost inevitably fakes made by machine, rather than hand-made, or are badly preserved or bear signs of faulty work-manship. In addition, street vendors will not be able to provide you with an official purchase receipt, needed to take goods out of the country.

Branches of the **ARTex** chain stock a good selection of CDs, records and cassettes. Another well-stocked music store is **Longina**, in Calle Obispo, Habana Vieja. Note that recordings of local music may not be available outside Cuba.

Paintings, sculpture and prints in the art galleries and in the *tiendas* of the Fondo de Bienes Culturales are sold with official authenticity certificates, which will be needed for export.

A squash stand in the Mercado de Cuatro Caminos, Havana

Shelves with cigars in a Casa del Habano

La Casa del Habano

Real Fábrica de Tabacos Partagás, Havana. **Tel** (7) 862 3772. Ave 1, esq. 64, Varadero. **Tel** (45) 667 843.

Shopping Center Marina Hemingway, Havana. **Tel** (7) 204 6772.

Tienda ARTex

Ave. L esq. 23, Havana. **Tel** (7) 838 3162. Calle San Rafael 110 esq. Industria, Havana. **Tel** (7) 860 8414. **www**.soycubano.com

HANDICRAFTS

Cuba does not have a long tradition of producing handicrafts. Today, however, market stalls are found every-where, selling all sorts of things from wood carvings and ceramics to embroidery, papier mâché objects and musical instruments. In Havana there is a daily handicrafts market behind the Castillo de la Real Fuerza and a second-hand book market in Plaza de Armas *(see p69)*. There is also a market on La Rampa in Vedado.

The market in Trinidad, near the central square, is a good place to look for embroidered linen and cotton. Crafts are also sold in state-run shops, in the Ferias de Artesanía and in the Galerías de Arte throughout the island.

MARKETS

The fruit and vegetable markets *(mercados agropecuarios)* in Cuba are lively and entertaining places to stroll around. Stalls sell fresh fruit and vegetables, pork and sausages, sweets, traditional food and flowers.

In Havana, the most central food market is in the Barrio Chino *(see p90)*, but the largest and most famous is the Mercado de Cuatro Caminos, south of the centre at Máximo Gómez (Monte) 256. The market is housed in a building constructed in 1922 and originally occupied by stalls selling Chinese food. It takes up a whole block.

Today the market extends out into nearby streets and includes stalls selling every-thing from meat to dried fruit. There are also cheap restaurants and stalls selling fritters, fruit shakes and juice.

Mercado de Cuatro Caminos

Máximo Gómez (Monte) 256, e/ Arroyo (Manglar and Matadero), Havana. ☐ *Tue–Sat, Sun am.*

A SOUVENIR IN FRONT OF THE CAPITOLIO

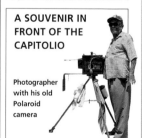
Photographer with his old Polaroid camera

In front of the Capitolio *(see pp82–3)* in Havana, visitors can have their picture taken with an original 1930s Polaroid camera, for one convertible peso. The photos develop immediately and the resulting picture, in black and white, looks just like a convincingly old photograph.

Embroidered table linen at the Trinidad market

What to Buy in Cuba

Apart from the famous Cuban cigars and excellent rum, there are many other good things to buy in Cuba: gold and silver jewellery, and hand-crafted objects made from local materials: wood, straw, papier mâché, shells, seeds, terracotta and glass. Cuban musical instruments are also popular choices. There are also toiletries and pharmaceutical products that are to be found nowhere else in the world, on sale in the international pharmacies and duty-free shops in the airport, where you can also buy books, video cassettes and CDs.

Dancing rag dolls

Rum
This classic brand of rum can be bought all over Cuba. Bottles are also sold in boxes (especially at the airport) to make them easier to transport.

Bauza
Cigars that do not meet the rigorous standards of the cigar-makers are labelled Bauza. However, they are still of very good quality. They are sold at authorized outlets at very reasonable prices.

A box of Vegas Robaina cigars

CIGARS
Packaged in elegant cedar boxes, Cuban cigars make a luxury gift *(see pp32–3)*. Make sure that the box has the branded label *"hecho in Cuba totalmente a mano"* (totally hand-made in Cuba), the official government seal, and the "Habanos" band. If they do not, they are not genuine.

Local Handicrafts
Raw material from the Caribbean (bamboo, shells and seeds) is used to make rustic household objects such as sonajeros, decorative wall hangings, and pretty, colourful necklaces.

A seed necklace

A seed and shell necklace

Musical Instruments
Many traditional Cuban musical instruments (see p31) such as claves, bongos, maracas, güiro, and tumbadora drums are made by craftsmen. They are sold in music stores and markets. Some, such as guitars, can be made to order.

Bongos

Hats and Baskets
Banana leaves and other plant fibres are used to weave typical hats and baskets of various shapes and sizes: an affordable, classic souvenir.

BLACK CORAL

Although the famous black coral from Cuban reefs makes delightful jewellery (earrings, rings, necklaces and pendants), bear in mind that conservation groups are anxious to discourage the plundering of fragile reefs. Authentic black coral commands high prices. Cheaper "black coral" pendants sold in handicrafts markets are unlikely to be genuine.

A black coral necklace

A cedar-wood cigar box

Silver and coral earrings and pendants

PAPIER MACHE

The *papier mâché* technique is a recent introduction to Cuba. It is used to produce masks, models, knick-knacks and toys. These articles are always painted in bright, decorative colours.

A mask representing the sun

African-style figures

WOOD

Cedar and rosewood are used to make small wooden figures that often draw inspiration from African tradition. Carved cedarwood cigar boxes always display elegant craftsmanship. Wooden objects can also be found on sale in the Galerías de Arte.

Doll

Model vintage cars

PERFUMES AND MEDICINES

The Suchel Camacho company produces very good perfumes, including spicy Coral Negro, flower-scented Mariposa and elegant Alicia Alonso, as well as quality face and body creams, at reasonable prices. The pharmaceutical sector is also in the avant-garde: PPG, an anti-cholesterol drug obtained from sugar cane, is also good for arteriosclerosis; shark cartilage strengthens bones in children and older people; and spirulina is a food supplement derived from algae. Excellent honey, with royal jelly and propolis (bee-glue), is also available.

Naïf Paintings
The Galerías de Arte sell naïf paintings of Afro-Caribbean inspiration depicting landscapes and views of Colonial towns, or Afro-Cuban divinities.

Eau de toilette

Moisturizing cream

ENTERTAINMENT IN CUBA

The possibilities for lively entertainment are diverse in a country where there is tremendous love of music, dance and theatrical display. Ballet, theatre, concerts, festivals and sporting activities are in full swing year round. In most major cities, there are theatres and concert spaces, and even in the smallest towns you will find a Casa de la Cultura

An Afro-Cuban dancer in Santiago

or Casa de la Trova, hosting performances of traditional music. Visitors opting for a vacation at Cuba's many all-inclusive beach resorts will find canned entertainment mostly performed by hotel staff. Beyond the resorts, any street corner may easily be turned into an improvised dance floor with just the help of a cassette recorder, and discos abound everywhere.

Attractive façade of the Teatro Tomás Terry in Santiago

INFORMATION & TICKETS

Major tourist hotels distribute brochures free of charge, but usually these refer only to the costliest tourist venues, and general information on cultural happenings and locales is scant. A good online resource is **Cubarte: The Portal of Cuban Culture** at www.cult.cu There are no regional ticket offices, although tickets for major cabarets and international events can usually be bought at hotel tour desks.

THEATRE

Regional theatre is more restrained than in Havana. An exception is Santiago – its more than a dozen theatre companies include several experimental ones that, for years, have boldly sought new forms of expression. These can be seen at the **El Mambí** theatre or the **Van Troi/Cabildo Teatral Santiago** hall. The **José Martí** theatre is more traditional. The modern and prestigious **José María Heredia** theatre is particularly active

during the Fiesta del Fuego in July *(see p35)*. The **Teatro Papalote** company, in Matanzas, performs in its own theatre and is acclaimed nationwide. The world-famous **Grupo Teatro Escambray** travels throughout the island, performing to rural communities. Other major venues include the **Teatro Tomás Terry**, in Cienfuegos; the **Teatro la Caridad**, in Santa Clara; and the recently restored **Teatro Principal**, in Camagüey.

BALLET AND CLASSICAL MUSIC

Founded in 1967, the acclaimed Ballet de Camagüey presents world-class classical dance productions in the Teatro Principal *(see Theatre)*. Camagüey is also home to the **Ballet Folkórico de Camagüey**, one of Cuba's foremost troupes. In the Oriente, **Ballet Folkórico Babul** is based at the Teatro Guaso in Guantánamo.

Most provincial capitals have theatres where classical music performances are hosted. Travelling symphonies can

be heard at Santiago's **Teatro Heredia**; the more intimate **Sala de Conciertos Dolores** is a venue for smaller ensembles.

FOLK AND TRADITIONAL MUSIC

Traditional Afro-based music and dance thrives in the provinces and is particularly strong in Oriente and Trinidad, where visitors should look for splendid African-derived performances by the Conjunto Folklórico de Trinidad, which also performs Bantu and Yoruba dances outside Cuba, as does Trinidad's Cocoró y su Aché, which performs at the **Palenque de los Congos Reales**. Trinidad holds a *Semana de la Cultura* (Culture Week) each January, when *madrugadas*, songs sung in the streets, are performed. Holguín's *Semana de la Cultura* is perhaps Cuba's most vibrant.

Santiago is the home of the **Conjunto Folklórico de Oriente** and the **Ballet Folklórico Cotumba**, whose rehearsals, held from Tuesday to Sunday, are open to the public. In the

Performance by the acclaimed Ballet Folklórico de Camagüey

A traditional **son** band performing in a Trinidad street

courtyard of the **Museo del Carnaval**, rehearsals of groups preparing for Carnival *(see p229)* are open to the public.

Don't miss the evening training sessions in the various *focos culturales* from Tuesday to Friday. The **Cabildo Carabalí Izuama** rehearses Carnival songs derived from African musical traditions, while in the *foco cultural*, founded by Haitian slaves in the late 1700s, 18th-century dances are accompanied by Bantu musical instruments. Here, too, both the **Casa del Caribe** and **Centro Cultural Africano Fernando Ortíz** hold *rumbas* on weekends *(see p290: Cultural Centres)*.

Guantánamo is the birthplace of many traditional dance forms, including *changuí*, and is home to the annual December Festival Nacional de Changuí. At other times, *changuí* and its derivative, *son*, are performed by the world-famous Orquestra Revé and other leading local proponents at the **Casa de la Música**, the Casa de la Trova *(see p290: Casas de la Trova)* and the **British West Indian Welfare Center**.

The **Casa de la Cultura in Pinar del Río** is known for its *controversias*, a form of song in which two singers pit themselves against each another in creative impromptu verse. The **Casa de la Cultura in Nueva Gerona** is a centre for the local music and dance form known as *sucusuco*, unique to the Isla de la Juventud. And Las Tunas has an annual **Jornada Cucalambé** Folkloric Festival where local songsters perform *décimas*, ten-syllable rhyming songs.

NIGHTCLUBS, CABARETS & DISCOTHEQUES

Most tourist villages and large-scale hotels in Cuba have clubs that open until late. Customers pay in convertible pesos; depending on location, Cubans may be barred, so don't expect to find a broad cross-section of Cuban society.

Outside tourist resorts, most nightclubs are associated with cabarets. The most important are the **Tropicana**, in both Matanzas and Santiago. Show-girls also kick up their heels at Santiago's touristy **Cabaret San Pedro del Mar**. Varadero also offers two excellent *cabarets espéctaculos*: the large-scale **Cabaret Continental**, and the **Cueva del Pirata**, where shows are held in an atmospheric natural cave. Every other major town has at least one cabaret, which turn into nightclubs with dancing once the show ends.

Most discos are based in the tourist resorts, concentrated in Varadero. These are large, modern discos featuring loud music (usually a mix of salsa and other Latin sounds with world-beat), neon lighting, and simple decor. The entry fee is in convertible pesos and is usually quite expensive. Several such discos are for hotel patrons only. For these reasons, the majority of the customers are foreigners. However, there is usually a sprinkling of young Cuban couples, as well as wayward singles waiting outside in the hope of partnering with a foreigner for entry (occasional police sweeps occur, when Cubans being too friendly with foreigners are arrested).

The best such clubs in Varadero are **Mambo Club**, the **Club Nocturno Havana Club**, and **Palacio de la Rumba**. All three are popular with Cubans, who often travel many miles to party until dawn. The most unusual venue is Trinidad's Disco Ayala, deep inside a cave.

You can also listen to modern "música popular" in Casas de la Música in a few major cities. The principal venue, the **Casa de la Música de Trinidad**, hosts concerts by local groups. Several open-air ruins in Trinidad are also used as nightclubs. The **Casa de la Música de Cienfuegos** is also bursting with energy on weekends; and the **Club Benny Moré** is a 1950s-style nightclub with disco following comedy and cabaret.

Santiago's venues come and go, but two venerable hot-spots are the **Patio de Artex**, and **Sala de Fiestas La Iris**.

One of the Tropicana dancers in a typically exotic costume

Live music and dancing at an intimate Casa de la Trova

CASAS DE LA TROVA

The traditional and intimate Casas de la Trova are clubs where people can listen to live music, dance or just relax over a cocktail. First opened in 1959 in almost all Cuban provincial capitals, these were originally places where older musicians, interpreters of traditional *trova*, could perform and educate younger people in their musical skills. Today, Casas de la Trova are found in virtually every town and even in rural villages and are usually the most important musical venues. Many also organize lectures, conferences, poetry readings and art exhibitions, thus maintaining their original spirit as keepers of tradition.

In some places, such as in Santiago and Trinidad, Casas de la Trova have geared themselves to tourists, with a bar offering different Cuban cocktails, and a shop selling CDs, DVDs, books and souvenirs. Whatever the style, Casas de la Trova continue to be popular with Cubans of all ages and offer plenty of atmosphere.

The most important Casas de la Trova are in **Santiago**, home of *son*, and **Trinidad**, where the classical tradition of the *trova* prevails. The *trova* at **Bayamo** has a faster rhythm and stronger Afro-Caribbean overtones, while **Camagüey** focuses more on melodic tunes. Some Casas de la Trova are associated with venerated musicians, such as Casa de la Trova "El Guayabero" in **Holguín**, where the esteemed Faustino Oramas "El Guayabero" Osorio still performs.

In some towns, traditional *trova* activities are held in the Casas de la Cultura, charged with a more broadly based mandate to preserve traditional culture. In **Baracoa** and **Sancti Spíritus**, for example, they put on performances by *repentistas* (improvisers). The Casa de la Cultura in **Pinar del Río** hosts performances of *punto guajiro*, country-style music centred around improvisation.

A less touristy alternative to the Casa de la Trova is the **Casa de las Tradiciones** in Santiago, a good place to see up-and-coming local groups.

CULTURAL CENTRES

The Casa de la Cultura is an institution in every Cuban city. These cultural centres foster various forms of artistic expression: the figurative arts, poetry and music. Trinidad and Santiago are the most active cities culturally.

In Santiago, those interested in anthropology and religion can visit the **Centro Cultural Africano Fernando Ortíz**, dedicated to the African influences in Cuba, and the **Casa del Caribe**, which organizes an annual Caribbean Cultural Festival. The eclectic fare at the **Ateneo Cultural** ranges from poetry readings to rap performances.

UNEAC (National Writers and Artists' Union), with branches in a number of cities, puts on exhibitions, conferences and concerts. The Holguín and Santiago branches are particularly active and host cultural debates, art shows and music shows, as well as poetry readings.

CHILDREN

Cuba has plenty of children's playgrounds, including rather basic fairgrounds in Santiago and other major cities. The most complete fairground is Varadero's **Todo En Uno**, which has a tiny roller-coaster, *carros locos* (bumper cars) and other attractions. Nearby, Parque Retiro Josone *(see p162)* has a miniature train, plus camel rides among its attractions for children. At the **Delfinario de Varadero**, daily dolphin shows delight children; swimming with these creatures is also permitted.

Cuba has three other provincial dolphin shows: at **Delfinario de Rancho Luna**, near Cienfuegos; **Acuario Cayo Naranjo**, at Guardalavaca; and Acuario Baconao *(see p235)*.

Children will also enjoy the small zoos in Ciego de Ávila, Sancti Spíritus, and Santiago. And several cities – notably Santa Clara and Bayamo – have goat-drawn cart rides for children in the main squares.

The **Teatro Guiñol de Holguín** is a puppet theatre founded in 1959. All year round, plays and puppet shows are performed, as they are in many other cities. Holiday villages provide safe play areas for small children, as well as shallow swimming pools; Cuban families are not allowed, so don't expect your child to be able to mix if you opt for a beach resort holiday.

Swimming with a dolphin at the Acuario Cayo Naranjo

DIRECTORY

THEATRE

El Mambí
Calle Bartolomé Masó
303, Santiago de Cuba.

**Grupo Teatro
Escambray**
La Macagua, Manicaragua.
Tel (42) 491 494.

José María Heredia
Ave. las Américas, Santiago
de Cuba. *Tel (22) 641 124.*

José Martí
Calle Félix Peña 313,
Santiago de Cuba.
Tel (22) 620 507.

Teatro la Caridad
Calle Marta Abreu, e/ Máx-
imo Gómez y Lorda, Santa
Clara. *Tel (422) 205 548.*

Teatro Papalote
Calle Daoíz y
Ayuntamiento, Matanzas.
Tel (45) 244 672.

Teatro Principal
Padre Valencia 64,
Camagüey.
Tel (32) 293 048.

Teatro Tomás Terry
Plaza Martí, Cienfuegos.
Tel (43) 513 361.

**Van Troi/Cabildo
Teatral Santiago**
Calle Saco 415, Santiago
de Cuba. *Tel (22) 626 888.*

BALLET &
CLASSICAL MUSIC

**Ballet Folkórico
Babul**
Paseo 855 e/ Cuartel y
Ahogados, Guantánamo.
Tel (21) 327 940.

**Ballet Folkórico
de Camagüey**
Calle Pobre, esq. Triana,
Camagüey.
Tel (32) 293 048.

**Sala de Conciertos
Dolores**
Aguilera, esq. Mayía Rod-
ríguez, Santiago de Cuba.
Tel (22) 653 857.

Teatro Heredia
Ave. las Américas, esq.
Ave. de los Desfiles,
Santiago de Cuba.
Tel (22) 643 834.

FOLK & TRADI-
TIONAL MUSIC

**Ballet Folklórico
Cutumba**
Calle Saco 170, Santiago
de Cuba. *Tel (22) 620 922.*

**British West Indian
Welfare Center**
Serafín Sánchez 663,
e/ Paseo y Narciso López,
Guantánamo.
Tel (21) 325 297.

**Cabildo Carabalí
Izuama**
Calle Pío Rosado, e/ San
Mateo y San Antonio,
Santiago de Cuba.

Casa de la Cultura
Calle 24 esq. 37,
Nueva Gerona.
Tel (46) 323 591.

Casa de la Cultura
Martí 65, Pinar del Río.
Tel (82) 752 324.

Casa de la Música
Calixto García e/ Crombet
y Gulo, Guantánamo.
Tel (21) 327 266.

**Conjunto Folklórico
de Oriente**
Calle Hartmann 407,
Santiago de Cuba.

Jornada Cucalambé
Ciego de Ávila.
Tel (31) 47 770.

Museo del Carnaval
Heredia 304, Santiago de
Cuba. *Tel (22) 626 955.*

**Palenque de los
Congos Reales**
Echerri 146, esq. Jesús
Menéndez, Trinidad.
Tel (41) 994 512.

NIGHTCLUBS,
CABARETS &
DISCOTHEQUES

Cabaret Continental
Hotel Varadero
Internacional, Varadero.
Tel (45) 667 038.

**Cabaret San Pedro
del Mar**
Carretera del Morro Km
7.5, Santiago de Cuba.
Tel (22) 69 1287.

**Casa de la Música
de Cienfuegos**
Calle 37 e/ Av. 4 y 6.
Tel (43) 552 320.

**Casa de la Música
de Trinidad**
Calle Rosario 3, Casco
Histórico.
Tel (41) 996 622.

Club Benny Moré
Avenida 54 2907, e/ 29 y
31, Cienfuegos.
Tel (43) 551 105.

**Club Nocturno
Havana Club**
Centro Comercial Copey,
Calle 62 final, Varadero.
Tel (45) 611 807.

Cueva del Pirata
Autopista Sur, Km 11,
Varadero.
Tel (45) 667 751.

Mambo Club
Club Amigo Varadero,
Carretera Las Morlas.
Tel (45) 668 565.

Palacio de la Rumba
Hotel Bella Costa, Ave. las
Américas, Varadero.
Tel (45) 668 210.

Patio de Artex
Heredia 304, Santiago de
Cuba. *Tel (22) 654 814.*

Sala de Fiestas La Iris
Aguilera 617, e/ Plácido y
Monseñor Bernada,
Santiago de Cuba.
Tel (22) 654 910.

**Tropicana de
Matanzas**
Autopista Varadero Km
4.5. *Tel (45) 265 555.*

**Tropicana de
Santiago**
Autopista Nacional Km
1.5. *Tel (22) 686 034.*

CASAS DE LA
TROVA

Baracoa
Calle Maceo 149.

Bayamo
Calle Martí esq. Maceo.
Tel (23) 425 673.

Camagüey
Calle Cisneros y Martí.
Tel (32) 291 357.

**Casa de las
Tradiciónes**
Calle Rab 154, Santiago
Tel (22) 653 892.

Holguín
Calle Maceo 174.

Pinar del Río
Gerardo Medina 108.
Tel (48) 754 794.

Sancti Spíritus
Casa de la Cultural,
Zerquera esq. Ernest
Valdes.

Santiago
Heredia 208.
Tel (22) 623 943.

Trinidad
Calle Echerri 29.
Tel (41) 996 445.

CULTURAL CENTRES

Ateneo Cultural
Félix Peña e/ Castillo
Duany y Diego Palacios.
Tel (22) 651 969.

**Centro Africano
Fernando Ortíz**
Manduley esq. Calle 5,
Santiago de Cuba.
Tel (22) 642 487.

Casa del Caribe
Calle 13 154, Santiago de
Cuba. *Tel (22) 642 285.*

UNEAC de Holguín
Libertad 148.
Tel (24) 474 066.

CHILDREN

**Acuario Bahía
Naranjo**
Carretera a Guardalavaca.
Tel (24) 430 439.

**Delfinario de
Rancho Luna**
Carretera a Pasacaballo.
Tel (43) 548 120.

**Delfinario de
Varadero**
Autopista Km 11. Vara-
dero. *Tel (45) 66 8031.*

Teatro Guiñol
Martí 119, e/ Libertad y
Maceo. *Tel (22) 628 713.*

Todo En Uno
Autopista Sur y Calle 54.
Varadero.

Spectator Sports

After the revolution, the government abolished professional sports and invested large amounts of money in physical education and amateur sports, and as a result some outstandingly successful sportsmen and women have emerged. Baseball and boxing are by far the most popular sports (baseball is virtually a national obsession), but volleyball, basketball, football and athletics are also widely practised. Major sporting events are held in Havana and televised throughout the island.

The Cuban national women's volleyball team in action

INFORMATION AND TICKETS

It is both easy and cheap to go to a baseball game; in fact, tickets cost only a few Cuban *pesos*, which is less than a dollar. Tickets can be purchased directly at the stadium box office just before the game.

The major stadiums have specially reserved seating areas for foreign spectators.

MULTI-PURPOSE SPORTS ARENAS

A new stadium, the **Estadio Panamericano** sports complex, was built in the Habana del Este quarter of the capital for the 1991 Pan-American Games. It is now a major venue for athletics. Cuba has produced some great athletes, including Javier Sotomayor, Ana Fidelia Quirot and Ivan Pedroso *(see p19)*. The centre also has pools for swimming competitions, water polo and synchronized swimming, tennis courts and a velodrome.

The **Sala Polivalente Ramón Fonst** in Centro Habana specializes in volleyball and basketball, while the **Coliseo de la Ciudad**

Deportiva in the Boyeros district hosts national and international volleyball, basketball, boxing and fencing matches.

BASEBALL

This is the national sport. It has been a passion here for over a century, and today's teams are world-class. The first baseball stadium in Havana was built in 1881 and the first amateur championship was held in 1905. The official baseball season is from November to March, and games are played on Tuesday, Wednesday and Thursday at 8pm, on Saturdays at 1:30 and 8pm and on Sundays at 1:30pm.

Watching a game is fun; many families attend and there is always a good atmosphere. Games are played in the **Estadio Latino-americano**, inaugurated in 1946, which has a seating capacity of 55,000.

BOXING

Cuba has won several Olympic boxing titles. The founder of the modern school of boxing is Alcides Sagarra, a trainer who has been active in the profession since 1960, producing such greats as Teófilo Stevenson, the Olympic heavyweight champion, who has since set up his own school.

At the annual Girardo Córdova Cardín tournament, expert boxers fight against emerging ones; this is part of the selection procedure for the Equipo Cuba, one of the best boxing teams in the world.

Fights can be seen at the **Sala Kid Chocolate**, located opposite the Capitolio in Centro Habana.

DIRECTORY

MULTI-PURPOSE SPORTS ARENAS

Coliseo de la Ciudad Deportiva
Ave. de Rancho Boyeros y Vía Blanca, Havana
Tel (7) 648 7047.

Estadio Panamericano
Carretera de Cojímar, km 1.5.
Tel (7) 766 4140.

Sala Polivalente Ramón Fonst
Ave. Rancho Boyeros y Bruzón, Havana. **Map** 2 E4.
Tel (7) 8820 000.

BASEBALL

Estadio Latinoamericano
Pedro Pérez 302, El Cerro, Havana.
Tel (7) 8706 526, (7) 870 6576.

BOXING

Sala Kid Chocolate
Paseo de Martí (Prado) y Brasil, Havana. **Map** 4 D3.
Tel (7) 8628 634.

Cuba's national baseball team during a game

Outdoor Activities

The logo of Cubadeportes

The varied Cuban landscape allows for a wide range of outdoor activities. Facilities for a variety of water sports along the coast are increasingly good, particularly in the north, and mountain ranges and nature parks have just as much to offer. Tourist centres are equipped with exercise gyms, swimming pools and tennis courts, and also organize trekking and horse riding excursions. For athletes and fitness fanatics who want to stay in good shape, the state-run Cuba-deportes organization makes it possible to experience Cuban sports at first-hand by arranging meetings with local athletes and the provision of special courses.

Beach volleyball at a tourist village on Cayo Largo

DIVING

With 5,746 km (3,570 miles) of coastline and over 4,000 small islands, Cuba is one of the supreme places in the Caribbean for diving enthusiasts. The crystal-clear water (with a temperature ranging from 23–30° C, 70–85° F) and variety of sea beds in particular make the Cuban sea a paradise for scuba divers at any time of year. Thanks to the coral reef and numerous offshore islands *(cayos)*, there are no strong currents along the coast and the horizontal visibility under water is hardly ever less than 40 m (130 ft).

There is an abundance of sites along the coral reef for both wall and platform dives. Besides all kinds of coral, on the sea bed divers can see gorgonian fans and sponges, multicoloured fish *(see p147)*, tarpons, barracuda, sea turtles, large lobsters, beautiful anemones, and perhaps even sharks. A family of pelagic sharks lives in the Boca de Nuevitas (near Playa Santa Lucía), and the area can be visited

with the guides and instructors from the **Shark's Friends** diving centre.

There are also fascinating shipwrecks to explore. In the past the island's bays were used as refuges for pirate galleons, and in some areas, such as Playa Santa Lucía, divers can still see anchors and cannons – relics of 19th-century and even more recent ships – lying on the sea floor. Underwater tunnels and grottoes add to the attractions.

The development in tourism has triggered the opening of new diving centres and the updating of existing ones. As a result, virtually every resort has at least one centre. Scuba centres have all the latest facilities as well as trained international-level instructors, and offer courses for all levels of ability. Some, such as the Hotel Colony on Isla de la Juventud *(see p150)*, also have decompression chambers. Divers can hire all the equipment

they need on site; however, it is advisable to bring along indispensable items such as a depth gauge and a knife. Underwater photographers are advised to bring spare film and batteries, as these items may be in scarce supply.

The most important diving centres *(centros de buceo)* are **El Colony** on Isla de la Juventud (best suited to experienced divers), the **Centro de Buceo María La Gorda**, **Acua** at Varadero, and the **Centro de Buceo Meliá** at Cayo Guillermo. It is possible to dive from the shore at Playa Santa Lucía and Playa Girón, two other prime dive sites.

The Jardines de la Reina islands are also wonderful places to dive, although they can only be reached by sea, and still have no tourist facilities to speak of: only a rather plain "floating hotel". Cruise yachts take scuba divers to sites with unspoiled sea floors, where sea turtles can be seen.

For information concerning diving in general, contact **Cubanacán Nautica**.

SURFING AND WINDSURFING

At the main seaside resorts (Varadero, Guardalavaca, Cayo Largo, Cayo Coco and Marea del Portillo) conditions are ideal for surfing and windsurfing, and at the larger holiday villages all the necessary equipment can be hired.

A scuba diver exploring a shipwreck off the Playa Santa Lucía *(see p206)*

Enjoying the sea on a catamaran hired from a tourist marina

SAILING AND MOTORBOATS

Thanks to its position at the entrance to the Gulf of Mexico, Cuba makes an ideal stopping-off point for yachts and sailing boats. The tourist marinas, many of which belong to the **Marinas Marlin** chain *(see p250)*, provide a series of facilities and services, including motorboats and catamarans for hire and yacht excursions.

Most sailing is done around the Archipiélago de los Canarreos, south of the mainland. The best season for sailing is from December to April, because the climate is mild, the winds are not too strong, and storms infrequent. However, Cuba is surrounded by generally tranquil waters, and there are plenty of bays if shelter is needed.

FISHING

Fishing enthusiasts will be in their element in Cuba. The northwestern coast is marvellous for deep-sea fishing, where the catch might include swordfish, tuna or mackerel, while fish such as tarpon can be caught off the southern coast.

Fishing is often one of the many activities provided by marinas and holiday villages. Holidays tailor-made for fishermen are organized by the **Havanatur Pesca y Caza** company.

In May, the Marina Hemingway *(see p137)* is the venue for the Ernest Hemingway International Marlin Fishing Tournament, a competition reserved for expert marlin fishermen. The original rules were established by the American author, who had a passion for deep-sea fishing.

The freshwater lakes and rivers around the island are very good for trout fishing.

TENNIS AND GOLF

Almost all the holiday villages and large hotel complexes have tennis courts. Non-residents usually make use of them by paying a fee.

The island also has two good golf courses: the nine-hole **Club de Golf Habana** and the 18-hole **Club de Golf Las Américas** at Varadero.

The sport is increasingly popular and there are plans to lay out even more golf courses in the main tourist resorts in the near future.

CYCLING

Touring the island by bicycle is an excellent way to enjoy the landscape and meet local people. The bicycles offered for rent to tourists (by larger hotels and most holiday villages) are of better quality than those the locals have to use. Cycling is not usually dangerous, particularly outside the towns where traffic is light. Beware, however, of potholes in the road. Fortunately, there are plenty of roadside workshops *(talleres)*, where repairs can be carried out.

Bikes should always be locked or left in supervised places (thefts are common), and remember to wear a helmet. Mountain bikes are best for rough terrain.

Hikers on a path near Topes de Collantes *(see p187)*

HIKING, EXCURSIONS AND BIRDWATCHING

Trekking on horseback is another very enjoyable way to see the Cuban landscape. In Havana the only horse riding centre is in Parque Lenin *(see p116)*, but hotels in the main resorts, eco-tourist centres and camping sites can provide horses as well as organized excursions. Both experienced and inexperienced riders are catered for.

Until recently, the only opportunities for hiking – either with official guides or on well-marked trails – were in the areas of Viñales, Topes de Collantes and Sierra Maestra (from Alto de Naranjo to Las Cuevas). However, in

Varadero's golf course, close to the sea

recent years eco-tourist principles have been spreading to all parts of Cuba and programmes have been devised to cater for a wider range of interests, such as speleology, botany and bird-watching. The Península de Zapata *(see pp164–7)* is a particularly good area for birders, since the marshland ecosystem is a haven for hundreds of different bird species. Migratory birds may also be seen in season.

For information, contact **Gaviota Tours** and **Ecotur**; the latter organization oversees the upkeep and improvement of the trails, and also arranges nature tours and programmes.

HUNTING

Cubans enjoy the thrill of hunting and the island has a number of hunting reserves *(cotos de caza)*, where people are allowed to hunt birds and small animals within rigorously defined limits and under the supervision of the forest rangers. The reserves are usually sited near lagoons, lakes or cays, and hunting is for wild duck, snipe, guinea fowl and pigeons, among other birds. In general, it is possible to hire all the equipment needed for hunting at these reserves, although prices can be high. The hunting season is from the end of October until the middle of March.

Cuba has no specialist hunting trip agencies, but **Havanatur Pesca y Caza** offers some organized holidays that include an element of hunting.

Horse riding among the *mogotes* in the Valle de Viñales

DIRECTORY

DIVING

Acua
Ave Kawama 201,
e/ 2 y 3, Varadero.
Tel (45) 668 063.

Centro de Buceo Meliá
Cayo Guillermo.
Tel (33) 301 627.

Centro de Buceo María La Gorda
La Bajada,
Pinar del Río.
Tel (48) 778 131.

Cubanacán Nautica
Calle 184 n. 123,
Reparto Flores,
Havana.
Tel (7) 273 6675.
Fax (7) 273 7520.

El Colony
Carretera de Siguanea,
km 41, Isla de la Juventud.
Tel (46) 398 181.
Fax (46) 398 420.

Shark's Friends
Hotel Brisa Santa Lucía,
Playa Santa Lucía,
Camagüey.
Tel (32) 336 317.
Fax (32) 336 255.

SAILING AND MOTORBOATS

Marea del Portillo
Marea del Portillo, Pilón.
Tel (23) 597 008.

Marina Cayo Coco-Guillermo
Cayo Coco, Archipiélago
Jardines del Rey.
Tel/ Fax (33) 301 737.

Marina Cayo Largo
Cayo Largo.
Tel (45) 248 384 (may be
closed due to hurricane
damage, phone ahead).

Marina Chapelin
Carretera de las Morlas,
km 21, Varadero.
Tel (45) 667 550.

Marina Guardalavaca
Playa Guardalavaca,
Holguín.
Tel (24) 430 185.

Marina Hemingway
Ave. 5 y 248, Santa Fe,
Playa, Havana.
Tel (7) 2041 150.

Marina Internacional Vita
Bahía de Vita, Holguín.
Tel (24) 430 445.

Marina Santa Lucía
Playa Santa Lucía, Cama-
güey. *Tel (32) 336 317.*

Marina Santiago
Ave 1, Punta Gorda,
Santiago de Cuba.
Tel (22) 691 446.

Marina Tarará
Via Blanca km. 18, Playa
Tarará, Havana.
Tel (7) 796 0242.

Marina Trinidad
Carretera María Aguilar,
Playa Ancón.
Tel (41) 996 205.

Marina Dársena Varadero
Carretera de las Morlas km
21, Varadero.
Tel (45) 667 755.

FISHING AND HUNTING

Havanatur Pesca y Caza
Edificio Sierra Maestra,
Calle 1, e/ 0 y 2, Playa,
Havana.
Tel (7) 203 9783.

GOLF

Club de Golf Habana
Carretera de Vento km 8,
Capdevila.
Tel (7) 338 919.
Fax (7) 338 820.

Club de Golf Las Américas
Ave. Las Américas,
Varadero.
Tel (45) 667 788.
Fax (45) 668 180.

TREKKING AND BIRDWATCHING

Ecotur
Ave Boyeros 116 esq.
Santa Catalina, Havana.
Tel (7) 641 0306.
Fax (7) 648 7649.

Gaviota Tours
Edificio La Marina, level 3,
Ave del Puerto 102 e/
Jústiz y Obrapía,
Havana. Map 4 F2.
Tel (7) 869 5773.
Fax (7) 869 5774.

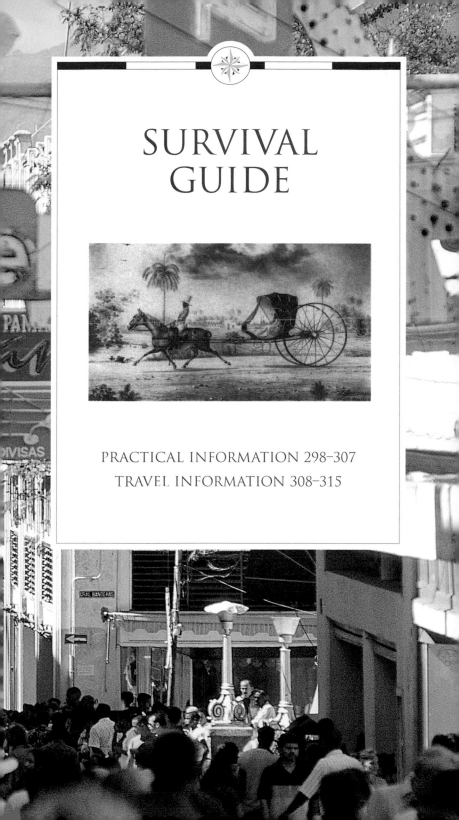

SURVIVAL
GUIDE

PRACTICAL INFORMATION

In the last 20 years Cuba has made great strides in the field of tourism and can now provide visitors with modern, international-level facilities. It is now possible for tourists to move about much more easily on the island, although advance planning is still essential, especially as regards transport around the island. An effective approach is to contact one of the many travel agencies in Cuba, which may have their own offices or be based in the major hotels. The latter also func-

Cuba,

**Logo of the Cuban
Tourist Board**

tion as tourist offices, providing practical information and often a booking service. However, although Cuban tourist operators are very good, visitors still need to be adaptable and flexible. The pace of life here is slow, as is the bureaucracy, so be prepared to waste a certain amount of time when trying to get things done. Whatever happens, try and remain optimistic. With a bit of patience and a lot of perseverance *"todo se resuelve"*, as they say in Cuba: a solution can always be found.

One of the Playas del Este at Havana, crowded with tourists and locals

WHEN TO GO

Apart from September to November, prime hurricane months, and July and August, when the torrid heat can make touring quite tiring (unless you spend your entire holiday at the seaside), any time of year is good for a visit to Cuba. It is possible to relax on the beach all year round, thanks to the mild climate.

The best period for visits is December to March, when there are more cultural events and the climate is warm without being unbearable.

VISAS AND PASSPORTS

To enter Cuba, European travellers must have a valid passport, a return ticket and a visa *(tarjeta de turista)* issued by a Cuban consulate, or the travel agency or the airline you bought your ticket from. This

visa is a yellow piece of paper which you have to fill in with your personal data and the name of the place where you are planning to stay. Visas are valid for one month and can be extended for another 30 days: in Havana, go to the **Main Immigration Office**. In other cities, you must go to the local Dirección Provincial de Inmigración. If, however, you are going to Cuba on business or to work as a journalist, you should apply to the Cuban embassy or consulate in your home country well in advance for a special visa.

For US-passport holders, special regulations apply *(see p308)*.

Sobre regulaciones de Aduana

Brochure illustrating customs regulations

Main Immigration Office
Calle 20 e/ Ave 3 y 5,
Miramar, Havana.

CUSTOMS INFORMATION

Besides their personal belongings, tourists are allowed to take into Cuba new or used objects whose overall value is no more than $250, plus 10 kg (22 lb) of medicines in their original packaging. Small appliances such as electric razors are allowed, but not objects such as telephone apparatus or fax machines. It is forbidden to import fresh food such as fruit and plants of any kind, as well as explosives, drugs, and pornographic material. Hunters with firearms must present their permits at customs.

If you intend to take more than 50 cigars out of the country you must be able to produce a receipt declaring their purchase at a state-run shop; their value must not exceed 2,000 convertible pesos.If you take out more than 50 you may well need to pay duty when you get home. Visitors can take no more than four bottles of rum or liqueur out of the country.

In order to export works of art that are part of the national heritage, you must have official authorization from the Registro Nacional de Bienes Culturales del Ministerio de Cultura.

Avoid purchasing items made from endangered species such as tortoiseshell, or bags or belts made from non-farmed reptile skins. These are covered under the Convention on International Trade in Endangered Species (CITES). The import and export of vaccinated domestic animals is allowed.

Rum for sale in a *tienda*, four per person for export

LANGUAGES

The official language in Cuba is Castilian Spanish, which is spoken with a distinctive local inflection and vocabulary *(see p335)*.

English is spoken fairly widely in Havana and in the main hotels and resorts.

FORMS OF GREETING

The most common greeting in Cuba is a kiss on the cheek, while shaking hands is common among men only in formal circumstances. It is polite to use proper titles when speaking to Cubans – *señor, señora, señorita, doctor, ingeniero* (engineer) and *profesor*. The word *compañero* (comrade) is not used as much as it once was and in any case is used only among Cubans, or at the very most with foreigners who are part of volunteer organizations on the island.

WHAT TO WEAR

The most suitable clothing for tourists is light and generally casual attire. In the winter a cotton or woollen sweater is useful in the evening, and may be useful at other times of year in places with air conditioning. A waterproof may come in handy all year round because of the tropical showers. Sunhats are recommended to protect the skin from the burning sun.

Two tourists in casual summer clothes

Except for evenings out at cabarets and nightclubs, there is usually no need for evening dress. However, Cubans do appreciate elegance and cleanliness. For a formal meeting or interview, men should not wear shorts or T-shirts, but trousers and a light shirt instead; and women should wear a dress or a skirt and blouse, but nothing too revealing.

LOCAL CUSTOMS

Cuba is a tolerant country but attitudes are still rather conservative. Nudism and topless sunbathing are not allowed on most beaches.

Despite the macho traditions in Cuba, the taboo concerning homosexuality has virtually disappeared, provided that common sense and modesty are respected. Cuban men feel virtually obliged to pay compliments to women passing by on the street: it is almost a form of

chivalry, a ritual, even if it is not always expressed with good taste. In any case, these kinds of comments should not be misinterpreted; no reaction is seriously expected, or at the very most a smile.

Women travelling alone should not experience problems, although they may be obliged to deal with frequent offers of assistance from men. The best way to put an end to undesired flirtation without offending is simply to say that you are married; this should be enough for most men to take the hint and leave you alone.

HITCH-HIKING

The lack of fuel and consequent scarcity of public transport in recent years has forced Cubans to resort to hitch-hiking *(pedir botella)* both in town and in the country. Everyone hitch-hikes, young and old, but it is never completely reliable. Students sometimes have to walk for miles and miles to get to their schools.

If you are driving a car, remember that picking up hitch-hikers is very much appreciated by Cubans, is generally not dangerous, and can provide an excellent opportunity to make friends. Cubans always pick up their fellow countrymen, but if they offer a foreigner a ride they may be fined by police unless they have a permit.

Hitch-hiking, often the only alternative to walking on a country road

JINETERISMO

The tourist boom and the economic crisis have given rise to a particular form of prostitution known as *jineterismo*, which consists of living off foreign tourists, not only through prostitution proper, but also by selling counterfeit goods (especially cigars), finding rooms for rent or *paladares* and receiving a commission from the owners. The *jinetera* (*jinetero* if male) accosts the tourist, and initiates a relationship that may last a night or several days. Sometimes the aim is not just to make money, but also to get an invitation to go abroad.

At first this social phenomenon was underestimated, but now the Cuban authorities are trying to limit its spread with severe measures, not against tourists but against Cubans acting in this way. To avoid difficult situations, be wary of "chance" meetings, above all outside hotels or in discos.

This mainly affects Havana and cities and resorts popular with tourists. Cubans are very friendly people so don't dismiss everyone as a *jinetero*.

CUBAN LAW

Foreign visitors may find it useful to know that in Cuba camping and sleeping in sleeping bags on the beach, or in areas not specifically used as a camping site, is strictly forbidden.

Cannabis may be offered on the street or outside a disco, but purchasing even a tiny amount of marijuana is illegal and could lead to immediate expulsion from the country.

Plaque at entrance to the Colonial Art Museum, Sancti Spíritus

Tourist brochures and maps published by Ediciones GEO

TOURIST INFORMATION

In all the hotels there are state-run tourist bureaux, such as Cubatur, Havanatur or Cubanacán, offering basic information, ticket booking and trips. Maps, guides and brochures are also available at these desks in airports and major cities. The Cuban publisher Ediciones GEO produces particularly good maps.

DISABLED TRAVELLERS

Only major airports, hotels and restaurants have wheelchair access for the disabled. However, a programme is under way to gradually add such facilities in airports and stations, public buildings, museums, offices and streets.

OPENING HOURS

Normal working hours on weekdays are from 8am to 5:30pm, while banks open at 8am and close at 3pm.

Museum opening hours vary, but in general they are from around 9am to 5pm, while on Sunday museums are open only half a day. Museum hours can be unpredictable, so if a visit is important to you, it is best to telephone ahead.

An entry fee is always charged at museums. Children pay half-price, Cubans pay in national *pesos* and tourists in convertible pesos. On average, the entrance fee is 1–3 convertible pesos. The same amount may be charged for permission to take photos in museums.

ELECTRICAL ADAPTORS

Electric current in Cuba is 110 volts AC (same as in US), so for European-type appliances and plugs you will need a voltage converter and an electric adaptor plug. Many recently built hotels also have 220-volt AC current.

CUBAN TIME

Cuba is five hours behind Greenwich Mean Time (GMT), like the US east coast, and in the summer there is daylight saving time, exactly as in Europe.

Personal Security

Compared with any other part of North, Central or South America, Cuba is a peaceful and safe place to travel in. However, in recent years, the great development of tourism, combined with the economic crisis, has triggered an increase in petty crime, especially in Havana and Santiago. Although the situation is under control, it is wise to take a few precautions: leave your valuables, documents and money in the hotel safe; never carry a large amount of money with you; do not wear showy jewellery; and keep an eye on your camera. If you have a hired car, it is always advisable to park near hotels or in pay car parks if possible, and do not leave any belongings open to view in the car.

A traffic policeman

CUBAN POLICE AND THE FIRE BRIGADE

Policemen in Cuba are usually polite and willing to help tourists. The officials who check passports in the airports, who belong to the Inmigración y Extranjería and wear green military uniforms, do their job slowly and with what might be considered excessive meticulousness, but problems are not common. Expect problems if you have not organized a place to stay, if only for the first few days. Tourists' luggage is often not checked, but it is best to adhere to the customs regulations to be on the safe side.

The policemen of the PNR (Policía Nacional Revolucionaria) wear blue trousers and a light grey shirt. Their role is to maintain public order, and they seldom stop foreigners. In some tourist areas such as Varadero and La Habana Vieja, you may see policemen in dark blue uniforms; they belong to a special corps that was created expressly to protect

A fire engine at Matanzas

tourists from pickpockets and to check the documents of suspicious individuals. They speak some English and can also provide information.

Different uniforms are worn by the traffic policemen (*policía de tránsito*) and firemen (*bomberos*).

Guards from the relatively new SEPSA organization provide security for banks and *tiendas* and also see to transporting valuables.

The telephone number for emergencies varies from province to province.

Road sign indicating a dangerous stretch of road

ROAD SAFETY

There are not that many cars in Cuba, even though traffic is increasing. While driving in the cities, watch out for cyclists, who do not always observe traffic regulations. The greatest potential dangers while travelling on roads and motorways through the countryside (*see p313*) are the animals grazing on the side of the road and the railway crossings without gates. The road surface is often bumpy, with sometimes deep potholes, so speeds should be kept down.

When it rains for several days in a row, the roads may easily become flooded.

THEFT AND LOST PROPERTY

To report the loss or theft of personal documents and belongings, either find a policeman, who should take you to the nearest police station, or ask for directions. Once there, be prepared for a long wait to make your report.

NATURAL DISASTERS

The greatest natural danger in Cuba is the possibility of being caught in a hurricane. Hurricane season runs from June through November. The autumn months are when hurricanes are most likely, with most occuring in October. Nowadays hurricanes are forecast well in advance, leaving plenty of time for adequate security measures, so the risk involved should not be that great. Should a hurricane occur, follow the instructions given by hotel staff. You will probably be told to wait in the hotel until it passes, and asked to keep away from windows.

DIRECTORY

EMERGENCY NUMBERS

Ambulance
Havana **Tel** (7) 838 1185, 838 2185. Santiago **Tel** (22) 623 300.

Police
Havana **Tel** 106.
Santiago **Tel** 106.

Fire Brigade
Havana **Tel** 105.
Santiago **Tel** 105.

Health and Medical Matters

A pharmacy sign

Thanks to the good health services, and the absence of most tropical diseases, a trip to Cuba should pose no unusual health risks. All the international hotels have a doctor on 24-hour call, and the first visit, as well as first-aid service, is free of charge. However, owing to the present economic difficulties in the country and the embargo, everyday pharmaceutical items are in very short supply. Normal pharmacies are rarely well stocked with medicines, and the well-supplied *farmacias internacionales* – international pharmacies which charge in convertible pesos – are not found in every town. It is best to bring your own supply of usual medicine – pain relievers, fever reducers, antibiotics and stomach treatments – as well as strong sunscreens and insect repellents.

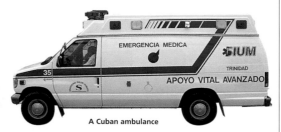

A Cuban ambulance

VACCINATIONS

No vaccinations or inoculations are required for visits to Cuba. Remarkably, almost all tropical diseases have been eliminated, and it is quite safe to travel around the entire island.

Malaria has also gone, thanks to a successful eradication campaign. There are restrictive sanitary regulations only for those arriving from countries in which yellow fever and cholera are endemic diseases.

MEDICAL TREATMENT

Cuban public health care is excellent, free of charge, and superior to that offered in any other Latin American country, though it has been put under severe pressure by the US embargo.

The national service is reserved for Cuban citizens. Foreign visitors are treated in international clinics or in public hospitals, where they will have to pay for treatment in convertible pesos. On the plus side, they are given more comfortable rooms.

PHARMACIES

The national pharmacies are not well stocked and generally reserved for Cubans. Medicines are sold only upon presentation of a prescription. In these pharmacies foreigners can only purchase medicines made from natural ingredients, including syrups, tinctures and vegetable essences, which are made on the premises. They are excellent, effective and cost virtually nothing (they can

be paid for in *pesos*). On the other hand, the international pharmacies, which are located in Havana and a few tourist resorts, stock various medicines that can be bought with or without a prescription, as well as over-the-counter products (sanitary pads, ear plugs, ointments for fungal infections and sunburn and so on) that cannot be found in the common *tiendas*.

PUBLIC WCS (RESTROOMS)

In Cuba public toilets are hard to find, and they are often dirty and without water. There is no such thing as toilet paper, except in the bathrooms in restaurants, hotels, luxury nightclubs and airports, so it is wise to carry a good supply with you.

ILLNESSES

Summer colds are quite common in Cuba, often caused by the contrast between the heat of outside and the chilly air in hotels and so on, where air conditioning is on maximum. It is a good idea to carry a light sweater or jacket for these occasions.

Asthma sufferers may find that the humid climate could trigger an attack; visitors to Cuba with respiratory problems should always carry their usual medicine and an inhaler with them. All the hospitals and *policlínicos* (the neighbourhood outpatient clinics) are well-equipped for these problems.

Entrance to the historic Taquechel pharmacy in Havana *(see p72)*

Wearing a hat and using sunscreen to avoid burns and heatstroke

Another fairly common nuisance in Cuba is diarrhoea, or worse, dysentery. This can generally be prevented by always drinking bottled water, or water that has been purified with tablets; another useful precaution is to avoid food and drinks sold on the street. It may be best to avoid ice in cocktails as well.

All these measures should also be enough to ward off giardiasis, a disease caused by a parasite that attacks the intestine and causes dysentery, nausea, fatigue and weight loss.

A bottle of Ciego Montero mineral water

Rare cases of yellow fever and dengue fever may occur in the summer in the marshy zones of Eastern Cuba (although in practice few tourists visit these areas). However, since these two diseases are spread by mosquitoes, it is advisable to use plenty of insect repellent when planning to tour marshy areas.

PROTECTION FROM THE SUN

The sun in Cuba is very strong and protection is necessary, especially in July and August. Wear a hat, whether in town or in the countryside, and use a strong sun lotion with a high screen factor. It is also advisable to drink a lot of water to prevent dehydration. High humidity and heat may cause heatstroke, with symptoms of thirst, nausea, fever, and dizziness. If this occurs, keep up fluid intake and take cold baths.

INSECTS

Mosquitoes are the main irritant in Cuba (and can cause disease). In swampy or lagoon areas, such as the Zapata swamp, pay particular attention to applying insect repellent, cover up in the evening and sleep with the fan or air conditioning on.

DIRECTORY

EMERGENCY NUMBERS

Ambulance and First Aid
Havana **Tel** (7) 838 1185, 838 2185. Santiago **Tel** (22) 626 485, 623 300.

INTERNATIONAL HOSPITALS AND CLINICS

Havana
Clínica Cira García,
Calle 20 n. 4101,
esq. 43, Miramar, Havana.
Tel (7) 2042 811.

Santiago de Cuba
Ave Raúl Pujol y Calle 10.
Tel (22) 642 589.

Varadero
Calle 60 y 1.
Tel (45) 667 711.

INTERNATIONAL PHARMACIES

Farmacia Internacional Miramar
Ave. 41 esq. 20, Miramar, Havana.
Tel (7) 204 4350.

Farmacia Internacional Habana Libre
Hotel Habana Libre, Ave. L, e/ 23 y 25, Vedado, Havana.
Map 2 E2. **Tel** (7) 838 4593.

HEALTH TOURISM

Servimed – Cubanacán Turismo y Salud
Ave 43 n. 1418, esq. 18, Miramar, Havana.
Tel (7) 204 1630.

HEALTH TOURISM

Thanks to its favourable climate, Cuba has long been regarded as an effective sanatorium, popular with an international clientele. By the 19th century, the first hotels had been built near springs of therapeutic mineral water. Beside the spas, there are now international clinics which provide general medical care and also specialize in anti-stress and skin treatments, as well as hospitals for the rehabilitation of alcoholics and drug addicts. These centres are located throughout the country and are in great demand: the waiting lists are not long, the prices are competitive, and the results are good. They are run by the state-run **Servimed** organization, part of the Cubanacán group.

Dermatological treatment in one of the specialist clinics

Communications

An unusual letter box

The telephone is by far the most widespread system of communication in Cuba. Unlike the postal service, which is not all that efficient, the telephone network run by ETECSA has improved considerably. Today there are new public telephones that work with pre-paid phone cards. The use of e-mail is spreading, if mainly in business. Cuba also has two national television channels and several national, regional and municipal radio stations. Many hotels have a satellite dish and broadcast a TV channel especially for tourists. The leading daily newspaper is *Granma*, while the weekly *Granma Internacional* is printed in various languages. *Business Tips on Cuba* is a business monthly on investments in Cuba.

HOW TO USE A PUBLIC TELEPHONE

1 Lift the receiver and wait for the dialling tone. The display will ask the user to insert a telephone card *(inserte su tarjeta)* in the slot above the receiver.

2 Once you have inserted the telephone card, the display will show how much credit remains on the card.

3 Dial the number you want to call. While you are dialling, the number you are calling will appear on the display. The readout will also say how much credit remains on the phone card.

Telephone cards

4 After the call is finished, place the receiver back on the hook. The phone card will be returned from the slot automatically. If the card expires while you are phoning, the connection will be interrupted and you will have to phone again.

DIALLING CODES

- Directory inquiries 113
- If you want to make a long-distance telephone call via the operator, dial 00.
- To make a reverse charge (collect) international telephone call via the operator, dial 09.
- To dial long-distance within Cuba from a phone card public telephone, add 0 in front of the area code.
- To make a direct-dial international telephone call from a public telephone with a phone card, dial 119, and from a hotel 88, followed by the country code (Australia 61; Ireland 353; New Zealand 64; UK 44; USA and Canada 1), the area code and then the local telephone number.

TELEPHONE NUMBERS

If you are calling from abroad, dial the international access code of your country (eg 00 in the UK), followed by the Cuba country code (53), the local area code, and lastly the local phone number you want to reach. The local area codes, which may have one or two digits, are given in brackets in front of all phone numbers listed in this guide. For local calls, there is no need to dial the area code. The number of digits of local numbers varies, since the phone network system is in the process of being updated.

5 centavos

20 centavos

Coins used for phoning

PUBLIC TELEPHONES

Throughout the country there has been an increase in the number of new public telephones, which can be used to make direct-dial international calls without the help of the operator. Magnetic telephone cards *(tarjetas telefónicas)* can be purchased at hotels, post offices, *tiendas* and ETECSA telephone centres for $10, $20 and $50.

There are also coin-operated telephones which take *pesos*. For a local call you must insert at least a five *centavos* coin (also known as *"medio"*), or one for 20 *centavos ("peseta")* to talk for a few minutes.

Local, long-distance and international calls can also be made from hotels. This is certainly the easiest way, since the operator does everything for you, but it is also the most expensive.

PRIVATE TELEPHONES

The only direct-dial calls that can be made from private telephones are local ones, while long-distance and international calls must be made through an operator. Calls to foreign countries are always reverse charge, unless you use an ETECSA telephone with a contract specifying payment in dollars. This type of telephone can be found in hotels, in travel agencies, in some public offices, and in the homes of foreigners who work in Cuba, rarely in Cubans' private homes.

POSTAL SERVICE

The Cuban postal service is slow, but is generally no worse than in any other Latin American country. For letters and postcards, use the stamps *(sellos)* that can be purchased in dollars in the hotels or in *pesos* in the post offices *(oficinas de correo)*. Whatever the postage, letters take a long time to arrive, although it may help a little to post mail in the *oficinas de correo* postboxes.

The safest, and comparatively the fastest, way to post documents, letters or parcels that are important or urgent, is via international courier services: **DHL, Cubapost,** or **Cubapack Internacional SA**.

Entrance to a post office *(oficina de correo)* in Havana

ADDRESSES

In Cuba the street number, preceded by "N." or "#", comes after the name of the street or square, followed by *"esq."* (*esquina* = corner) and the name of the cross street, or by *"e/"* (*entre* = between) and the name of two streets *(see p118)*. This is followed by the number of the apartment, if it has one, or by *"altos"* (first floor) or *"bajos"* (ground floor) if it is a private house, followed by the name of the *"reparto"* (quarter) or district, and then by the locality.

A crowded news-stand in Pinar del Río

RADIO AND TELEVISION

There are four main Cuban television channels. Cubavisión broadcasts soap operas, films, news, music and US drama series around the clock. Tele Rebelde specializes in news and sports programmes and airs school lessons during the day and documentaries in the evening, as do Canal Educativo and Canal Educativo 2. Each province has its own local channel. Canal Habana and Multivisión, for example, broadcast from Havana.

Hotels have a selection of channels such as CNN, Discovery ESPN, Cinemax, HBO and The Cartoon Network, all of which are not allowed in family homes.

There is also a tourist channel which can be viewed in hotels. *Canal del Sol* features mainly films and sports.

A good radio station is *Radio Taíno*, with music and information in English and Spanish (1180 AM in Havana and 1100 AM in Varadero). *Radio Rebelde* has news, music and sports; *Radio Habana Cuba* broadcasts for an overseas audience; and *Radio Reloj* broadcasts news 24 hours a day.

NEWSPAPERS AND PERIODICALS

The daily newspaper with the widest circulation in the country is *Granma*, the official organ of the Cuban Communist Party, which also publishes a weekly version for foreigners, *Granma Internacional*.

Masthead of the daily *Granma*

There are also several provincial dailies: *Trabajadores* (Monday to Saturday only) and *Tribuna de La Habana* in Havana; *Guerrillero* in Pinar del Río; *Girón* in Matanzas; *5 de Septiembre* in Cienfuegos; *Adelante* in Camagüey; *Ahora* in Holguín; *Sierra Maestra* in Santiago de Cuba; and *Victoria* in Isla de la Juventud.

Among Cuba's magazines are *Bohemia*, a cultural weekly, and a periodical for investors and foreign tourists, *Business Tips on Cuba*, which is printed in several languages.

INTERNET AND FAX

E-mail is used increasingly in Cuba, mainly in offices, while surfing the Internet is still limited to the "privileged few". You can log onto the Web in many hotels, and a few cyber cafés.

Fax services are available in all the international post offices in the large cities as well as in all the major hotels.

DIRECTORY

COURIER SERVICE

Cubapack Internacional SA
Calle 22 n. 4115, e/ 41 y 47,
Playa, Havana.
Tel (7) 2042 817,
(7) 204 2134,
(7) 204 2817.

Cubapost
Calle 21 n. 1009, e/ 10 y 12,
Vedado, Havana.
Map 1 B4.
Tel (7) 836 9790,
(7) 836 9791.

DHL
Calle 26, esq. 1, Playa, Havana.
Tel (7) 204 0998,
(7) 204 1578,
(7) 204 1876.

Banking and Local Currency

Cuba's currency is the *peso cubano* (CUP), but most visitors primarily use the *peso convertible* (CUC), or convertible peso. You can buy and pay for everything in convertible pesos. The US dollar was valid in Cuba until 2005 when the law changed, and it is now the least desirable major currency to bring to the country as, although exchangeable in banks, it is subject to a 10% surcharge. Credit cards and travellers' cheques issued by banks in the US are not accepted anywhere in Cuba. American Express cards, regardless of where they were issued, are not accepted either. Euros are now widely accepted in hotels in Varadero, Jardines del Rey, Holguín, Santa Lucía and Cayo Largo del Sur.

BANKS AND BUREAUX DE CHANGE

Banks are usually open from 8am to 3pm from Monday to Friday. Among those that carry out foreign currency transactions the best prepared are the **Banco de Crédito y Comercio** (BANDEC) and the **Banco Financiero Internacional** (BFI), branches of which exist in the major tourist resorts and provincial capitals. Bank commissions on travellers' cheques is 2 or 3 per cent.

Bureaux de change, especially those located in hotels, have longer opening hours than banks. The commission for cashing travellers' cheques is around 4 per cent. The **CADECA Casas de Cambio**, often located near shops or markets, are the best places to buy *pesos cubanos*.

Money can also be withdrawn using a credit or debit card (VISA or Mastercard). An increasing number of Automated Teller Machines (ATMs) accept foreign cards, though ATMs are still nonexistent in many towns. Remember that cards issued by US banks are not accepted.

The logo of the Banco Financiero Internacional

CREDIT CARDS

The vast majority of hotels, some restaurants and many convertible peso-charging shops accept credit cards, though only those issued by non-US banks and never American Express. If you encounter a problem using a credit card, contact the **Centro de Tarjetas de Crédito in Havana**.

In many small towns, and even in some remote tourist resorts, credit cards will be useless, so it is wise to carry a certain amount of cash with you (this is essential outside of the major cities and tourist resorts). Wherever you are cash will be needed for tips and small purchases.

CURRENCY

The dual economy of the *peso cubano* and the *peso convertible* (convertible peso) can be confusing, especially as both currencies are often referred to as *pesos*. Even the symbol ($) used to denote them is the same. The most common terms to differentiate them are *"moneda nacional"* or CUP for the *peso cubano*, and *"divisa"* or CUC for the convertible peso.

There are currently 24 *pesos cubanos* to the convertible peso. Visitors will use the convertible peso almost exclusively, while the *peso cubano* is used mostly just by Cubans. However, it is the only valid currency on local buses, at most cinemas and sports stadiums, so it may be a good idea to carry a small amount with you. Some services, such as museum fees, are charged to Cubans in *pesos* and to foreigners in convertible pesos.

The handsome Neo-Classical façade of a bank in Santa Clara

DIRECTORY

BANKS

Banco Financiero Internacional
5ta Ave. no.9009 esq. 92,
Miramar, Playa,
Havana.
Tel (7) 267 5000.
Fax (7) 267 5001.

Banco de Crédito y Comercio
Amargura no.158 esq. Cuba,
Habana Vieja,
Havana.
Tel (7) 861 4533.
Fax (7) 866 8968.

BUREAUX DE CHANGE

CADECA Casa de Cambio
Aeropuerto José Martí, Terminal 3, Havana. ⬤ *24 hours daily.*

CADECA Casa de Cambio
Obispo no.257, e/ Aguiar y Cuba, Habana Vieja, Havana.
⬤ *8am–10pm daily.*

CADECA Casa de Cambio
Hotel Nacional, Calle 0 esq. 21, Vedado, Havana.
⬤ *8am–noon & 1–11pm Mon–Sun.*

CADECA Casa de Cambio
Aeropuerto de Varadero.

CREDIT CARD ASSISTANCE

Centro de Tarjetas de Crédito
Calle 23 (La Rampa), e/ L y M, Vedado, Havana.
Tel (7) 835 6400, 838 4407.

Coins

There are 100 centavos (cents) to a national peso. Cuban coins come in 1 centavo *("kilo"), 2* centavos, *5* centavos *("medio" – used for calls), 20* centavos *("peseta", also used for phone calls); and 1 and 3 pesos (the latter bearing Che Guevara's portrait).*

3 pesos

1 peso

20 centavos

5 centavos

Pesos Cubanos

Cuban bank notes come in units of 1, 3, 5, 10, 20, 50 and 100 pesos. Each note has a different colour. Twenty-four pesos correspond to one peso convertible: be careful not to confuse the bank notes.

5 pesos

10 pesos

20 pesos

Pesos Convertibles
(Convertible Pesos)

Bank notes of the peso convertible *circulate in units of 1, 3, 5, 10, 20, 50 and 100 pesos. The coins come in units of 5, 10, 25, 50 cents and 1 peso. These* pesos convertibles *are not valid anywhere outside Cuba.*

1 peso convertible

25 centavos

10 centavos

5 centavos

1 centavo

10 pesos convertibles

TRAVEL INFORMATION

The majority of foreign tourists arrive in Cuba by aeroplane. Charter and regular scheduled flights arrive from Europe, Canada, Central and South America, and there are even some special flights from the US. The internal connections within Cuba are good, and there is at least one airport in every province; 9 are international and 21 domestic. Taxis are available at the airport for hotel transfers, if these have not been previously arranged, or cars may be hired (driving is the most efficient way of getting around Cuba). From José Martí airport in Havana, a modern coach service, part of the Vaivén company line, provides a link with the city centre. On Cayo Largo, one of Cuba's most well-known island resorts, there is an airport with international links, and Isla de la Juventud is linked to the rest of Cuba by a domestic airport as well as by ferries and catamarans.

Logo of Cuba's national airline

ARRIVING BY AIR

Cuba is connected to Europe and the rest of the world by flights operated by several major airlines, with scheduled and charter flights.

Most arrivals from Britain are charter flights; scheduled direct flights from London to Havana are rare. **Monarch Airlines** offers flight-only deals from Gatwick to Holguín and Varadero, as well as a range of package holidays. The Cuban national airline is **Cubana de Aviación**, and has regular flights between the United Kingdom and Havana.

Most scheduled routes from Britain involve a stopover in a third country, though **Virgin Atlantic** flies direct from Gatwick to Havana. **Air France** flights depart from Heathrow and other UK airports to Havana

Entrance to the José Martí airport in Havana

via Paris. **Iberia** flights (from London and Manchester) go via Madrid in Spain.

In Canada, regular Cubana de Aviación flights go from Toronto and Montreal. Cubana de Aviación also operates flights from Mexico – with services departing from Cancún and Mexico City airports.

US TRAVELLERS

American law means that it is illegal for US-passport holders to travel to Cuba as tourists or on business, but it is possible to apply for a licence from the **US Treasury Department**. These can be given for religious or humanitarian interest trips, to freelance

CITY	AIRPORT	ℹ INFORMATION	DISTANCE FROM CITY OR TOURIST CENTRE
Havana	José Martí	(7) 266 4133	Town centre: 25 km (15 miles)
Varadero	Juan Gualberto Gómez	(45) 247 015	Town centre: 6 km (4 miles)
Cayo Largo del Sur	Vilo Acuña	(45) 248 146	*(in the middle of the cay)*
Camagüey	Ignacio Agramonte	(32) 261 010	Town centre: 9 km (5.5 miles)
Holguín	Frank País	(24) 462 512	Town centre: 13 km (8 miles)
Santiago de Cuba	Antonio Maceo	(22) 698 614	Town centre: 5 km (3 miles)
Manzanillo	Sierra Maestra	(23) 577 401	Town centre: 8 km (5 miles)
Ciego de Ávila	Máximo Gómez	(33) 309 161	Cayo Coco: 80 km (50 miles)
Cienfuegos	Jaime González	(43) 552 047	Town centre: 5 km (3 miles)

journalists (full-time journalists need no specific licence), and to students whose university has applied for a licence. Regulations tend to change, so check the current situation.

The **Center for Cuban Studies** has its own licence and can therefore arrange group and individual travel for US-passport holders of the above categories and also provides updates and advice.

Some US travellers choose to go without a licence, flying via Mexico, Canada or the Caribbean. These trips cannot be arranged through US travel agents, and it is vital to avoid having your passport stamped by the Cuban authorities.

Sign for the international terminal at Havana airport

AIRPORTS

Cuba has 9 international and 21 domestic airports. The main international airport is José Martí, 18 km (11 miles) south of Havana. Charter flights land at Terminal II, scheduled flights at Terminal III, while Terminal I is reserved for domestic flights.

Most of the other international airports (other than in Havana) are for charter flights for tourists en route to holiday resorts. Of these, Varadero is the busiest.

ARRIVING BY SEA

Because of the US embargo, Cuba is not connected to North and South America by ferries, and few cruise ships dock here. But private yachts are welcome at Cuba's many harbours, including Marina Hemingway in Havana (special rules applies for US passport holders – see above). The following documents are needed: the passports of all those on board, the ownership documents, the name and registration

number of the boat, and the customs document *(zarpe)* issued at the last port the ship called at. The *Cruising Guide to Cuba* by Simon Charles is a good source of information.

ORGANIZED TOURS AND PACKAGE HOLIDAYS

Air fares vary depending on the airline and time of year. Fares tend to be higher at peak periods, that is in July and August and at Christmas and Easter. The best value is often to buy a package including charter flights from a tour operator; your travel agent can help you decide which is the most suitable for your needs. There are usually reductions for children under 12 years. From the UK, charter flights are available to Cuba from both Gatwick and Manchester.

Mainstream UK tour operators include **Thomas Cook** and **The Holiday Place**. Specialist operators, who can help independent travellers plan a tailor-made visit, include **Captivating Cuba, Havanatur, Journey Latin America** and **Regent Holidays**. **Dance Holidays** *(see pp250–51)* offers arrangements including music and dance tuition.

Special interest holidays, especially those involving diving, water sports and salsa are particularly popular, and eco-tourism is also a developing area *(see p250)*. Among the tour operators offering special interest holidays are **Scuba en Cuba** and **Voyager Cuba**.

An aeroplane landing at Cayo Largo, an international holiday resort

DIRECTORY

AIRLINES

Air France
www.airfrance.com
Tel 0845 084 5111 (UK).

Cubana de Aviación
www.cubana.co.cu
Tel 020 7537 7909 (UK).

Iberia
www.iberiaairlines.co.uk
Tel 0845 609 0500 (UK).

Monarch Airlines
www.flymonarch.com
Tel 01582 400 000 (UK).

Virgin Atlantic
www.virgin-atlantic.com
Tel 01293 562 345 (UK).

US TRAVELLERS

Center for Cuban Studies
www.cubaupdate.org
Tel (212) 242-0559 (US).

US Treasury Department
www.treas.gov/ofac
Tel (202) 622-2000 (US).

TOUR OPERATORS

Captivating Cuba
www.captivatingcuba.com
Tel 0870 887 0123 (UK).

Havanatur UK
Tel 01707-646 463 (UK).

Holiday Holiday
www.holidayholiday.co.uk
Tel 0870 251 2523 (UK).

Journey Latin America
www.journeylatinamerica.co.uk
Tel 020-8747 8315 (UK).

Regent Holidays
www.regent-holidays.co.uk
Tel 0870 499 1311 (UK).

Scuba en Cuba
www.scuba-en-cuba.com
Tel 01895-624 100 (UK).

South American Experience
www.southamericanexperience.
co.uk
Tel 020 7821 4060 (UK).

The Holiday Place
www.theholidayplace.com
Tel 020 7644 1755 (UK).

Thomas Cook
www.thomascook.com
Tel 0870 750 5711 (UK).

Voyager Cuba
www.voyagercuba.co.uk
Tel 01580 766 222 (UK).

Getting Around Cuba

If your time is limited, the best way to get around the island is without doubt by aeroplane, because this is the only really fast means of transport in Cuba. The network of domestic flights is good and connections are made via Cubana de Aviación and Aerocaribbean airlines. Trains are much cheaper, but they are also much slower. Tourist coach services, on the other hand, have greatly improved. They are becoming more numerous and comfortable and provide services to all the tourist resorts and provincial capitals.

Nueva Gerona national airport, Isla de la Juventud

BOOKING AND CHECK-IN FOR DOMESTIC FLIGHTS

There are flights from Havana to the following destinations: Baracoa, Bayamo, Camagüey, Cayo Coco, Cayo Largo, Ciego de Ávila, Cienfuegos, Guantánamo, Holguín, Las Tunas, Manzanillo, Moa, Nueva Gerona, Playa Santa Lucía, Santa Clara and Santiago de Cuba.

It is not necessary to go in person to the **Cubana de Aviación** or **Aerocaribbean** airline offices to book a domestic flight; any travel agency will contact these airlines for you and make your reservation without any extra charge. However, bear in mind that you should book early, especially for flights in high season. Check-in is 60 minutes before take-off, and the maximum luggage weight allowance is 20 kg (44 lbs).

Domestic flights cost about twice as much as trains or coaches, but if you book one together with an international flight with Cubana, there is a saving of 25 per cent. Children under two travel free of charge, and young people under 18 pay 33 per cent of the normal fare.

The aeroplanes are not always new, and the service may lack frills, but the staff are experienced and reliable.

A Cubana de Aviación plane for domestic flights

SHIPS AND FERRIES

If time is not an issue, it is possible to travel to Isla de la Juventud by sea rather than by air. Departure is from the port of Batabanó, on the southern coast of Havana province, 60 km (37 miles) from the capital. The journey once took up to six hours by ferry, but nowadays a catamaran built by Damex Shipbuilding & Engineering does the journey in about two and a half hours. Tickets for the catamaran can be bought at the quay and there is no need to book ahead of time.

A recent development is a daily service between Varadero and Havana in elegant catamarans that belong to the Dodero Argentine shipping line and are run by Cubanacán. The catamarans depart in the morning from Marina Chapelín, in Varadero, and dock at the cruise ship terminal in Havana; the return trip is in the late afternoon. The trip takes two and a half hours and cruising speed is 35 knots. This air-conditioned ship has a seating capacity of 380, and facilities include a solarium.

In the cities of Havana, Santiago and Cienfuegos,

A *lanchita*, a waterbus connecting the various towns around the bay of Havana

you can also find waterbuses or ferries called *lanchas* or *lanchitas*, which operate around their respective bays, linking towns or providing a crossing to the opposite side.

Small ferries connect the coast north of Pinar del Río with Cayo Levisa.

TRAINS

Cuba has 4,881 km (3,030 miles) of public railway lines, serving all the provincial capitals. In recent years the service has been extended and slightly improved, although the carriages are by no means modern and clean. Refreshments may not be available, so take supplies.

There is at least one train per day on each of the main lines, but do not count on it arriving on time.

The trains known as "*especiales*", which cover long-distance routes such as Havana-Santiago, have air conditioning (though it may not always function as it should), reclinable seats, and a refreshment service.

Information on timetables and tickets (tourists have to pay in convertible pesos) can be obtained in Havana railway station at the **Ferrotur** offices. An alternative is the LADIS agency, which also sells tickets for long journeys.

The advantage in travelling by train is that it is almost always possible to find a seat without booking in advance, even in high season. If you have time, patience and are on a tight budget, railway travel can be a very pleasant and sociable way of travelling around Cuba.

Façade of the railway station in Morón

COACH SERVICES

The modern coaches operated by the **Víazul** company provide transport to the main cities and towns and tourist resorts in Cuba. They connect Havana with Santiago (passing through Santa Clara, Ciego de Ávila, Camagüey, Las Tunas, Holguín and Bayamo), Varadero, Trinidad and Viñales. There is also a direct service between Varadero and Trinidad.

A minibus for tourists

On the positive side, Viazul coaches are very comfortable and arrive on time – the disadvantage is that, at least on the stretch between Havana and Santiago, the frequent intermediate stops in all the provincial capitals make for rather a long journey. The seats can be reclined (a little), and there are toilets and a minibar for passengers. The air conditioning is always turned on full, so that if you do decide to use this means of transport, always carry a sweater or jacket.

Travel agencies also supply hotels with minibus shuttle services to take guests to nearby tourist resorts.

DIRECTORY

AEROCARIBBEAN

Havana
Calle 23 n. 64, Vedado.
Map 2 F2. **Tel** *(7) 8797 524,
(7) 8797 525.*

CUBANA DE AVIACIÓN

Camagüey
Calle República 400.
Tel *(32) 291 338.*

Holguín
Calle Libertad, esq. Martí.
Tel *(24) 464 148, 464 149.*

Havana
Calle 23, e/ P e Infanta, Vedado.
Map 2 F1. **Tel** *(7) 834 4446.*

Santiago de Cuba
Calle Enramada esq. San Pedro.
Tel *(22) 651 578.*

Varadero
Ave 1ra e/ 54 y 55.
Tel *(45) 611 823-5.*

FERROTUR

Havana
Estación Central de Ferrocarriles,
Egido y Arsenal. **Map** 4 E4.
Tel *(7) 862 1920.*

VÍAZUL

Havana Main Office
Ave 26 y Zoológico, Nuevo
Vedado. **Tel** *(7) 8811 413 or
(7) 882 0645.*
Fax *(7) 883 6092.*

Varadero
Calle 36 y Autopista.
Tel *(45) 614 886.*

Santiago de Cuba
Ave de los Libertadores,
esq. Yarayó.
Tel *(22) 628 484.*

A Víazul line coach

Travelling by Car

The best way to see a lot of Cuba's hinterland is to travel by car. With a car it is possible to discover places and scenery that it would be difficult to see on an organized tour, and even more so if you travel by air. It is best to plan an itinerary and stopovers in advance, and a good road map is essential. A few precautions should be taken. Keep speed down and always park in supervised car parks. In summer, because of the heat, it is advisable to travel early in the morning. You will see many people hitch-hiking on the road; you are not obliged to pick them up, but it is a normal way of life in Cuba and the lift will be appreciated *(see p299)*.

Example of a new road sign
seen outside cities

A lorry picking up hitch-hikers on the Autopista Nacional (motorway)

THE HIGHWAY CODE

In Cuba traffic drives on the right. The speed limits for cars are 20 km/h (12 mph) in parking areas, 40 km/h (25 mph) near schools, 50 km/h (30 mph) in town, 60 km/h (37 mph) on dirt roads and in tunnels, 90 km/h (55 mph) on asphalt roads and 100 km/h (62 mph) on the motorway.

Every so often on the *Autopista* (motorway) you will see signs telling you to reduce your speed to around 50 km/h: do not ignore these instructions, as they are often followed by road blocks. In general, the police are quite tolerant with tourists, but speeding may invalidate car hire insurance.

In town, headlights should be kept dipped. Seat belts are only fitted in the more recent models of car. Their use is both recommended and compulsory.

The road signs are the usual international ones, but there are also others on the country roads that warn drivers they are approaching a junction or a stretch of dangerous road *(see p301)*.

THE ROAD NETWORK

The carretera central is an old, narrow and not particularly comfortable road linking Pinar del Río to Guantánamo, via all the provincial capitals. The only motorway in Cuba is the Autopista Nacional, or "Ocho Vías"; it goes from Pinar del Río to Jatibonico, near Sancti Spíritus (the Holguín–Santiago de Cuba stretch is under construction) and is toll-free. It is in good condition but should be used as if it were an ordinary road, without

exceeding the speed limit, because every so often the road is crossed by unmarked railway lines or you may come across wandering animals.

The worst roads, with potholes and bumps, are found in Eastern Cuba, but the surfaces of city streets are by no means perfect either.

PETROL

Fuel is distributed through the many Servi-Cupet and Oro Negro service stations through-out the island. They sell petrol for convertible pesos and are open 24 hours a day. However, there are fewer stations outside the towns, so it is best to keep the tank topped up, just in case.

Ask the car hire company for a free copy of an *automapa*, which shows where the Servi-Cupet service stations are located across the island.

ROAD MAPS

A good road map is essential. *Tiendas* and the book shops in hotels and elsewhere sell good road maps which are published by Ediciones GEO.

Maps and brochures are also distributed free of charge in travel agencies and by the car hire companies.

A hire car at a Servi-Cupet service station

NUMBER PLATES

Cuban car number plates come in different colours, indicating the type of ownership. Above the number is a word indicating the category of the vehicle: *"estatal"* means it belongs to a state-run organization, *"particular"* means it is a private car, *"turismo"* is used for cars rented by tourists and *"empresa"* for joint venture companies.

Official plate

Private plate

Tourist plate

ROAD SAFETY

The most serious danger on Cuban roads is posed, in fact, by slow vehicles: carts and carriages, tractors and cyclists tend to occupy the middle of the road, and before overtaking them it is a good idea to sound the horn.

It is also a good rule of thumb to sound the horn before making a sharp turn or when passing a lorry (they often do not have rear-view mirrors).

It is forbidden to keep your car lights on during the day, unless there is heavy fog. It is advisable not to drive outside town at night unless absolutely necessary, because of poor visibility. Roads are not lit and you may run into animals, pedestrians and even cyclists, whose bicycles are rarely equipped with front lights and rear reflectors.

At any time of day, take extra care after rainy weather, because road surfaces may become flooded (*see p301*). In mountain areas there may be some danger of falling rocks.

Tourists on a scooter

CAR HIRE

In order to hire a car in Cuba visitors must have a valid driver's licence from their own country or an international licence, be over 21 years of age, and have a valid passport to show to the car rental company. The three main agencies are **Transautos**, **CubaCar** and **Vía Rent a Car**. Transautos, the bigger chain, has a number of branch offices in hotels throughout the island and in Servi-Cupet service stations, so that they are able to provide a good network of support. CubaCar and Via Rent a Car have offices only in the main cities.

Cars can be picked up and dropped off at most of the airports, but it is advisable to book them well in advance, especially in high season, when the smaller and cheaper models are very much in demand. Payment is made in advance, and you must either leave a cash deposit (which is refunded) or leave an imprint of your credit card. A car may be dropped off at a different office from the one where it was hired, but there will be a high charge. A penalty will also have to be paid if the contract for car hire is lost.

There are two kinds of optional insurance for hire cars. Plan A covers accidents but not theft, and Plan B covers all risks except for loss of a tyre.

In the event of an accident you must obtain a copy of the police report, which should then be handed over to the car hire company.

For exploring certain parts of the island, including the extreme west and far east, it may be best to hire a four-wheel drive (off-roader) to negotiate the pitted roads.

Larger groups of visitors might prefer to rent a minibus from **Cubamar**, **Cubanacán** or **Transgaviota**. It is also possible to hire scooters.

DIRECTORY

CAR HIRE

Cubacar
Calle 3rd y 164, Miramar, Havana.
Tel (7) 273 1157, (7) 273 0600.

Rex
Ave. de Rancho Boyeros y Calzada de Bejucal, Havana.
Tel (7) 683 0303, (7) 273 9166.

Vía Rent a Car (Gaviota)
Calle 9na y 98, Playa.
Tel (7) 2043 606.

MINIVAN HIRE

Cubacar
Calle 164 esq. 3ra, Reparto Flores, Havana.
Tel (7) 273 2277, (7) 835 0000, (7) 272 5986, (7) 272 5985.

Micar
Calle 110 e/ 5 y 3, Playa Habana, Havana.
Tel (7) 206 9778, (7) 204 3457.

Transtur
Calle 1ra esq. 26, Playa Habana, Havana. *Tel/Fax* (7) 2045 532.

A hired four-wheel drive: a good choice of vehicle for the road conditions in Cuba

Getting Around Havana

In Havana, road traffic is on the increase but is still nowhere near the levels of a normal European or American city. Getting around using public transport can be a major undertaking, unless you use the local tourist bus service, HabanaBusTour. On the other hand, there are plenty of taxis as well as *cocotaxis*, which offer a safe and fast way of getting around town. In Habana Vieja and Centro Habana, the most pleasant way to explore is to hire a rickshaw or to stay on foot.

HabanaBusTour, the best and cheapest way to explore Havana

A rickshaw near the Capitol building

WALKING IN HAVANA

Havana is an immense city and every district *(municipio)* extends for miles. However, if you are staying in the city centre (the area described on pages 56–105) then it should be quite feasible to do a lot of exploring on foot. Besides, walking along the Malecón seaside promenade, or through the tree-lined streets in the Vedado quarter, or the old Colonial section of town, is a very pleasant occupation. Visitors have the chance to discover hidden corners and details of buildings that would not be noticed in a car.

The best places for hailing taxis are the main arteries such as Calle 23 in Vedado. Should you get lost, ask a local passer-by for help; Cubans are usually very courteous and helpful with foreign tourists.

BUS SERVICES

Travelling by bus in the city can be something of an adventure. However, it is made easier by the hop-on/ hop-off air-conditioned tourist bus service, HabanaBusTour, with three different routes around town. Two of the routes start in Parque Central and go as far as Marina Hemingway to the west and Playas del Este to the east, for the daily price of five pesos convertibles.

Take the local buses to visit the areas not covered by the tourist buses, but be prepared to devote plenty of time and patience to each journey. The ability to speak Spanish will help, and be sure to make a note of the number of the bus you have to take as well as its route, because there are no route maps at the bus stops to indicate the various stops. At any bus stop you must generally ask who is the last (*último* or *última*) in line for the *ruta* (destination) you want. There is a queue even though you may not be aware of it, which will re-form in an organized way once the bus arrives.

Passengers get on the front of the bus, where the conductor or driver should be paid the fare in small change in national *pesos*. The cost is usually forty Cuban cents, though you can also pay five centavos convertibles per journey. Buses are usually very crowded, so feel lucky if you find an empty seat. The heat can often be suffocating. Allow plenty of time to get out, because passengers tend to block the exit door. Hold wallets and bags close to deter pickpockets.

The colourful metrobus service has now substituted the old *camellos*. The buses are more comfortable and run more often. Vaivén minibuses also link the airport to the city centre, stopping at the main hotels. Fares are cheap and there is air conditioning, but it might take you a while to get to your destination.

The modern Metrobus has replaced the old *camello*

TAXIS

Certainly the safest and most comfortable way of getting about in Havana is by taxi. There are many cars bearing the word TAXI, but not all of them are authorized to pick up tourists. Official taxis can be recognized easily because they are new and well-kept, comfortable, and almost always have air conditioning. Avoid illegal taxis, which have no accident insurance and may often be more expensive. The official taxi company is **Cubataxi**.

Taxis can be summoned by phone or hailed in the street. Taxi ranks are found in front of hotels, at the airport and in the following two places in Habana Vieja: by Plaza de Armas behind el Templete, and at the corner of Calle Empedrado and Tacón. A quirky alternative is to hire an old American convertible car, which are also official taxis; easily recognisable because they are in perfect condition and have the Grand Car sign and logo on both sides. These can usely be found outside the Hotel Nacional (see p255).

COCOTAXIS

An original and unusual means of transport is the *cocotaxi*, an egg-shaped yellow scooter that can carry two passengers as well as the driver. It costs more or less the same as a taxi, but has no meter and the driver does not give receipts. It is very useful for

A state-owned taxi, the best way to get from one district to another

short rides. Besides Havana, *cocotaxis* are now used in almost all Cuban cities. In Trinidad, for example, they shuttle from the city to Playa Ancón.

The yellow *cocotaxi*, an unusual three-seater scooter

HORSE-DRAWN VEHICLES

In Habana Vieja it is possible-to go on an enjoyable sight-seeing tour in horse-drawn carriages – perfectly restored old carts or Colonialstyle carriages, quite unlike those used by Cubans outside of town. These vehicles are not cheap, but can be a romantic and picturesque way of exploring the city.

The carriage and gig rank is located in the square between Calle Empedrado and Calle Tacón, at one end of the handicrafts market.

RICKSHAWS

A more environmentally friendly but slower alternative to taxis is to use a rickshaw, or bicitaxi, as they are known in Cuba. These are used by Cubans and tourists for short rides in the centre.

They circulate mostly in Habana Vieja, or can be found outside hotel entrances.

DRIVING IN HAVANA

People who are used to heavy traffic in big cities will not find driving in Havana too difficult. But it is important to stay alert at all times and watch out for the many cyclists, pedestrians and even dogs, which often run free in the streets. Keep speeds low in order to be able to spot and avoid the many potholes and bumps. The road signs and markings are reasonably good.

In the city centre there are three tunnels. Two pass under the Almendares river, connecting Vedado and Miramar (see p109). The other, which begins in Plaza Mártires del 71, behind the Castillo de la Punta, takes you rapidly to the other side of the bay and the Morro and Cabaña fortresses (see pp110–11). The latter is especially useful for those heading for the beaches in Habana del Este (see p113). The alternative is the long, winding port road, though it is easy to get lost.

DIRECTORY

TAXIS

Cubataxi
Tel 855 5555.

Tel 873 5712.

Tel 204 1446.

Tel 204 9518.

A horse-drawn carriage in Calle Obispo, Habana Vieja

General Index

Acknowledgments

Fabio Ratti Editoria would like to thank the following staff at Dorling Kindersley:

Map Co-Ordinator
Dave Pugh.

DTP Manager
Jason Little.

Managing Editor
Anna Streiffert.

Managing Art Editor
Jane Ewart.

Director of Publishing, Travel Guides
Gillian Allan.

Publisher
Douglas Amrine.

Dorling Kindersley would like to thank all those whose contribution and assistance have made the preparation of this book possible.

Main Contributor
Irina Bajini, a scholar who specializes in Hispanic-American languages and literature, lives in Milan and Havana. Among her publications are a conversation handbook, a Cuban-Italian dictionary published by Vallardi, and a book on the santería religion: *Il dio delle onde, del fuoco, del vento* (The God of the Waves, Fire and Wind), published by Sperling&Kupfer. She has also translated a number of Cuban books.

Other Contributors
Alejandro Alonso, an expert in Cuban art, is a journalist and critic who has published essays and curated exhibitions in Cuba and abroad. The former deputy director of the Museo de Bellas Artes, Alonso now heads the Museo Nacional de la Cerámica (National Ceramics Museum) in Havana, which he founded in 1990.

Miguel Angel Castro Machado, the second *historiador de la ciudad* of Baracoa, teaches Hispanic-American literature at the University of Santiago de Cuba.

Andrea G Molinari is executive director of Lauda Air Italia airline and a passionate smoker of, and expert on, Cuban cigars. He is the author of *Sigaro. La guida per l'apprendista fumatore di sigari cubani* (Cigars. A Guide for Newcomers to Cuban Cigar Smoking), published by IdeaLibri.

Marco Oliva is a diving instructor and an expert on diving in the Caribbean. He holds various specialist licences, including those for underwater photography, scuba-diving on wrecks, and marine biology.

Francesca Piana, a journalist and specialist on Latin America, has written numerous travel articles as well as guides to Greece, Mexico, Ecuador and Chile for the Touring Club.

Editorial and Design Assistance
Alejandro Alonso, Walfrido La O (Academia de la Historia de Cuba, Havana), Juan Romero Marcos.
For Dorling Kindersley: Monica Allende, Claire Baranowski, Julie Bond, Ernesto Juan Castellanos, Conrad van Dyk, Juliet Kenny, Kathryn Lane, Maite Lantaron, Carly Madden, Naomi Peck, Helen Peters, Rada Radojicic, Marisa Renzullo, Mary Scott, Helen Townsend.

Proof Reader
Stewart J. Wild.

Special Thanks
Archivo fotográfico e histórico de La Habana; Archivo ICAIC; Laura Arrighi (Lauda Air Italia); Bárbara Atorresagasti; Sandro Bajini; Freddy L Cámara; Casa de África, Havana; Aleida Castellanos (Havanatur Italia); Pedro Contreras (Centro de Desarrollo de las Artes Visuales, Havana); Vittoria Cumini (Tococoro restaurant, Milan); Juan Carlos and José Arturo de Dios Lorente; Alfredo Díaz (Tococoro restaurant, Milan); Mariano Fernández Arias (Gaviota); Cecilia Infante (José Martí publishers, Havana); Jardín Botánico del Parque Lenin; Lien La O Bouzán; Manuel Martínez Gomez ("Bohemia" archives); Adrian Adán Gonzalez (Tococoro restaurant, Milan); Guillerma López; Chiara Maretti (Lauda Air Italia); Stefano Mariotti; François Missen; Annachiara Montefusco (Cubanacán Italia); Jorge A Morente Padrón (Archipiélago); Orencio Nardo García (Museo de la Revolución); Eduardo Núñez (Publicitur); Mariacarla Nebuloni; Oficina del Historiador de la Ciudad, Havana; Sullen Olivé Monteagudo (Arcoiris); Angelo Parravicini (Lauda Air Italia); Milagros Pérez (Havanatur Italia); Alicia Pérez Casanova (Horizontes); Josefina Pichardo (Centro de Información y Documentación Turísticas); Richard Pierce; Poder Popular de Isla de la Juventud; Carla Provvedini (Ufficio Turistico di Cuba, Milan); Quinta de los Molinos, Havana; Gianluca Ragni (Gran Caribe); Celia Estela Rojas (Museo de las Parrandas de Remedios); Federica Romagnoli; Aniet Venereo (Archipiélago); Yoraida Santiesteban Vaillant; Lucia Zaccagni.

The Publisher would like to thank Andrea G Molinari in particular for the enthusiasm and willingness with which he supported the preparation of this guide.

Picture Sources
Geocuba, Havana; Habanos SA.

Reproduction Rights
The Publisher would like to thank all the museums, hotels, restaurants, shops and other sights of interest for their kind assistance and authorization to photograph their premises.

Specially Commissioned Photos
Drinks: Paolo Pulga, courtesy of the Tocororo restaurant, Corsico (Milan).

Additional Photography
Julie Bond, Ernesto Juan Castellanos, Maite Lantaron, Ian O'Leary, Daniel Stoddart.

Picture Credits
key: t = top; tl = top left; tlc = top left centre; tc = top centre; trc = top right centre; tr = top right; tra = top right above; cla = centre left above, ca = centre above; cra = centre right above; cl = centre left; c = centre; cr = centre right; cla = centre left above; crb = centre right below; cb = centre below; bl = bottom left; br = bottom right; b = bottom; bc = bottom centre; bcl = bottom centre left; bcr = bottom centre right; (d) = detail.

Every effort has been made to trace the copyright holders. The publisher apologizes for any unintentional omissions and would be pleased, in such cases, to add an acknowledgment in future editions. The publisher would like to thank all the individuals, local bodies and associations and photographic agencies for permission to reproduce their photographs.

Works of art have been reproduced with the permission of the following copyright holders: Augustín Cárdenas *Figure 1953* © DACS, London 2006 95c; Wilfredo Lam *Third World* 1966 © ADAGP, Paris and DACS, London 2006 26c.

ALAMY IMAGES: John Birdsall 273tl; Rolf Brenner 288cl; Adam Eastland 125clb; isifa Image Service s.r.o. /PHB 212tr; Mike Kipling Photography 124br; Sergio Pitamitz 125tr; Robert Harding Picture Library Ltd/Bruno Morandi 290tl; Tribaleye Images/Jamie Marshall 290br.

ALEJANDRO ALONSO, HAVANA: 93cl, 95c.

ARCHIVIO MONDADORI, MILAN: Andrea and Antonella Ferrari 153t.

ARCHIVIO RADAMÉS GIRO, HAVANA: 30br, 30bl.

PIERFRANCO ARGENTIERO, SOMMA LOMBARDO: 32bl (all the photos), 33br, 33b, 286cla, 286clb.

MARCO BIAGIOTTI, PERUGIA: 19bl, 27cl, 87t, 91c, 110c, 132, 139c, 139clb.

CAPITAL CULTURE: James Sparshatt 125br.

CASA DE ÁFRICA, HAVANA: 9 (insert), 40bl, 42–3c, 42cl, 42bl, 73b.

CENTRO DOCUMENTAZIONE MONDADORI, MILAN: 46tr, 47bl, 49tr, 49tl, 52b, 87br, 114cl, 114cr, 114b, 117bl, 167b.

CENTRO HISTÓRICO DE LA CIUDAD DE LA HABANA, HAVANA: 28c, 28br, 29tr, 40, 41, 43t, 44, 45, 46bl, 47b, 48tr, 48b, 49bl, 50cl, 59b, 151cl, 219t.

GIANFRANCO CISINI, MILAN: 57bl, 80tr, 111br, 165b, 173tl, 174c, 175t, 176t, 188c, 221clb, 231c.

CORBIS: Jose Fuste Raga 10cl, 11tl; Reuters/Claudia Daut 126bl; Reuters/Susana Vera 124tc.

4CORNERS IMAGES: SIME/Schmid Reinhard 11br.

RAÚL CORRALES, HAVANA: 50–51c.
Cubanacán, Milan: A Cozzi 303b.

MARTINO FAGIUOLI, MODENA: 24cra, 24clb, 51tl, 86cr, 182tr, 220b, 224c, 225tl, 225tr, 225c, 226tl, 227b, 226br, 228tl, 229 cla, 229c, 229br, 233tl, 233b, 234c, 235c, 236t, 236b, 242c, 242b, 243t, 243b.

FARABOLAFOTO, MILAN: 49cr, 50tr, 51tr, 52tr, 53bl, 57tl, 66cl.

GETTY IMAGES: National Geographic/Steve Winter 11clb; Photographer's Choice/Louis Quail 272cl.

PAOLO GONZATO, MILAN: 14tl, 18c, 20crb *(aura tiñosa)*, 20crb (ox), 29c, 30tr, 31tr *(claves)*, 31tr *(güiro)*, 53cb, 75br (all the photos), 130br, 155, 160t, 163t, 172t, 172b, 173cb, 173bl, 173br, 178, 180b, 182tl, 182clb, 184tl, 184tr, 184c, 188cra, 188clb, 188crb, 188b, 189t, 192b, 194c, 201b, 212tl, 213t, 220t, 231t, 234t, 236c, 248b, 272tl, 274cr, 275clb, 284t, 286tl, 286tr, 286clb, 287tl, 287b (all the photos), 289t, 300t, 302c, 312t, 312b.

GRAZIA GUERRESCHI, MILAN: 23ad, 23bd, 37as.

HOTEL HABANA LIBRE, HAVANA: Sven Creutzmann 248t.

ICAIC, HAVANA: 27bl, 29bl, 29br, 37b.

IMAGE BANK, MILAN: 21 clb (flamingo), L Abreu 5t, 215b, C Ansaloni 156b, 165ca, 166tr, 166b, G Bandieri, 58cra, A Cavalli 16c, 18t, 21tra, 23bd, 23bl, 53br, 54–5, 58cla, 59tr, 59cr, 67tl, 81c, 81br, 88t, 102tl, 113br, 116t, 134c, 152c, 153c, 154, 157t, 170b, 176c, 177tr, 182cl, 185t, 192t, 193t, 198tl, 216tl, 234b, 238c, 239t, 249c, 287cl, 298c; M Everton 294b; GW Faint 126t; L King 303t; A Mihich 294t; A Pistoleli 21cra, 144–45, 148b, 150c, 211b, 235b, 244b, 245t; GA Rossi 4b, 14,

20tr, 20cra, 33tr, 57tr, 58br, 61t, 65b, 66b, 72tr, 72cr, 75cb, 85ca, 85b, 87bl, 96, 105b, 110t, 111b, 115tr, 115b, 130cr, 131tl, 133, 152t, 152b, 156t, 162t, 163b, 168c, 179, 198c, 232t, 233c, 249b, 270t, 270c, 293ca, 309b; E Vergani 113t, 165c.

LONELY PLANET IMAGES: Doug McKinlay 273cb.

STEFANO MARIOTTI, MILAN: 32br.

MUSEO NACIONAL DE BELLAS ARTES, HAVANA: 26, 27tr, 27cr, 38, 92, 93, 94, 95.

PAOLO NEGRI, MILAN: 80cla, 80b, 148tl, 148c, 150b, 274t, 275b, 275br.

MARCO OLIVA, MILAN: 75cla, 89c, 134b, 136b, 137tr, 137c, 137b, 138t, 138bl, 146t, 147 (all the photos), 150t, 173tr 191t, 207b, 232c, 250c, 250b, 293b.

OLYMPIA, MILAN: 19cr, 53t, 64b, 292t, 292b.

PRENSA LATINA, HAVANA: 28tr, 30bc, 31tl, 31bc, 36c, 47tr, 50bl, 51br, 51bl, 52c, 124b, 171b, 202c, 238b.

LAURA RECORDATI, MILAN: 118t, 118b, 271c.

REUTERS: Oswaldo Rivas 288br.

LUCIO ROSSI, MILAN: 3, 18b, 20tl, 20cla, 20clb

(woodpecker), 20clb *(cartacuba)*, 20bl, 21tl, 21trb, 21clb *(gavilán)*, 21crb *(zunzuncito)*, 21crb (lizard), 21bl, 21 br, 22ca, 22cb, 23tl, 25br, 33cra, 34t, 35tr, 59cl, 69b, 72tl, 72b, 87crb, 98cl, 109b, 114t, 131tr, 131b, 136tr, 136c, 139tl, 142t, 142c, 143t, 146c, 146b, 153b, 164tl, 164tr, 164bl (all photos), 165tl, 166tl, 167t, 167c, 180t, 192c, 193b (all photos), 197t, 197c, 197b, 198tr, 198b, 199c, 199b, 209, 210b, 218b, 220c, 221t, 222tr, 224tr, 229t, 229cra, 230b, 237c, 237b, 239b, 240–41, 242tl, 242tr, 244t, 244c, 245c, 245b, 248c, 249t, 250t, 271t, 295, 301b, 305t, 315b.

ALBERTO SALAZAR, HAVANA: 31c.

SOUTH AMERICAN PICTURES: Rolando Pujol 124cl.

STUDIO FALLETTI, MILAN: 33tr, 33cla, 33cr, 33clb, 138cr, 139tr, 139crb.

WIKIPEDIA, THE FREE ENCYCLOPEDIA: NASA 36bl.

JACKET
Front - ALAMY IMAGES: Martin Norris main image; DK IMAGES: Lucio Rossi clb. Back - CORBIS: Jose Fuste Raga bl; DK IMAGES: Heidi Grassley cla, clb. Getty Images: Stone tl. Spine - ALAMY IMAGES: Martin Norris t; DK IMAGES: Lucio Rossi b.

All other images © Dorling Kindersley.
For further information see:
www.dkimages.com

SPECIAL EDITIONS OF DK TRAVEL GUIDES

DK Travel Guides can be purchased in bulk quantities at discounted prices for use in promotions or as premiums. We are also able to offer special editions and personalized jackets, corporate imprints, and excerpts from all of our books, tailored specifically to meet your own needs.

To find out more, please contact:
(in the United States) **SpecialSales@dk.com**
(in the UK) **travelspecialsales@uk.dk.com**
(in Canada) DK Special Sales at **general@tourmaline.ca**
(in Australia) **business.development@pearson.com.au**

Phrase Book

The Spanish spoken in Cuba is basically the same as the Castilian used in Spain with certain deviations. As in the Spanish-speaking countries in Central and Southern America, the "z" is pronounced like the "s", as is the "c" when it comes before "e" or "i". Among the grammatical variations, visitors should be aware that Cubans use *Ustedes* in place of *Vosotros*, to say "you" when referring to more than one person. It is notable that some Indian, African and English words are commonly used in present-day Cuban Spanish. This basic phrase book includes useful common phrases and words, and particular attention has been paid to typically Cuban idioms in a list of Cuban Terms.

Cuban Terms

apagón	apag**on**	black-out, power cut
babalawo	babala-wo	a priest of Afro-Cuban religion
bohío	bo-ee-o	traditional rural house with palm leaf roof
carro	karro	car
casa de la trova	kasa deh la troba	club where traditional music is played
batey	batay	village around sugar factory
cayo	ka-yo	small island
chama	chama	child
criollo	kr-yo-yo	Creole (born in Cuba of Spanish descent)
divisas	deebeesas	dollars (slang)
guagua	gwagwa	bus
guajiro	gwaheero	farmer
guarapo	gwarapo	sugar cane juice
ingenio	eenhen-yo	sugar factory complex
jama	hama	food, meal
eva	eba	woman
jinetera	heenetaira	prostitute, or female hustler
jinetero	heenetairo	male person hustling tourists
libreta	leebreta	rations book
moneda nacional	moneda nas-yonal	pesos ("national currency")
moros y cristianos	moros ee krist-yanos	rice & black beans (Moors & Christians)
paladar	paladar	privately-owned restaurant
puro	pooro	authentic Cuban cigar
santero	santairo	santería priest
tabaco	tabako	low-quality cigar
tambor	tambor	Afro-Cuban religious musical feast
tienda	t-yenda	shop that only accepts dollars
trago	trago	alcoholic drink
tunas	toonas	prickly pears
zafra	safra	sugar cane harvest

Emergencies

Help!	¡socorro!	sokorro
Stop!	¡pare!	pareh
Call a doctor	Llamen un médico	yamen oon medeeko
Call an ambulance	Llamen a una ambulancia	yamen a oona amboolans-ya
Police!	¡policía!	poleesee-a
I've been robbed	Me robaron	meh rrobaron

Communication Essentials

Yes	sí	see
No	no	no
Please	por favor	por fabor
Pardon me	perdone	pairdoneh
Excuse me	disculpe	deeskoolpeh
I'm sorry	lo siento	lo s-yento
Thanks	gracias	gras-yas
Hello!	¡buenas!	bwenas
Good day	buenos días	bwenos dee-as
Good afternoon	buenas tardes	bwenas tardes
Good evening	buenas noches	bwenas noches
Night	noche	nocheh
Morning	mañana	man-yana
Tomorrow	mañana	man-yana
Yesterday	ayer	a-yair
Here	acá	aka
How?	¿cómo?	komo
When?	¿cuándo?	kwando
Where?	¿dónde?	dondeh
Why?	¿por qué?	por keh

How are you?	¿qué tal?	keh tal
It's a pleasure!	¡mucho gusto!	moocho goosto
Goodbye, so long	hasta luego	asta lwego

Useful Phrases

That's fine	está bien/ocá	esta b-yen/oka
Fine	¡qué bien!	keh b-yen
How long?	¿Cuánto falta?	kwanto falta
Do you speak a little English?	¿Habla un poco de inglés?	abla oon poko deh eengles
I don't understand	No entiendo	no ent-yendo
Could you speak more slowly?	¿Puede hablar más despacio?	pwedeh ablas mas despas-yo
I agree/OK	de acuerdo/ocá	deh akwairdo/oka
Certainly!	¡Claro que sí!	klaro keh see!
Let's go!	¡Vámonos!	bamonos

Useful Words

Large	grande	grandeh
Small	pequeño	peken-yo
Hot	caliente	kal-yenteh
Cold	frío	free-o
Good	bueno	bweno
Bad	malo	malo
So-so	más o menos	mas o menos
Well/fine	bien	b-yen
Open	abierto	ab yairto
Closed	cerrado	serrado
Full	lleno	yeno
Empty	vacío	basee-o
Right	derecha	dairecha
Left	izquierda	isk-yairda
Straight	recto	rrekto
Under	debajo	debaho
Over	arriba	arreeba
Quickly/early	pronto/temprano	pronto/temprano
Late	tarde	tardeh
Now	ahora	a-ora
Soon	ahorita	a-oreeta
More	más	mas
Less	menos	menos
Little	poco	poko
Sufficient	suficiente	soofees-yenteh
Much	mucho/muy	moocho/mwee
Too much	demasiado	demas-yado
In front of	delante	delanteh
Behind	detrás	detras
First floor	primer piso	preemair peeso
Ground floor	planta baja	planta baha
Lift/elevator	elevador	elebador
Bathroom/toilet	servicios	sairbees-yos
Women	mujeres	moohaires
Men	hombres	ombres
Toilet paper	papel sanitario	papel saneetar-yo
Camera	cámara	kamara
Batteries	baterías	bataireе-as
Passport	pasaporte	pasaporteh
Visa; tourist card	visa; tarjeta turistica	beesa; tarheta tooreesteeka

Health

I don't feel well	Me siento mal	meh s-yento mal
I have a stomach ache	Me duele el estómago	meh dweleh el estomago
headache	la cabeza	la kabesa
He/she is ill	Está enfermo/a	esta enfairmo
I need to rest	Necesito descansar	neseseeto dekansar
Drug store	farmacia	farmasee-ya

Post Office and Bank

Bank	banco	banko
I want to send a letter	Quiero enviar una carta	k-yairo emb-yar oona karta
Postcard	postal tarjeta	postal tarheta

| Stamp | sello | se-yo |
| Draw out money | sacar dinero | sakar deenairo |

Shopping

How much is it?	¿Cuánto cuesta?	kwanto kwesta
What time do you open/close?	¿A qué hora abre/cierra?	a ke ora abreh/s-yairra
May I pay with a credit card?	¿Puedo pagar con tarjeta de crédito?	pwedo pagar kon tarheta deh kredeeto?

Sightseeing

Beach	playa	pla-ya
Castle, fortress	castillo	kastee-yo
Cathedral	catedral	katedral
Church	iglesia	eegles-ya
District	barrio	barr-yo
Garden	jardín	hardeen
Guide	guía	gee-a
House	casa	kasa
Motorway	autopista	owtopeesta
Museum	museo	mooseh-o
Park	parque	parkeh
Road	carretera	karretaira
Square, plaza	plaza, parque	plasa, parkeh
Street	calle, callejón	ka-ye, ka-yehon
Town hall	Ayuntamiento	a-yoontam-yento
Tourist bureau	buró de turismo	booro deh tooreesmo

Transport

Could you call a taxi for me?	¿Me puede llamar un taxi?	meh pwedeh yamar oon taksee?
Airport	aeropuerto	a-airopwairto
Train station	estación de ferrocarriles	estas-yon deh fairrokarreeles
Bus station	terminal de autobús	tairmeenal deh owtoboos
When does it leave?	¿A qué hora sale?	a keh ora saleh?
Customs	aduana	adwana
Boarding pass	tarjeta de embarque	tarheta deh embarkeh
Car hire	alquiler de carros	alkeelair deh karros
Bicycle	bicicleta	beeseekleta
Insurance	seguro	segooro
Petrol/gas station	estación de gasolina	estas-yon deh gasoleena

Staying in a Hotel

Single room/double	habitación sencilla/doble	abeetas-yon sensee-ya/dobleh
Shower	ducha	doocha
Bathtub	bañera	ban-yaira
Balcony	balcón, terraza	balkon, tairrasa
I want to be woken at…	Necesito que me despierten a las…	neseseeto keh meh desp-yairten a las…
Warm water/cold	agua caliente/fría	agwa kal-yenteh/free-a
Soap	jabón	habon
Towel	toalla	to-a-ya
Key	llave	yabeh

Eating Out

What is there to eat?	¿Qué hay para comer?	keh I para komair?
The bill, please	la cuenta, por favor	la kwenta por fabor
Glass	vaso	baso
Cutlery	cubiertos	koob-yairtos
I would like some water	Quisiera un poco de agua	kees-yaira oon poko deh agwa
Have you got wine?	¿Tienen vino?	t-yenen beeno?
The beer is not cold enough	La cerveza no está bien fría	la sairbesa no esta b-yen free-a
Breakfast	desayuno	desa-yoono
Lunch	almuerzo	almwairso
Dinner	comida	komeeda
Raw/cooked	crudo/cocido	kroodo/koseedo

Menu Decoder

aceite	asayteh	oil
agua mineral	agwa meenairal	mineral water
aguacate	agwakateh	avocado
ajo	aho	garlic
arroz	arros	rice
asado	asado	roasted
atún	atoon	tuna
azúcar	asookar	sugar
bacalao	bakala-o	cod

café	kafeh	coffee
camarones	kamarones	prawns
carne	karneh	meat
congrí	kongree	rice with beans & onions
cerveza	sairbesa	beer
dulce	doolseh	sweet, dessert
ensalada	ensalada	salad
fruta	froota	fruit
fruta bomba	froota bomba	papaya
helado	elado	ice cream
huevo	webo	egg
jugo	hoogo	fruit juice
langosta	langosta	lobster
leche	lecheh	milk
marisco	mareesko	seafood
mantequilla	mantekee-ya	butter
pan	pan	bread
papas	papas	potatoes
postre	postreh	dessert
pescado	peskado	fish
plátano	platano	banana
pollo	po-yo	chicken
potaje/sopa	potaheh/sopa	soup
puerco	pwairko	pork
queso	keso	cheese
refresco	refresko	drink
sal	sal	salt
salsa	salsa	sauce
té	teh	tea
vinagre	beenagreh	vinegar

Time

Minute	minuto	meenooto
Hour	hora	ora
Half-hour	media hora	med-ya ora
Monday	lunes	loones
Tuesday	martes	martes
Wednesday	miércoles	m-yairkoles
Thursday	jueves	hwebes
Friday	viernes	b-yairnes
Saturday	sábado	sabado
Sunday	domingo	domeengo
January	enero	enairo
February	febrero	febrairo
March	marzo	marso
April	abril	abreel
May	mayo	ma-yo
June	junio	hoon-yo
July	julio	hool-yo
August	agosto	agosto
September	setiembre	set-yembreh
October	octubre	oktoobreh
November	noviembre	nob-yembreh
December	diciembre	dees-yembreh

Numbers

0	cero	sairo
1	uno	oono
2	dos	dos
3	tres	tres
4	cuatro	kuatro
5	cinco	seenko
6	seis	says
7	siete	s-yeteh
8	ocho	ocho
9	nueve	nwebeh
10	diez	d-yes
11	once	onseh
12	doce	doseh
13	trece	treseh
14	catorce	katorseh
15	quince	keenseh
16	dieciséis	d-yeseesays
17	diecisiete	d-yesees-yeteh
18	dieciocho	d-yes-yocho
19	diecinueve	d-yeseenwebeh
20	veinte	baynteh
30	treinta	traynta
40	cuarenta	kwarenta
50	cincuenta	seenkwenta
60	sesenta	sesenta
70	setenta	setenta
80	ochenta	ochenta
90	noventa	nobenta
100	cien	s-yen
500	quinientos	keen-yentos
1000	mil	meel